HISTORIC PHOTOS OF
APPALACHIA

TEXT AND CAPTIONS BY
KEVIN E. O'DONNELL

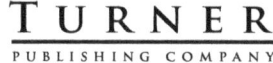

TURNER
PUBLISHING COMPANY

In the decades after the Civil War, the Tennessee town of Jonesborough prospered with the coming of the railroad. Jonesborough was founded in 1779, serving briefly as the capital of the state of Franklin. Unofficially the fourteenth state in the Union, Franklin was never recognized by Congress and was dissolved in 1788.

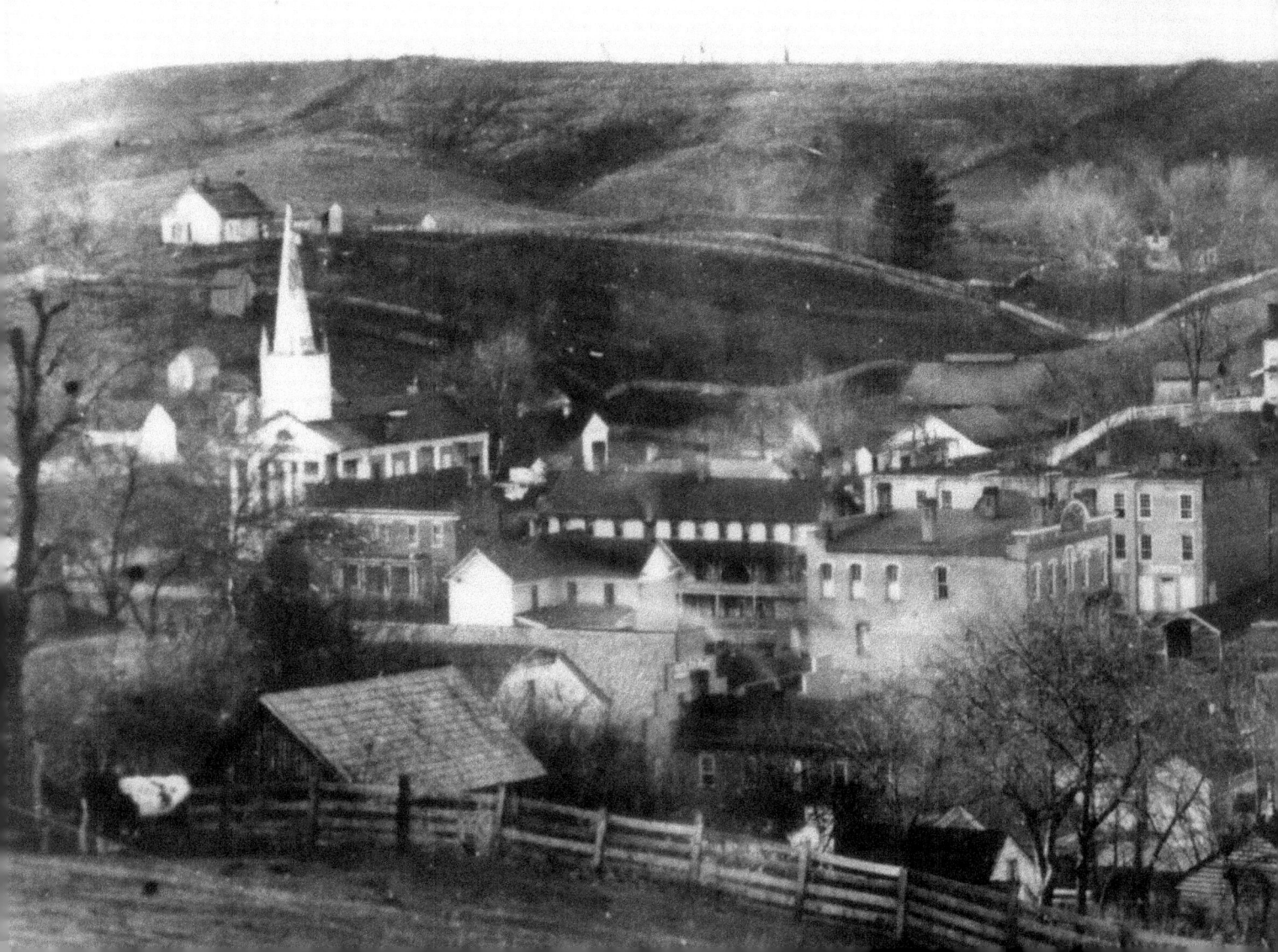

HISTORIC PHOTOS OF
APPALACHIA

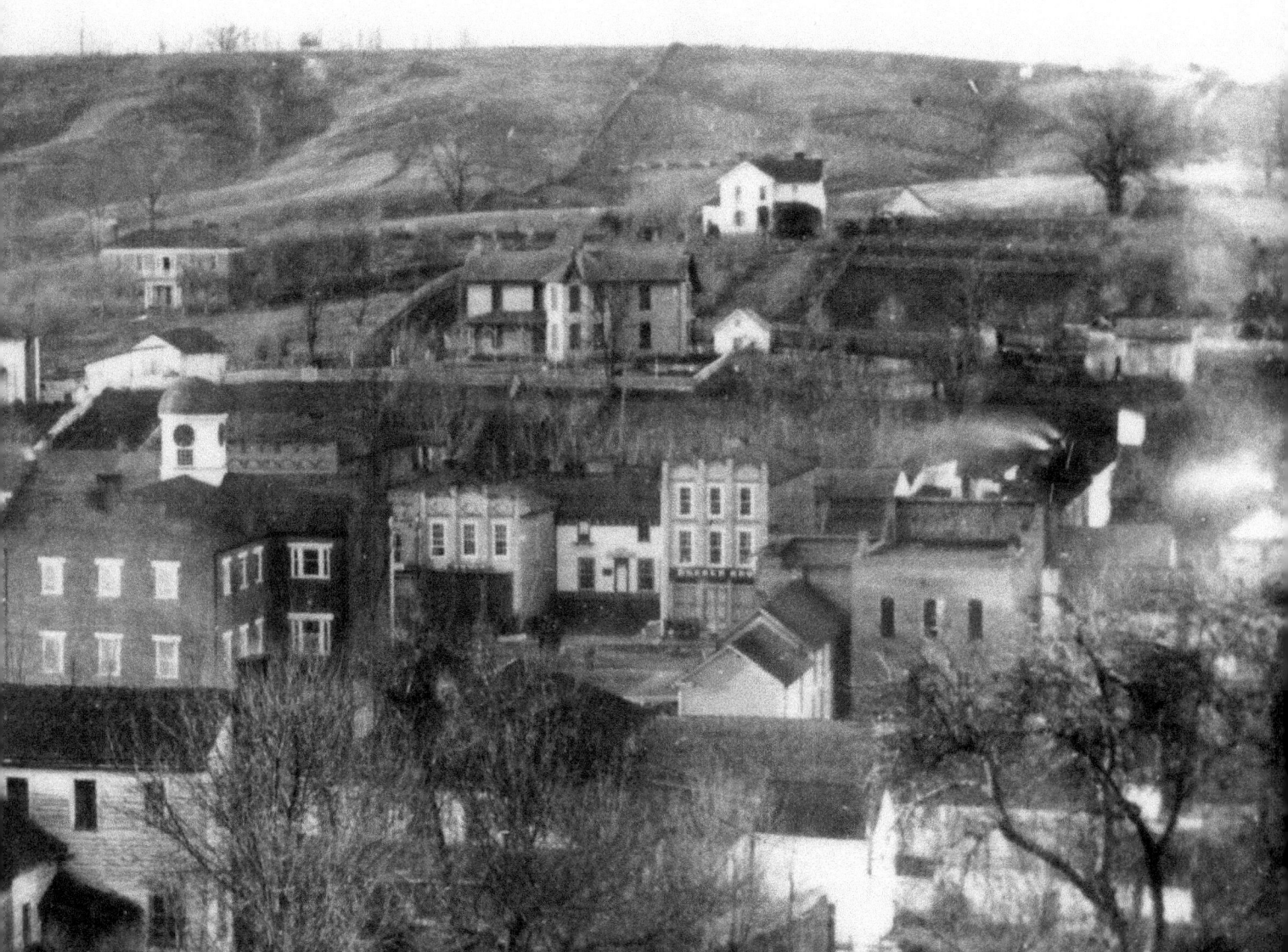

Turner Publishing Company
www.turnerpublishing.com

Historic Photos of Appalachia

Copyright © 2009 Turner Publishing Company

Library of Congress Control Number: 2009922660

ISBN: 978-1-59652-540-5

Printed in United States of America

ISBN 978-1-68442-090-2 (hc)

CONTENTS

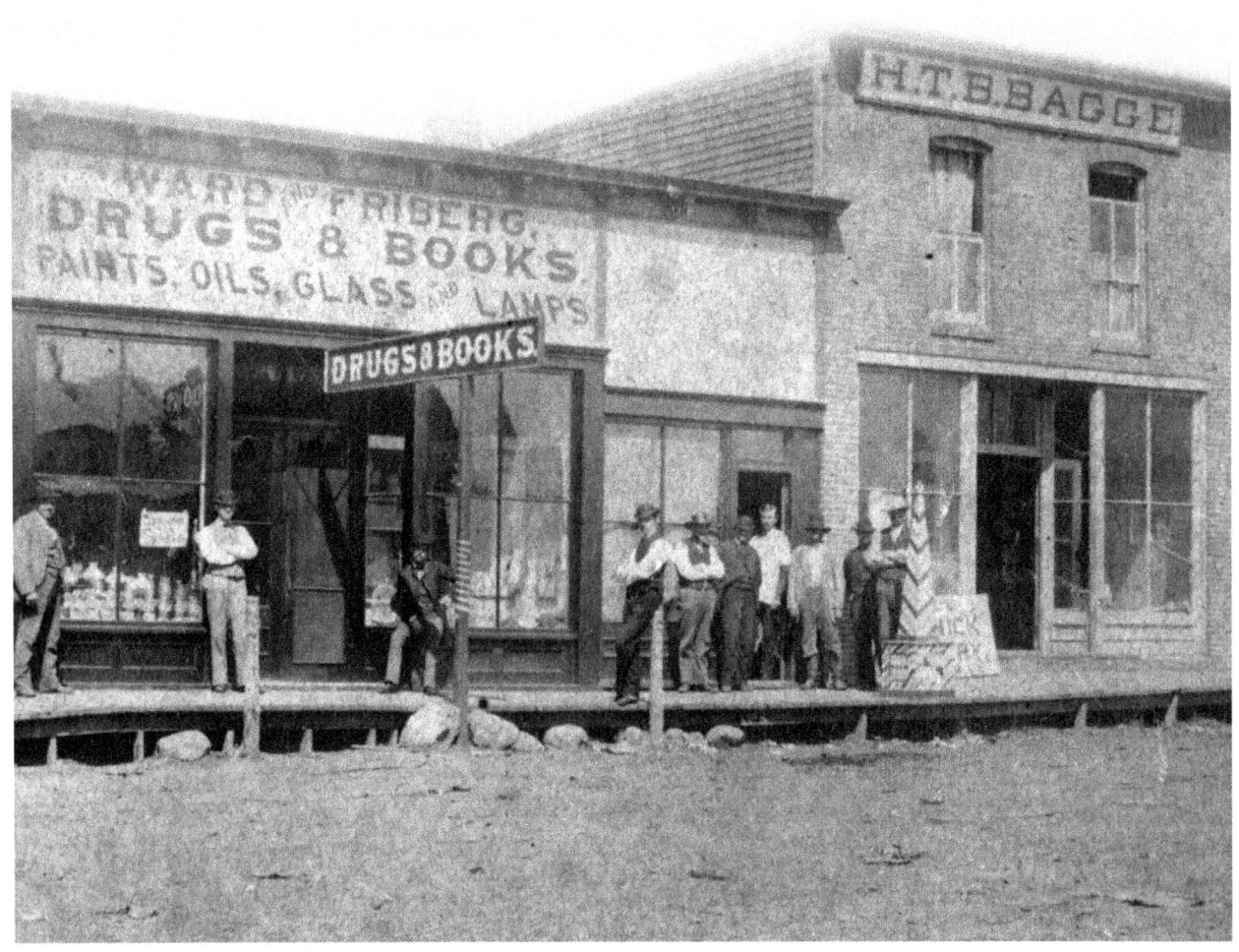

Originally a stereograph, this view of an Appalachian town in the 1880s features a mud street and wooden boardwalk adorning shopfronts.

ACKNOWLEDGMENTS

This volume, *Historic Photos of Appalachia,* is the result of the cooperation and efforts of many individuals and organizations. It is with great thanks that we acknowledge their generous support. The W. L. Eury Appalachian Collection at Appalachian State University in Boone, North Carolina, made available a large number of images, from several of its holdings: The Cratis Dearl Williams Papers; Leo Finklestein Papers; Tennessee Valley Authority Collection of Photographs; William D. Hoyt Photographs; Hotel Roanoke Photographs; C and O Railroad Photographs; Norris Dam Photograph; Shulls Mills Photographs; Smyth County, Virginia Lifetime Collection; Linville Valley, NC Photographs; Jonesborough, Tennessee Photographs; David Worth Papers; Harper's Ferry Photograph; German Fraternal Order Photograph; Virginia Cascade Stereograph; Delaware Water Gap Stereograph; and Natural Bridge Stereograph. Thanks also to the Forest History Society in Durham, North Carolina.

Three-fourths of the photographs came from the Archives of Appalachia, a division of the Center for Appalachian Studies and Services at East Tennessee State University. Included are images from fifteen of their collections: The Appalachian Photographic Archives; Pollyanna Creekmore Collection; James T. Dowdy, Sr., Photographs; Burr Harrison Photographs; Kyle Huddle Photograph Collection; Johnson City Foundry and Machine Works Records; Kelly and Green Company Collection; Mildred S. Kozsuch Collection; Erlene Ledford Photographs; Clifford A. Maxwell Photographs; Pressmen's Home Photograph Collection; Range Family Papers; Jeanne M. Rasmussen Collection; Jack Underwood Photograph Collection; and the Hugh L. White Collection.

Thanks to Georgia Greer and John Fleenor, of the archives staff, to Norma Meyers, archives director, and to Roberta Herrin, director of CASS, for their help with this book. Thanks also to Bob Cox, a contributing writer to the *Johnson City Press* and an East Tennessee historian. I don't know Mr. Cox personally, but his newspaper columns and "Yesteryear" Web site, bcyesteryear.com, have been invaluable resources in the preparation of this book.

—*Kevin E. O'Donnell, Johnson City, Tennessee, July 2009*

PREFACE

Appalachia comprises the southern highlands of Virginia, West Virginia, Tennessee, and North Carolina. The borders of the region, however, are variously defined. By most definitions, the region extends north into the hill country of Pennsylvania and Ohio, and south into the mountainous parts of Georgia, Alabama, and South Carolina. By any definition, the region is enormously diverse, in terms of both physical geography and human culture.

No collection of photographs, of course, could ever definitively represent such a region. The photographs in this volume came mainly from two archives: the Archives of Appalachia, at East Tennessee State University, in Johnson City, Tennessee, and the W. L. Eury Appalachian Collection at Appalachian State University, in Boone, North Carolina. Because those archives are located in east Tennessee and western North Carolina, respectively, this collection tends to emphasize those parts of Appalachia and, to a lesser extent, West Virginia and southwestern Virginia. Nonetheless, this volume includes images from across the region. These pictures provide snapshots, partial views, slices, and vignettes, which together suggest the broad range of landscapes, scenes, and experiences that make up Appalachia.

More than most other American regions, Appalachia tends to be associated with certain stock or stereotypical images: the homespun hillbilly, the feckless moonshiner, the shoeless child, the debris-strewn mountain homestead. Some of those stock images can be demeaning and misleading, even when they have a basis in history. With this collection, an effort has been made to move beyond the stereotypes, to represent a broader and more interesting range of Appalachian experience.

The photographs here include everyday views. Stores, schools, churches, and street scenes are pictured in abundance. They include sensational train and automobile wrecks as well as floods and other disasters—popular subjects for photographers, especially in the late nineteenth and early twentieth centuries. And they include iconic images: Virginia's Natural Bridge, for example, had been the common subject of oil paintings and engravings for more than a century before the photograph included here was taken.

The images also emphasize the industries that have dominated Appalachia's economy since the 1870s: railroads, timber, and coal. They show the tourists and travelers drawn to the region in large numbers in the decades following the Civil War. And they depict the classic, scenic mountain vistas that have drawn those visitors, ever since landscape painters began setting up their easels in the mountains in the early nineteenth century.

With the exception of touching up imperfections that have accrued with the passage of time and cropping where necessary, no changes have been made. The focus and clarity of many images is limited by the technology and the ability of the photographer at the time they were taken. These photographs were mostly taken by amateurs, and most of the photographers remain anonymous. The earliest photos date from the 1870s, when photography equipment first became widely available in America. Where possible, identifying information is included. In some cases, specific information about particular photographs is unknown, but in such cases the pictures speak for themselves.

—*Kevin E. O'Donnell*

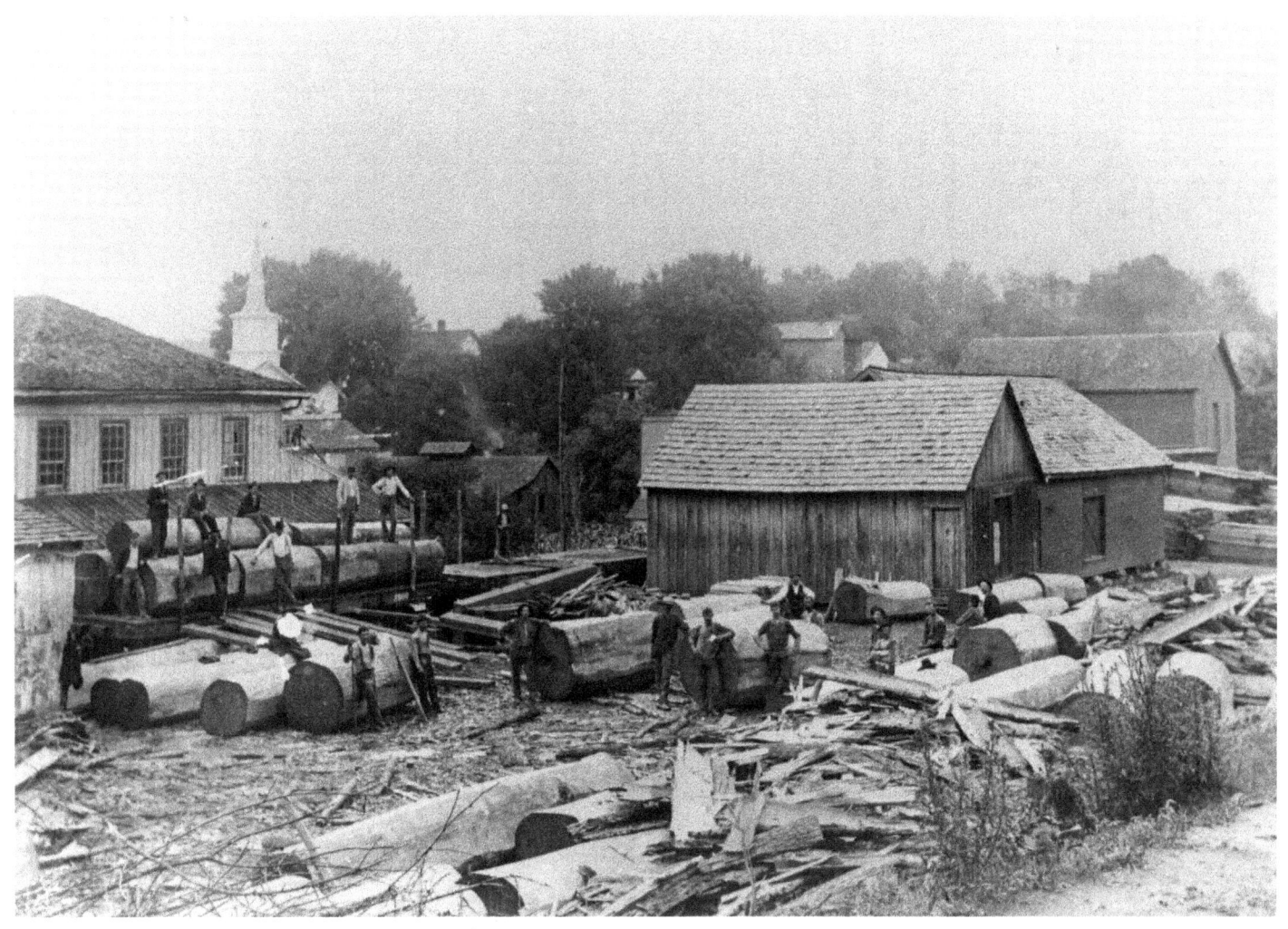

Logs are unloaded at a southern Appalachian milling operation. The long, warm growing season and high rainfall of the southern mountains can produce enormous deciduous hardwoods. The development of railroads and the emergence of steam-powered logging equipment in the 1880s initiated an era of industrial logging in Appalachia. Between 1880 and 1920, the great ancient forest was almost entirely clearcut. Much of the old housing stock of America's eastern seaboard was built with southern Appalachian timber.

An American Region Industrialized

(1870–1899)

When Spanish conquistadores, in Florida in the 1500s, encountered a native tribe north of the Florida peninsula, they called the tribe "Apalatchi." The term is "Span-dian"—a Spanish version of the Indian self-appellation that, no doubt, was pronounced quite differently by the Spanish from the version used by that now-vanished tribe. In any event, the conquistadores soon began using the word to refer broadly to the entire region north of Florida—to them a mysterious, forbidding region, to us today known as the American southeast.

For centuries, the strange hybrid word gained little purchase, until New Englanders in the mid nineteenth century began using it, almost as a substitute for the word "Alleghenies," to refer to the entire eastern mountain range that rises around Birmingham, Alabama, and sinks into the sea northeast of Maine. By the end of the century, the term "Alleghenies" generally referred to the northern part of that range, while "Appalachia" described the southern part, the unglaciated portion of the range that begins somewhere below the Delaware Water Gap, rises above the Shenandoah Valley, and reaches its heights in the Blue Ridge, Black, and Great Smoky Mountains, centering on the jagged border between the states of Tennessee and North Carolina.

After the Cherokees were forcibly removed, in 1830, and before the Civil War, the lives of the region's inhabitants of European descent were shrouded in mist and myth. Images of a de-volved, unlettered, and irreligious white mountain people abound in American writings of the period. But the reality was always more complex than the myth. The region was isolated, before the railroads, but never so backward and inbred as it was portrayed. Pockets of Cherokees, as well as immigrants not only from the British Isles but also from Germany and other parts of Europe, and even from the Far East, contributed to an ethnic and cultural diversity that belied the common notion.

After the Civil War, international commerce and industry reached into the region and transformed it forever. Northern and international corporations—"syndicates"—discovered the region in the 1870s, 1880s, and 1890s. A frenzy of railroad building, natural resource extraction, and economic growth resulted.

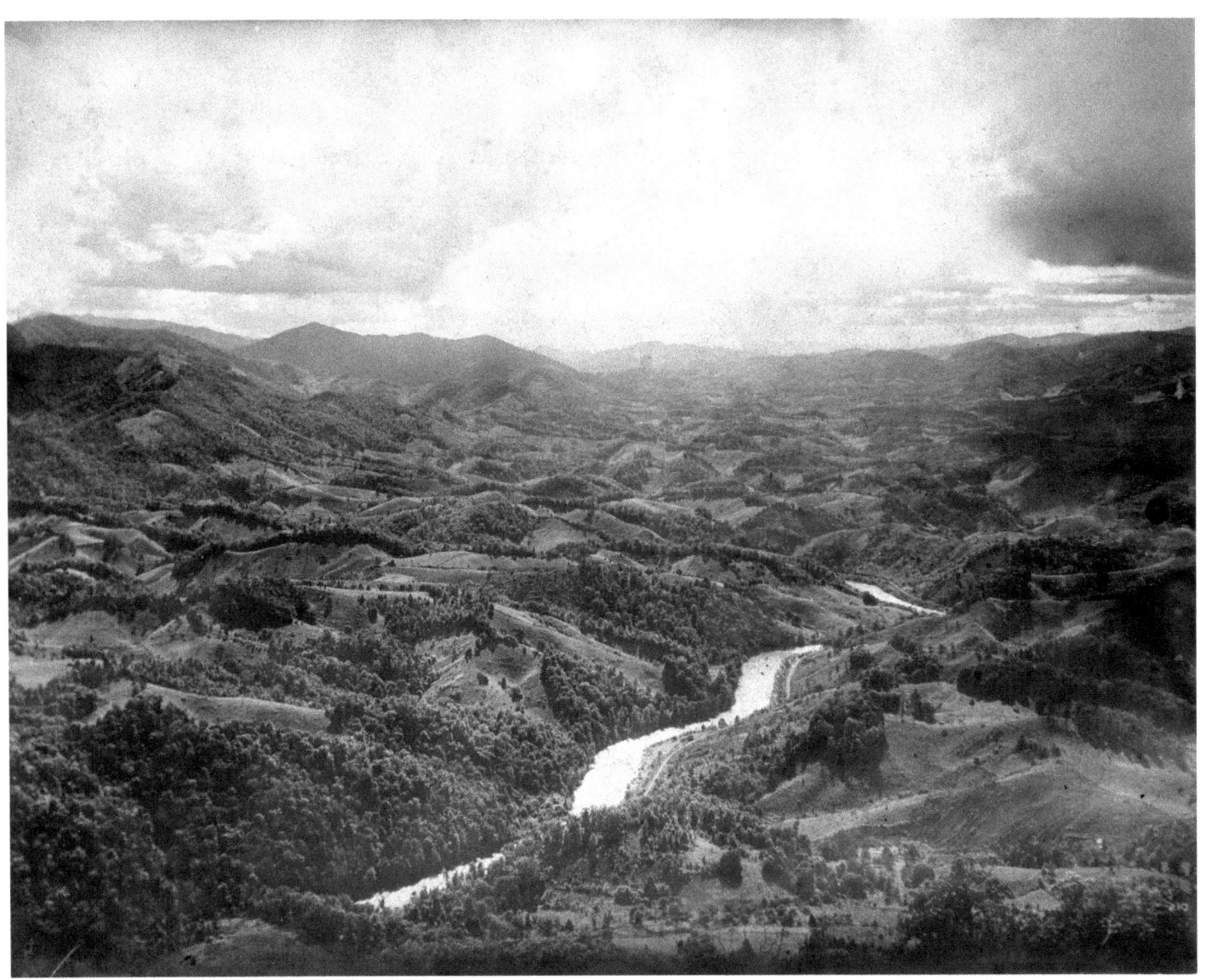

This nineteenth-century view shows the Watauga River Valley in Carter County, Tennessee, near North Carolina. In the eighteenth century, this land was near the Proclamation Line, a boundary dividing the eastern half of the continent between the British and the French. The Watauga Valley was considered to be on the "wrong" side of the line, and thus beyond the jurisdiction of official government. Inhabitants of the region have had a reputation for independence ever since.

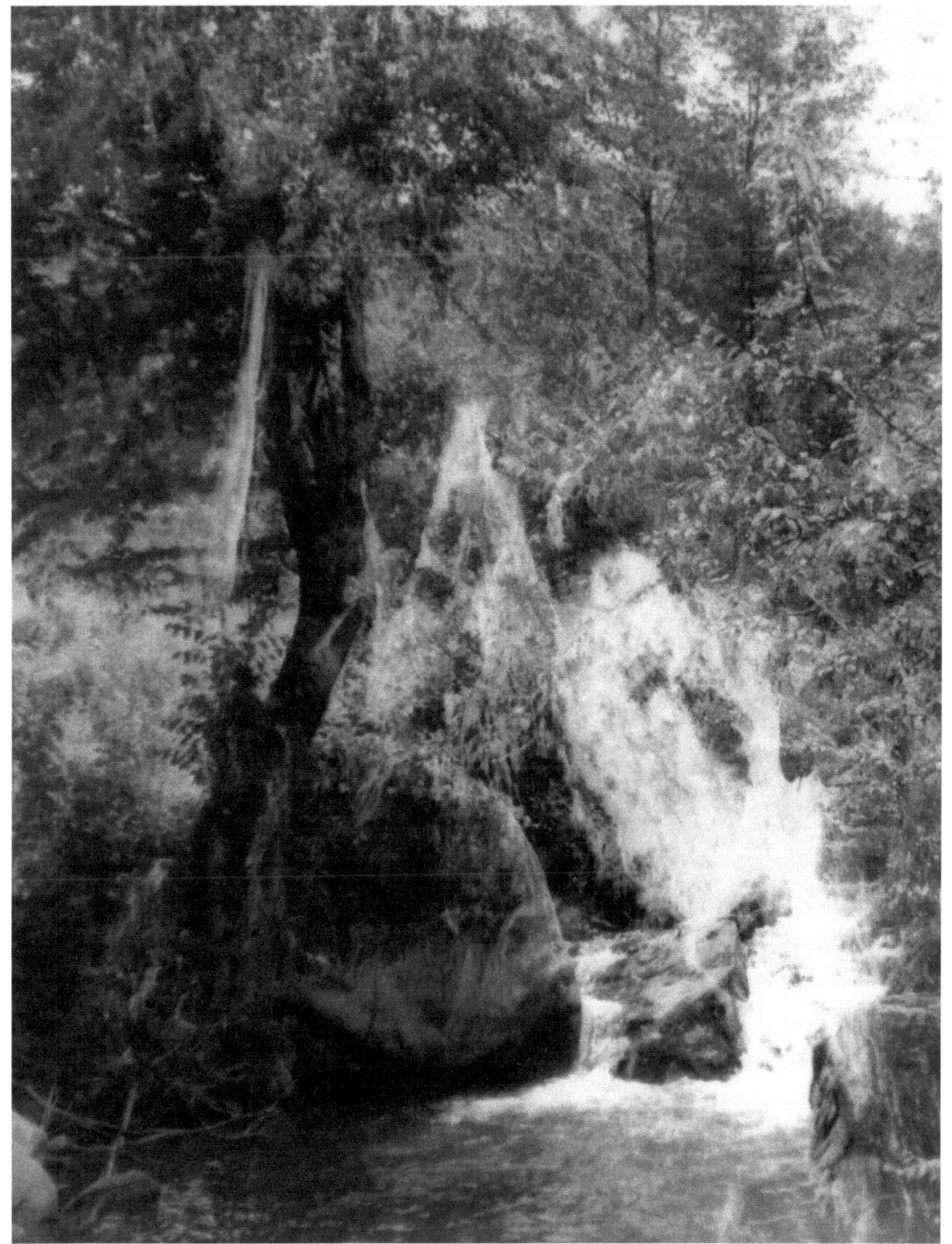

Classic view of a mountain stream. The Appalachian mountains are well-watered: some areas near the Smokies have historically averaged close to 90 inches of rain a year. The mountains serve as a water source for the eastern United States.

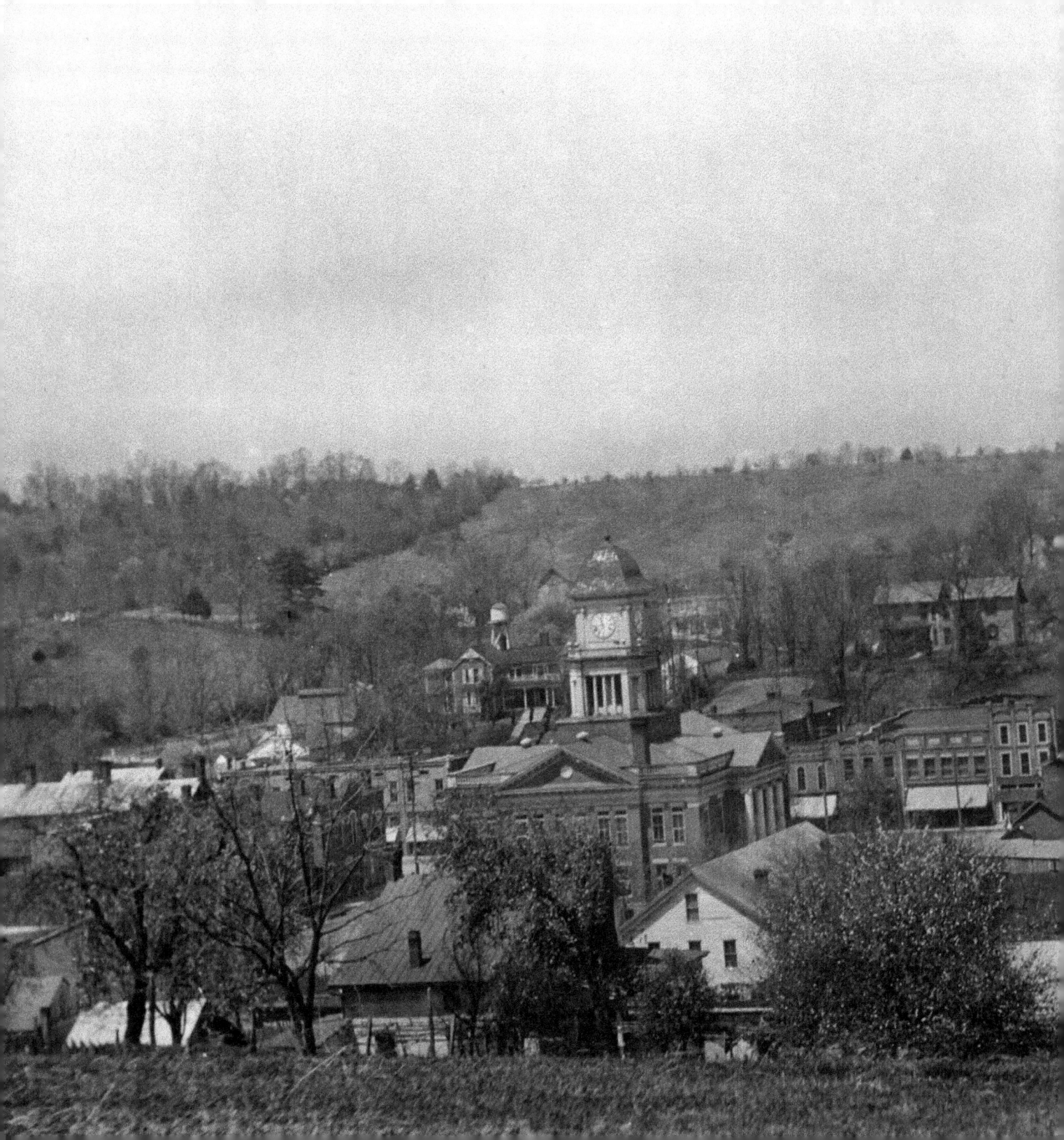

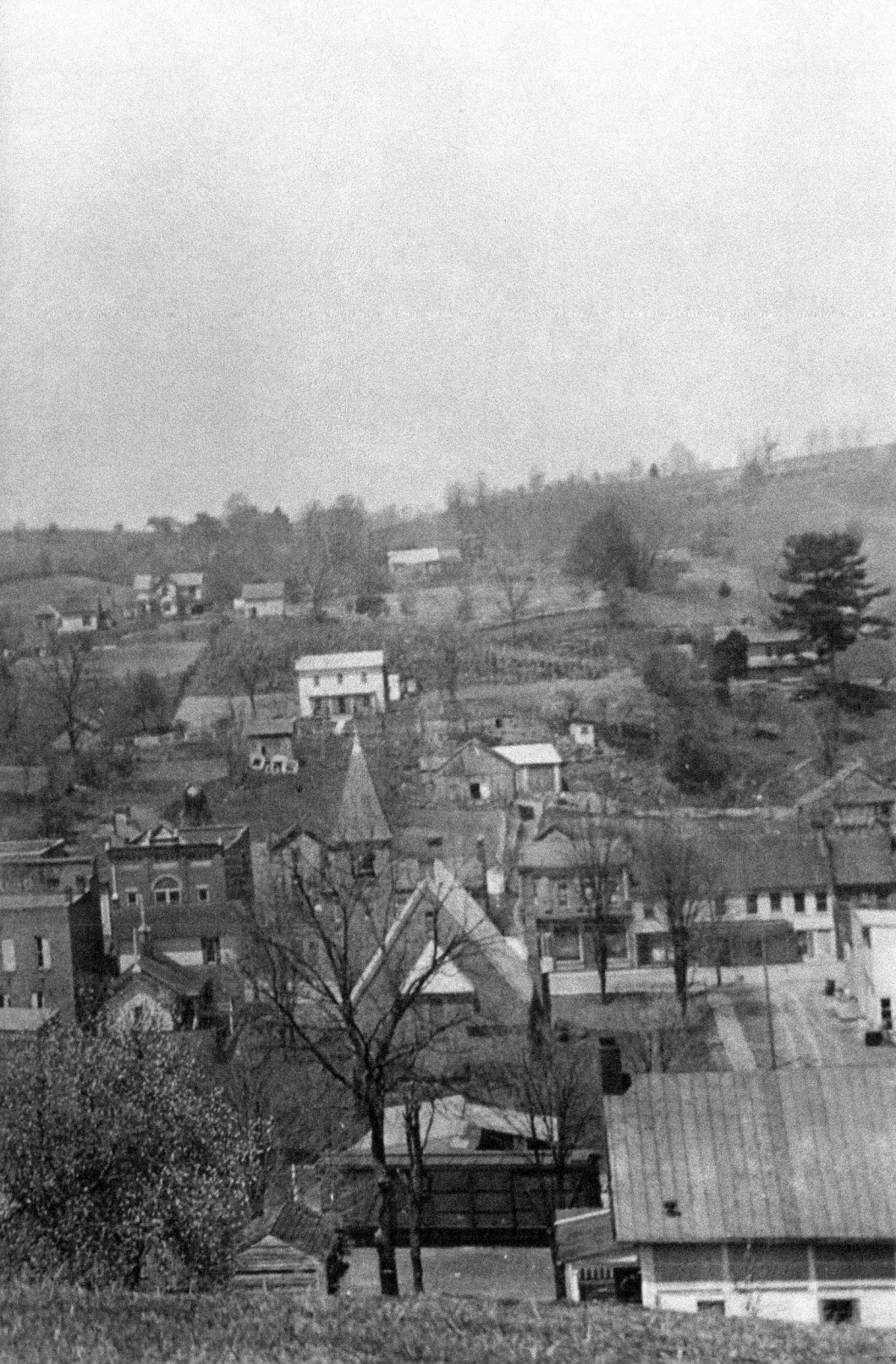

Jonesborough, Tennessee, holds claim to being the state's oldest town. It was founded during the early years of the American Revolution, along a stagecoach road that followed the Great Road of Virginia through the upper Tennessee Valley, down off the Cumberland Plateau, to a site on the Cumberland River which was known then as Fort Nashborough—today as Nashville.

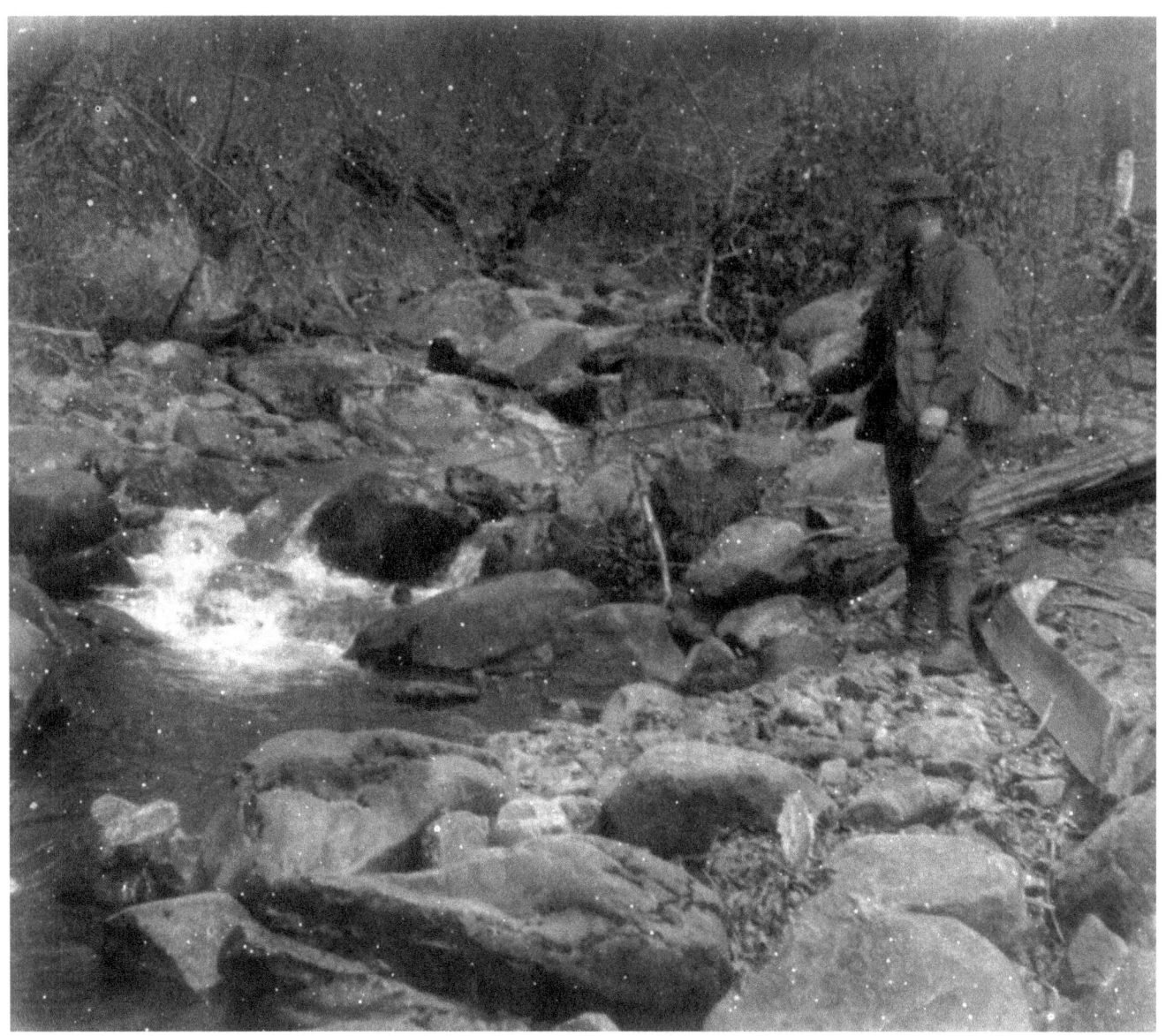

Appalachian streams have drawn trout fishers to the region since the early 1800s. Trout streams are now imperiled by an infestation of an aphid-like insect, the hemlock woolly adelgid, which is killing the eastern hemlocks of Appalachia. The hemlocks grow along stream banks, and their tightly woven evergreen branches keep the streams cool enough to support trout populations.

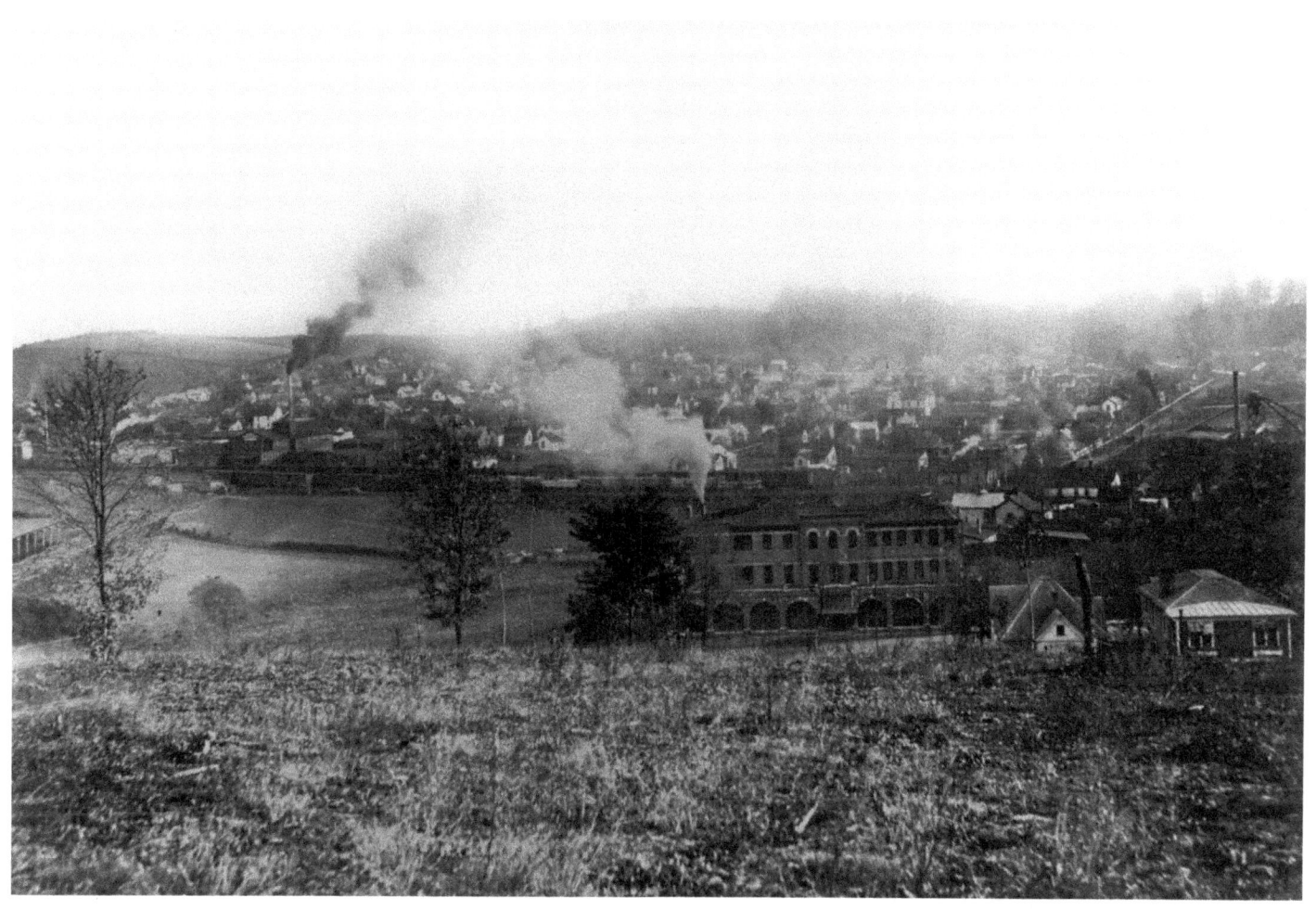

During the mid nineteenth century, railroads spurred the growth of towns, especially in the "ridge and valley" province of southern Appalachia. Johnson City, Tennessee, was sited along the corridor for the East Tennessee and Virginia Railroad. The settlement was originally known, in the late 1850s, as "Johnson's Tank," because trains stopped there to take on water. By the late 1880s, the community was a thriving town. The old Hotel Franklin is visible here in the foreground.

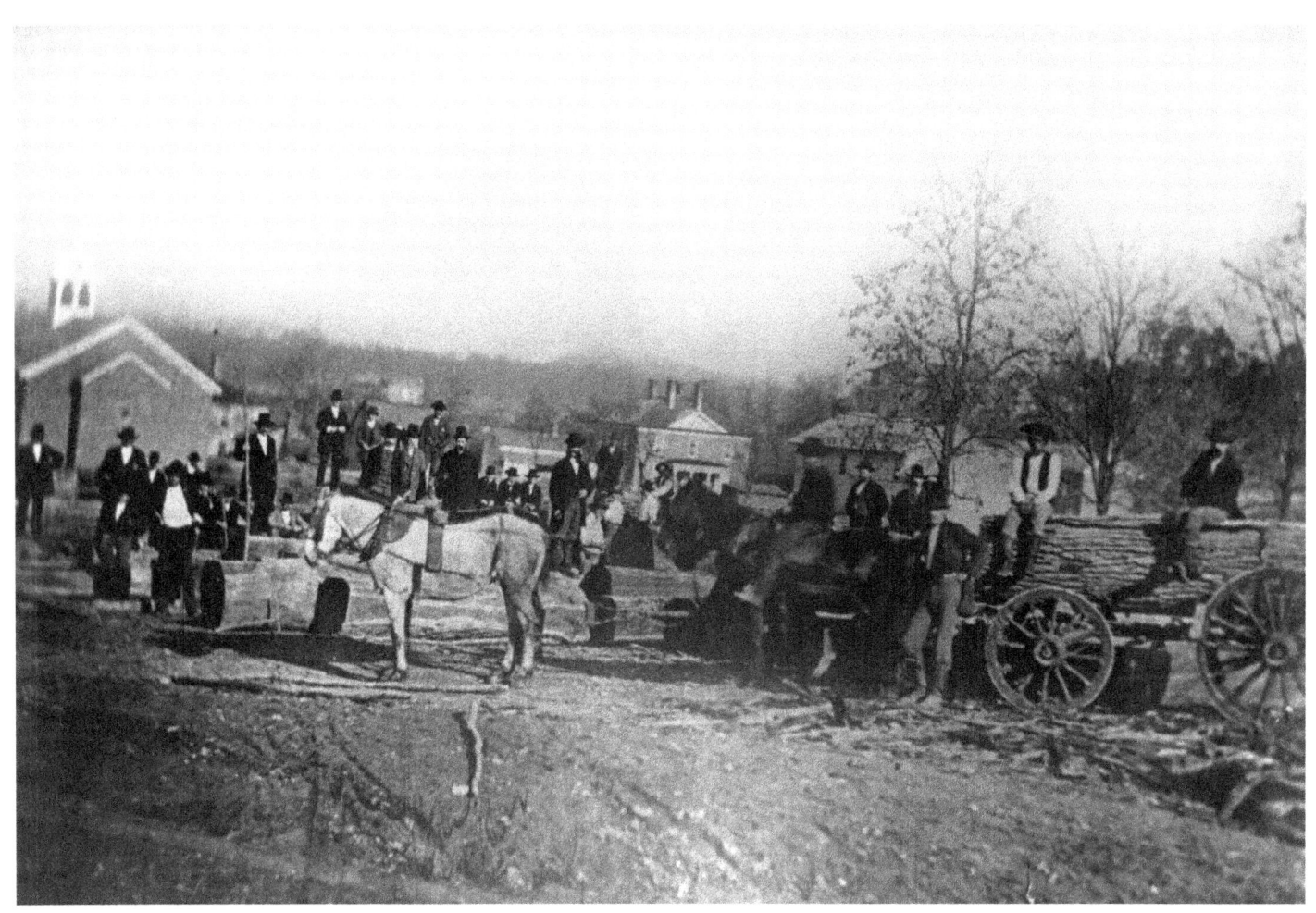

This photograph depicts Johnson City in the 1870s. A handwritten caption of unknown origin says that its subject is "possibly a log pulling contest." One such log sits in the wagon on the right.

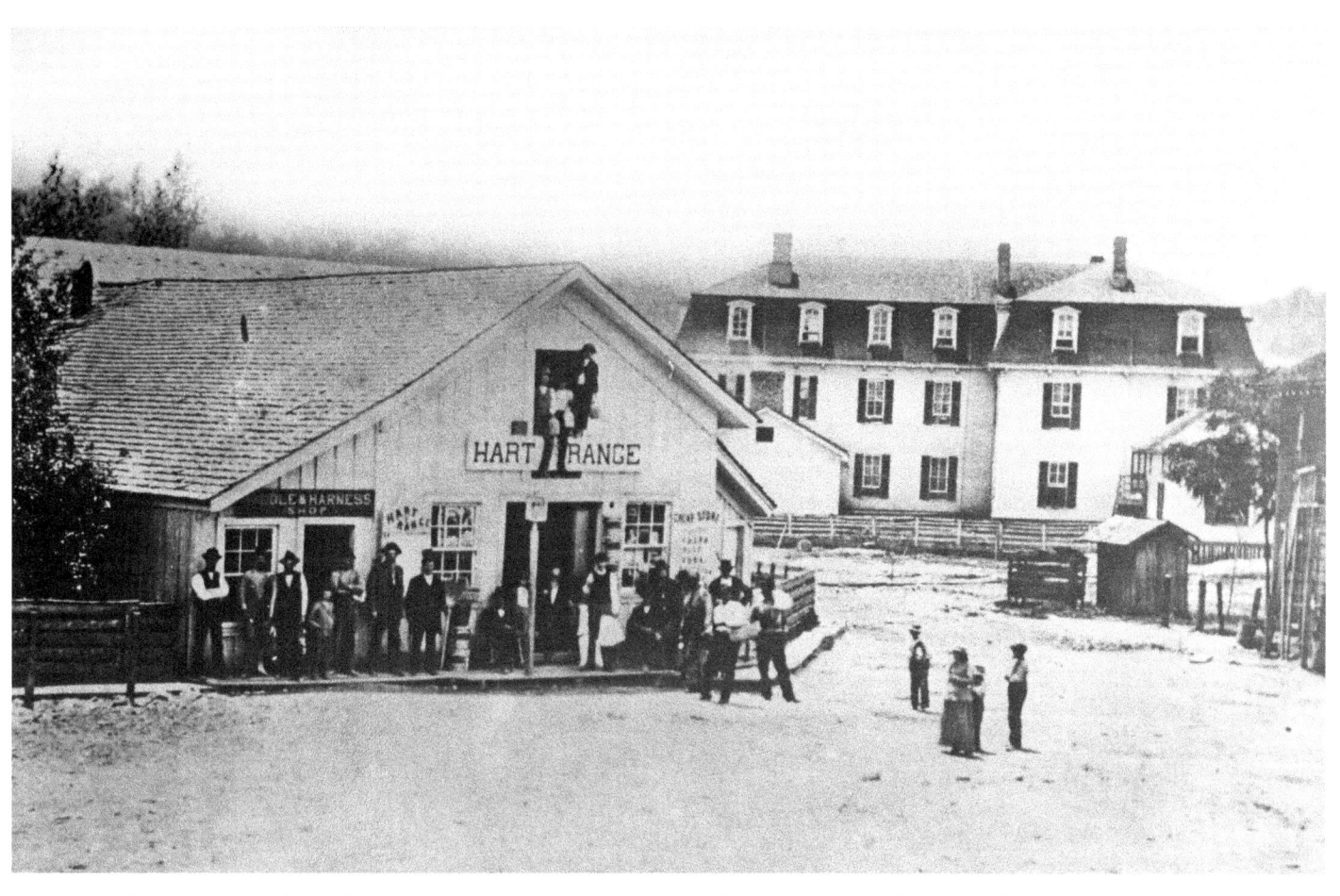

This early 1870s photo of what is now downtown Johnson City, Tennessee, shows the Hart and Range Saddle and Harness Shop, beside the City Hotel, later named the Piedmont Hotel. Johnson City historian Ray Stahl writes that "the harness shop was a popular gathering spot in that day."

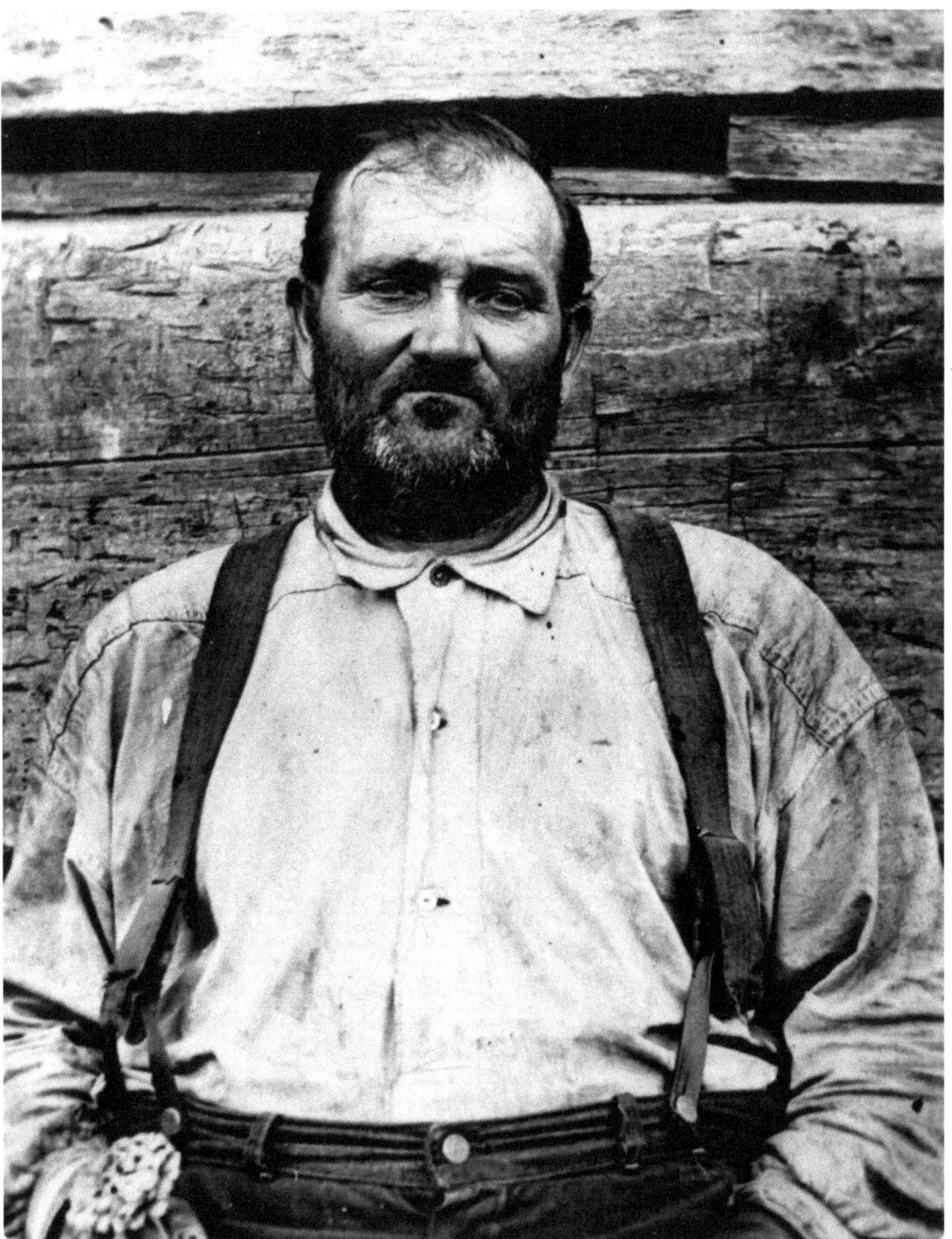

Nineteenth-century mountaineers were hardy people, yet able to appreciate the delicate. Standing in front of a structure built of immense hewn logs, this fellow holds a cut flower.

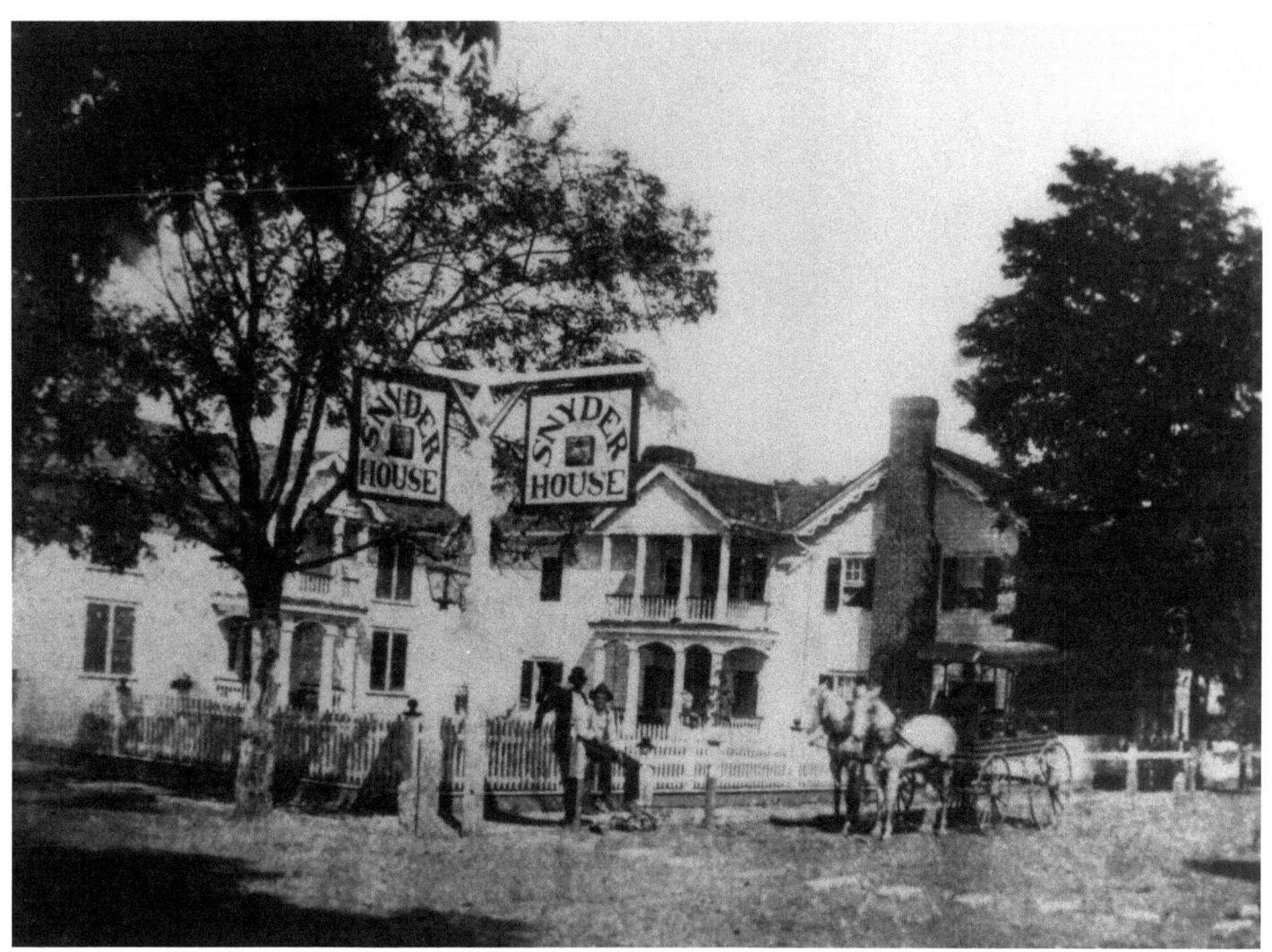

The Snyder House, said to be the first hotel in Elizabethton, Carter County, Tennessee, was located at First Street and Main, and operated by Henry Helm Snyder.

This photograph of Main Street in front of the old Washington County Courthouse, in Jonesborough, Tennessee, was taken in the 1880s. The gathering appears to be for an election day. Stepped gables on the structure, visible here in the upper-right-hand corner, beneath the cupola, are a characteristic of Jonesborough architecture of the period. The old courthouse was torn down in 1913 to make room for a new one.

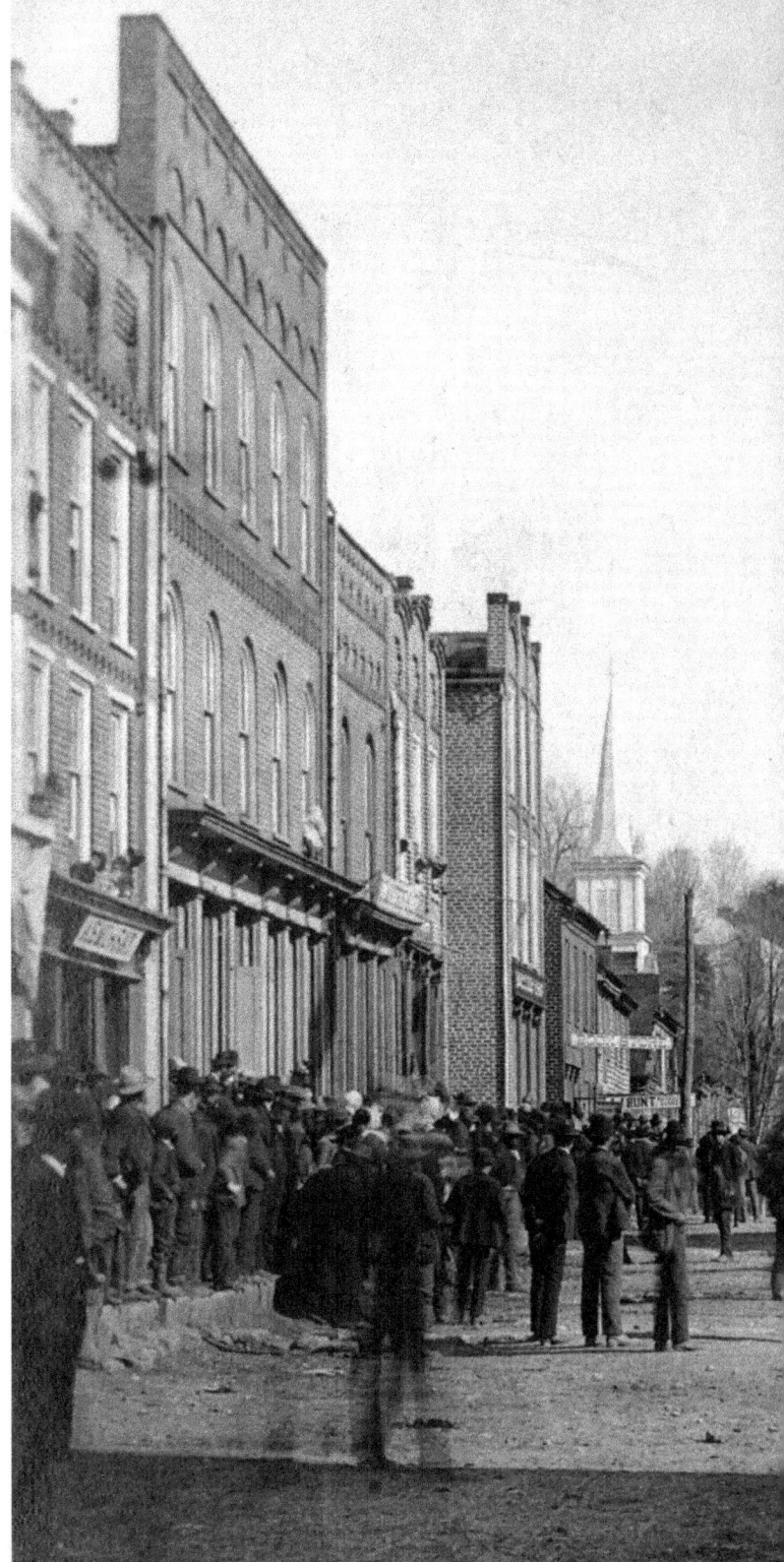

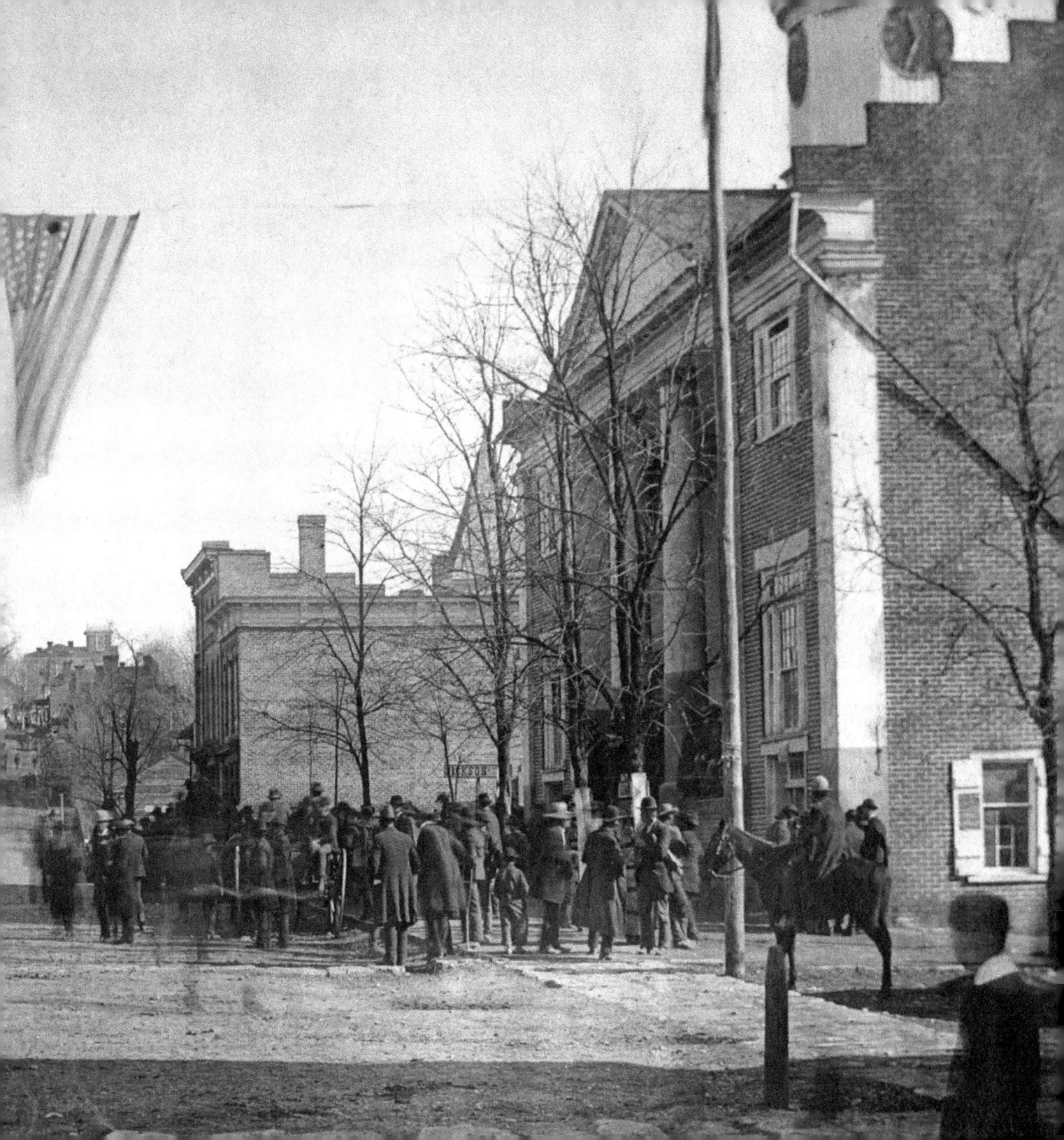

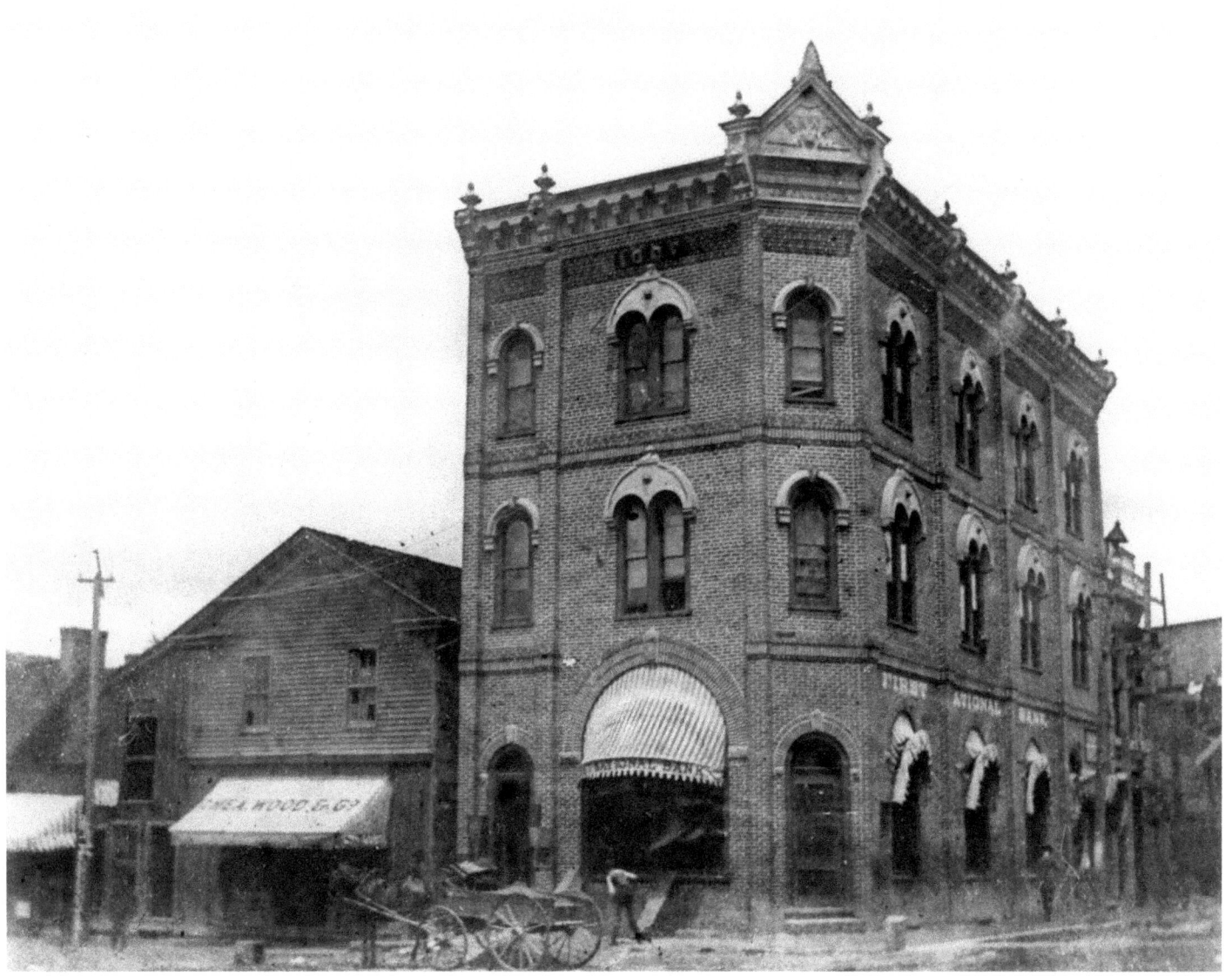

Though often perceived as isolated backwaters, many southern Appalachian towns participated fully in the American economic boom of the 1870s and 1880s—an era dubbed "the Gilded Age" by Mark Twain—and likewise participated in the international economic bust known as the Panic of 1893. The First National Bank, shown here in Johnson City, Tennessee, was established in 1886 and folded during the Panic.

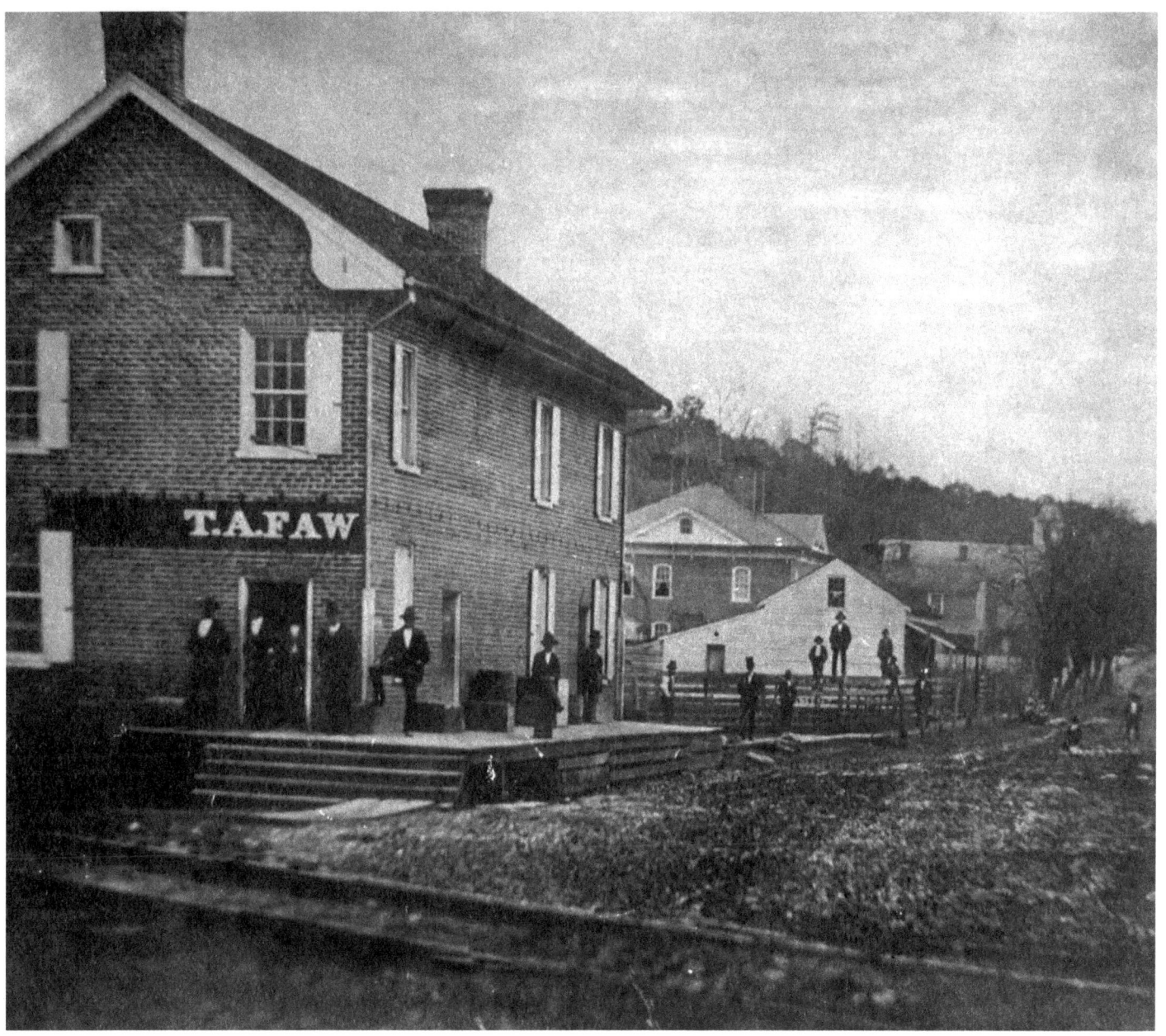

After the Civil War, commerce sprang up along railroad lines throughout Appalachia. The T. A. Faw store, operated by Walter, the son of Judge T. A. Faw, in Johnson City, Tennessee, was located beside the lines of the Southern Railroad.

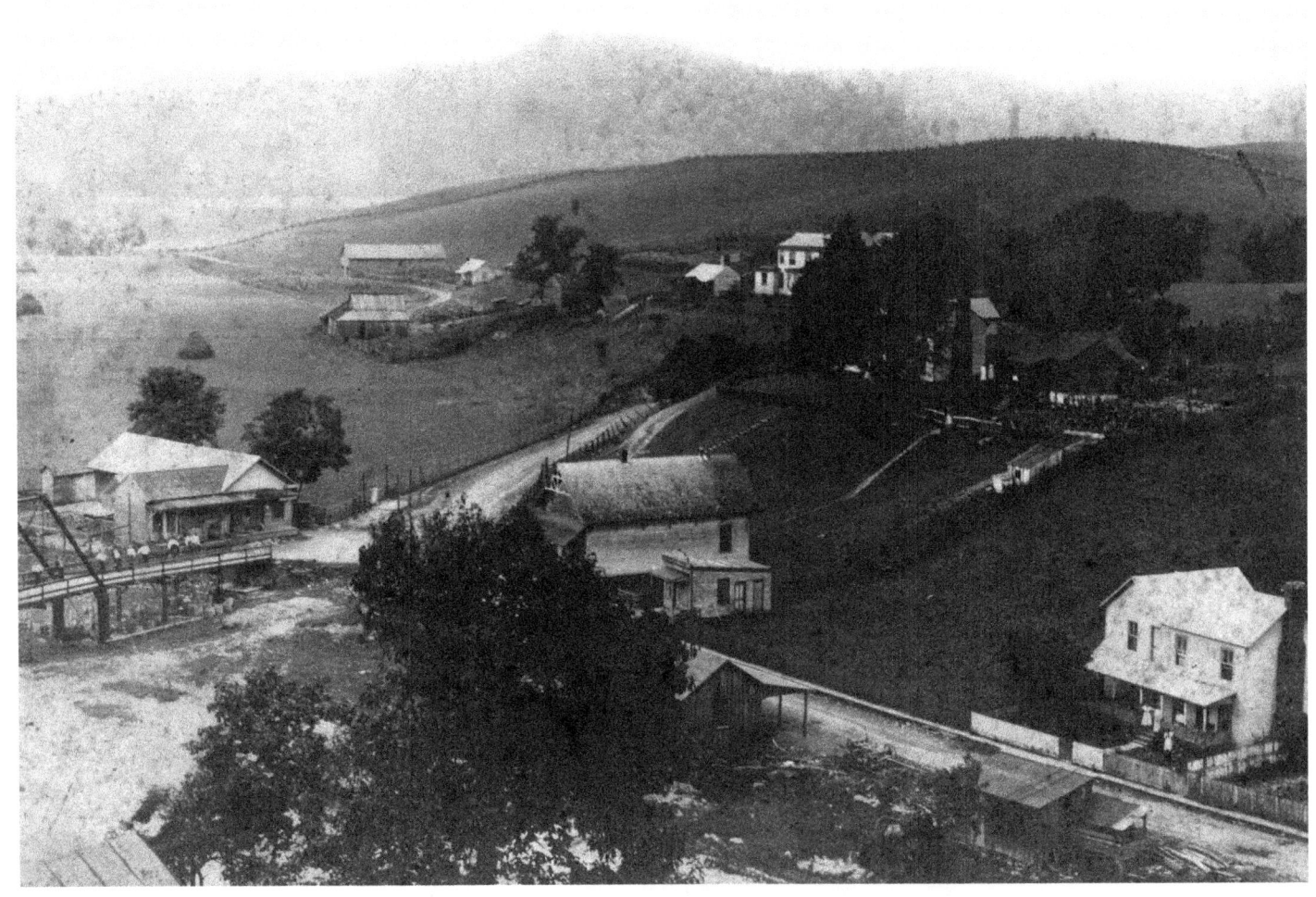

This nineteenth-century scene in Smyth County, southwest Virginia, shows how early communities developed as clusters of homes and farms along streams and roads in the habitable bottoms of the "Ridge and Valley" province of Appalachia. As early as the 1780s, one writer reported that all the habitable land of the upper Tennessee Valley between Kingsport and Knoxville was already being farmed.

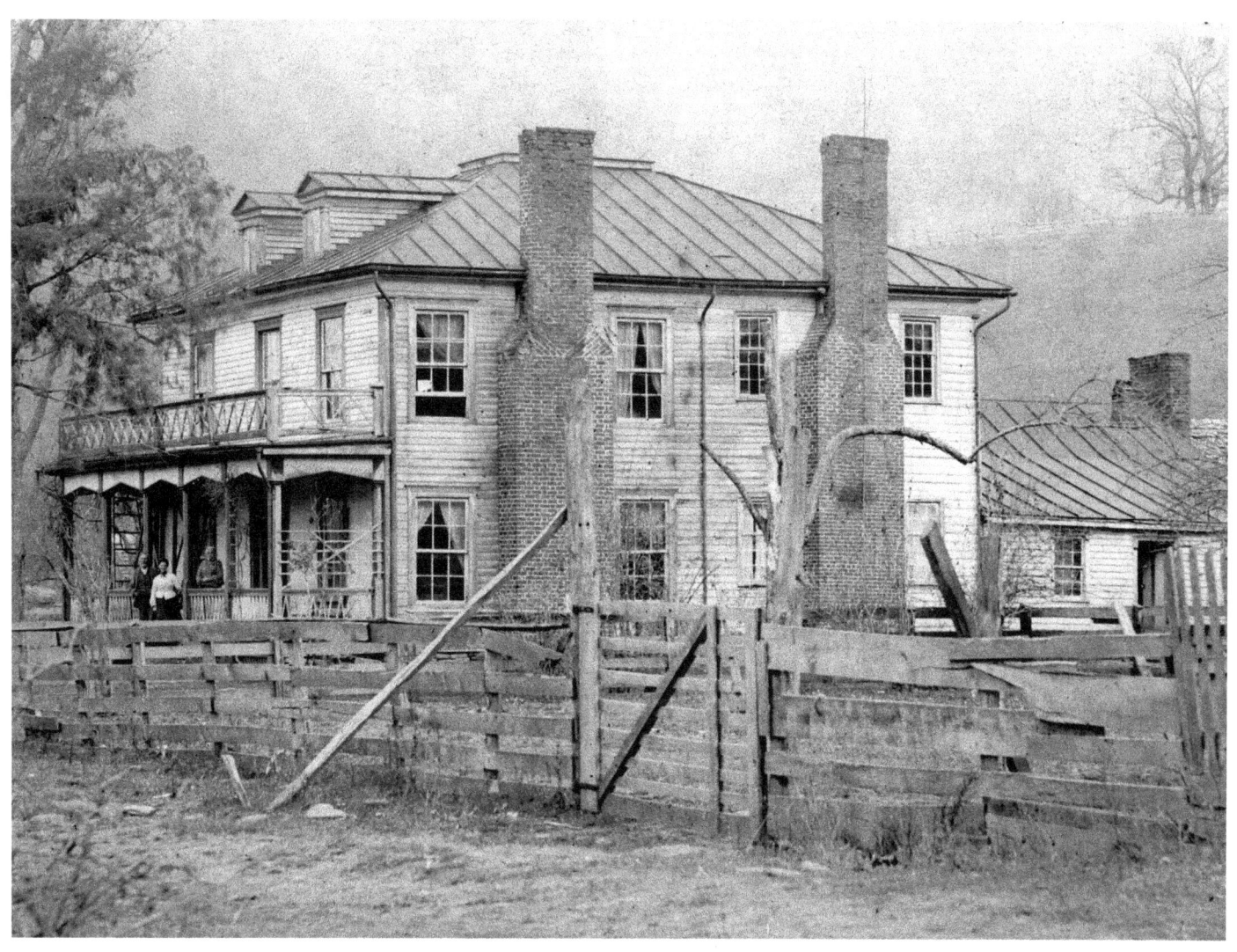

This photograph of the David Worth Home, in the town of Creston, in Ashe County, North Carolina, was taken around 1880. Worth was a tanner by trade, and became a prosperous merchant and prominent citizen in the mountainous border region near Tennessee.

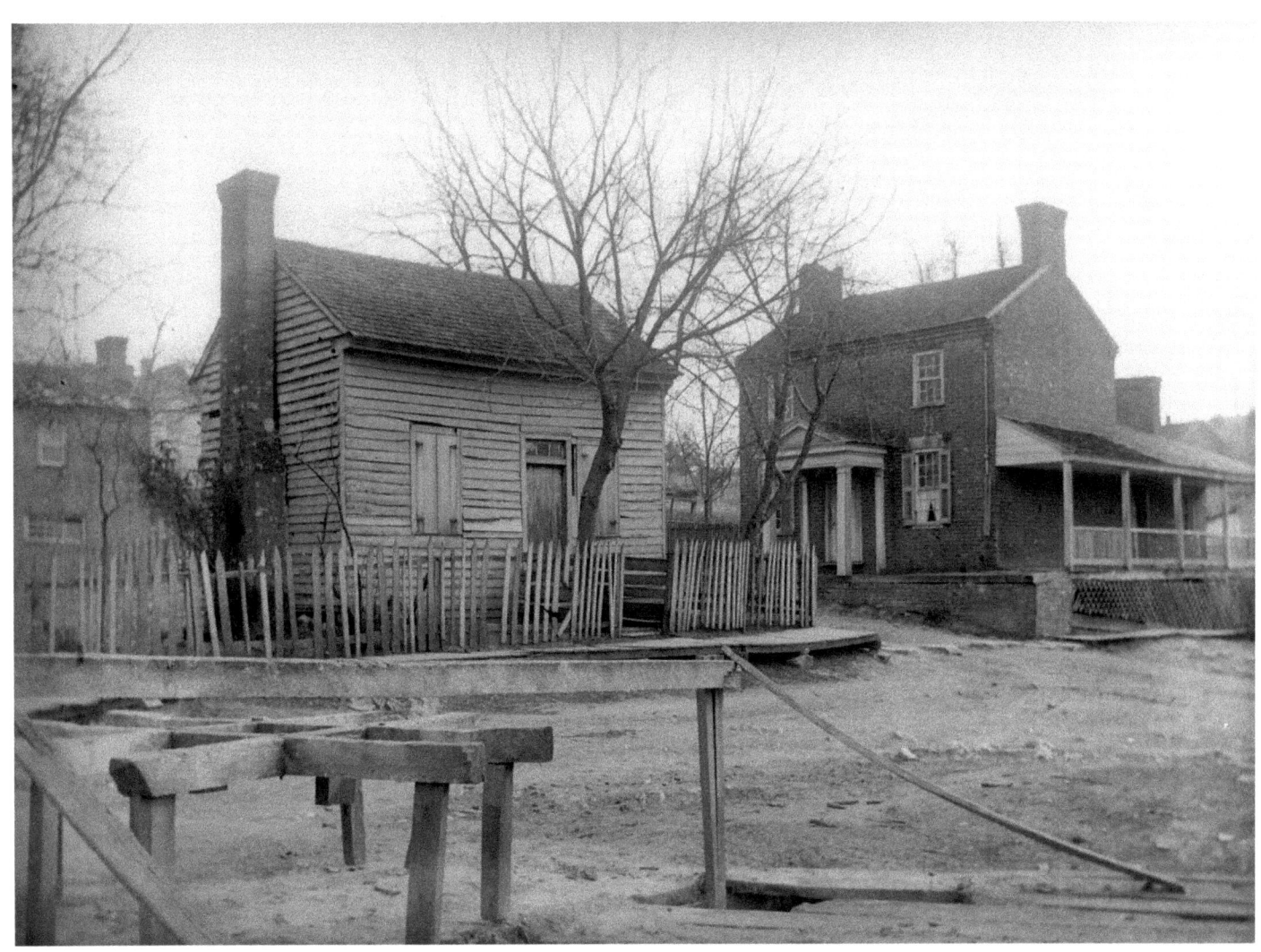

The Andrew Johnson home and tailor shop, in Greeneville, Tennessee—shown here around the time of Johnson's death in 1875—is now a National Historic Site. Like many residents of southern Appalachia, Johnson was pro-Union. Abraham Lincoln selected him as his vice-presidential running mate in 1864. As president, Johnson survived two attempts by Congress to remove him from office. He became a reviled figure throughout much of the country but remained well-respected in East Tennessee.

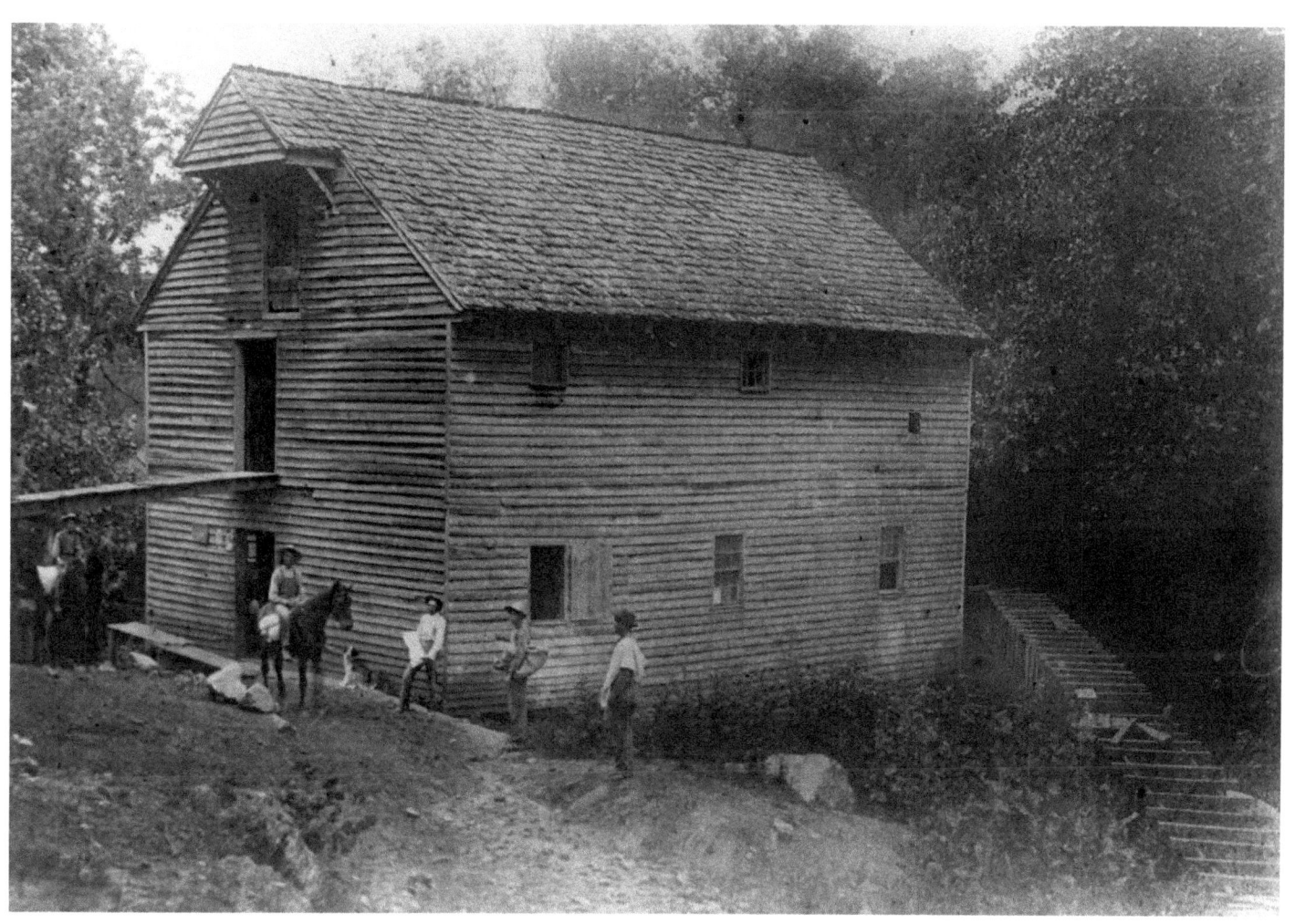

Benjamin Horn built this mill in the 1860s, in Sullivan County, Tennessee, in a community now known as Huddle Mill. Mills were important institutions in nineteenth-century Appalachia, and a water-powered mill such as this one often became the center of a settlement. This mill still stands, having been rebuilt after it was washed out by floods.

A number of the structures visible in this view, facing east along Main Street in Jonesborough, Tennessee—the seat of Washington County— are still standing today.

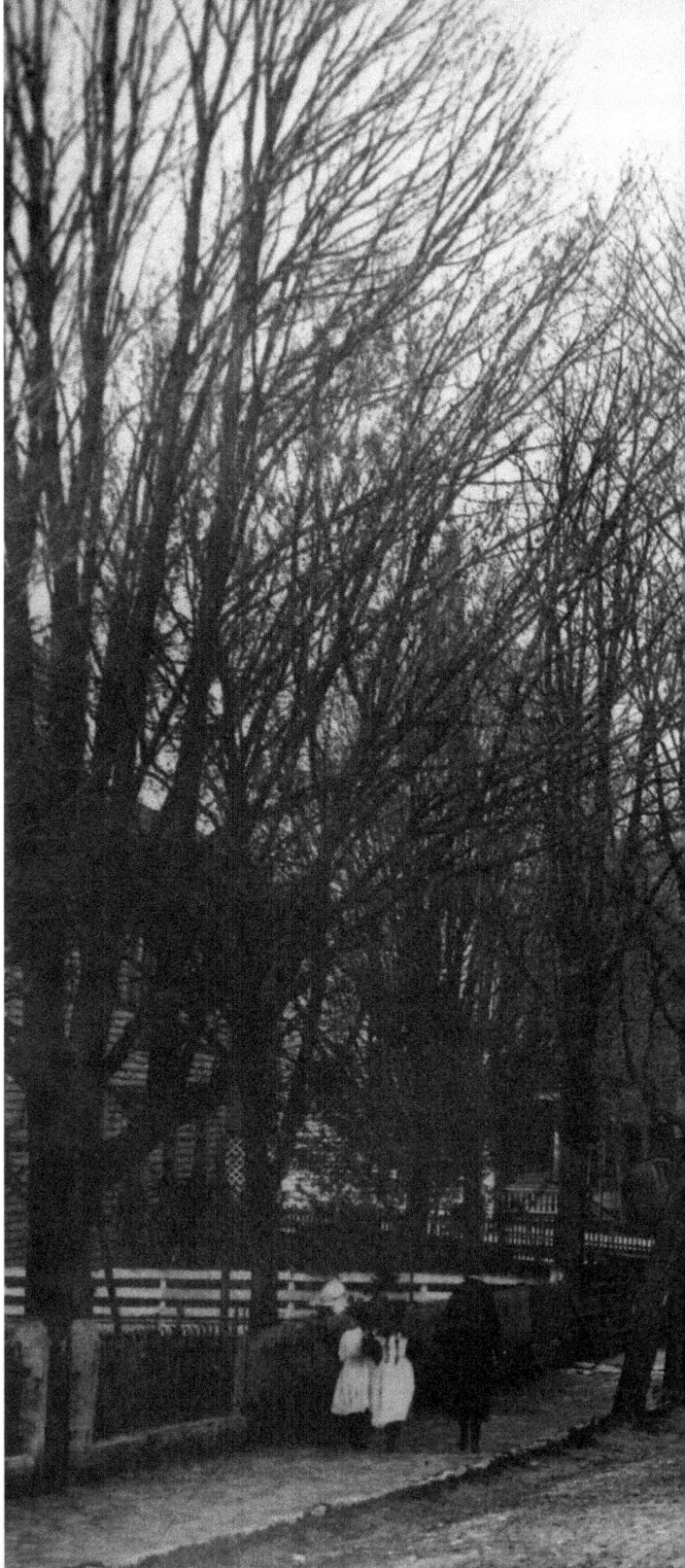

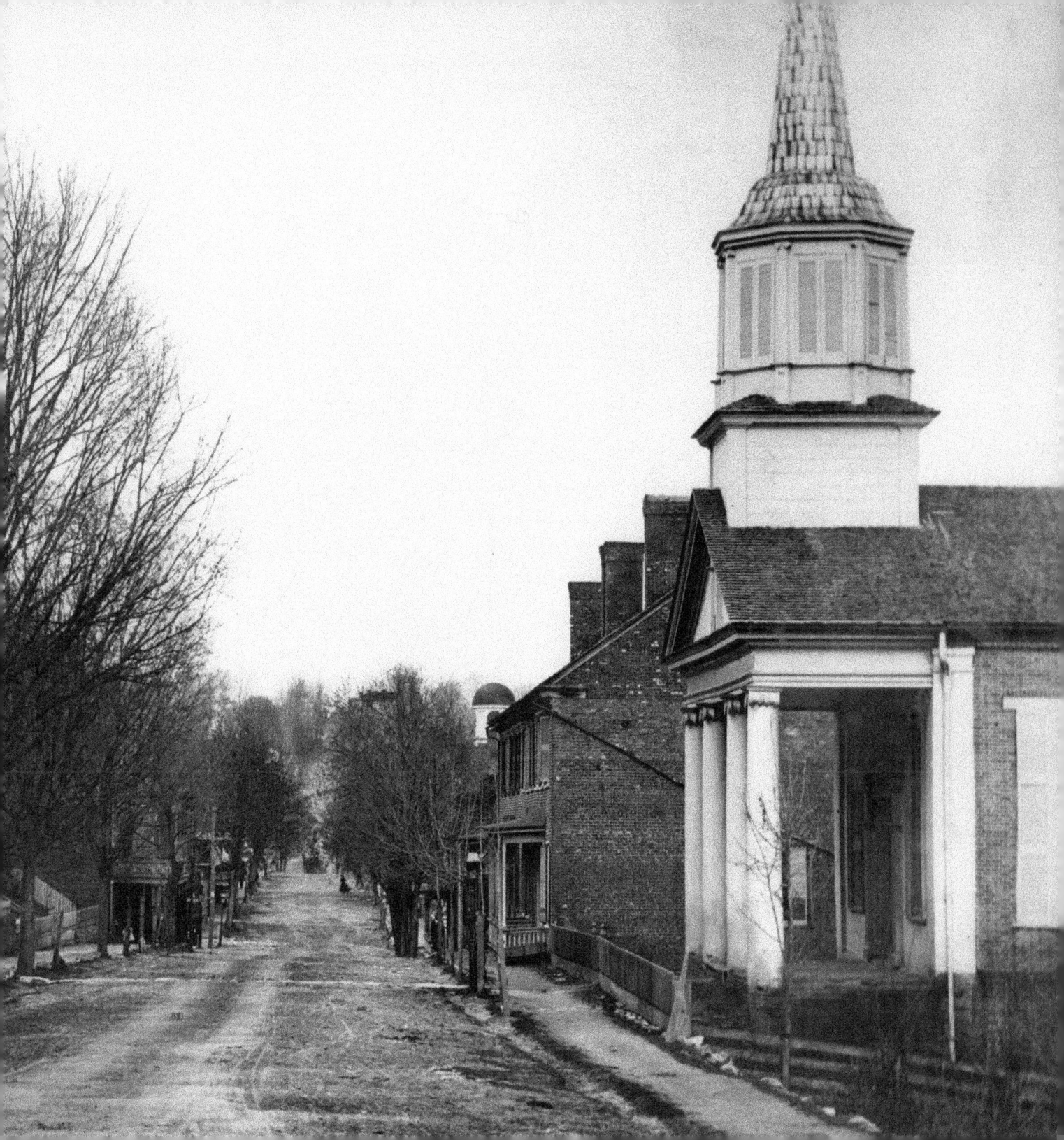

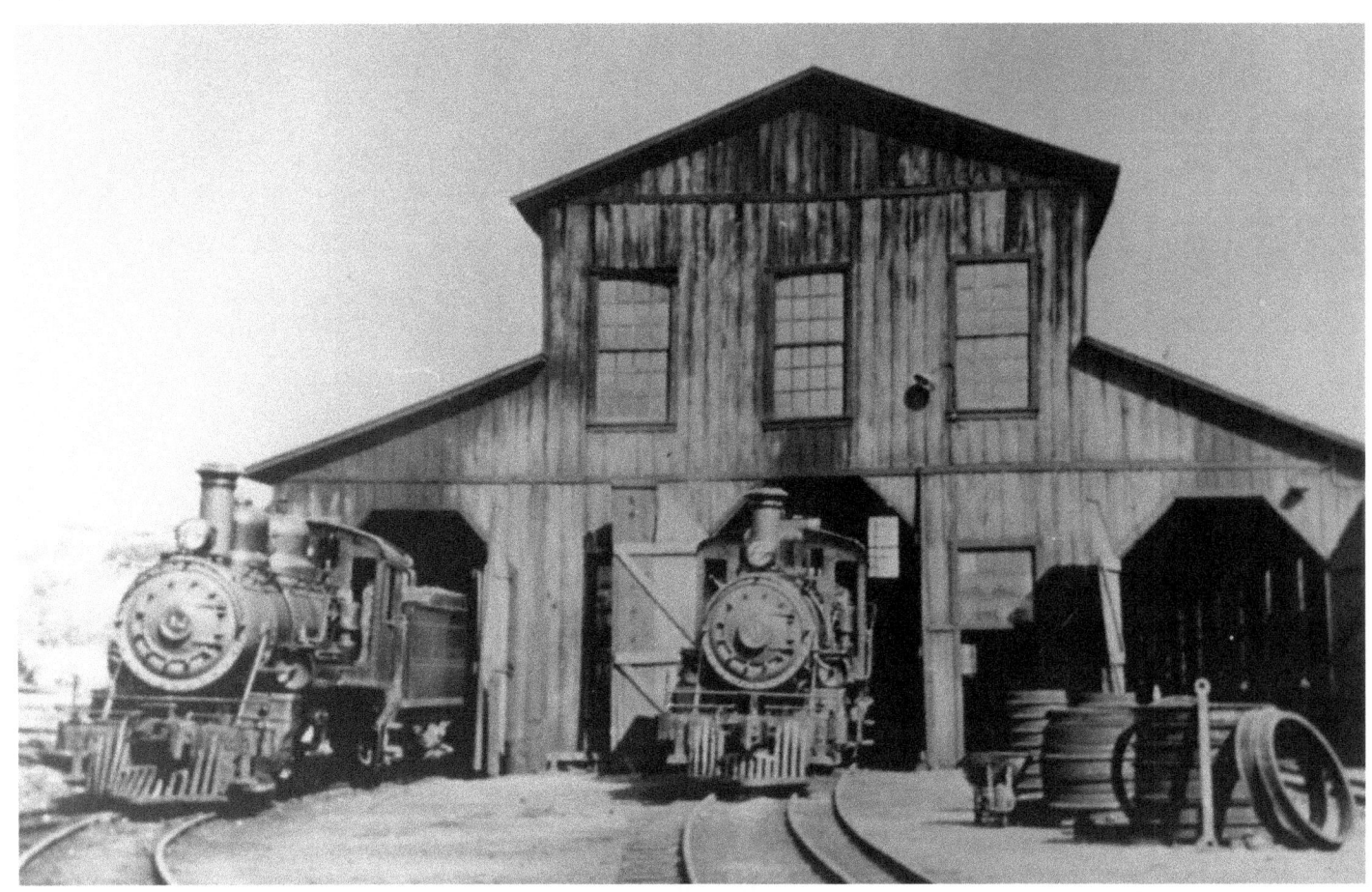

This is the old East Tennessee and Western North Carolina Railroad (E.T.&W.N.C.) shop, in Johnson City. The narrow gauge railroad ran through some of the most rugged country in the east, between Johnson City and Boone, North Carolina. It was instrumental in the harvesting of old growth timber, and later served as a passenger and excursion railroad, until the line was abandoned in 1950.

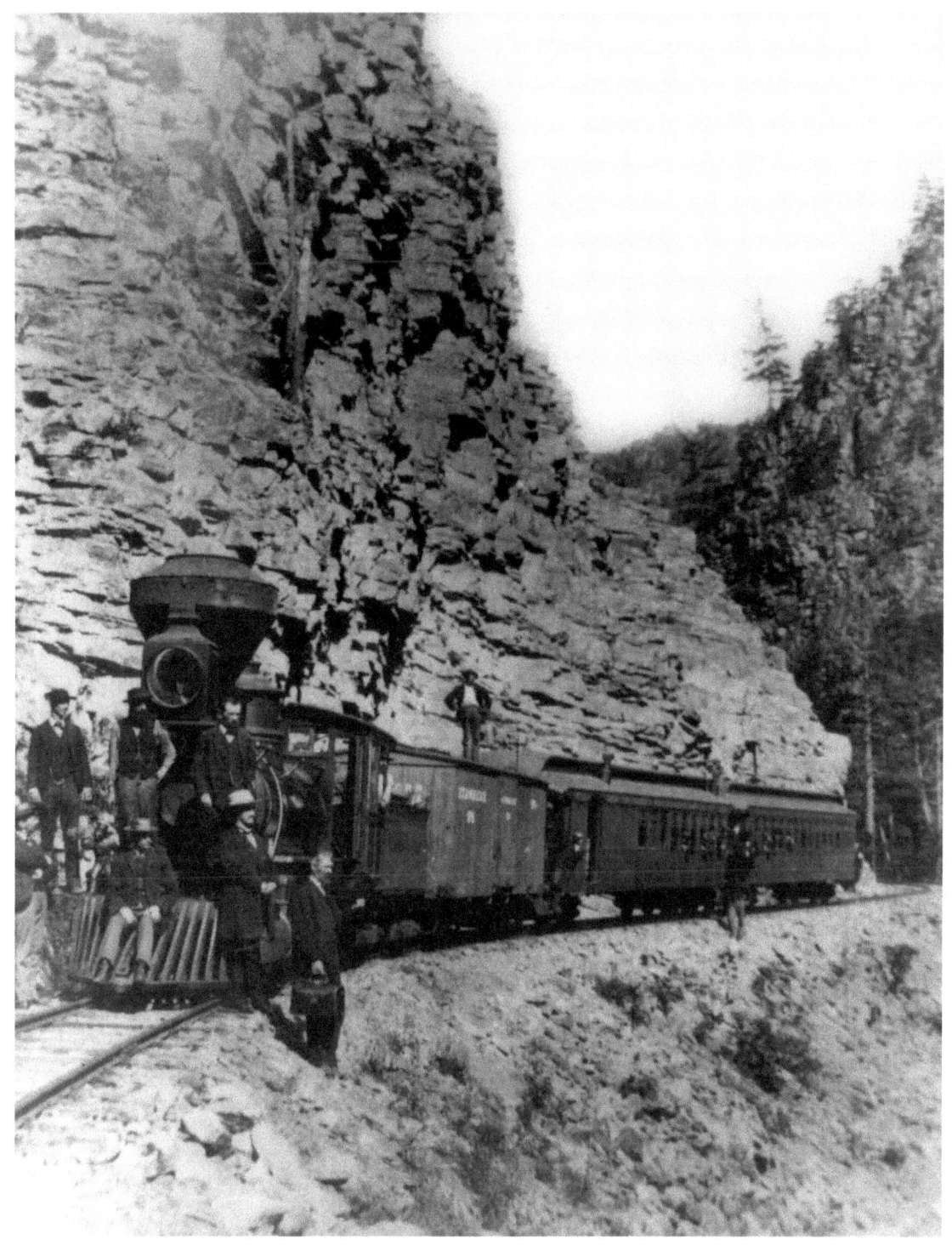

One of the first passenger trains to run on the E.T.&W.N.C. narrow-gauge line is pictured here, in the early 1880s, in the Doe River gorge, pulled by wood-burning Engine no. 1. A yard jockey figurine is mounted on the front of the engine, above the cowcatcher, atypical in images of early steam engines. By the early twentieth century, the E.T.&W.N.C. was nicknamed "Tweetsie Railroad," supposedly by children at summer camps near Grandfather Mountain, North Carolina, who mimicked the sound of the train whistle.

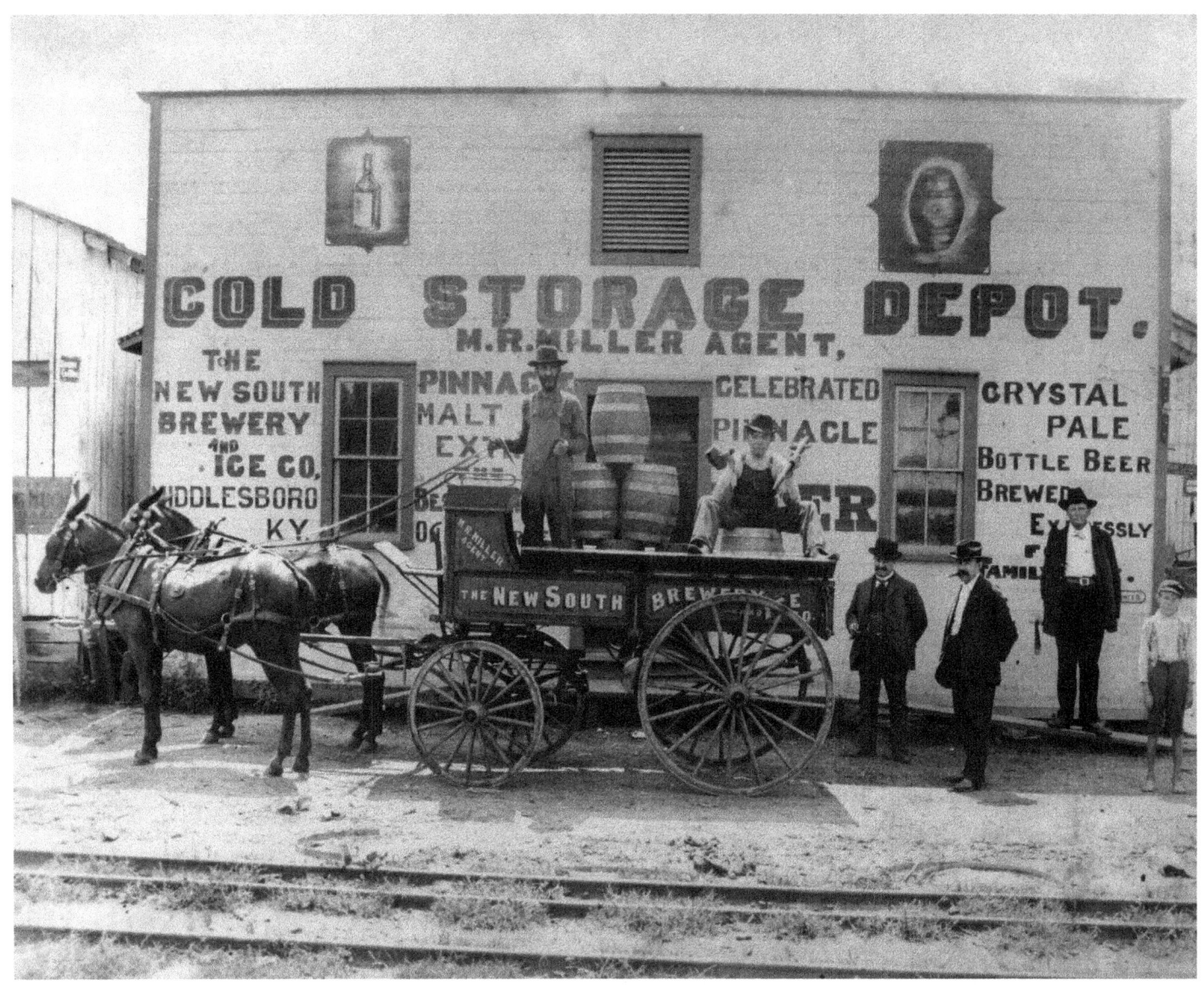

"Cold Storage Depot" was the somewhat euphemistic term applied to this beer warehouse located on Legion Street in Johnson City, Tennessee. The discovery of pasteurization, and advances in rail transportation and cold storage technologies, after the Civil War, made higher-quality beer widely available throughout Appalachia by the late nineteenth century.

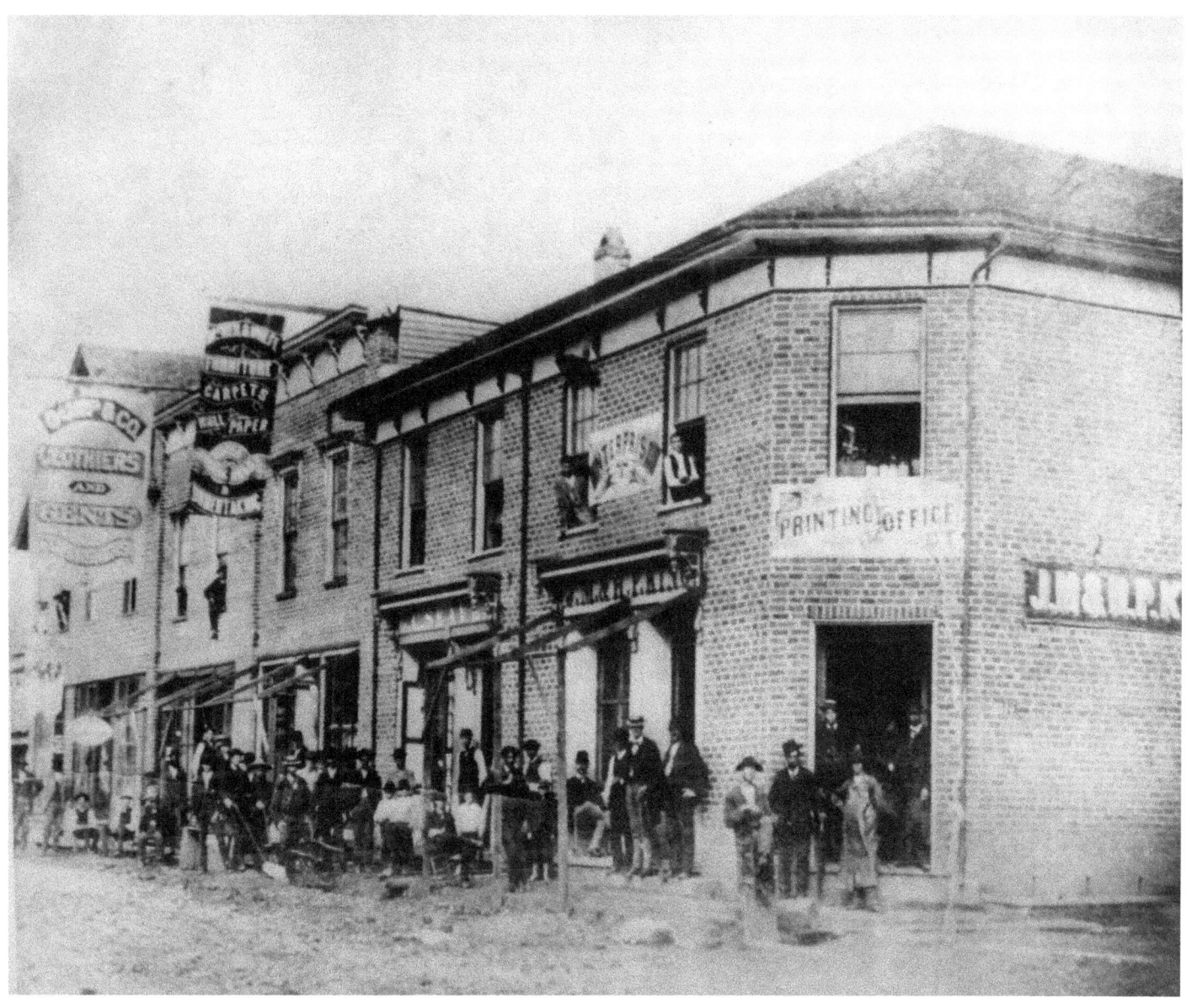

The office of the *Enterprise,* the first newspaper in Johnson City, in the 1880s. Like other small, regional newspapers, the Enterprise did job (commercial) printing, in order to stay in business. Also pictured are G. C. Seaver (saddle and harness shop) and McNeil and Wolfe (furniture, carpets, wallpaper, and undertaking).

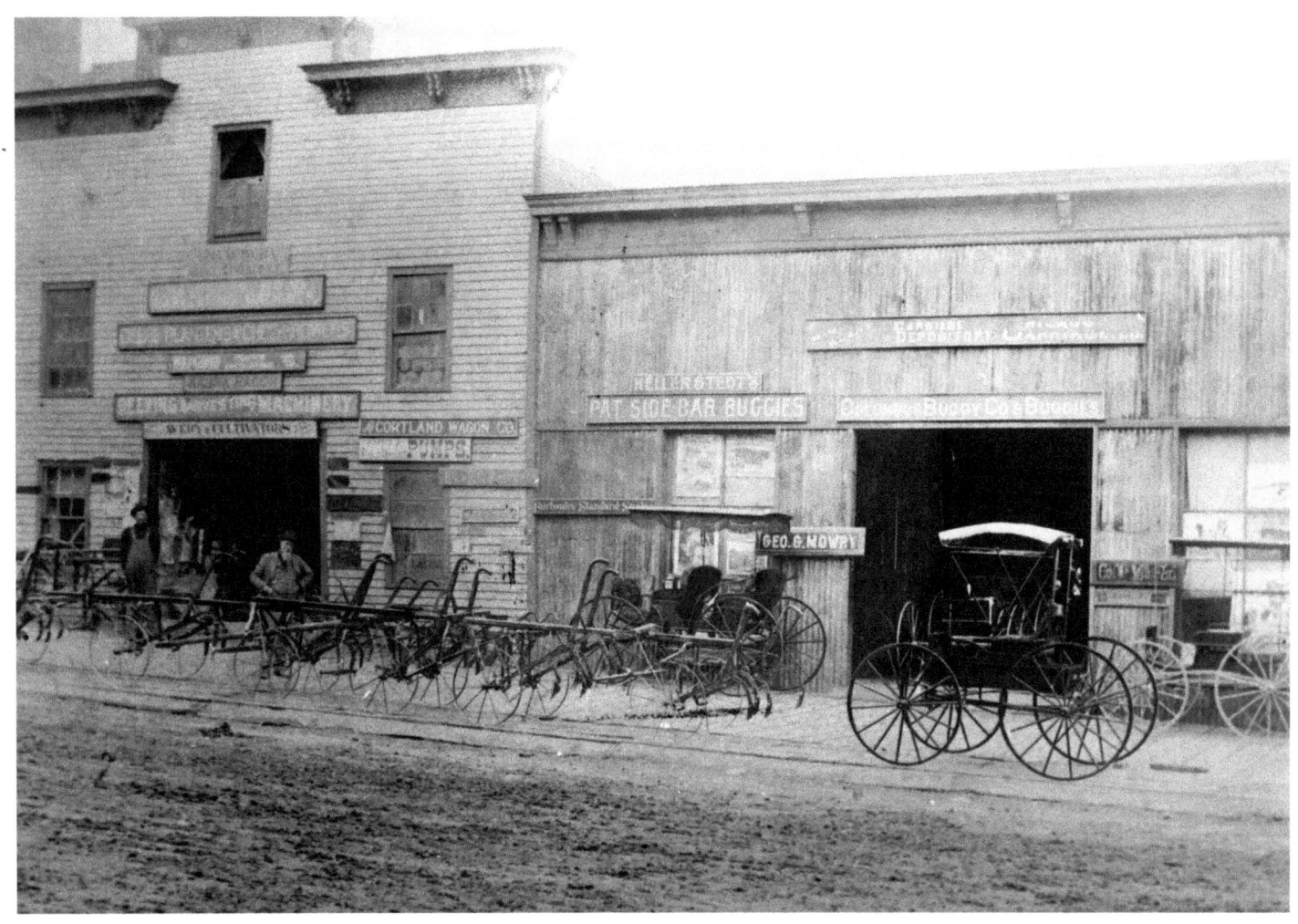

This East Tennessee farm implement store sold wagons, buggies, cultivators, and plows. One sharp-looking buggy and a long line of horse-drawn cultivators are on display here.

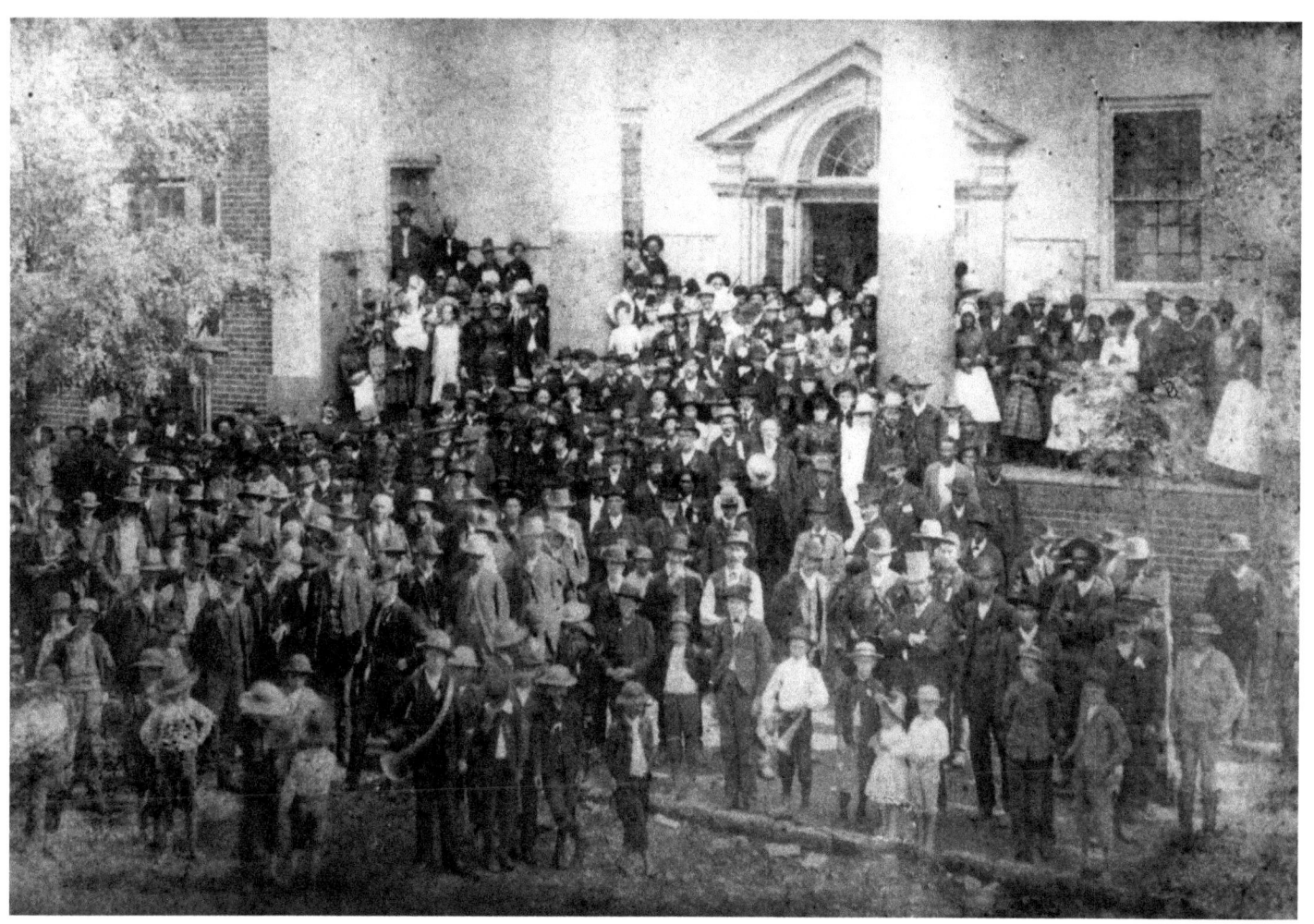

In 1887, Tennessee's General Assembly passed a resolution calling for a statewide vote on an amendment to the state constitution which, if passed, would ban the possession or sale of "intoxicating liquors." The special election that followed drew an unusually large turnout. The people of Tennessee voted against prohibition, 145,000 to 118,000. This photograph shows the scene on election day at the Washington County Courthouse.

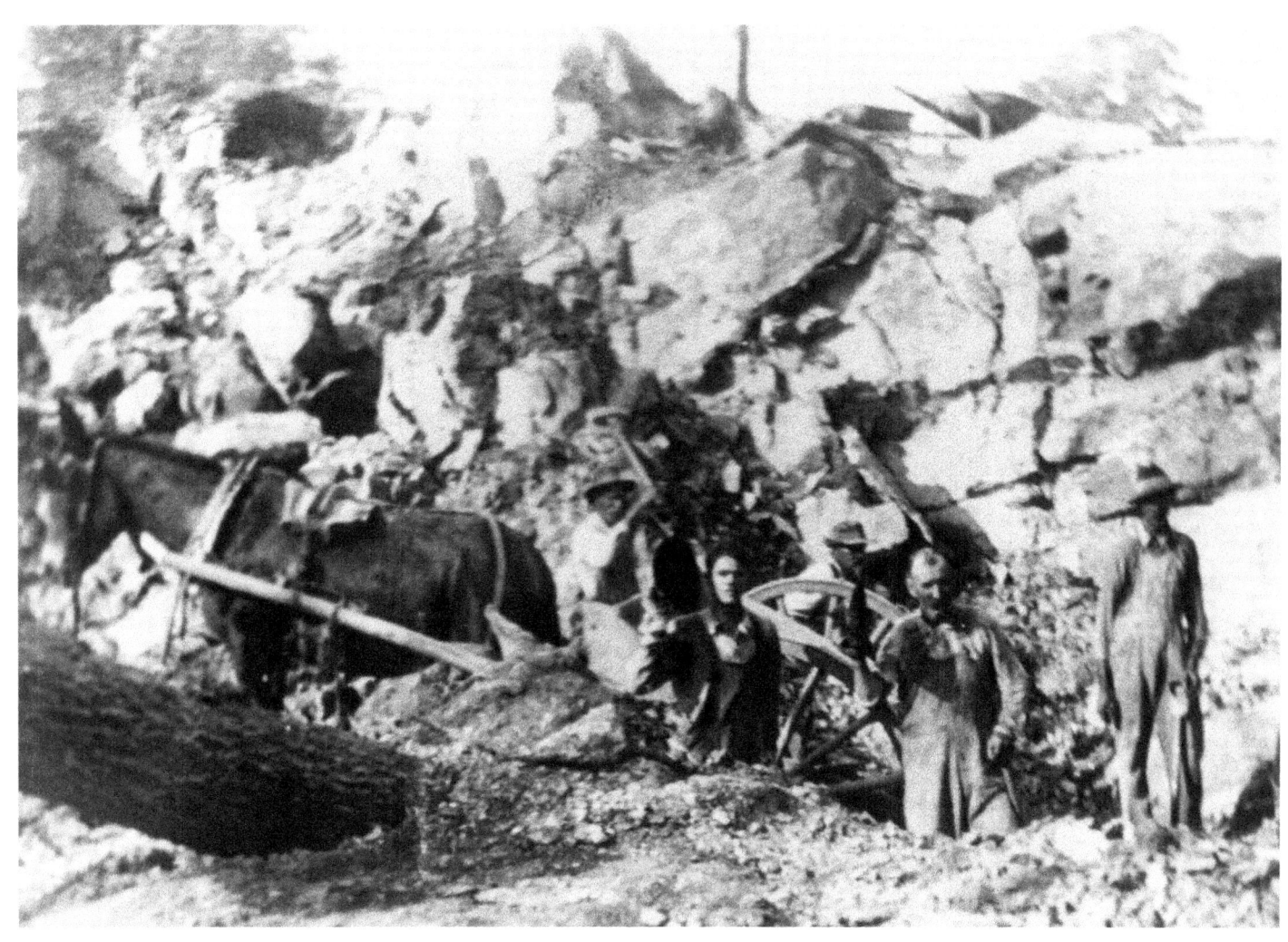

An excavating crew works with a mule cart, probably building a railroad bed, while several crewmembers doff their hats to the photographer. A wheelbarrow rests on the ledge above.

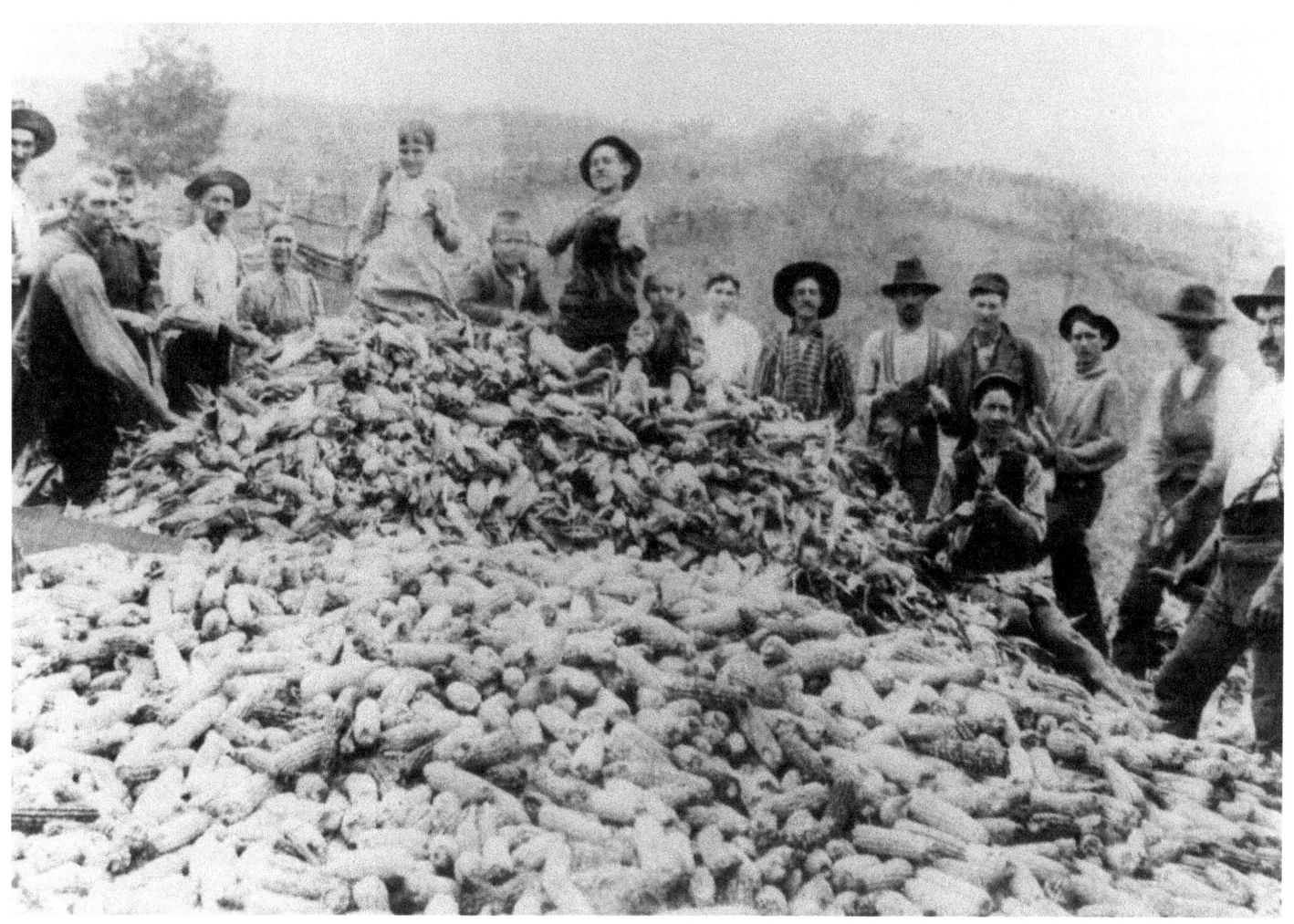

In the nineteenth century, corn-husking parties were popular events for young and old in Appalachia. By the first decades of the twentieth century, high-production grain farms in the Midwest led to a dramatic decline of grain production in Appalachia. At the top of this heap, several youngsters and their puppy dogs are "kings of the mountain."

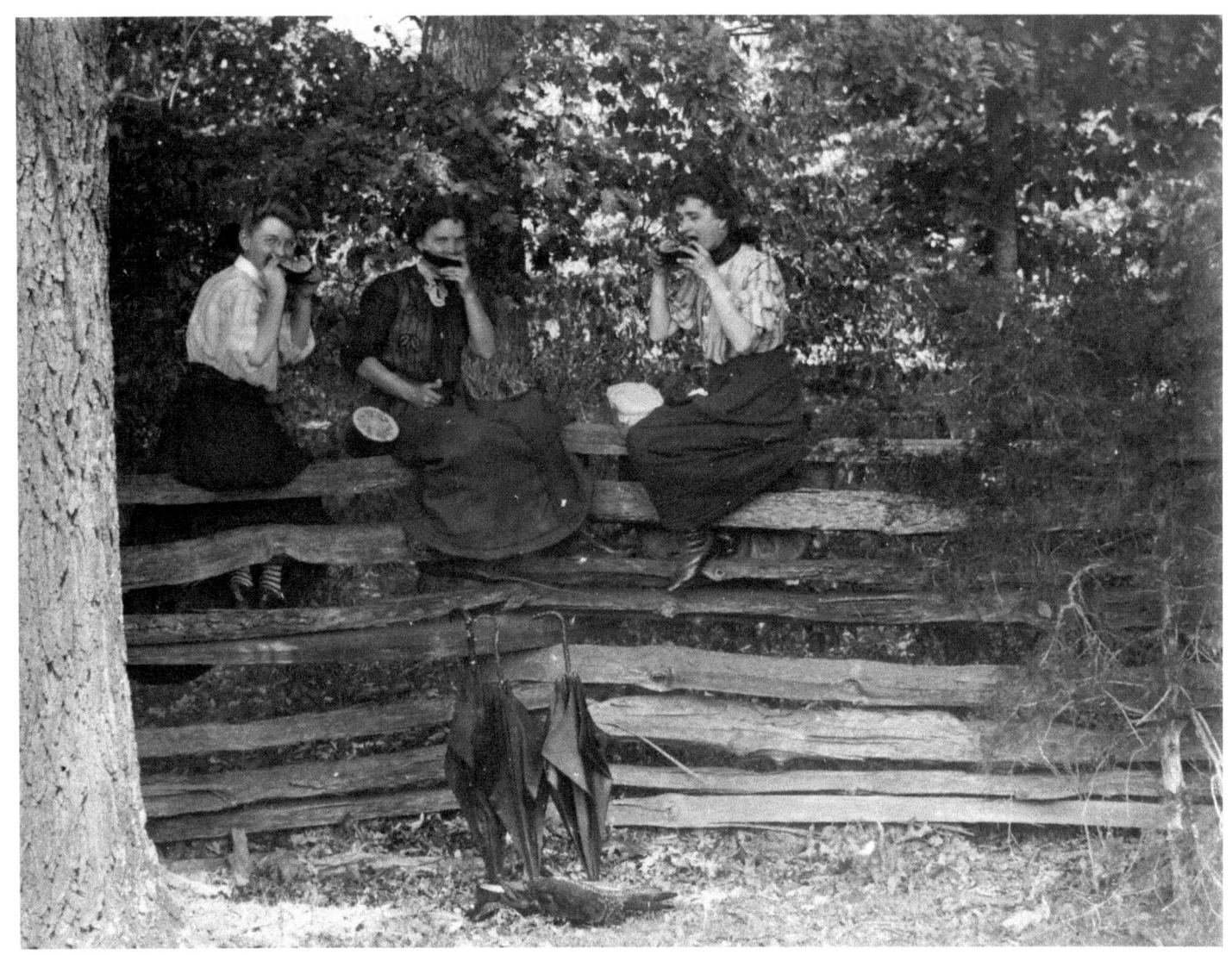

Three young women atop a split-rail fence enjoy melons on a nineteenth-century summer day. Leaning against the fence are their umbrellas, commonly used in that era as parasols, to ward off the harsh rays of the sun.

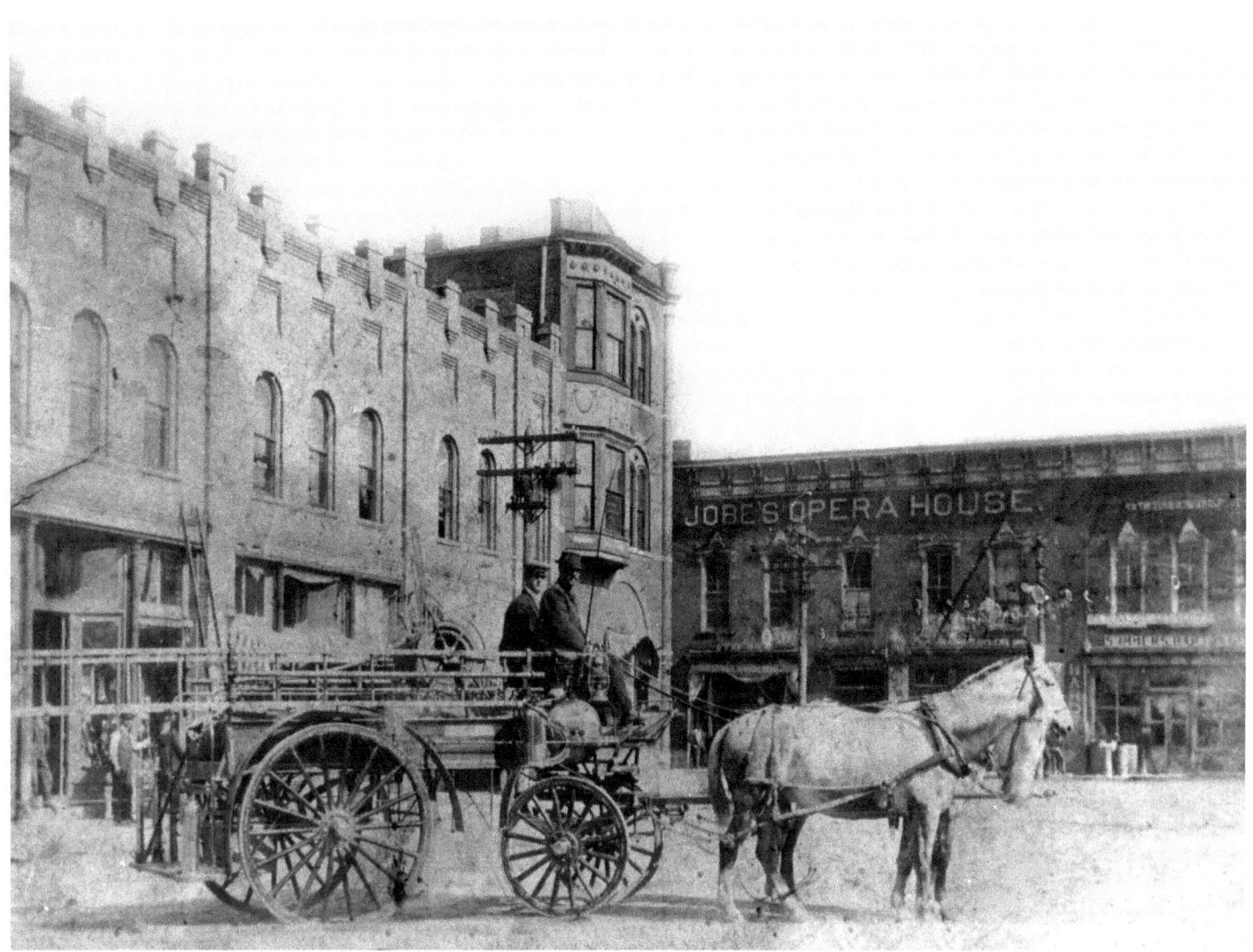

A horse-drawn fire wagon poses in the Johnson City, Tennessee, public square, in 1890, in front of Jobe's Opera House. The 900-seat, two-story auditorium was opened in 1885. Used for theater productions by traveling "dramatic troops," as well as for lectures, musical and comedic performances, and sporting events, the house closed around 1907, put out of business perhaps by the rise of motion pictures.

This private residence on Pine Street in Johnson City, Tennessee, seems to feature the family in their Sunday best, with Junior astride his favorite pony and Grandpa seated beside a potted colocasia, commonly known as elephant ear.

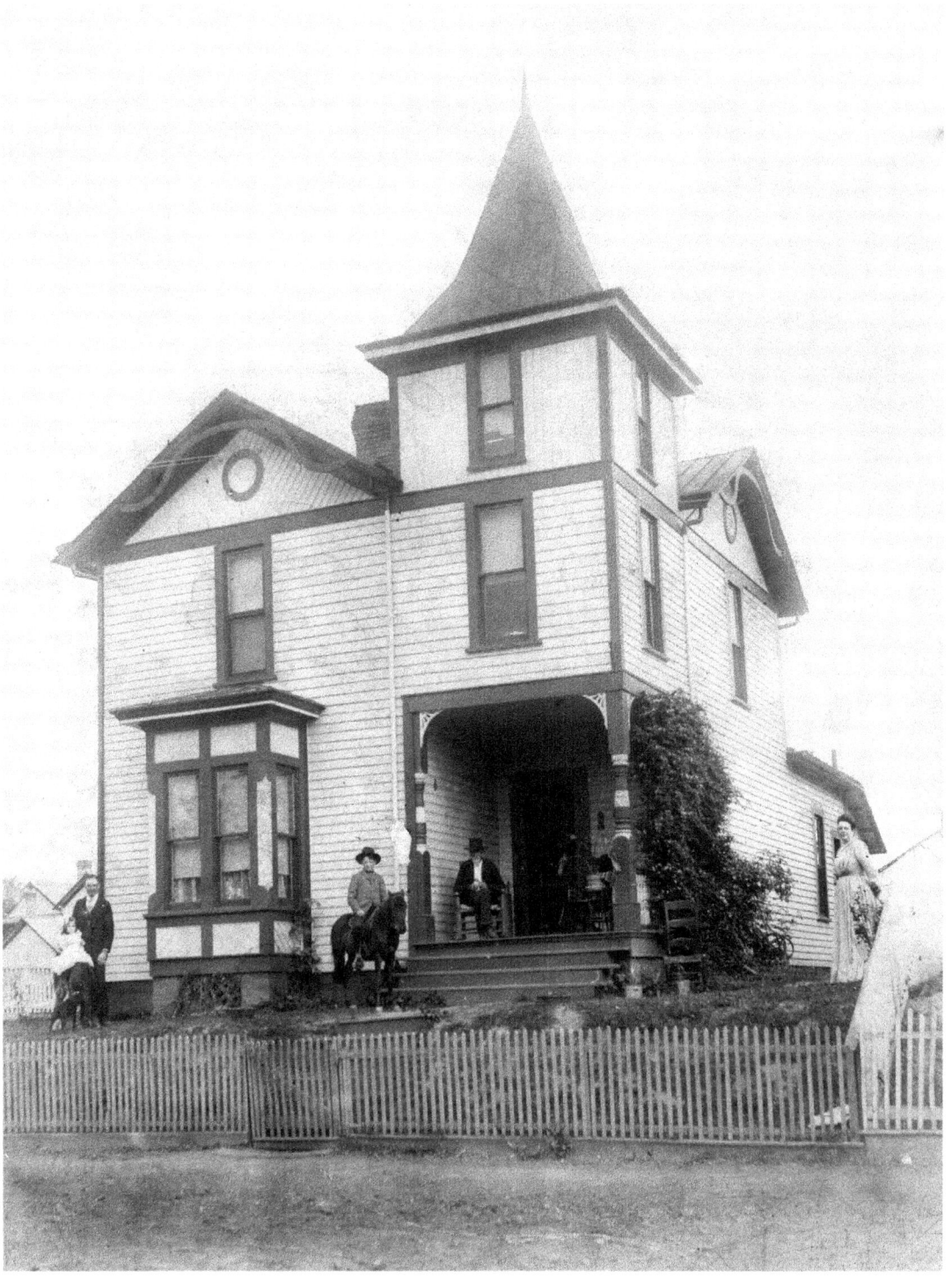

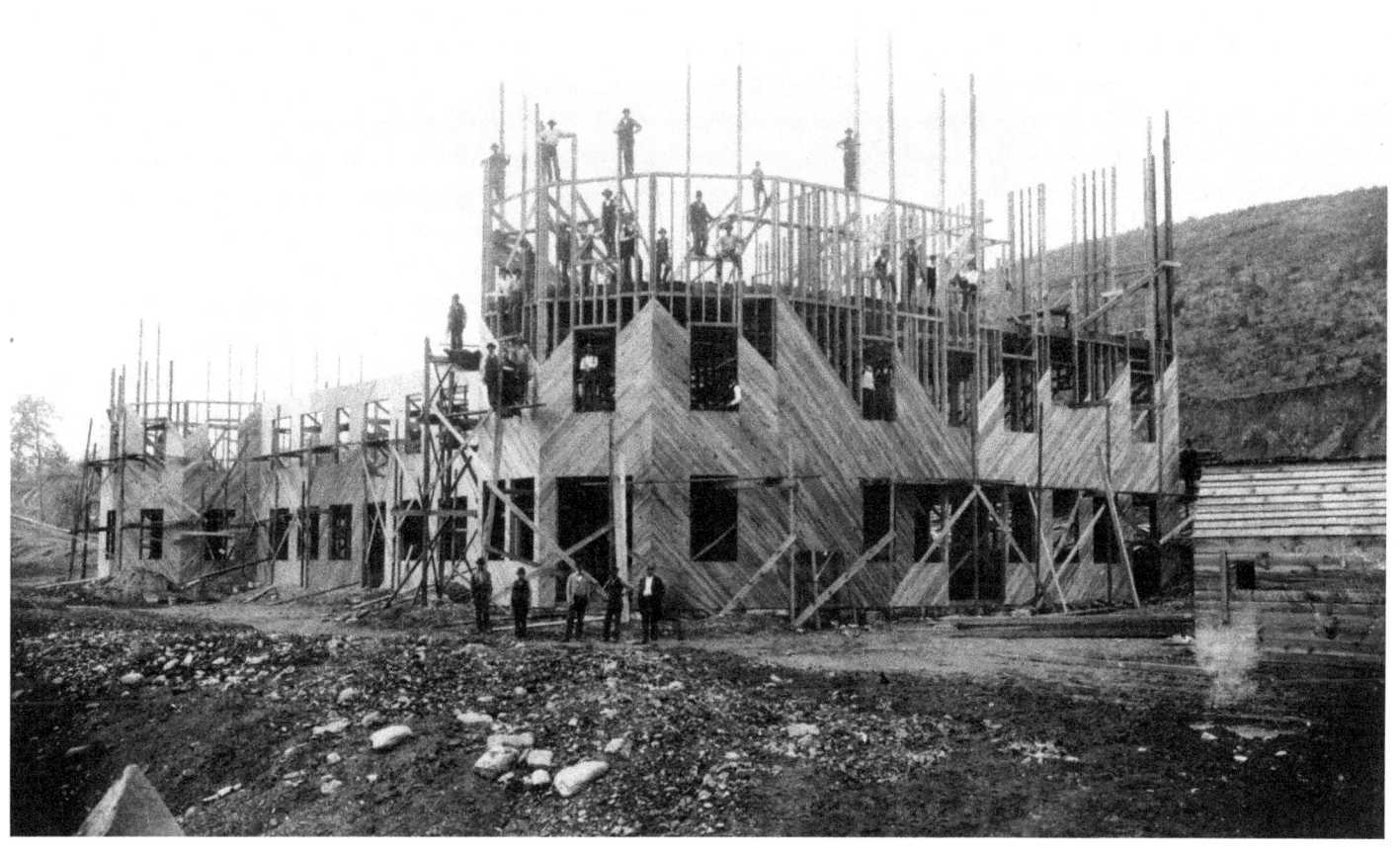

Workers pose on the Gladys Inn during construction in Clifton Forge, Virginia, in the early 1890s. A construction boom was being driven by the expansion of the Chesapeake and Ohio Railroad. The inn was named in honor of the daughter of M. E. Ingalls, at that time president of the railroad.

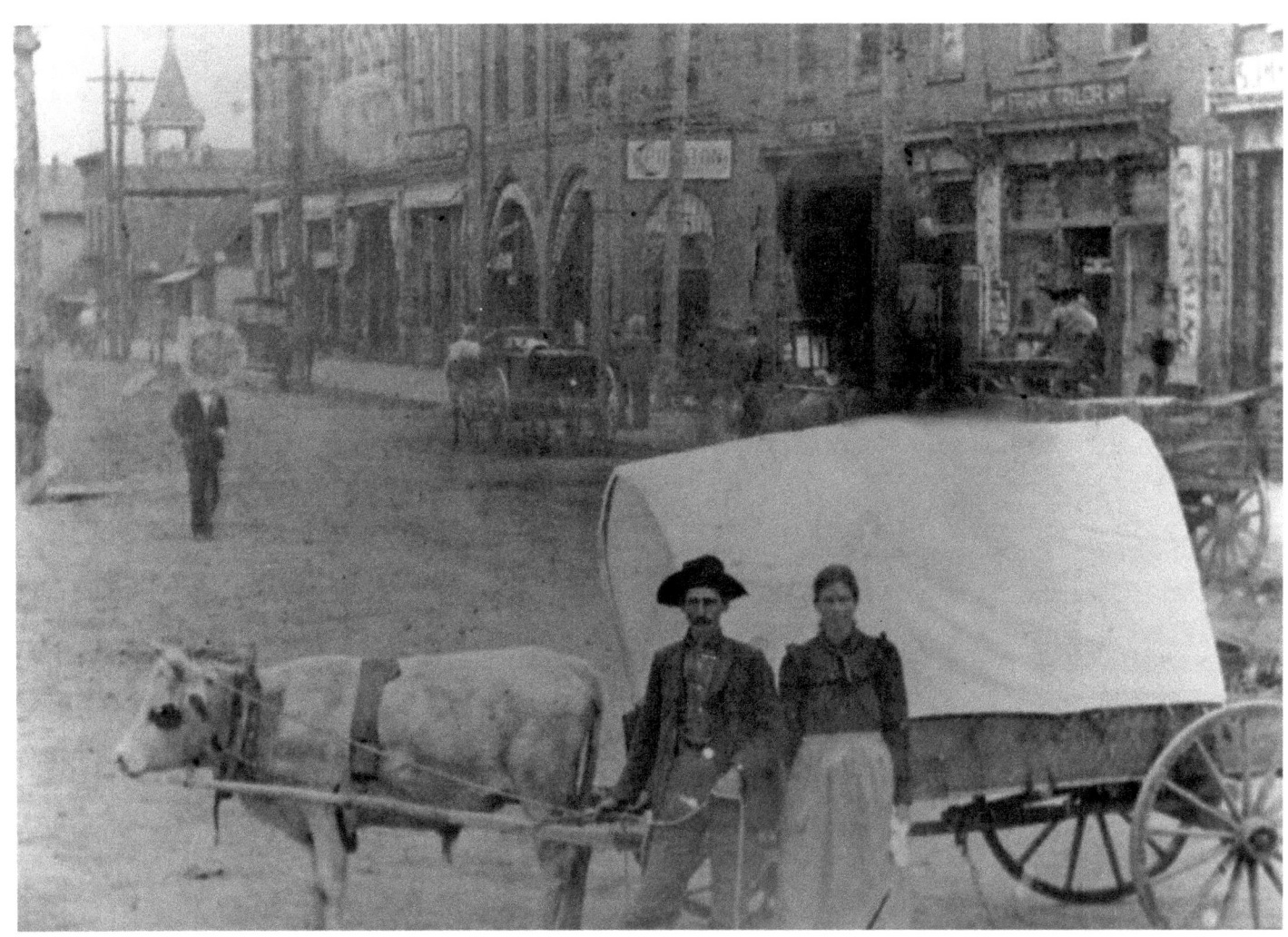

In the 1890s, apple sellers have brought their wares down from high mountain orchards, in the fall, in an ox-drawn covered wagon, to sell at the market in Johnson City, Tennessee.

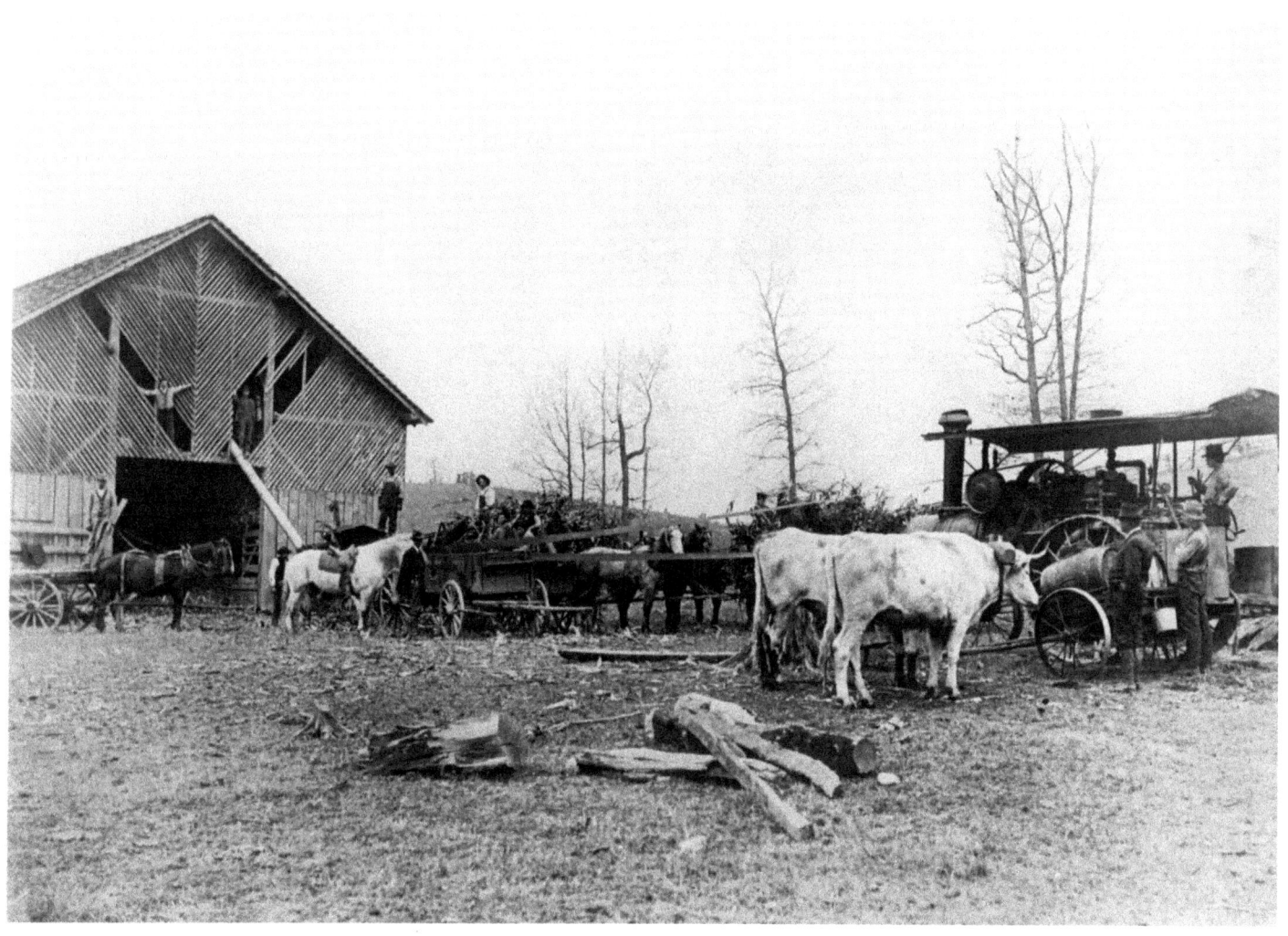

This farm scene of Appalachia in the 1890s shows a steam-powered threshing machine, or "thrasher," perhaps one of the first such machines in the region. Steam power had replaced horse power as the favored means of threshing—separating grain from chaff and straw—as well as much of the other work of row-cropping, but horse power continued as a necessity well into the twentieth century.

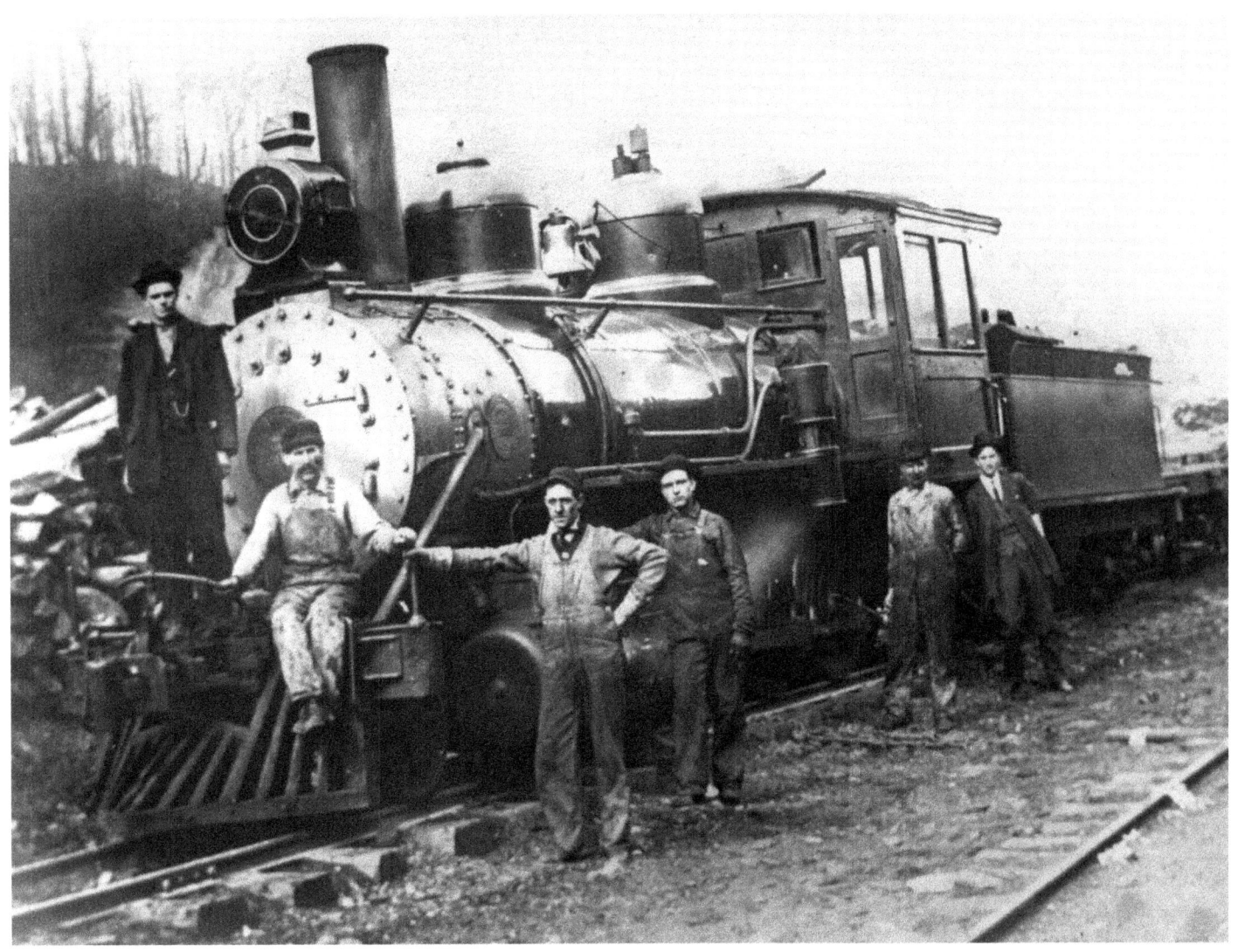

East Tennessee and Western North Carolina Railroad's engine no. 3 idles at Cranberry, North Carolina, in the 1890s. The narrow-gauge railroad hauled freight and passengers between Boone, North Carolina, and Johnson City, Tennessee. Cranberry was the site of a high-grade iron ore mine in the nineteenth century, but, like most Appalachian iron ore veins, miners had depleted the deposit by the early twentieth century.

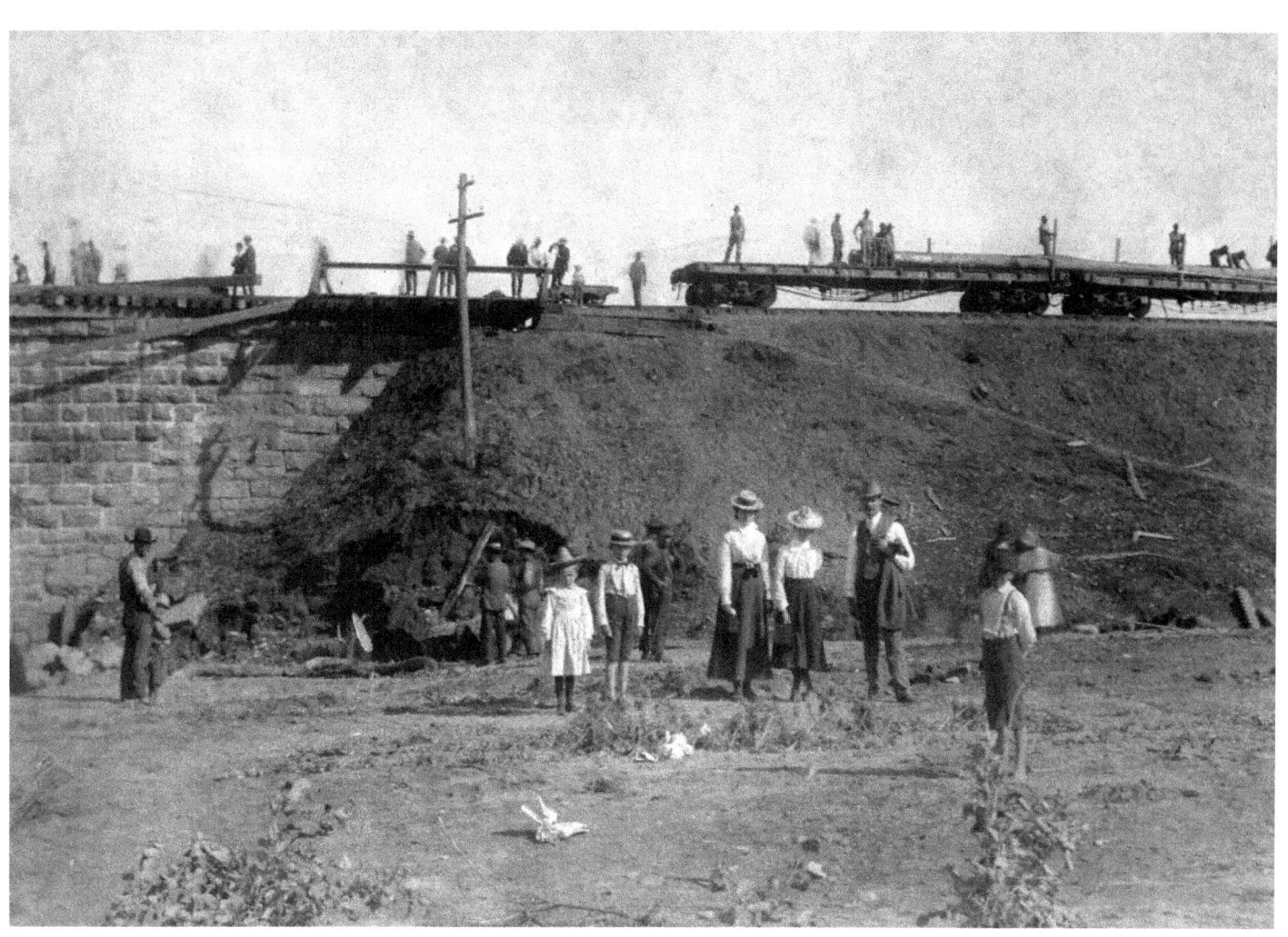

Construction is shown here at a Southern Railroad bridge over the Watauga River in East Tennessee, in the 1890s. This bridge was later washed out by flooding. The Watauga River originates at Grandfather Mountain in Watauga County, North Carolina, flowing across the state line into Tennessee.

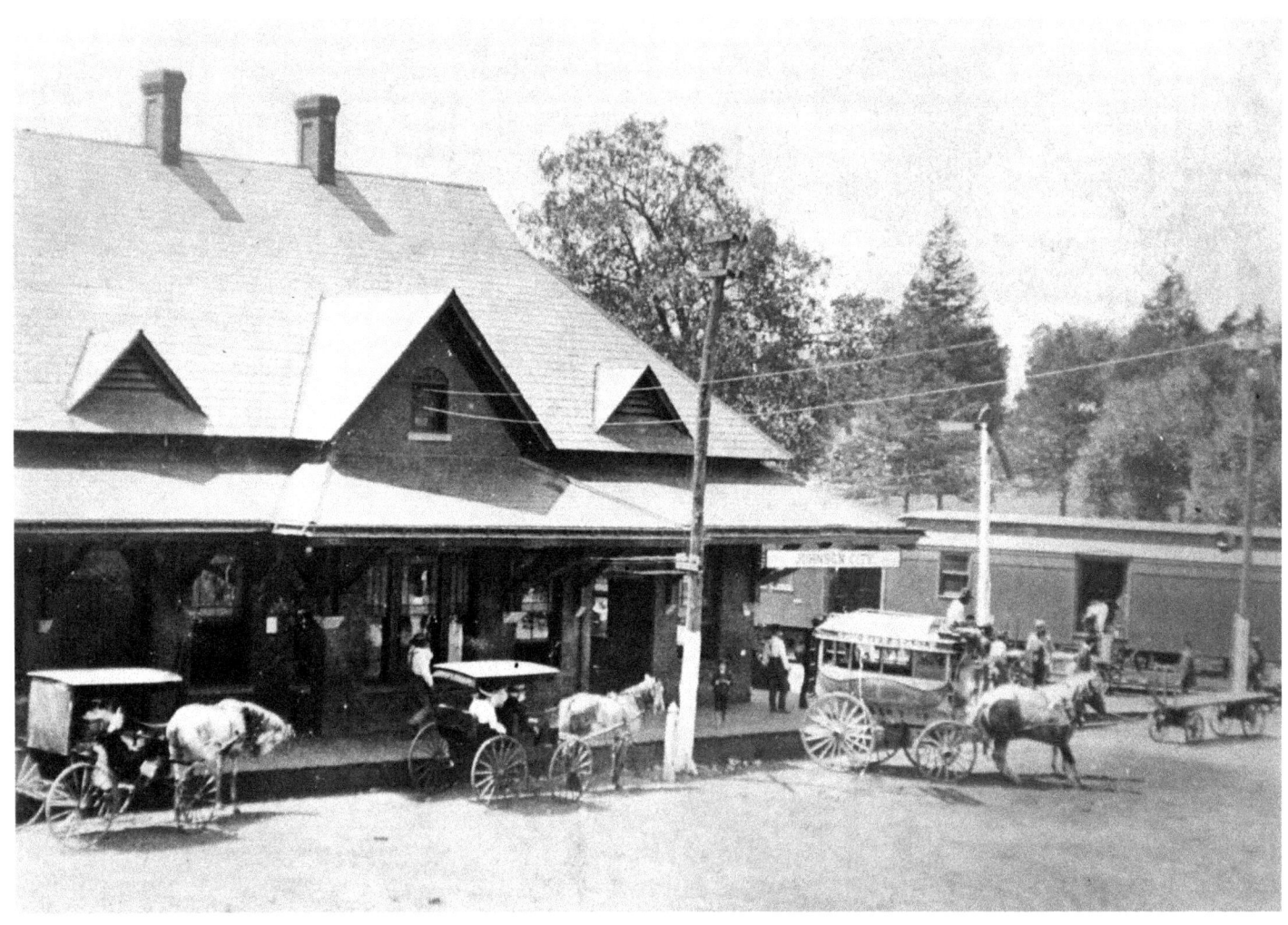

A bustling Johnson City, Tennessee, railroad depot in the 1890s. Founded in 1856 as a railroad station, the town was originally known as Johnson's Depot. Today it is the eight-largest city in the state.

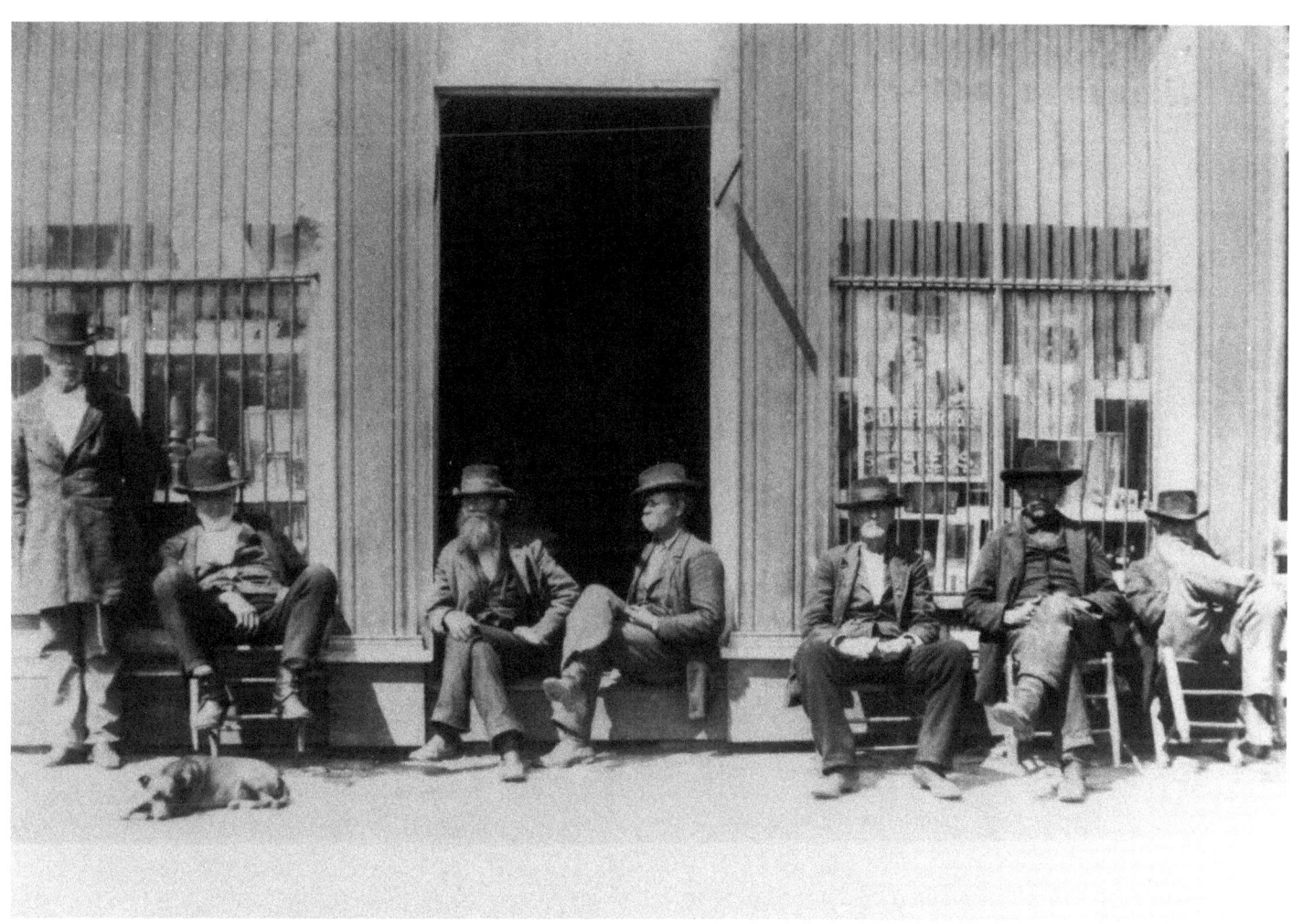

Locals sit outside an Appalachian country store in a classic pose: leaning back in cane-bottom chairs. Not to be outmaneuvered, the community dog appears equally eager to share in the moment.

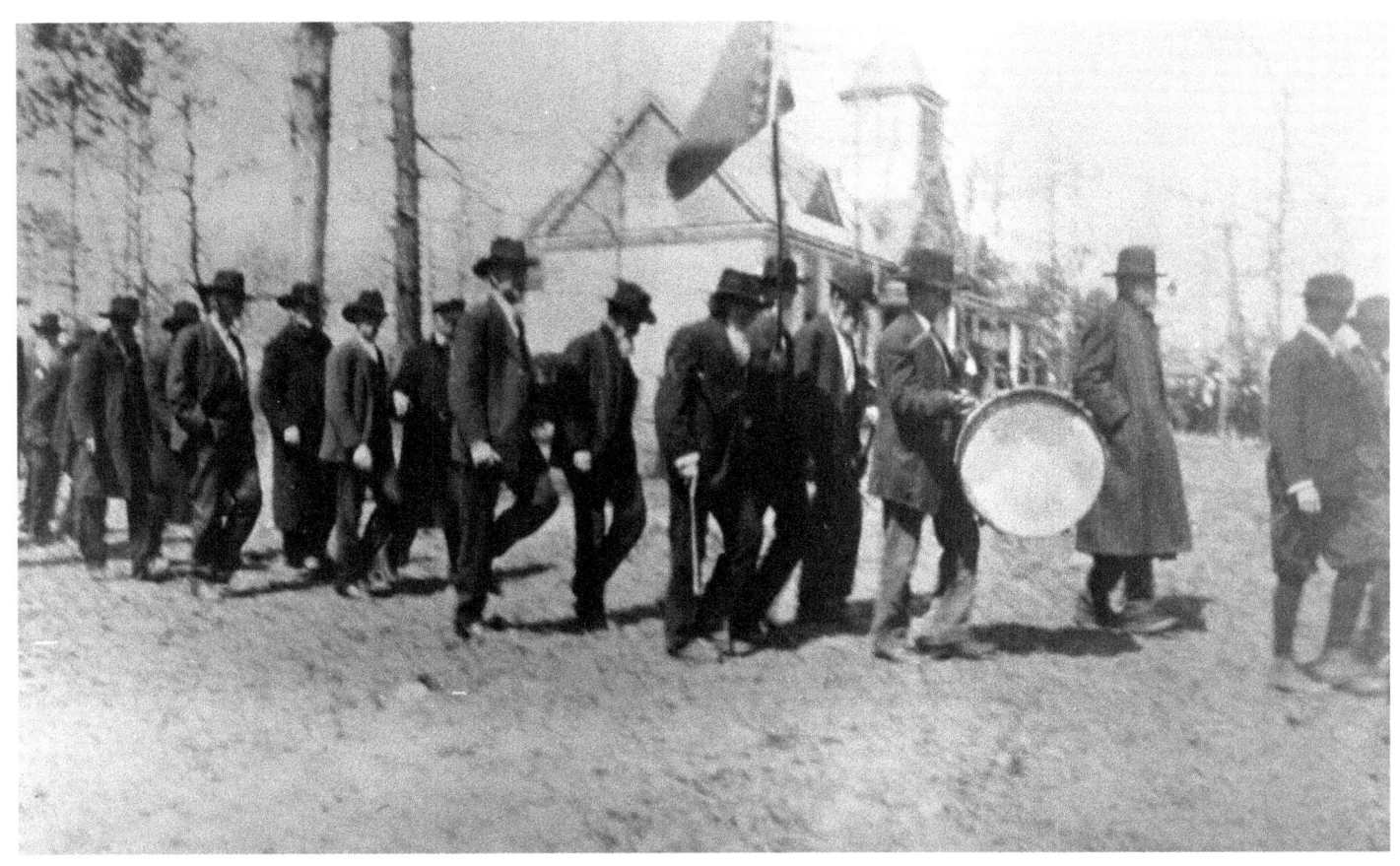

This appears to be a reunion of Confederate Civil War veterans in Watauga County, North Carolina, in the 1890s. The people of southern Appalachia were divided during the Civil War, with many southern mountaineers remaining loyal to the Union. By the 1890s, the general sentiment was toward reconciliation, and it was common for Union and Confederate veterans to join together in commemorative parades.

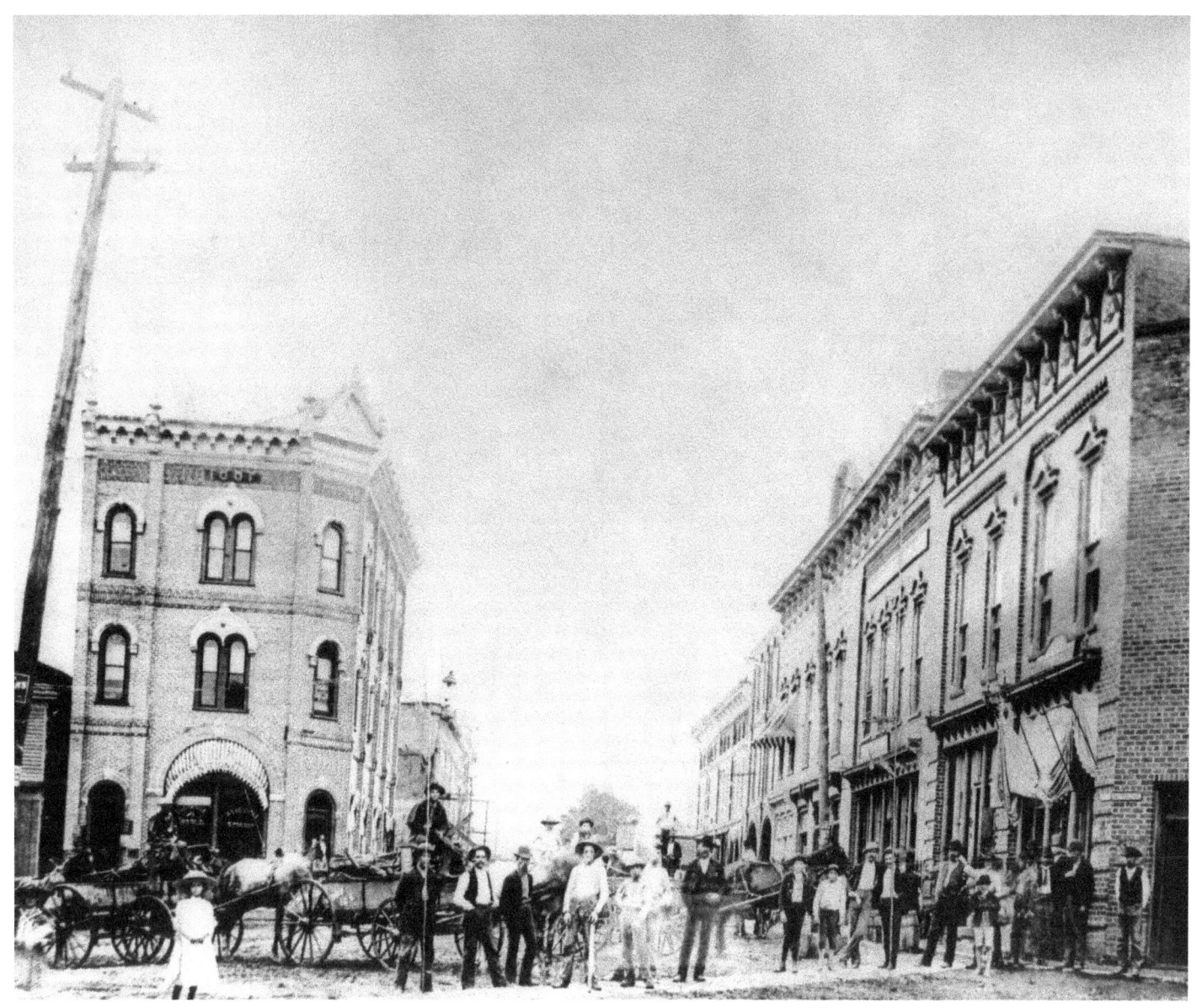

Johnson City, Tennessee, a railroad and market town, bustled with commercial activity in the years just prior to the Panic of 1893.

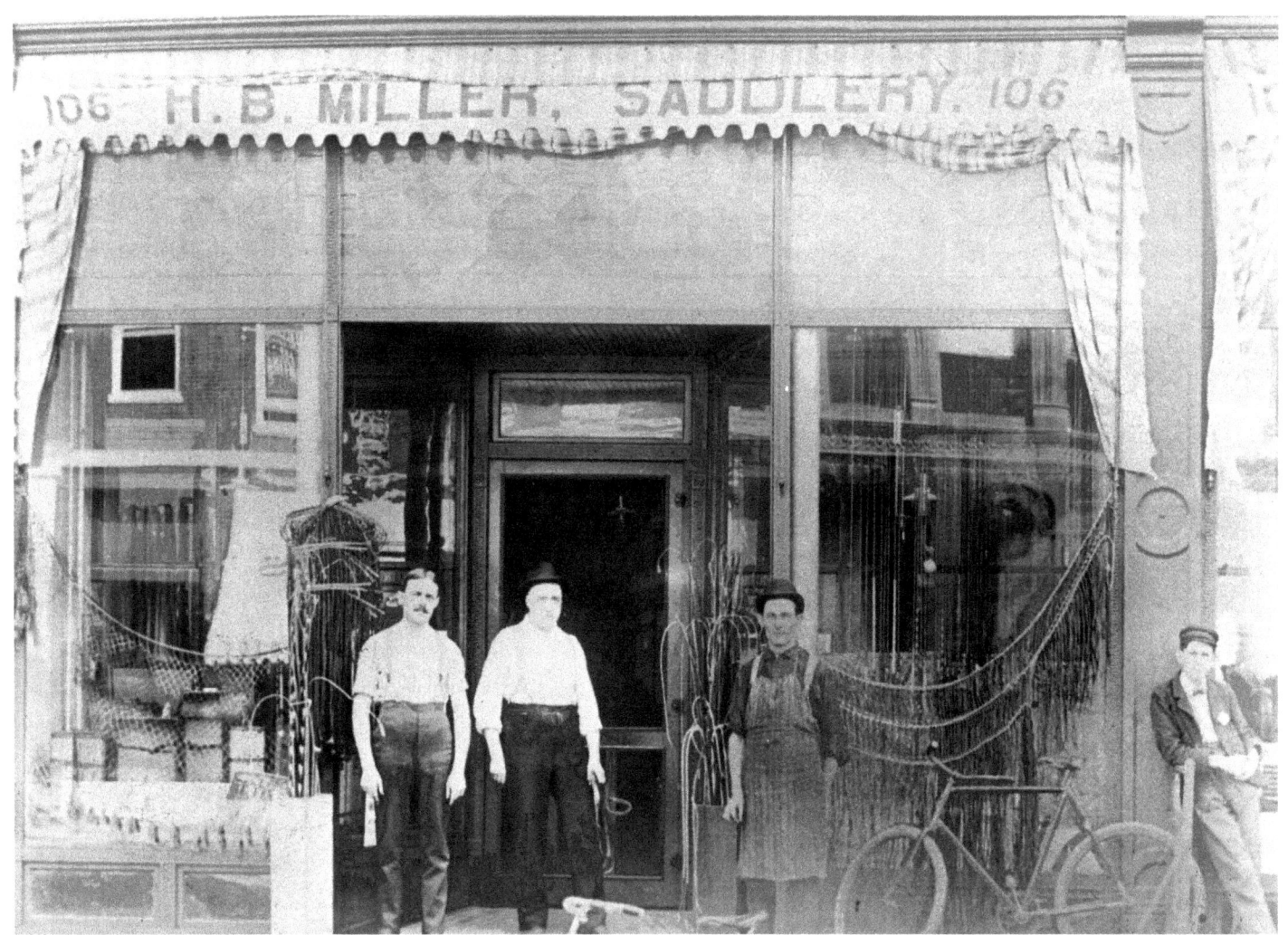

H. B. Miller Saddlery is shown in downtown Johnson City in the 1890s. Early high-wheeled bicycles known as penny farthings had recently given way to the modern type shown at right.

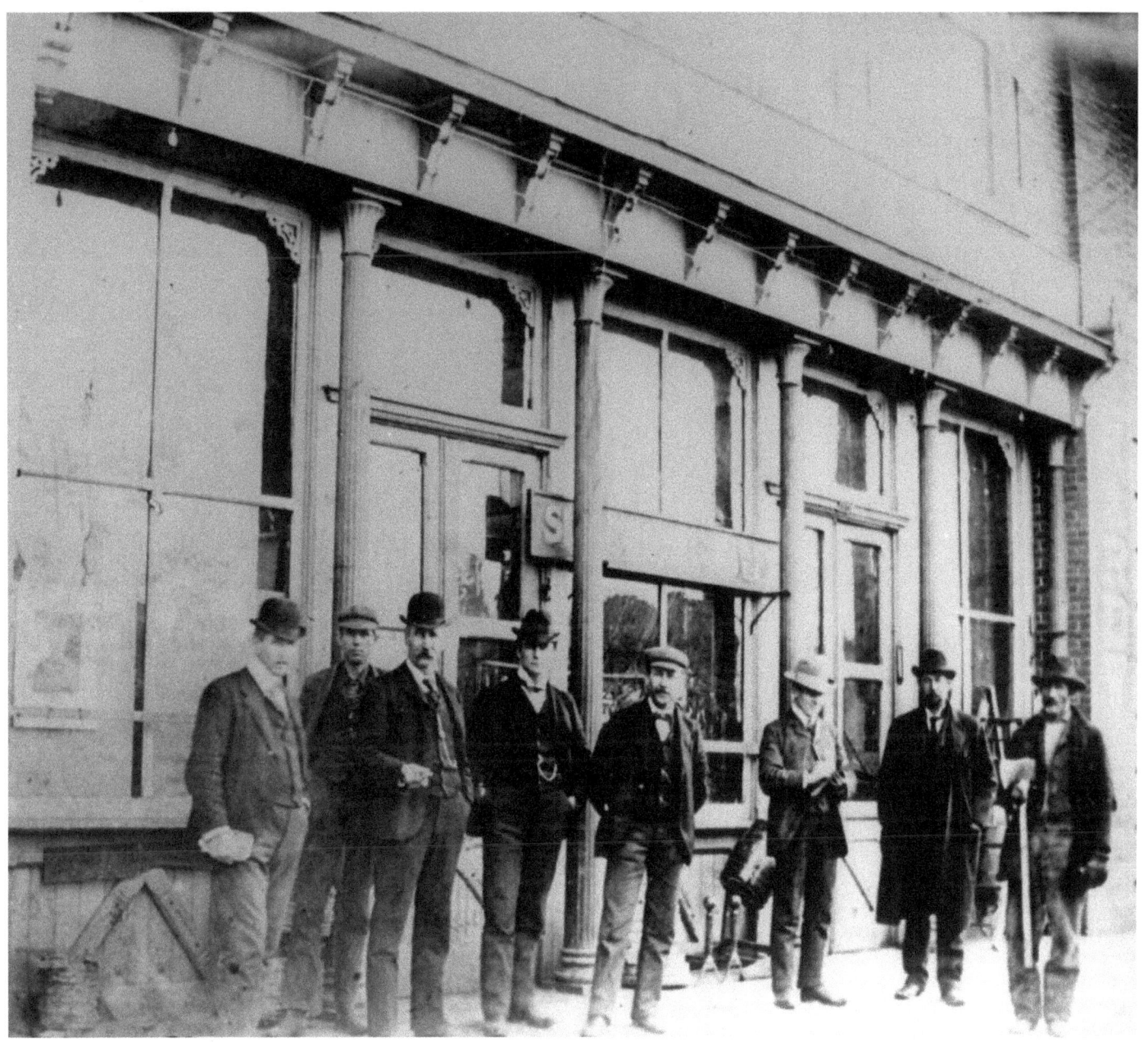

The cast-iron facade of Summers Hardware in downtown Johnson City, Tennessee. Cast iron had become popular during the era for commercial facades. Summers Hardware still operates today, out of a "new" building erected in 1910.

McMillon and Acuff Groceries, purveyors of notions and fancy groceries in Washington County, Tennessee, is open for business here in the 1890s.

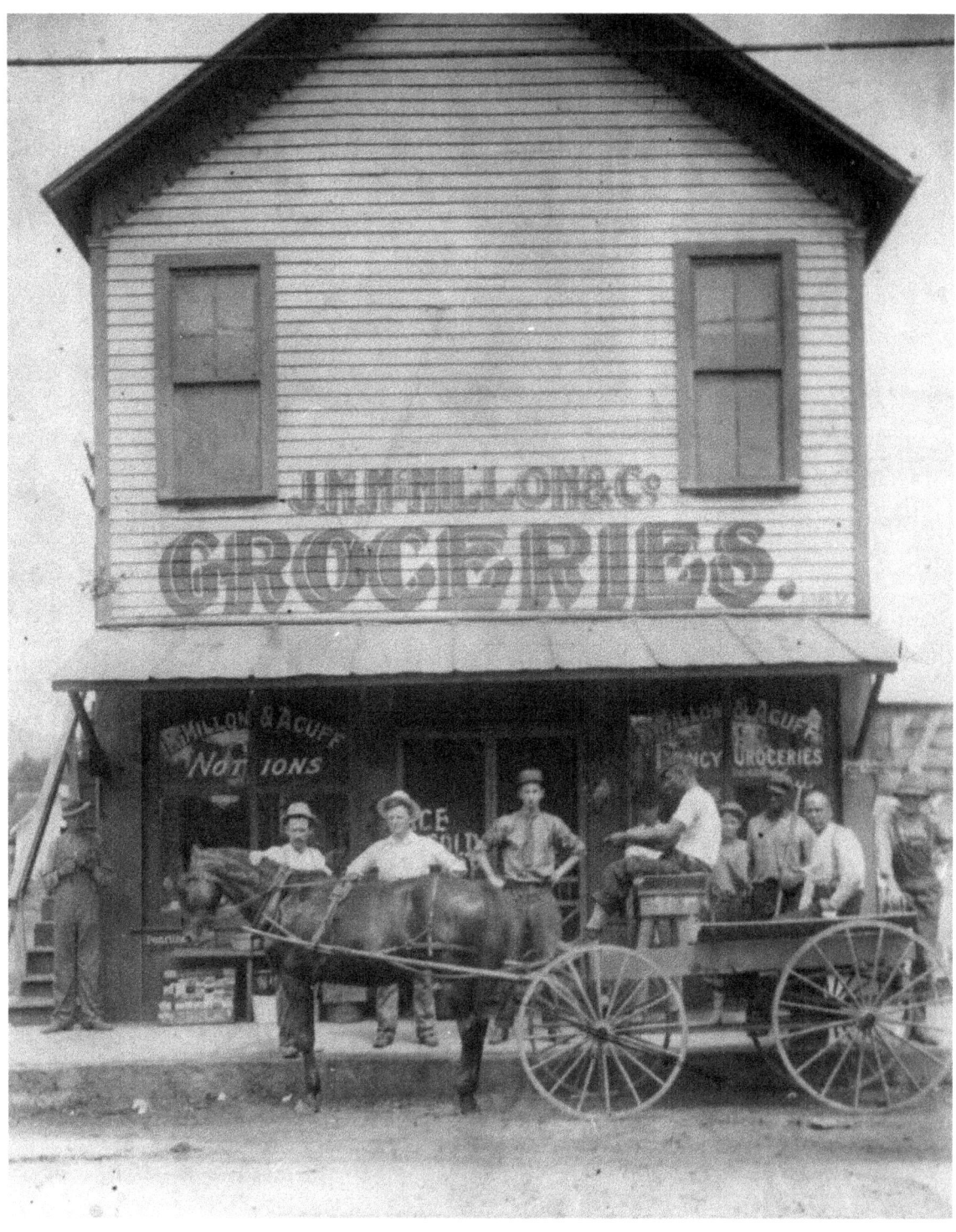

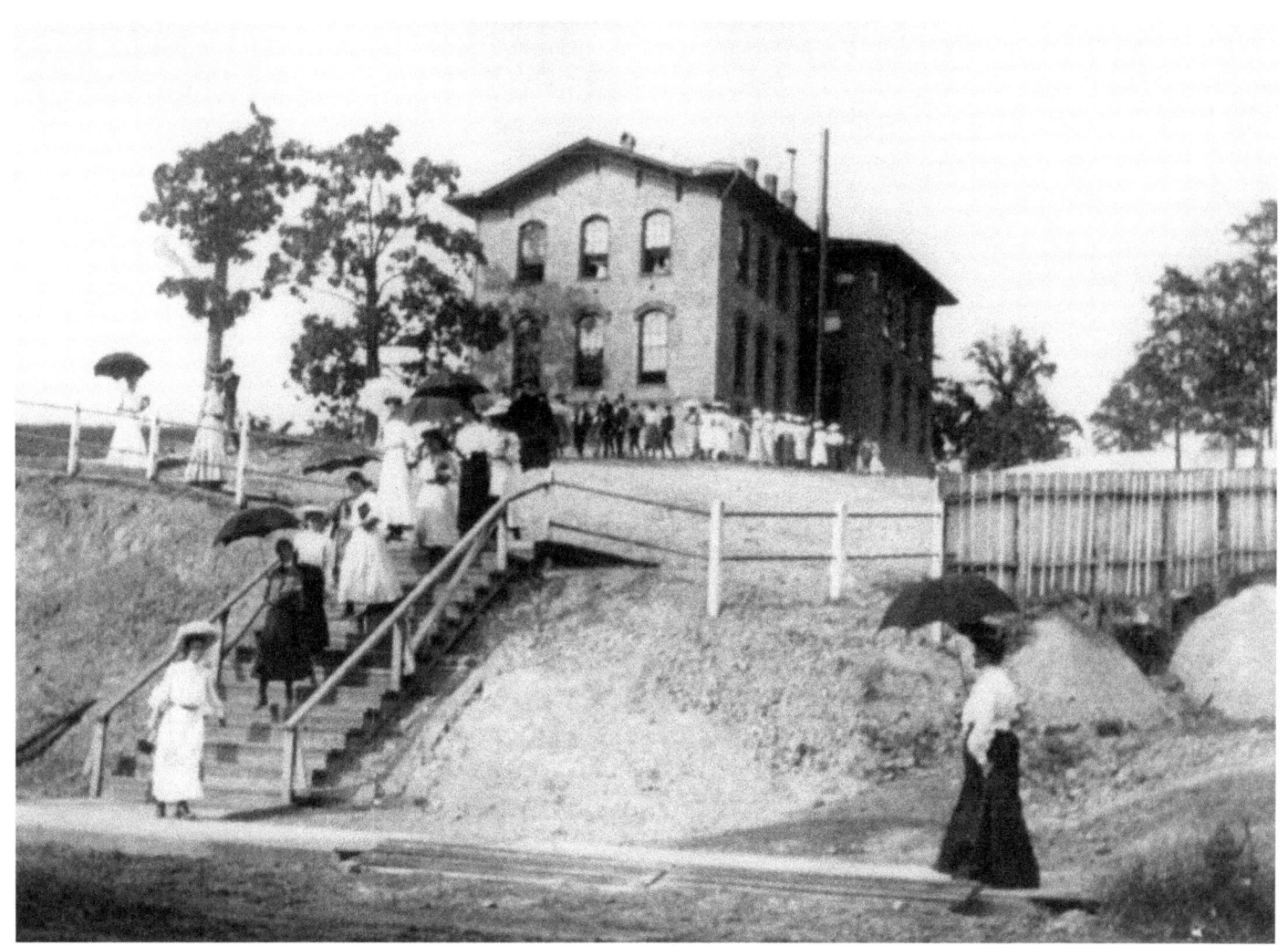

The Science Hill Male and Female Institute—on the site of what is now Science Hill High School, in Johnson City—is shown here in the 1890s, an era when umbrellas were employed to block sun rays. The building was constructed in the late 1860s, with volunteer labor and handmade bricks, made on site. The graduating class of 1899 had fifteen members.

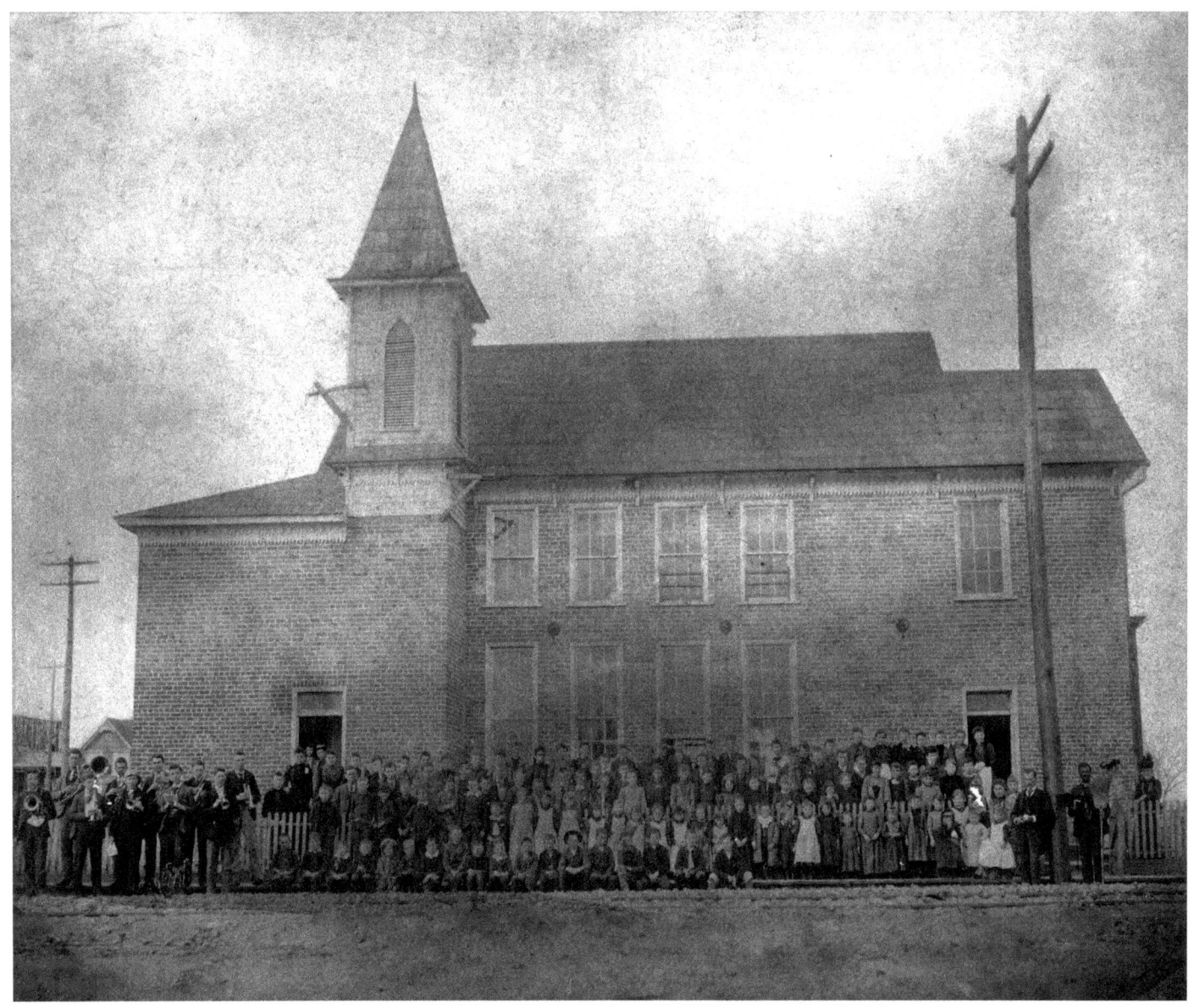

This is Lusk School, a grammar school in Johnson City, Tennessee. Students and teachers have assembled for a group shot here in the early 1890s.

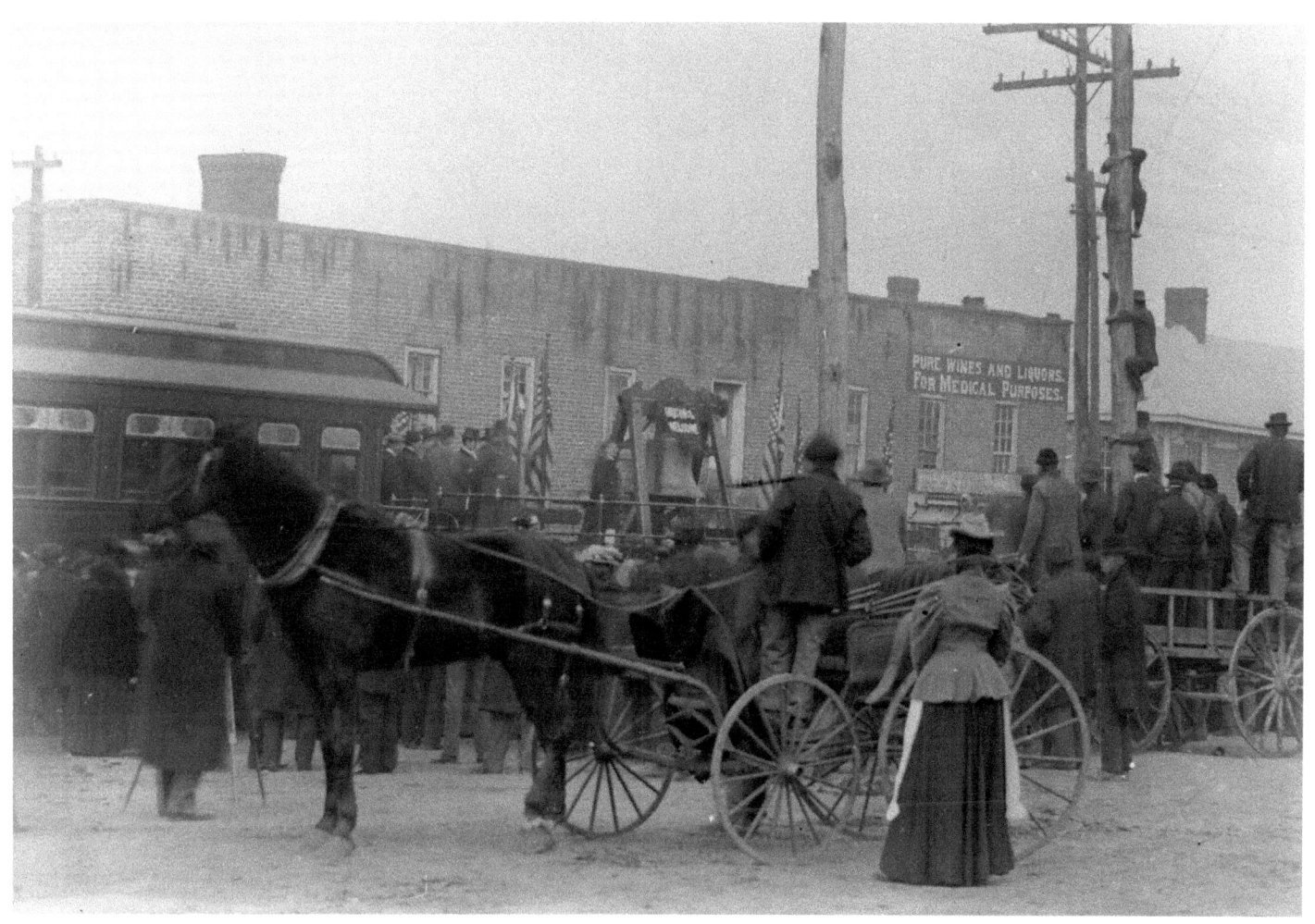

The Liberty Bell is displayed at the railroad station in Johnson City, sometime in the late nineteenth century. After the 1876 Centennial in Philadelphia, the bell was borrowed from Independence Hall and toured the country extensively, including its display at the three-months-long Cotton States and International Exhibition in Atlanta, Georgia, in 1895. On the route between Philadelphia and Atlanta, it was displayed at railroad stations as a national relic.

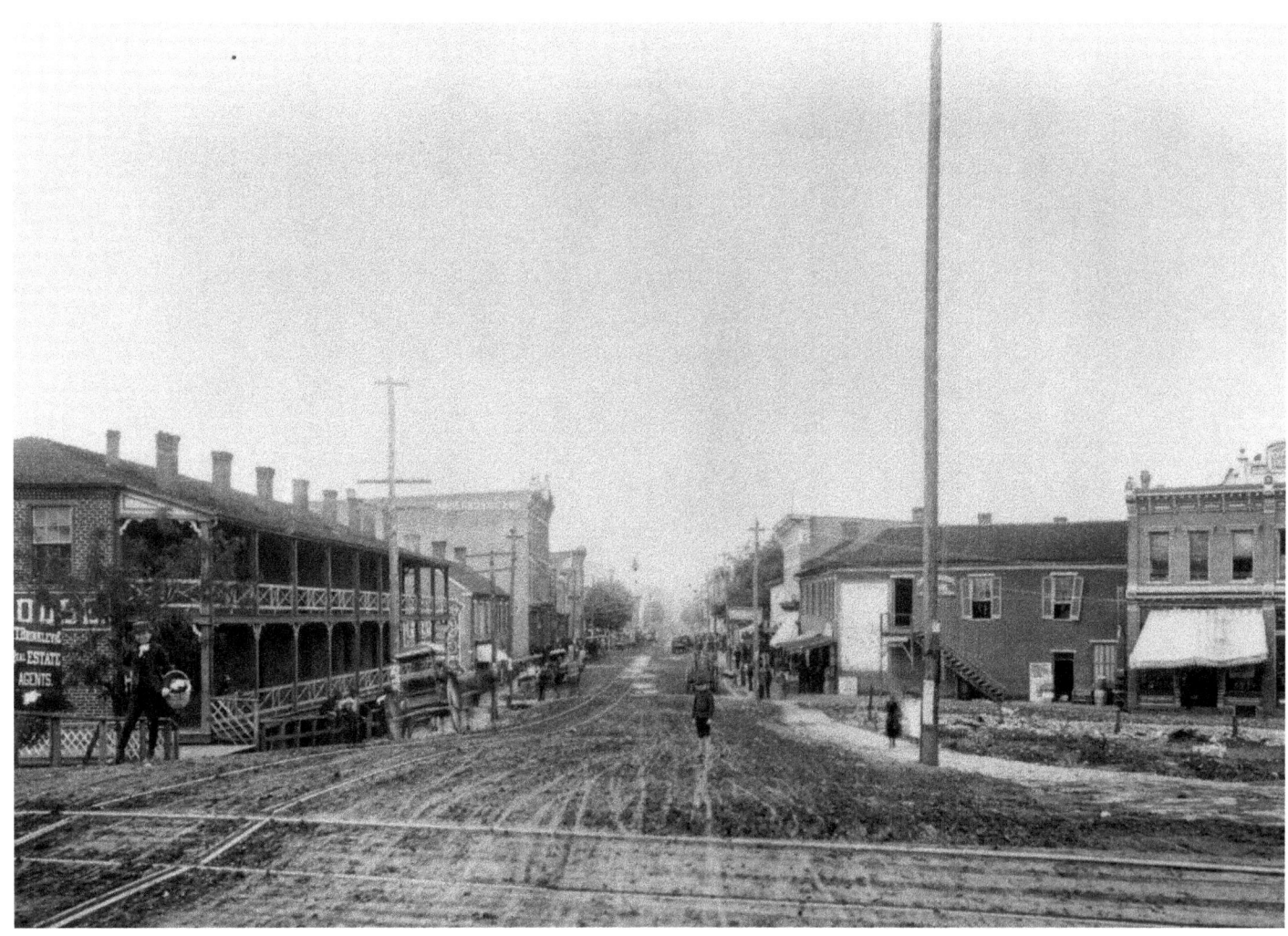

State Street, in Bristol, Tennessee and Virginia. The line dividing the two states runs through the center of town. At the turn of the century, developers envisioned that Bristol would become a great steel manufacturing center, but the iron ore veins in the Appalachian region were not as extensive as anticipated. When the vast ore deposits of the Mesabi Range in upper Minnesota were opened to extraction, steel production shifted to the north.

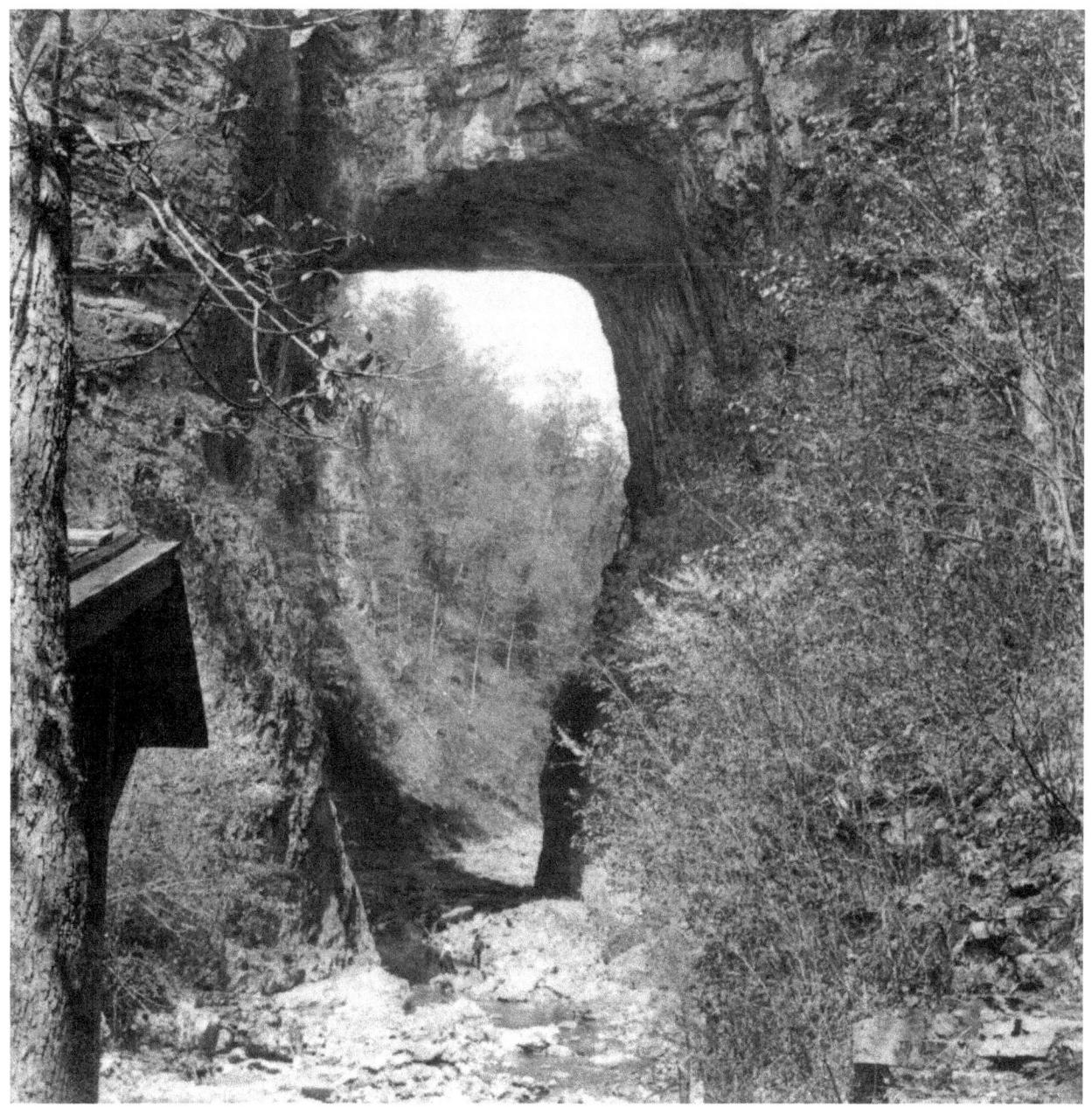

The Natural Bridge, in eponymous Rockbridge County, Virginia, was celebrated by Thomas Jefferson and was a popular tourist destination among travelers in the nineteenth century. A famous 1852 oil painting by F. E. Church shows much the same view seen here. The immense size of the feature dwarfs the two visitors posing for a photograph on rocks along the river below.

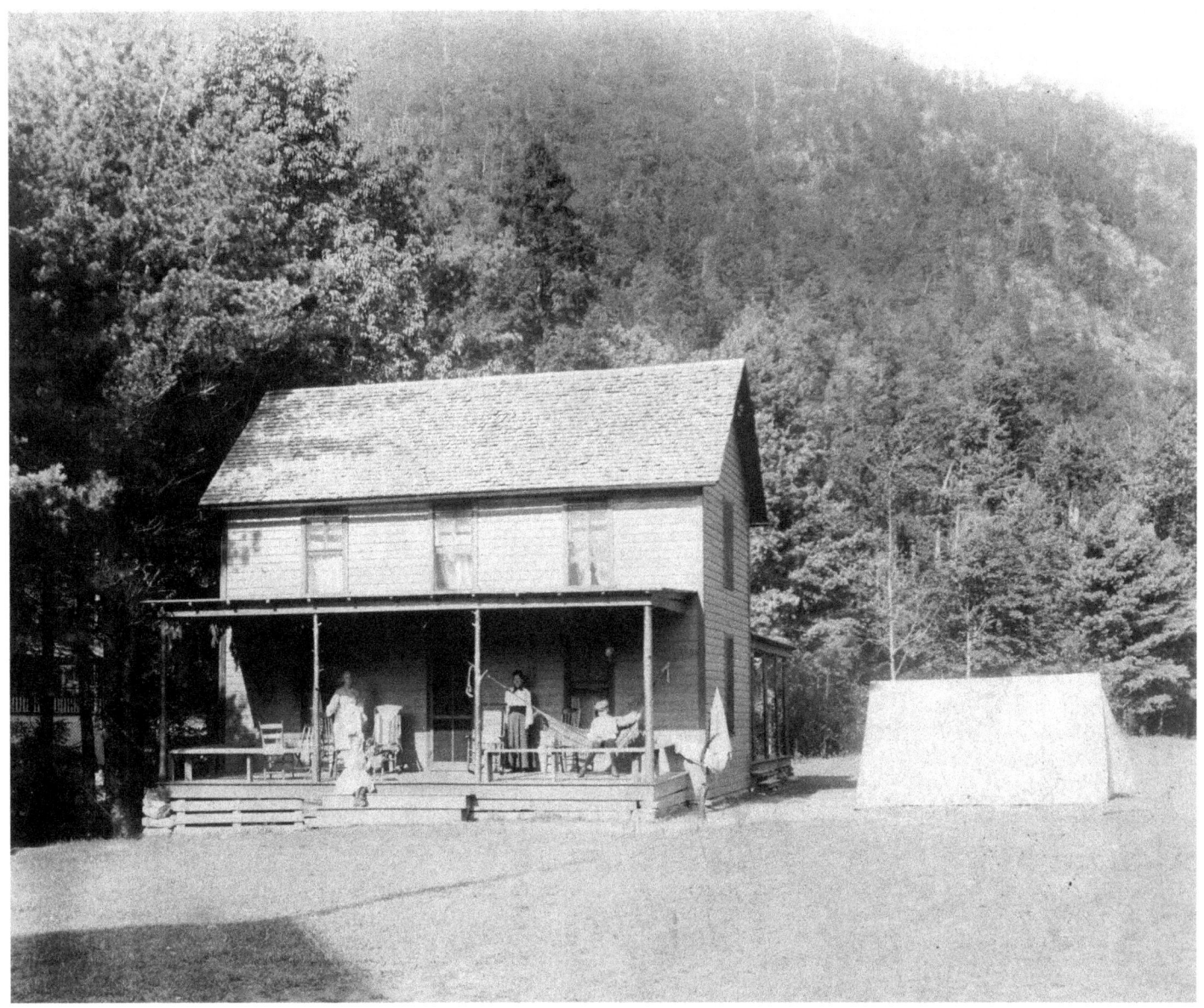

This cottage was on the grounds of Unaka Springs, Unicoi County, Tennessee, one of many mineral springs that drew visitors to Appalachia around the turn of the century. A brochure for Unaka Springs advertised "Dancing, Bathing, Mountain-climbing, and general amusements." In the 1890s, owners built a 40-room hotel with modern plumbing, with water supplied by gravity from a spring. The Nolichucky River gorge is visible in the background.

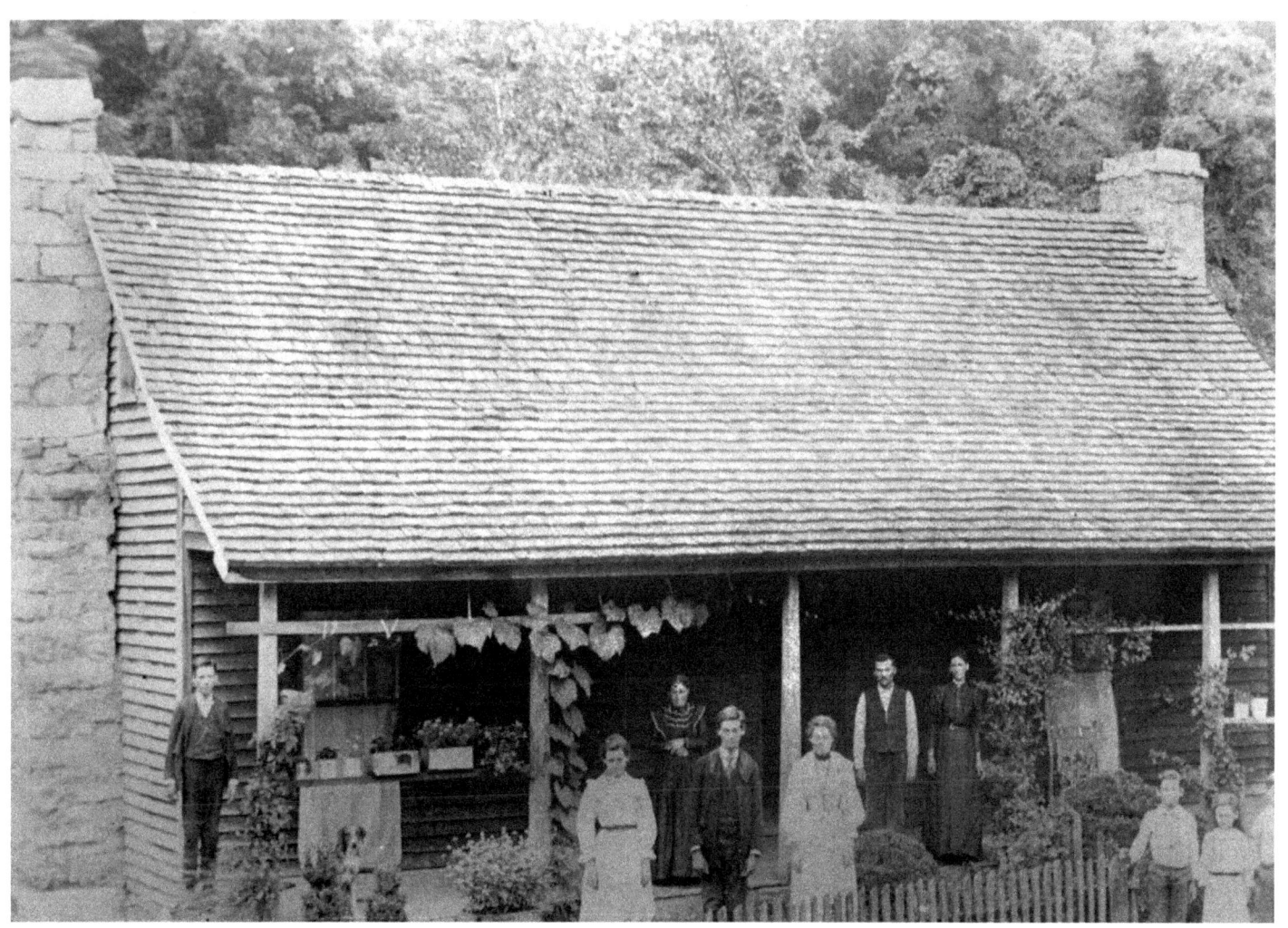

The Keplinger family poses for a photograph in Dry Creek, Tennessee. What appears to be a squash vine has found support along the porch posts at center-left.

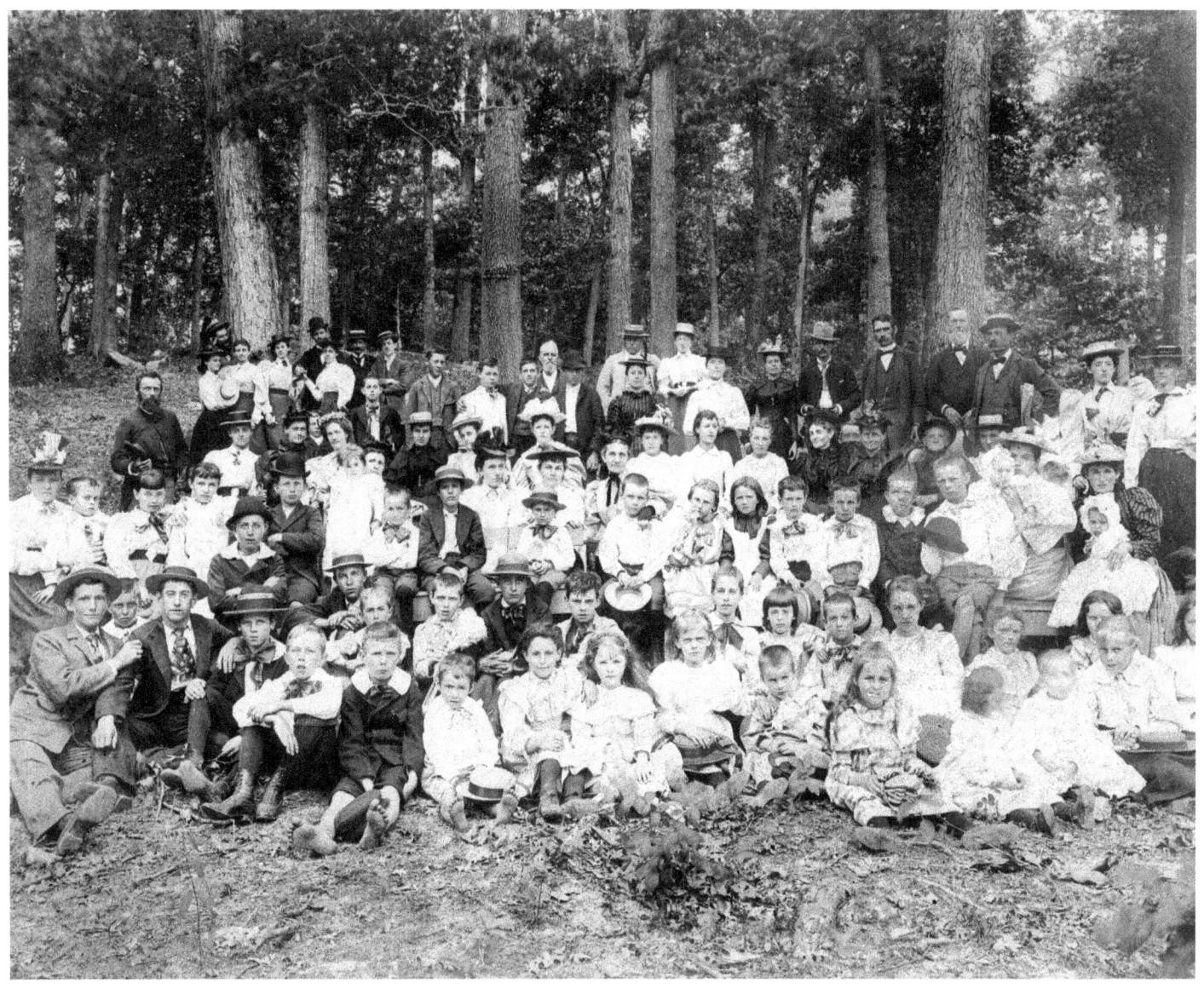

This unidentified gathering of people at a wooded retreat in East Tennessee near the turn of the century shows how fashions of dress were changing with the times. For men, bowler hats were giving way to boaters, and for women, dark clothing to lighter shades.

Like many Appalachian towns, Clifton Forge, Virginia, near Roanoke, grew up with the railroad. By the late nineteenth century, it was home to a large maintenance facility for the Chesapeake and Ohio Railroad. The C&O's development corporation erected many buildings in Clifton Forge at that time, including this Y.M.C.A., which provided lodging and a social center for many of the new workers that the railroad drew to town.

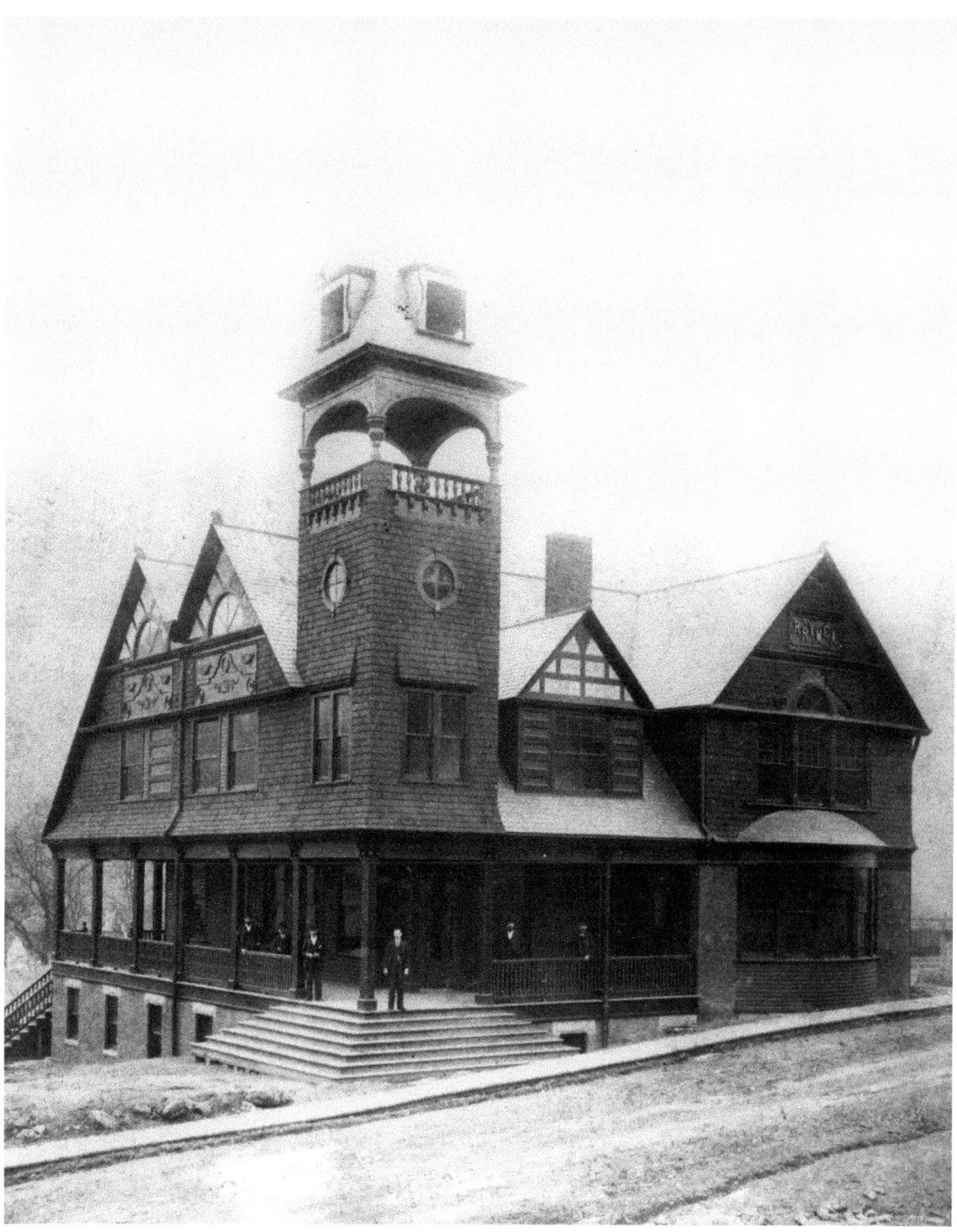

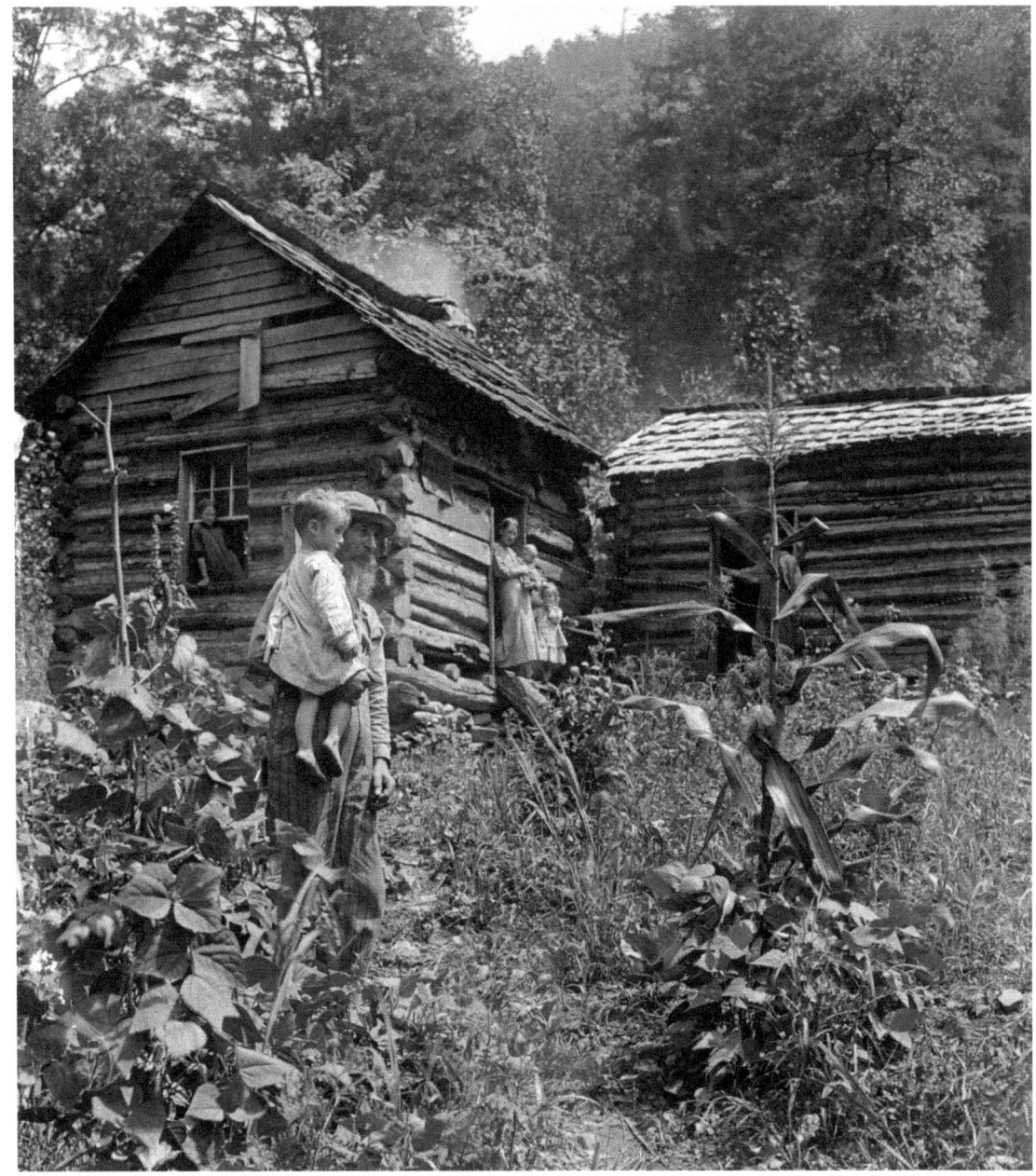

This family in Linville Valley, North Carolina, exemplifies the old mountain ways. The garden is a traditional interplanting of the "three sisters"—corn, beans, and squash. In this arrangement, corn provides support for the beans; beans stabilize the corn and fix nitrogen in the soil; and leaves from the squash vine serve as a natural mulch, discouraging weed growth.

TOURISM, EDUCATION, MODERNIZATION, AND THE GREAT WAR

(1900–1919)

Even as corporate logging operations were removing vast swaths of Appalachia's ancient forest, tourists were discovering the wild, natural beauty of the region. Increased mobility—by way of trains and, before long, automobiles—along with the rise of white-collar jobs and standard vacation periods, not to mention urbanization, which increased the need for respite from the city, led to increased travel to Appalachia for pleasure.

Meanwhile, residents of Appalachia themselves were becoming more educated and sophisticated. The Common School movement of the nineteenth century led to an emphasis on schooling in the early twentieth. Likewise, new forms of entertainment increased the ferment of ideas and culture: Traveling circuses and shows, which had passed through the region in the nineteenth century, became more frequent and more sophisticated. Motion pictures emerged, bringing fashions and ideas from far and wide.

As everywhere else in the nation, so, too, in Appalachia, new technologies brought about modernization. New roads were built and old ones paved to accommodate automobiles. Electricity was made widely available in cities, and electric trolley lines were laid to move people around those cities. In the countryside, steam-powered farm equipment began to transform agriculture.

As the world came to Appalachia, Appalachia went out into the world. The region has a historically high rate of military voluntarism. Tennessee as a whole is known as the Volunteer State, and the University of Tennessee at Knoxville, as the Volunteers, or "Vols." When the Great War—World War I—began, young Appalachian men went in droves. Those who returned from the war did so to build a new, modern Appalachia. The war machines had impressed them with the power of technology. The international culture and fashion that they encountered had changed their tastes, and was reflected in new products on the shelves of Appalachian stores and shops.

Railroad-building, logging, and an economy reliant on other natural resources, meanwhile, continued apace.

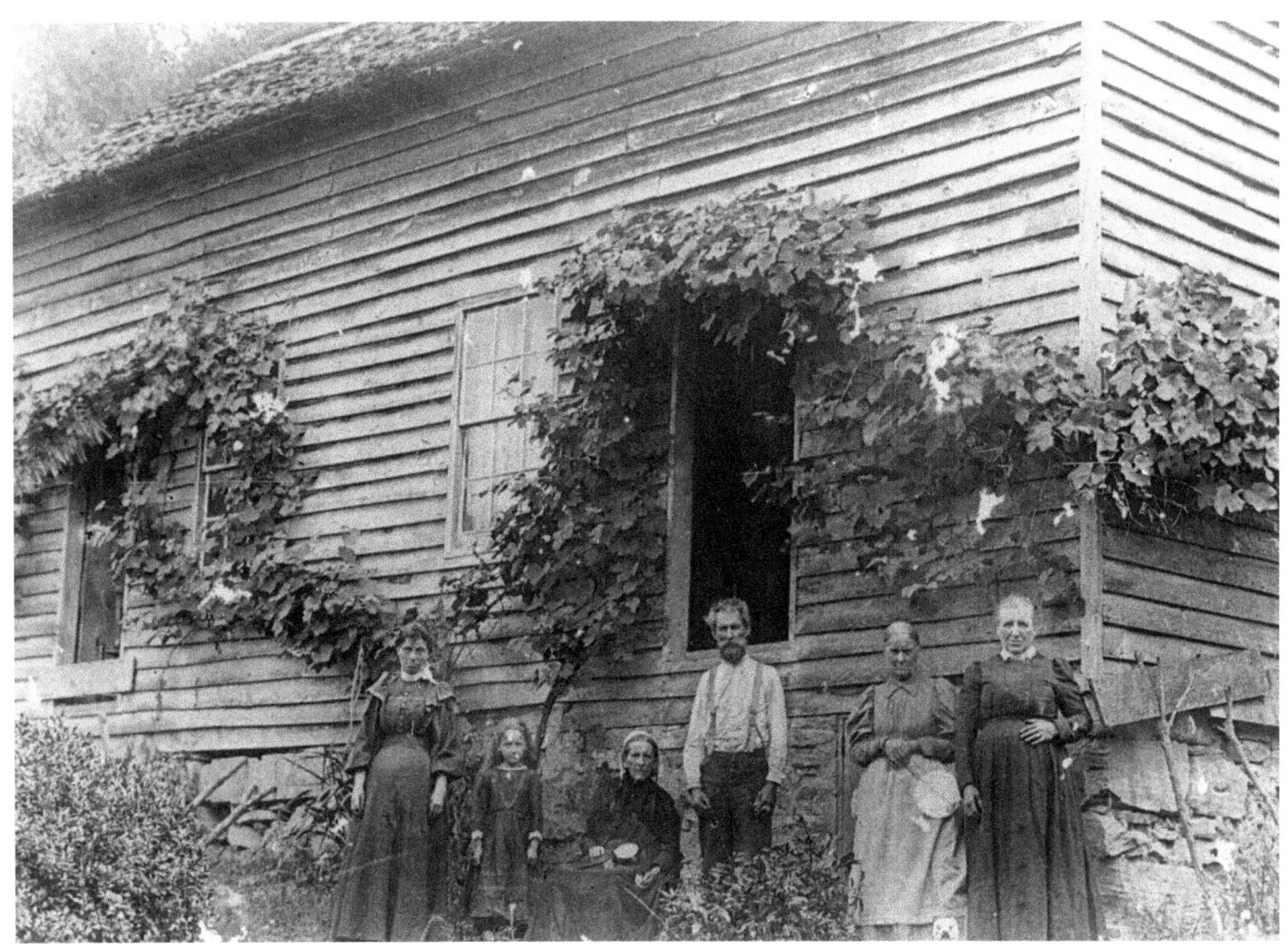

This East Tennessee family poses for a photographer in September 1901. Grapevines festoon the house, which is sided with unpainted clapboard. Loose boards are propped against the stone foundation, perhaps to plug gaps.

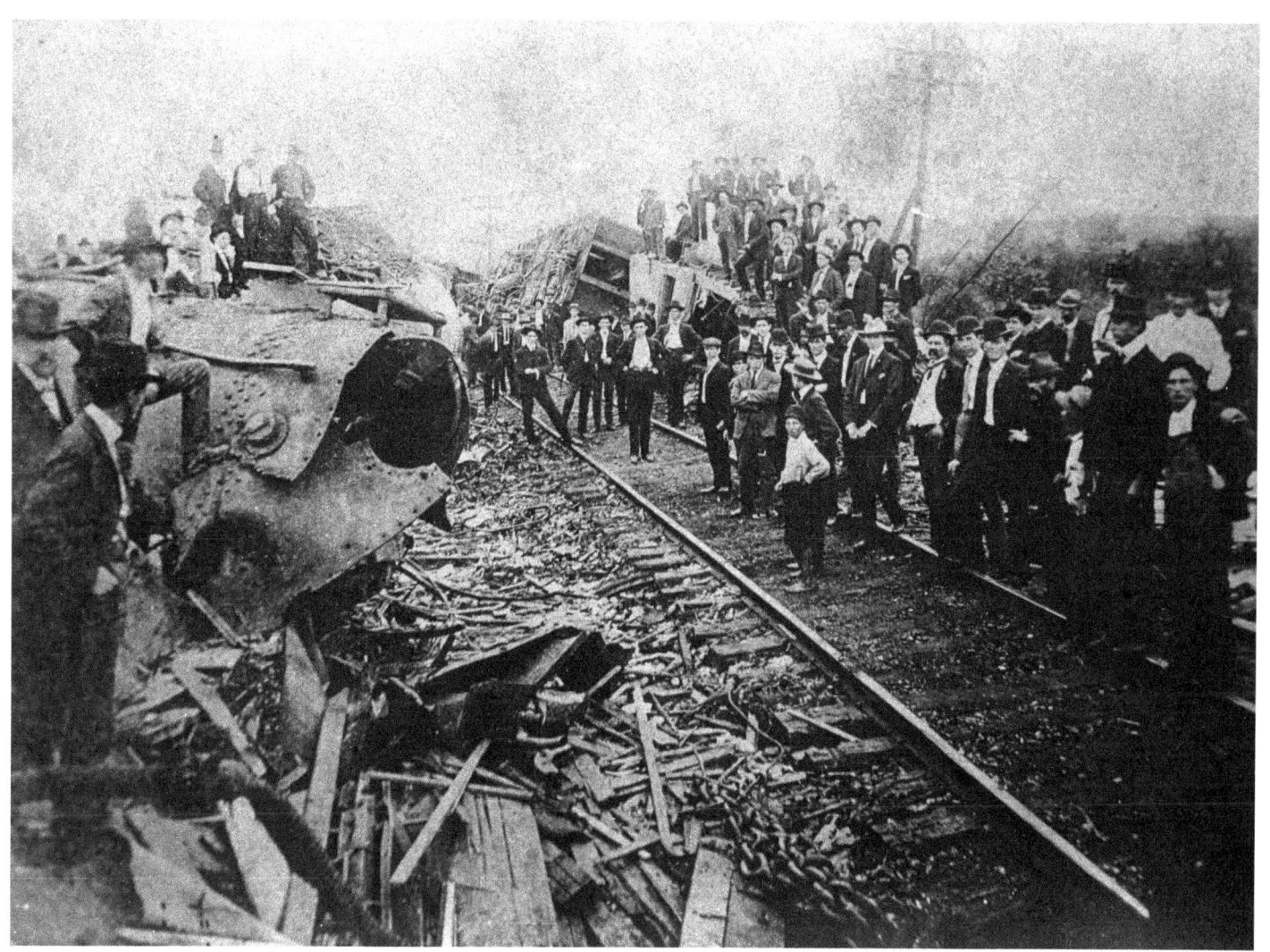

A crowd gathers around the scene of a terrible train wreck near New Market, Tennessee, outside Knoxville. On September 24, 1904, two passenger trains on the Southern Railroad collided head-on, at full speed. Estimates of the number killed range from 65 to 115.

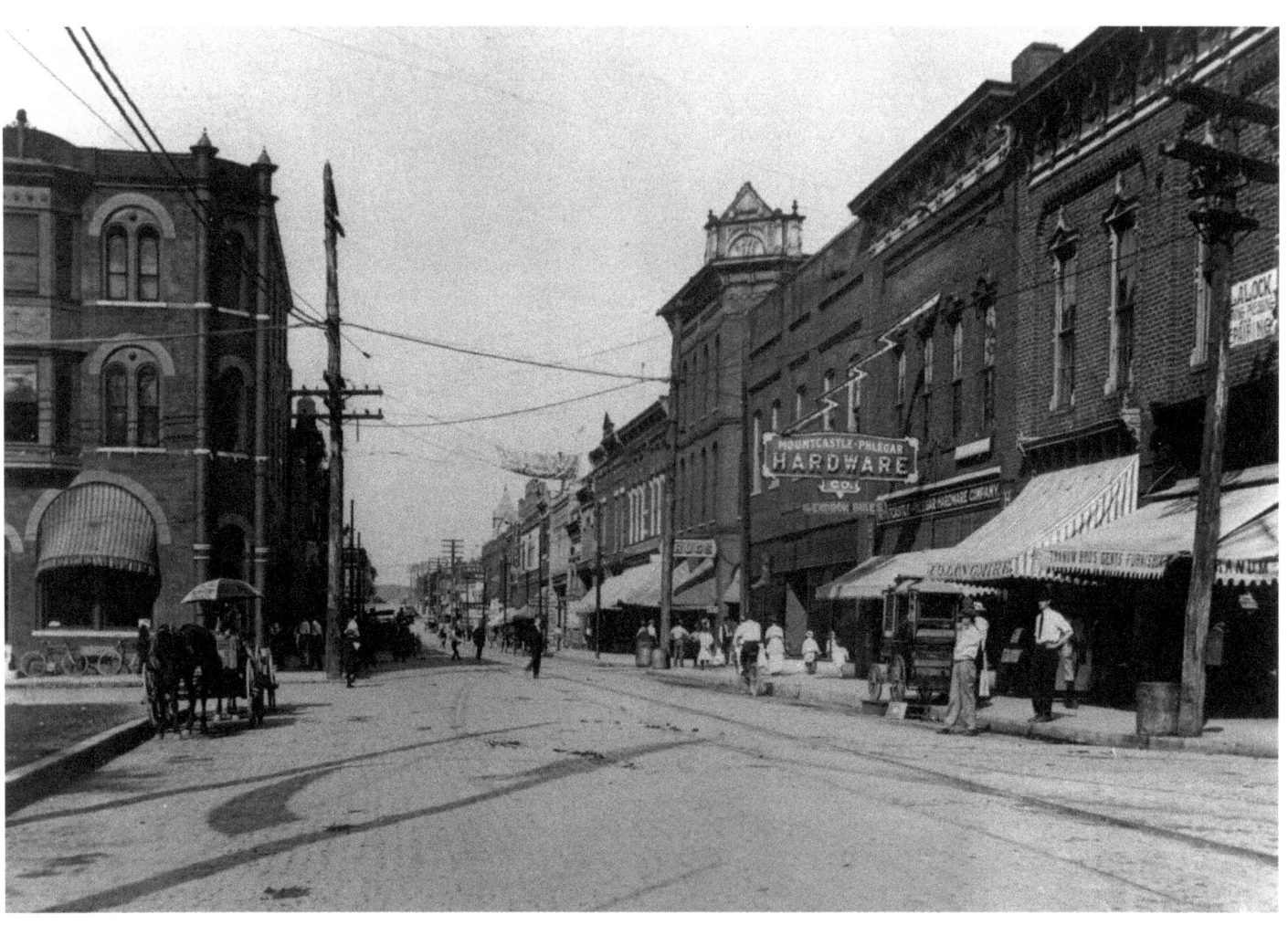

Downtown Johnson City, Tennessee, is pictured here as it appeared in the early twentieth century. In 1908, the streets were paved with brick, and the city was ready for the influx of automobiles, which would soon become popular.

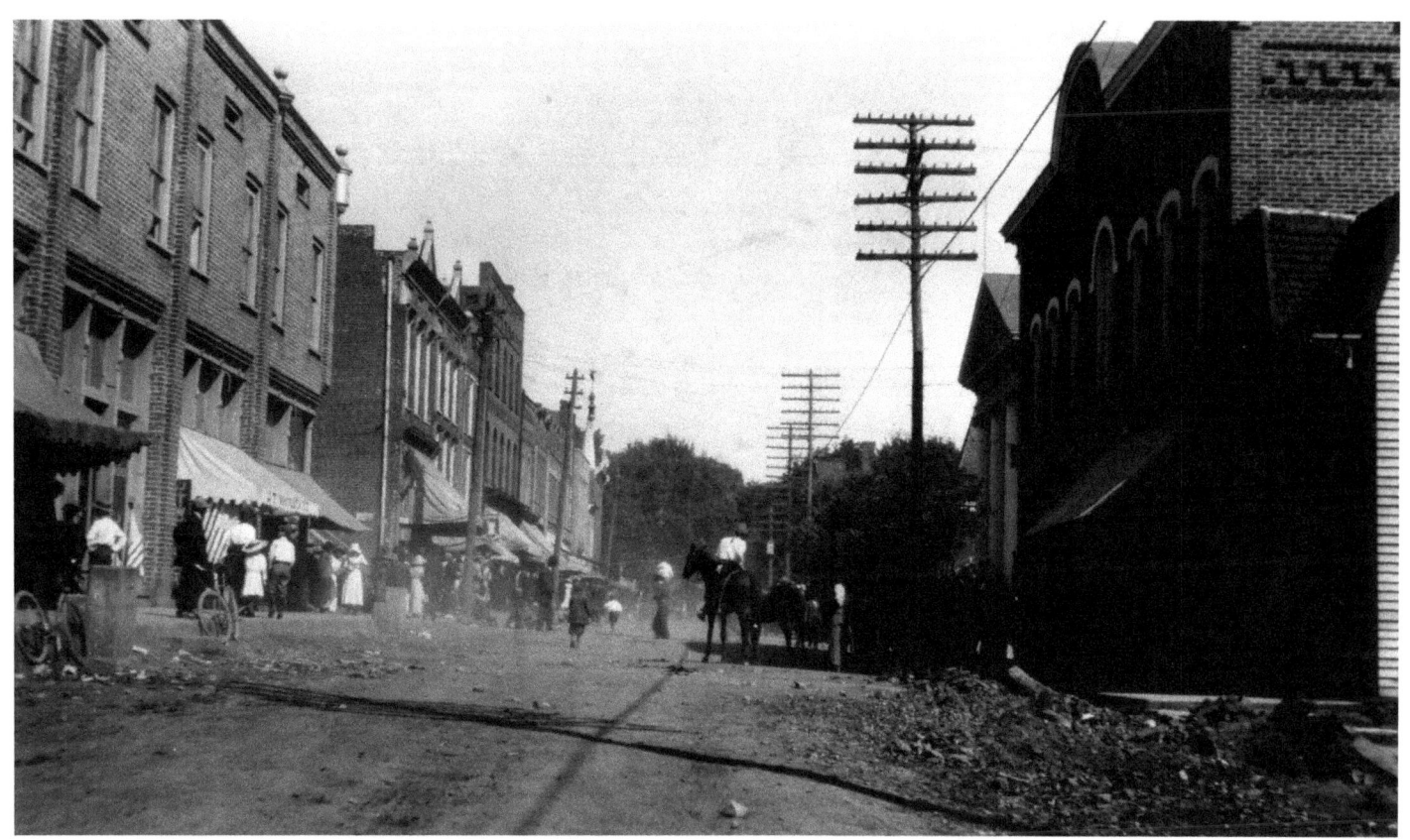

This shot of Main Street in Jonesborough, Tennessee, reveals the scene before roads were surfaced for automobile traffic. "Upping blocks," on the left side of the street, were used by ladies in long skirts and petticoats, to mount side-saddle on horses.

Following Spread: Panorama of Harper's Ferry, West Virginia. Located at the confluence of the Potomac and Shenandoah rivers, the town is now the site of the headquarters of the Appalachian Trail Conservancy. The Appalachian National Scenic Trail, a 2,200-mile continuous footpath that runs along the Appalachian Mountains from Georgia to Maine, is operated and maintained by volunteers, whose work is coordinated by the conservancy.

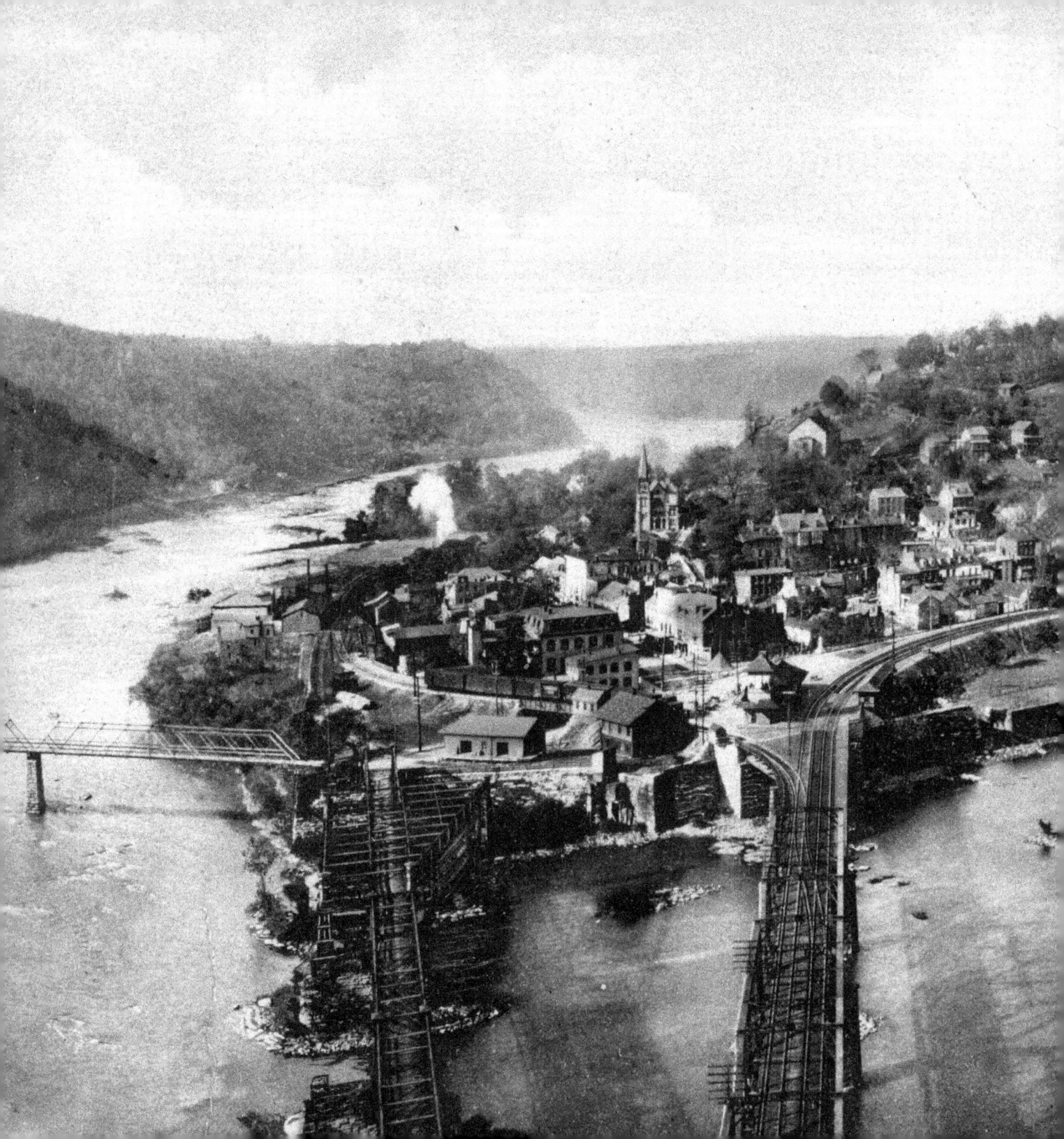

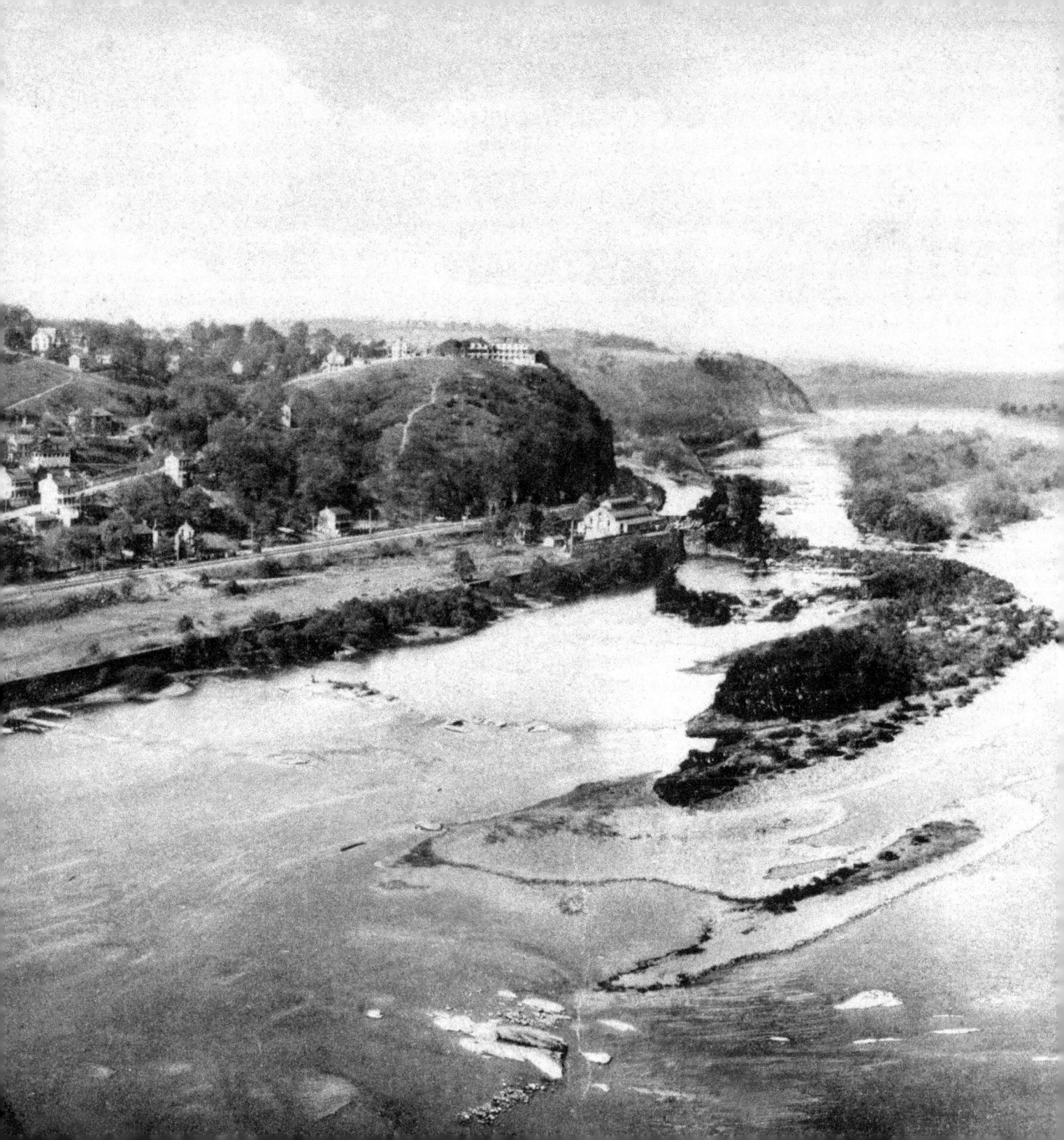

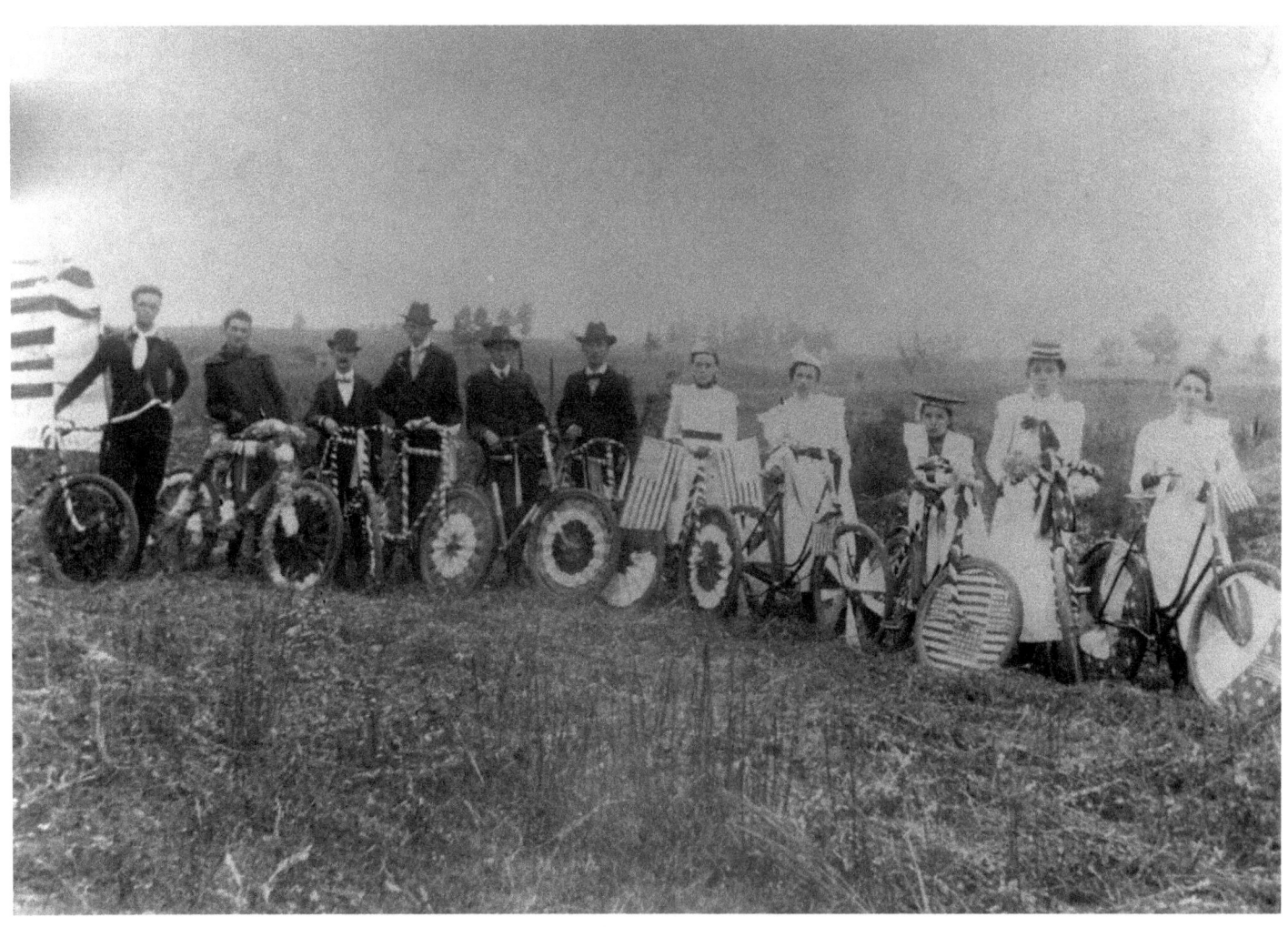

The growing popularity of bicycles is reflected in these preparations for an early-twentieth-century Fourth of July parade in East Tennessee.

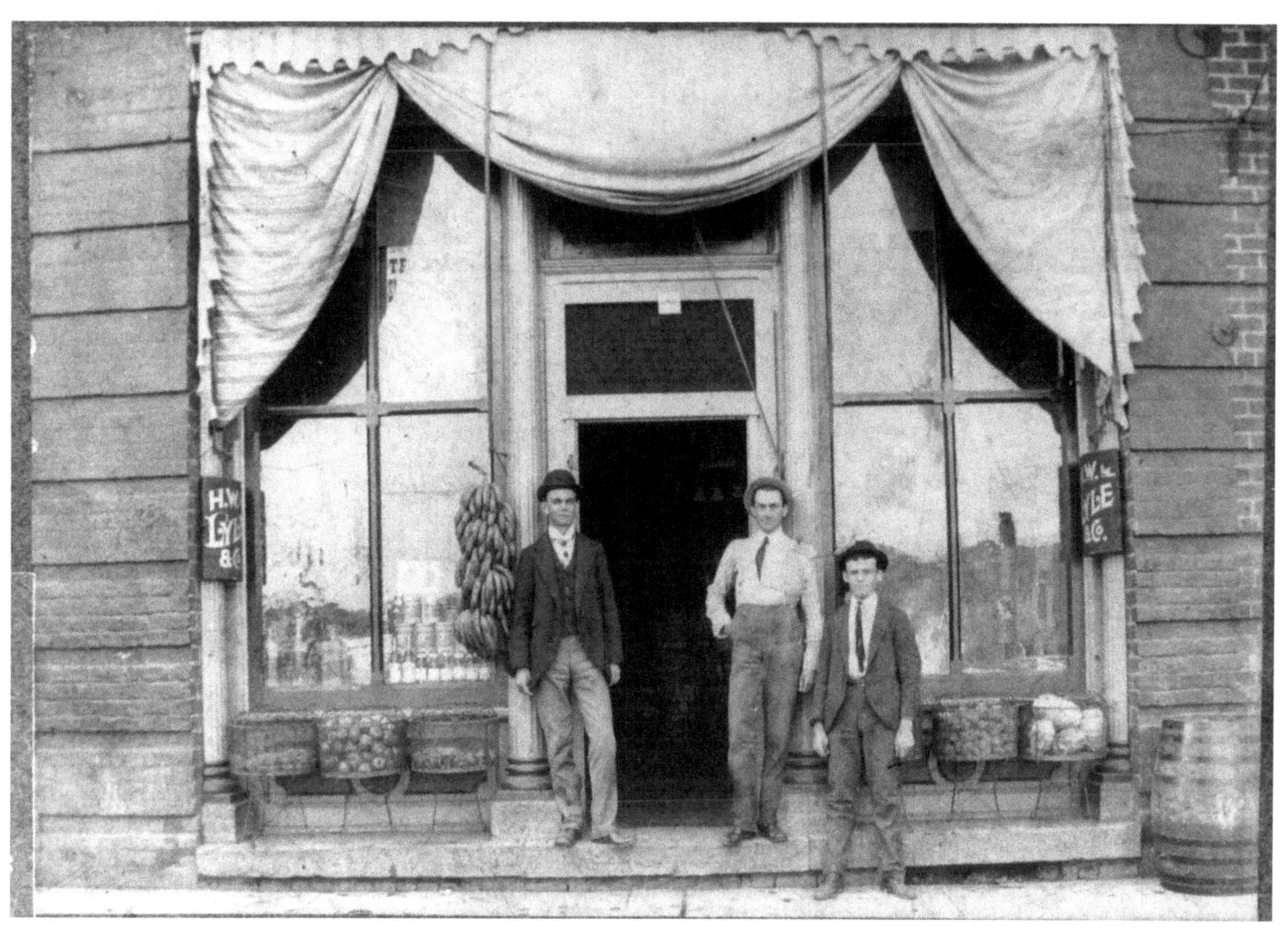

Bananas hanging beside the door of the Harry W. Lyle store in Johnson City, Tennessee, are a testament to the reach of global commerce into Appalachia in the early twentieth century.

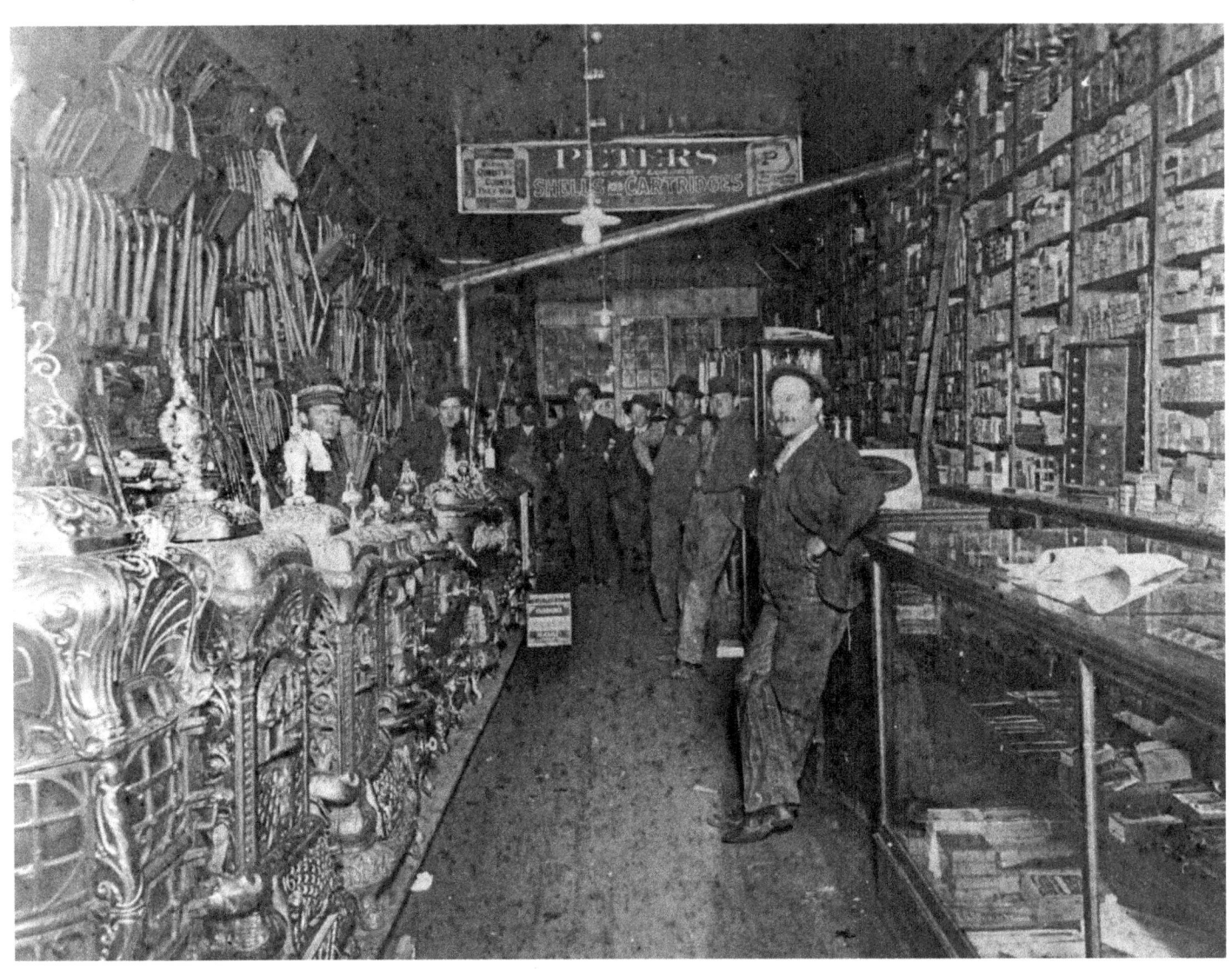

The well-stocked retail department of Summers-Parrott hardware store, in Johnson City, Tennessee, was a gathering place for locals. The cast-iron stoves at left reflect an era when many homes were heated directly by wood and coal, though by this time steam radiator systems had also become common.

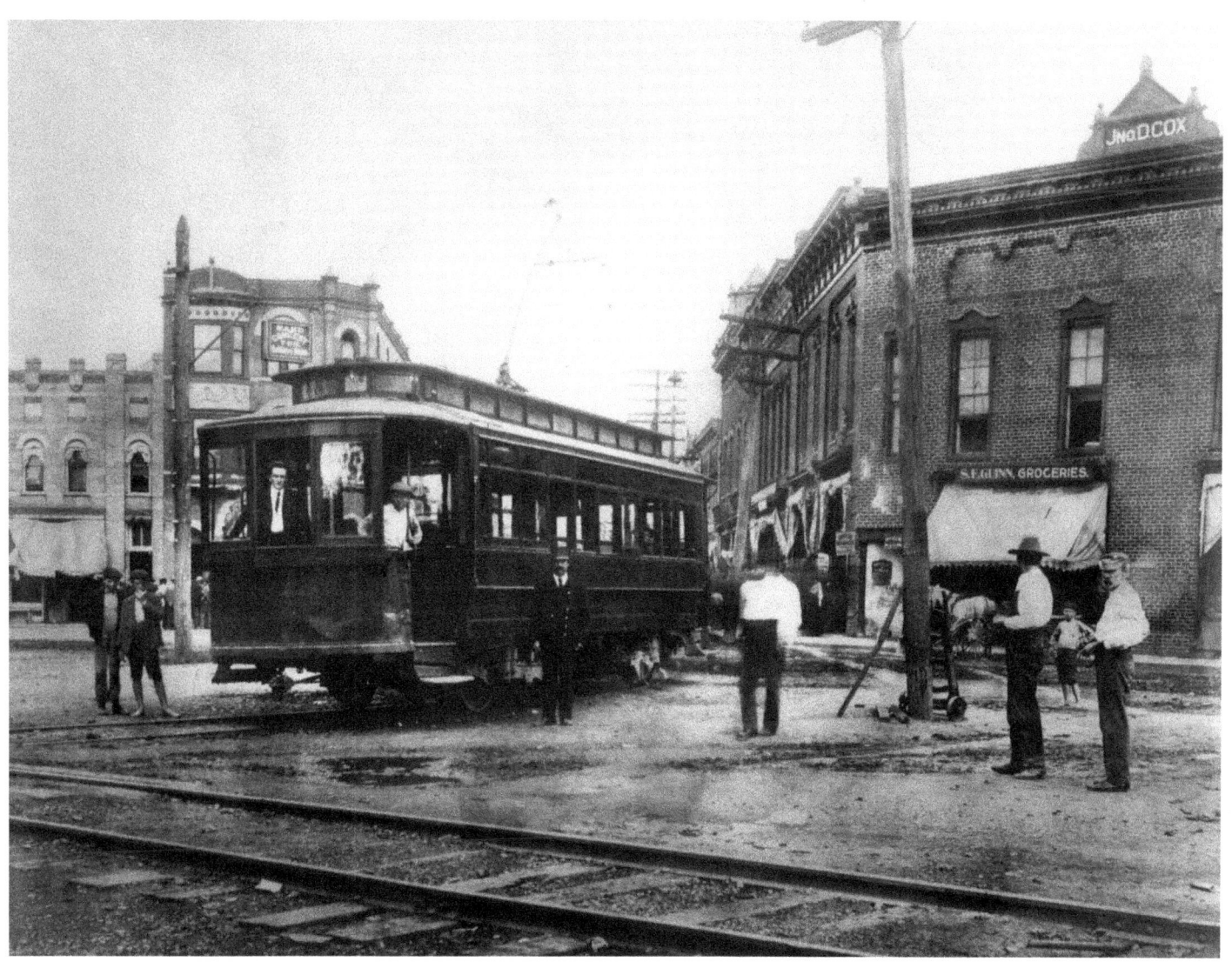

The first electric trams or trolleys appeared in Europe in the 1880s. By the early 1890s, they were in use in some Appalachian cities. The Johnson City and Carnegie Street Railway was established in 1892, and served the city until the 1930s. A car is shown here at Fountain Square in the early twentieth century.

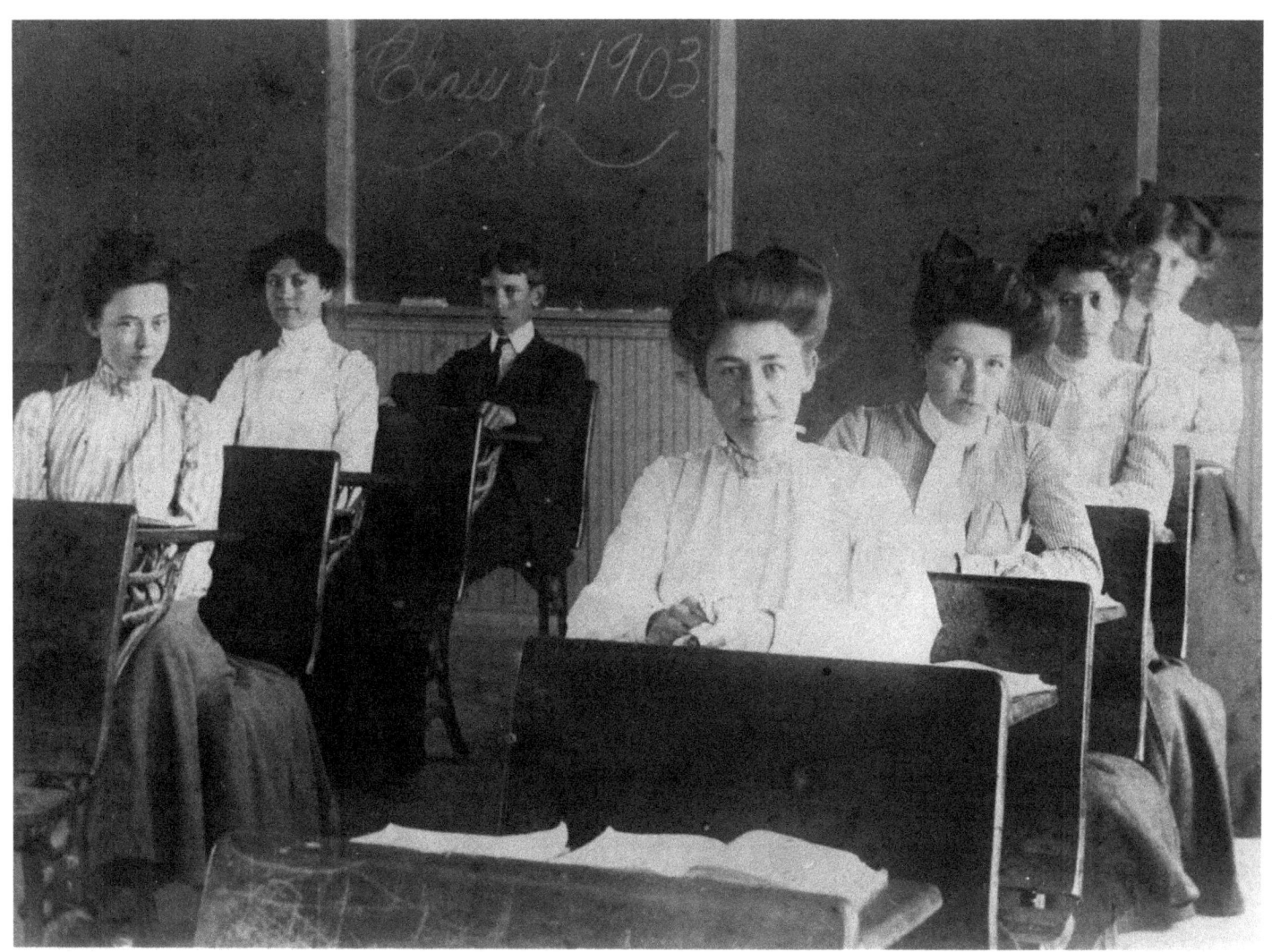

Science Hill Academy, shown here in 1903, was originally established as "Science Hill Male and Female Institute" in the early 1870s, in Johnson City, Tennessee.

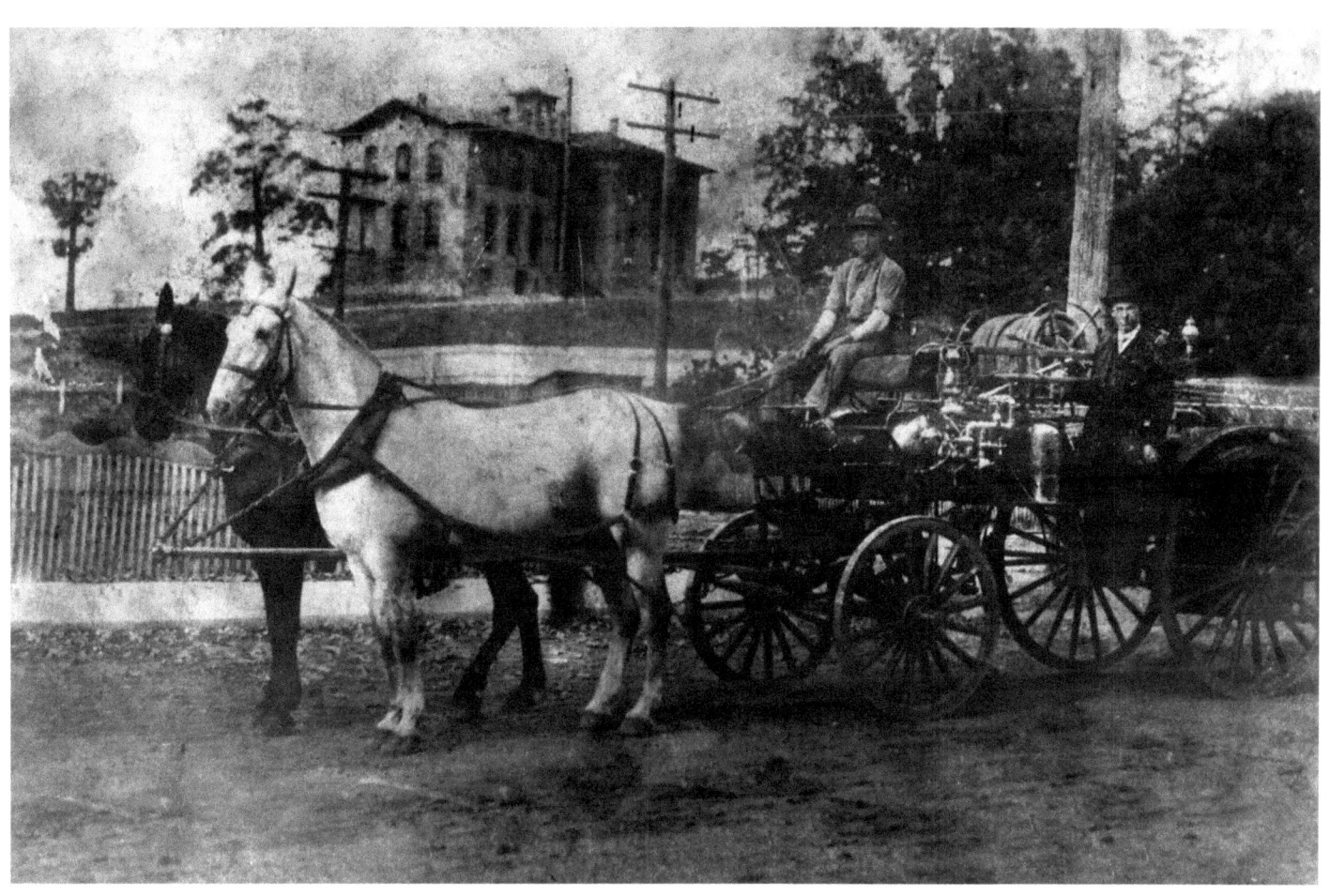

A chemical wagon purchased by the Johnson City Fire Department from the Chicago Fire Extinguisher Company is on display here in 1902. Johnson City residents at the time reported that the wagon caused a great deal of excitement when it raced through the street, pulled by strong horses, with its bells clanging. Science Hill Academy stands in the background.

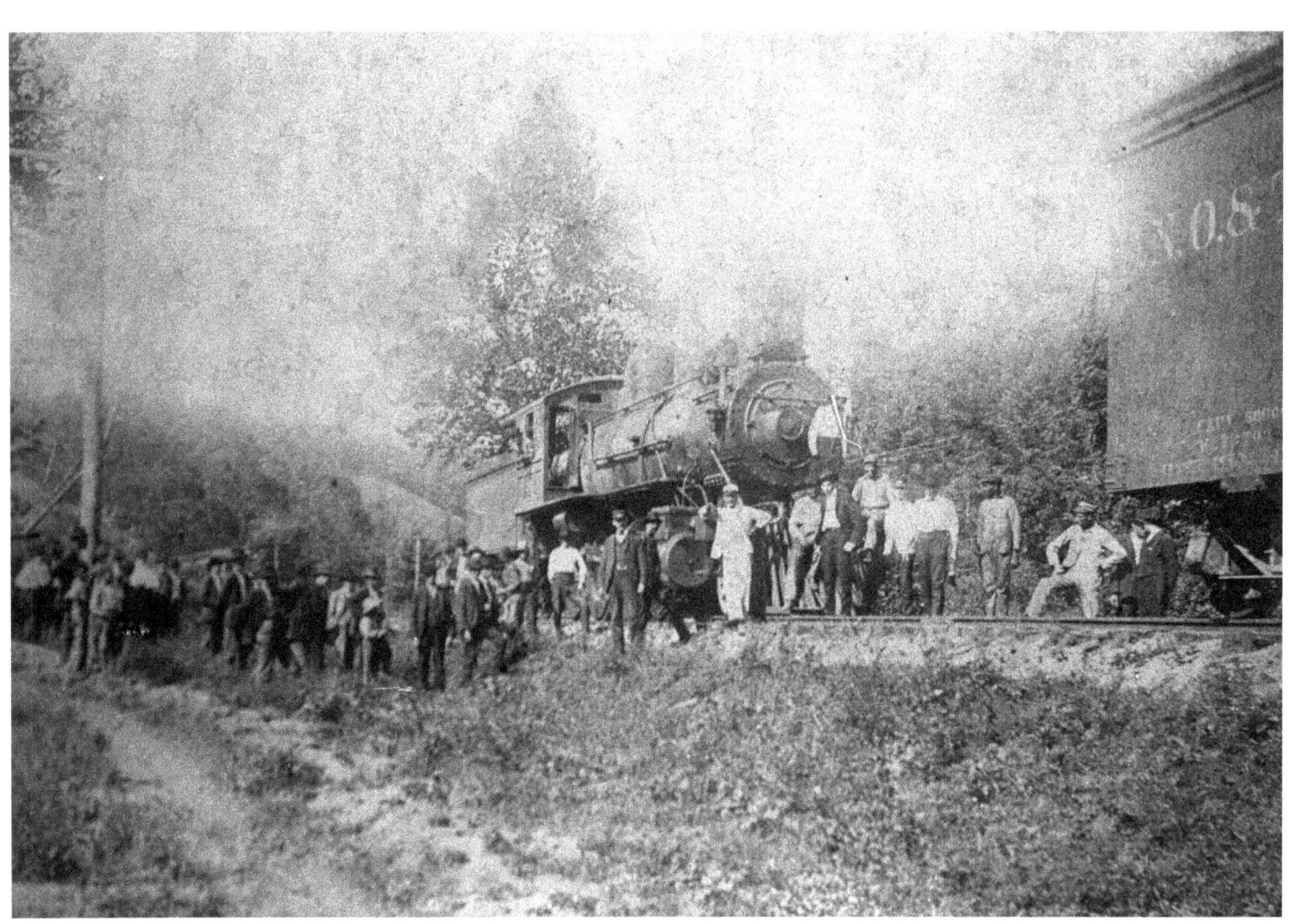

Workers for the Southern Railway pose in front of an engine. The initials partly visible at right, C.N.O.&T.P., name the Cincinnati, New Orleans, and Texas Pacific Railway, part of the Southern system.

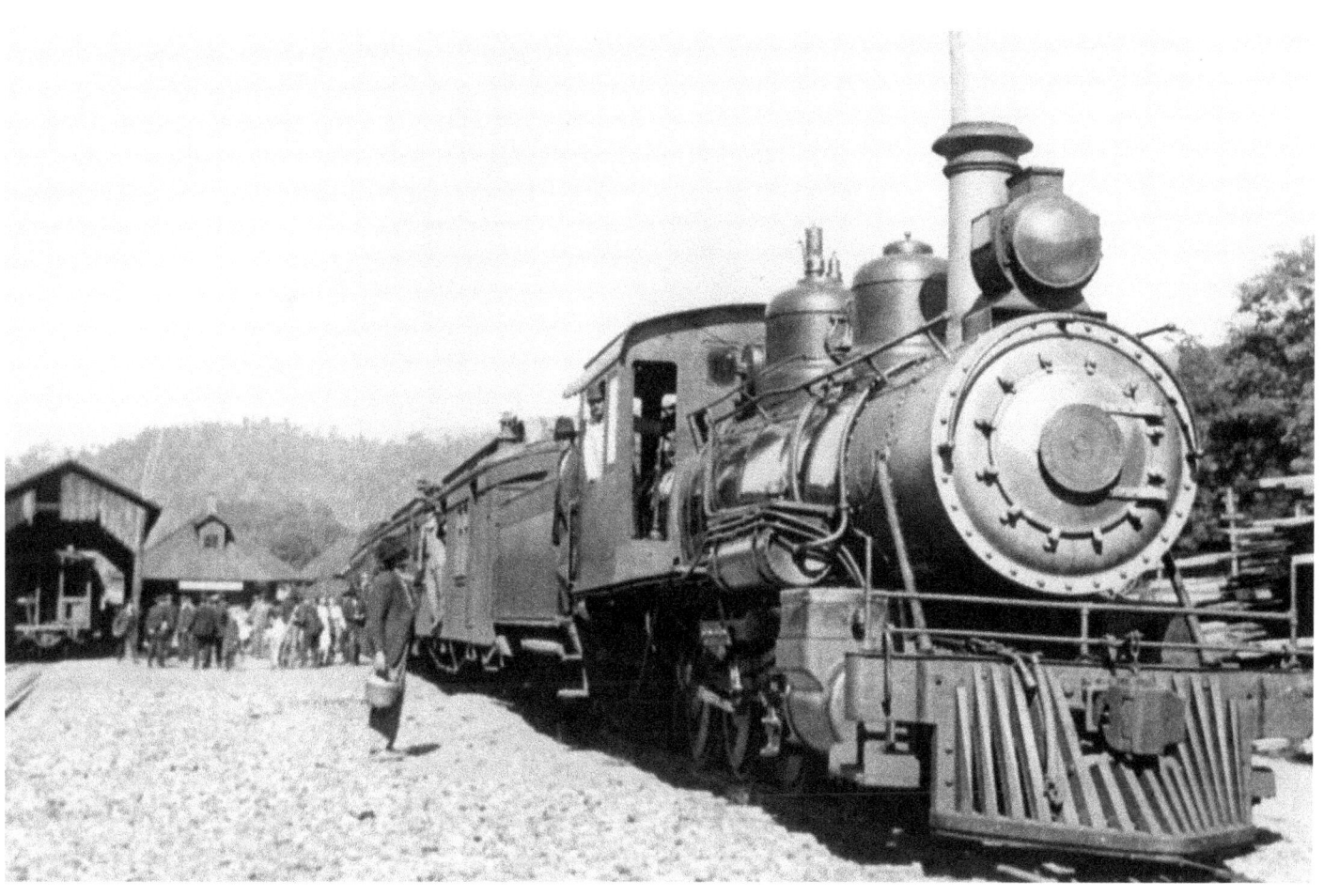

At Cranberry, North Carolina, passengers board a train pulled by Engine no. 9 of the East Tennessee & Western North Carolina (Tweetsie) and Linville River Railroad. The narrow gauge railway hauled passengers and freight through some of the most spectacular scenery in the East. Cranberry, near the Tennessee border, was a transfer point between the North Carolina and Tennessee portions of the rail route.

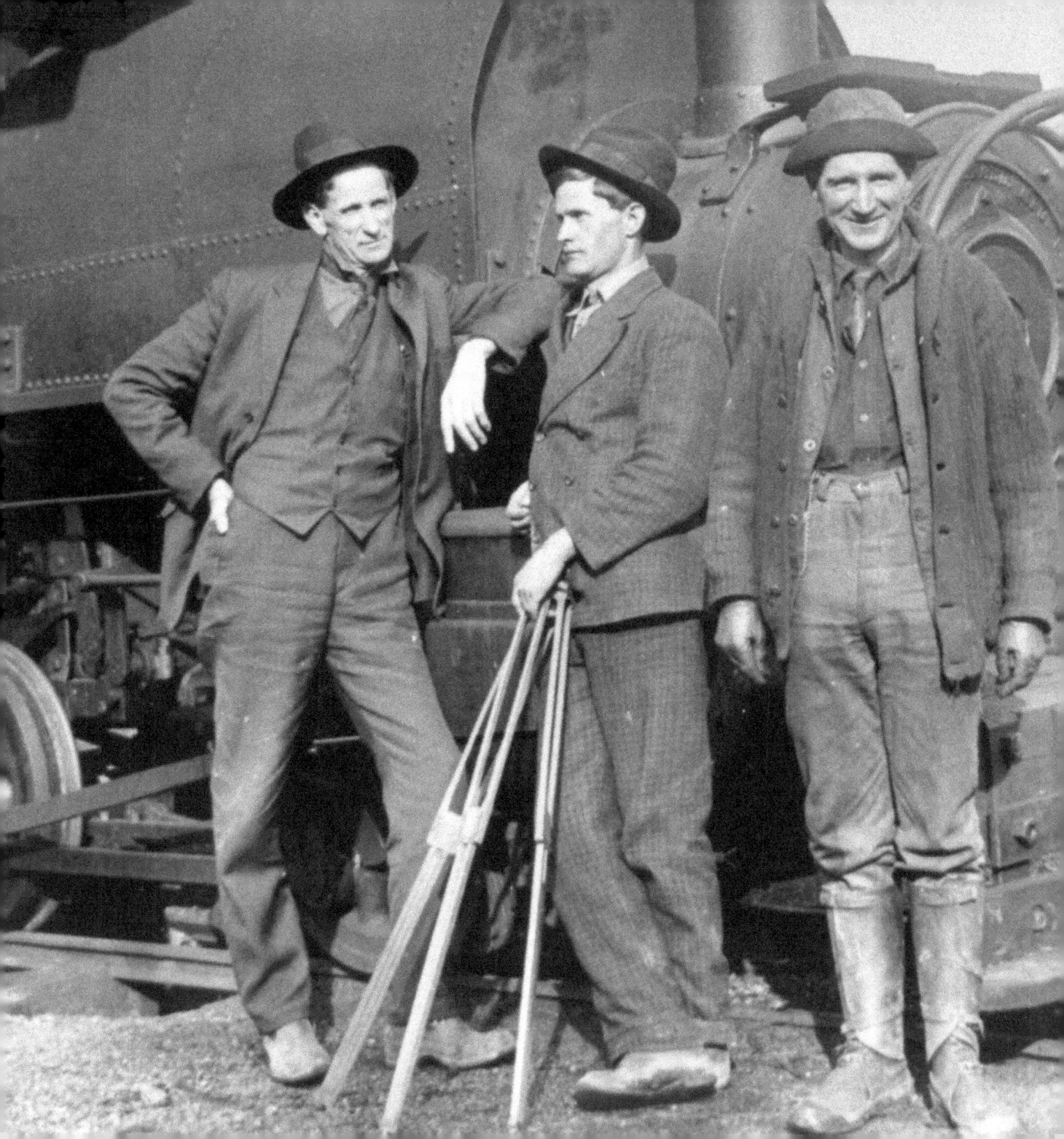

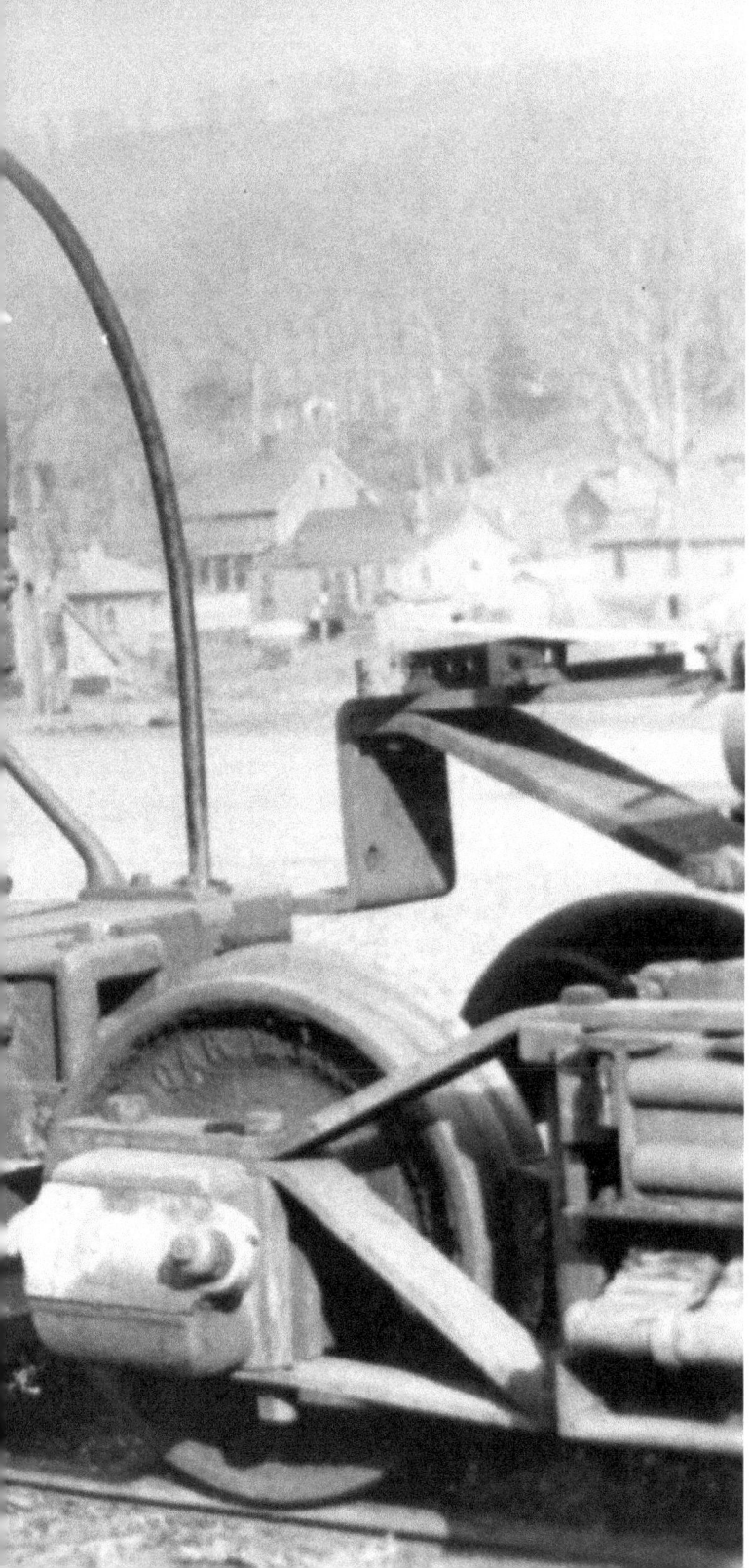

These men pose in front of an E.T.&W.N.C. engine used exclusively at the Cranberry mines. Cranberry was a company town, formed by the Cranberry Iron and Coal Company in the 1880s to mine nearby iron deposits. By 1900, the town was home to about 2,000 people. Yet early in the twentieth century, the deposits began to play out, and the mine was closed and the town itself shuttered in 1930.

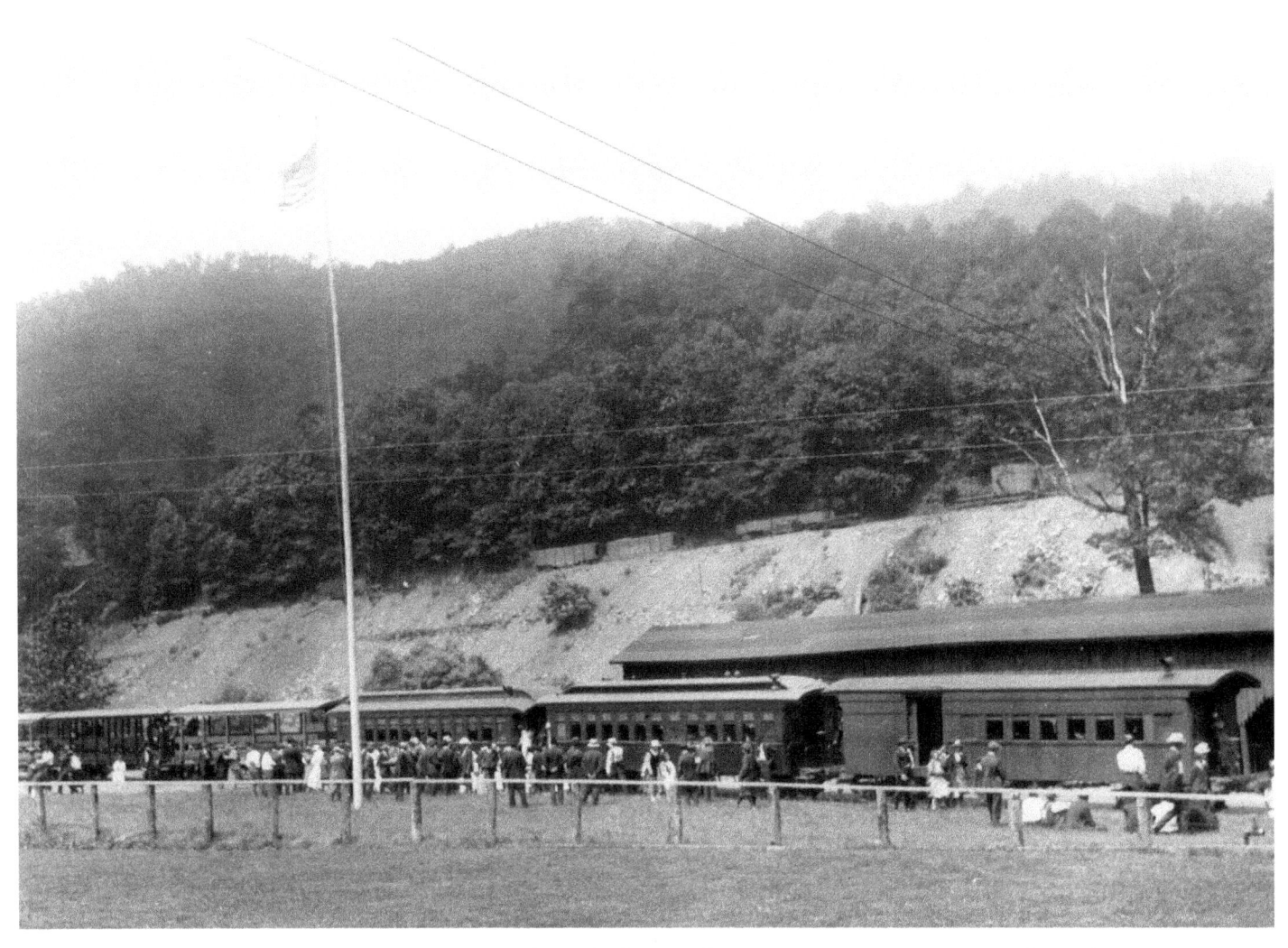

Passengers and excursionists stand outside the cars of an East Tennessee & Western North Carolina (Tweetsie) train.

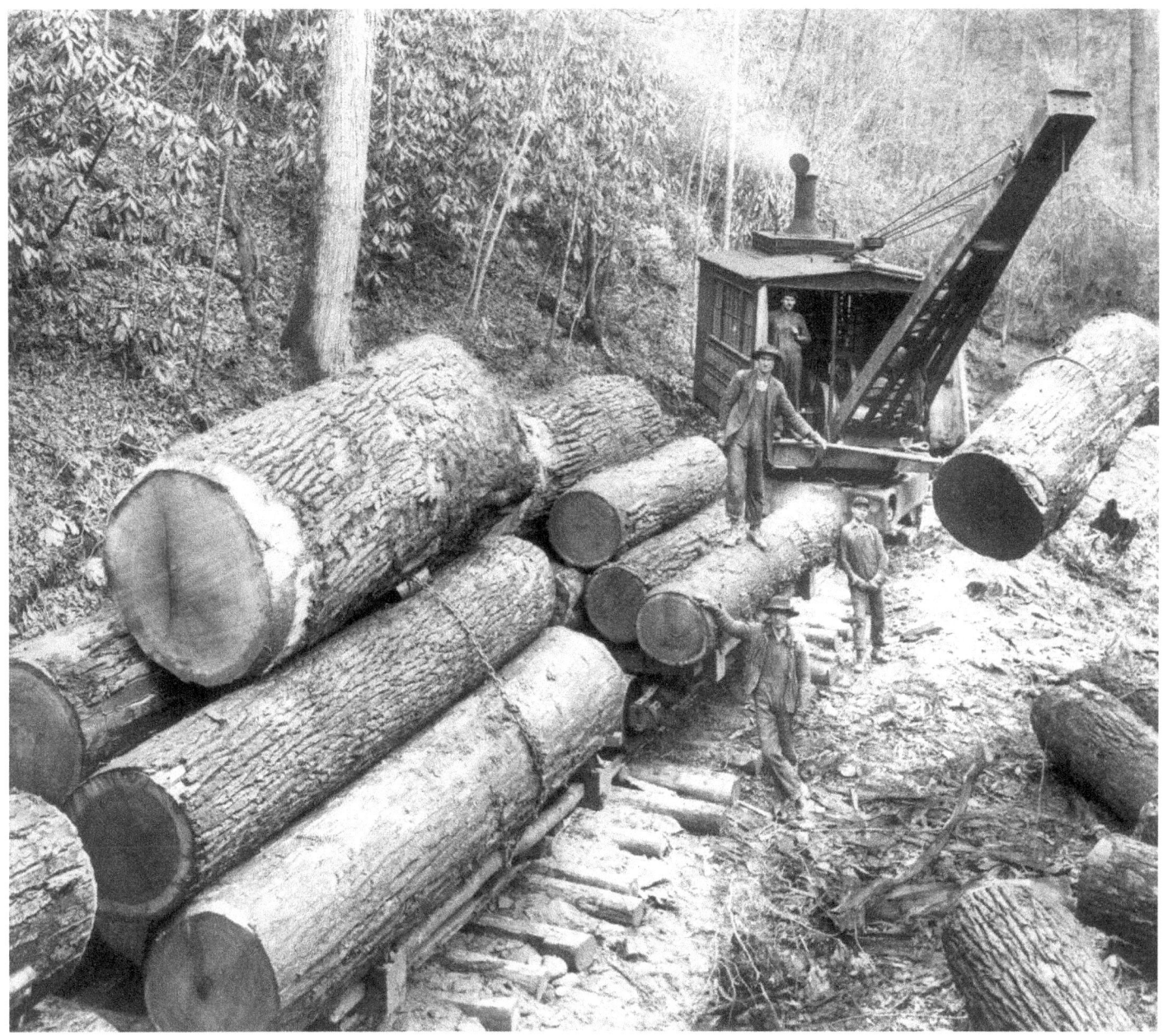

Workers in West Virginia use steam-powered equipment to load yellow poplar logs around 1910. During the era of industrial logging in Appalachia, from about 1880 to 1920, one of the greatest deciduous forests in the world was stripped of much of its timber. Today, despite the widescale encroachment of coal strip-mines, West Virginia is widely replanted with young forests, many decades short of yielding logs the size of those shown here.

Members of the Hugh L. White family take a dramatic perch aboard a flatcar, for an excursion into the mountains. White owned a lumberyard in Butler, Tennessee, and a sawmill in Elk Park, North Carolina, near Cranberry, as well as some logging railroad spurs.

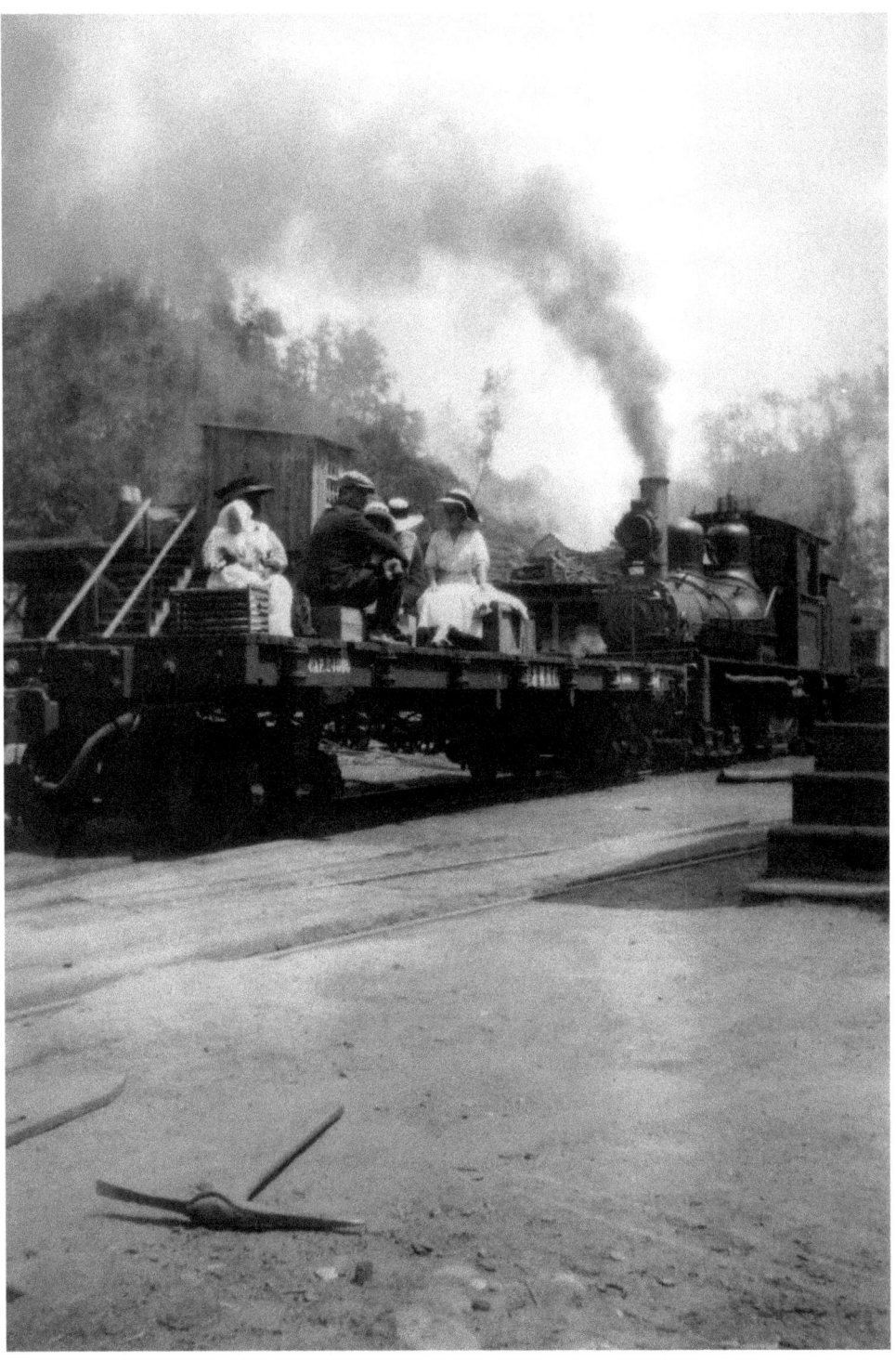

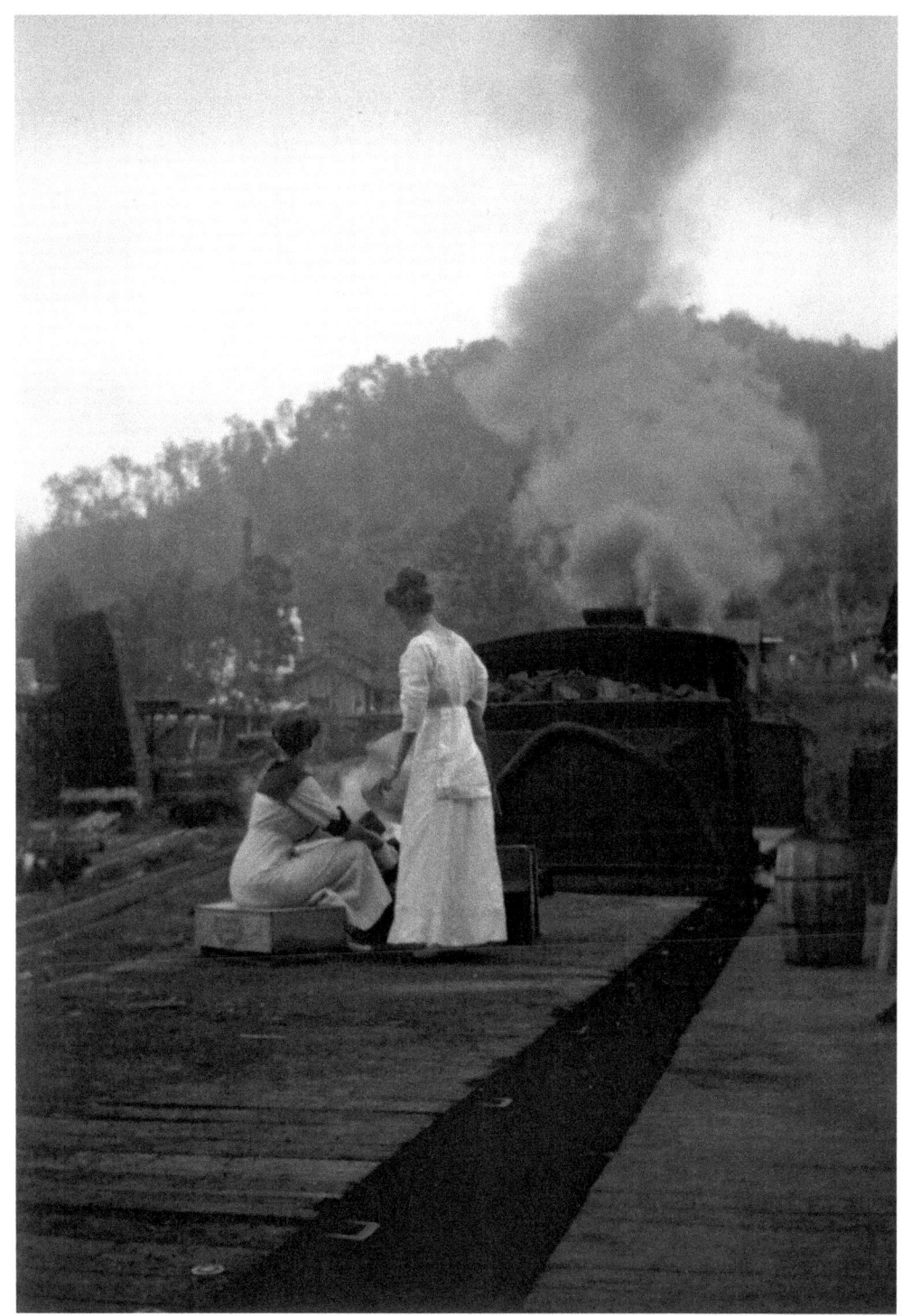

These women, perhaps members of the Hugh L. White family, take a daring excursion aboard a logging railroad flatcar. In addition to his sawmill and lumberyard, White owned logging railroad spurs in East Tennessee, including the Laurel Fork Railway in Carter County, and the Peavine Railroad in Greene County. This appears to be a scene on the Laurel Fork Railway.

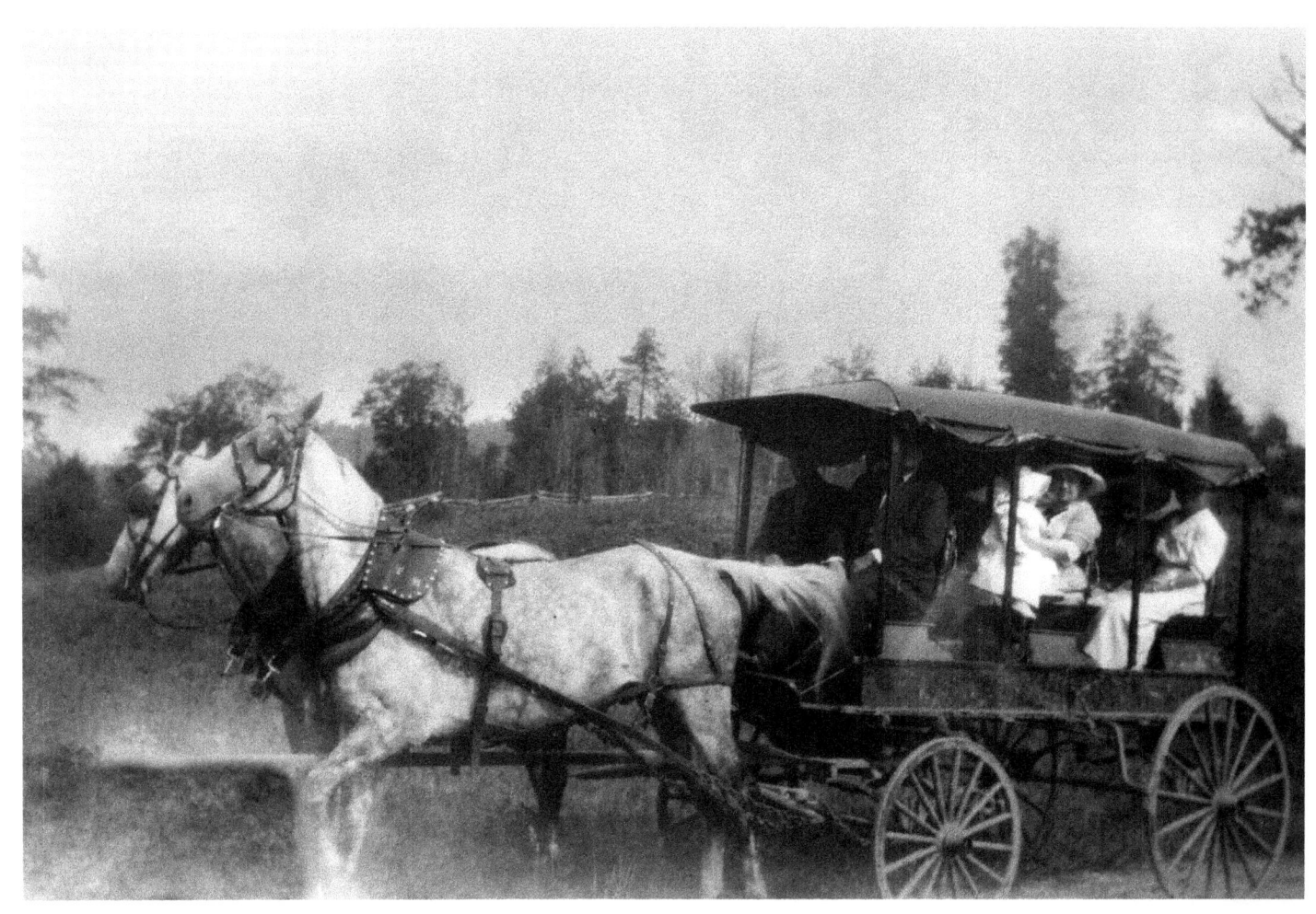

A mill owner's family members enjoy a carriage ride.

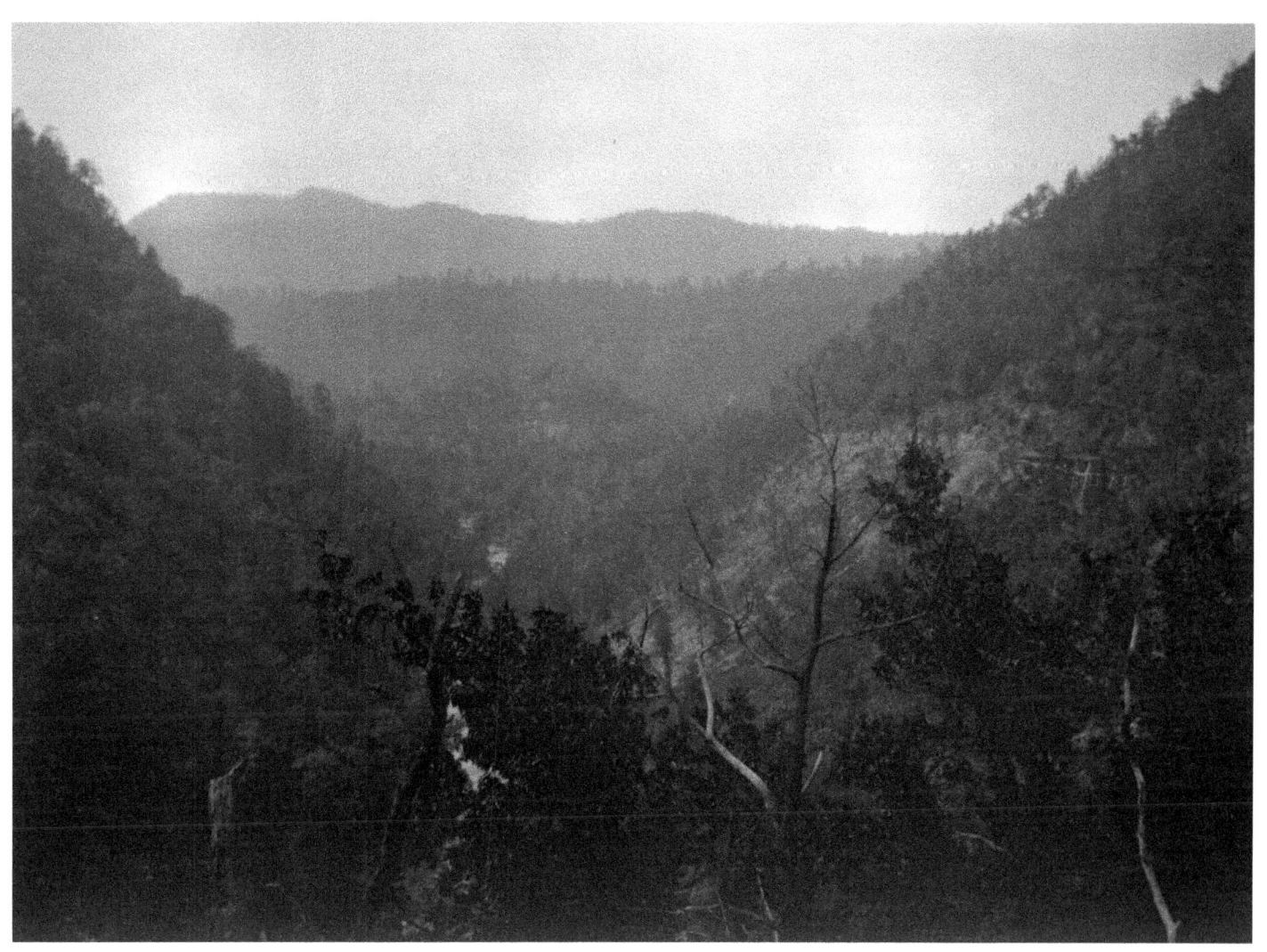

In this rugged, southern Appalachian scene, signs of logging are visible in the middle ground. This is Carter County, Tennessee, around 1910.

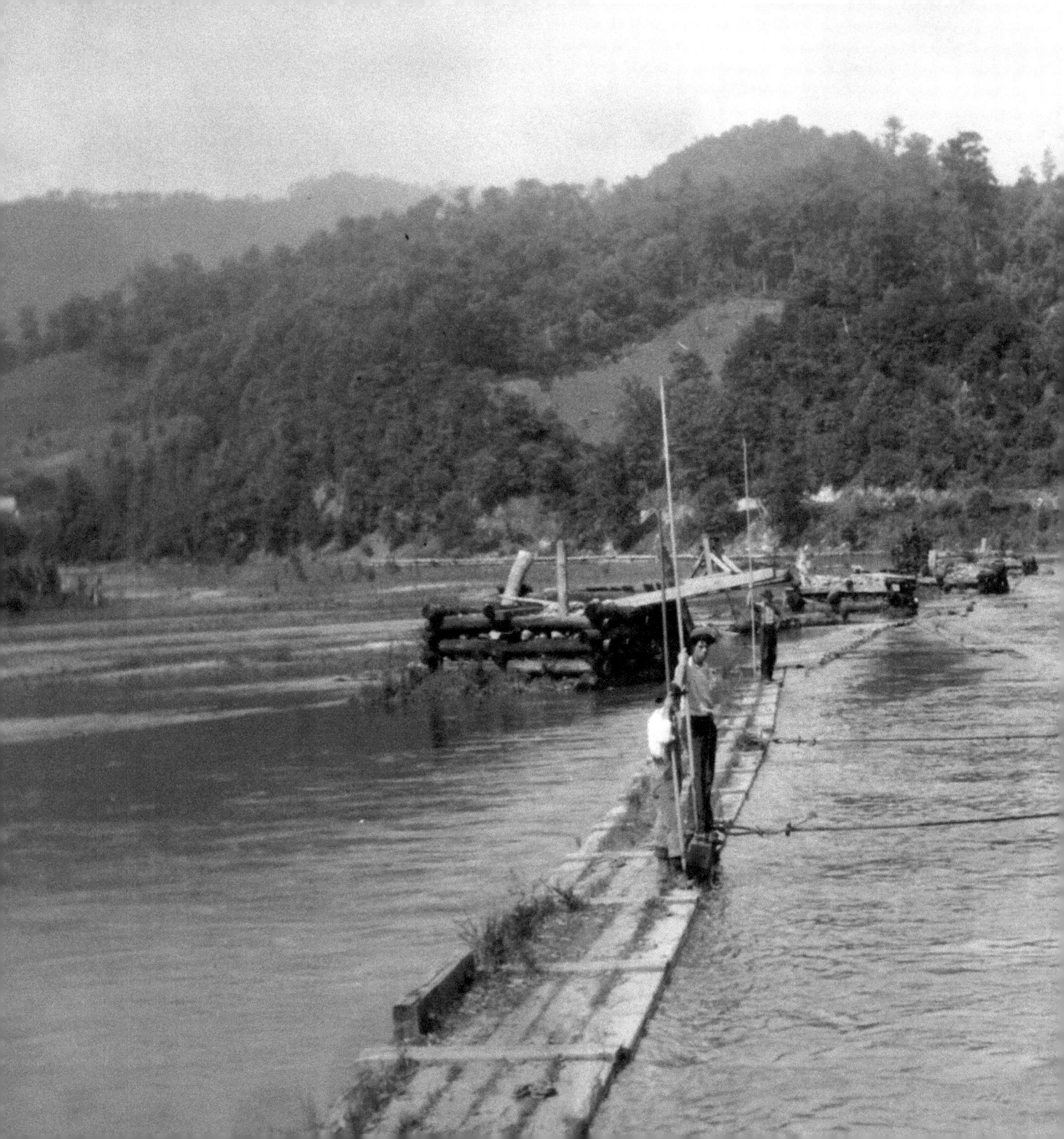

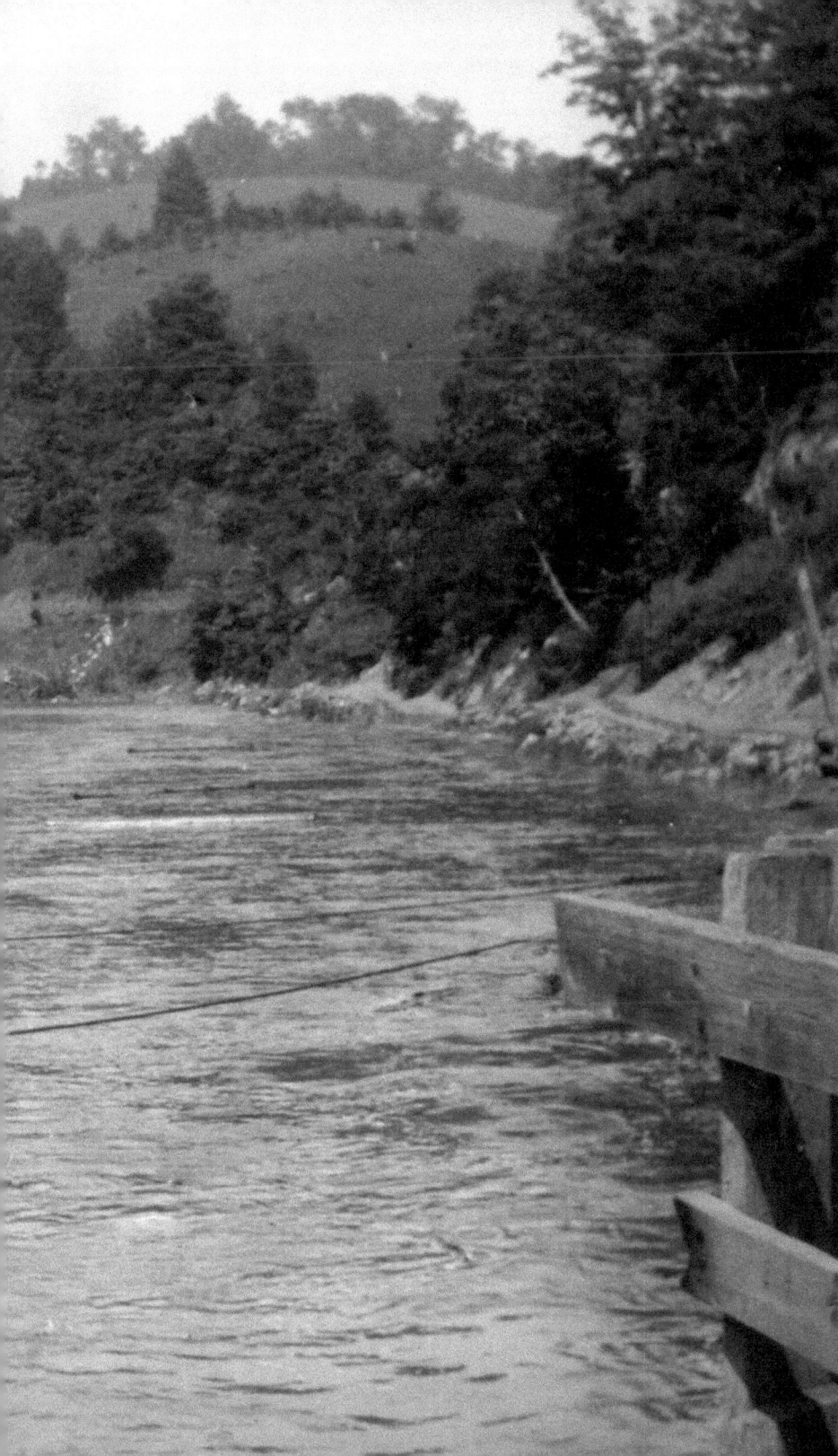

This splash pond for timber was part of a Whiting Lumber Company operation at Shulls Mill, in North Carolina.

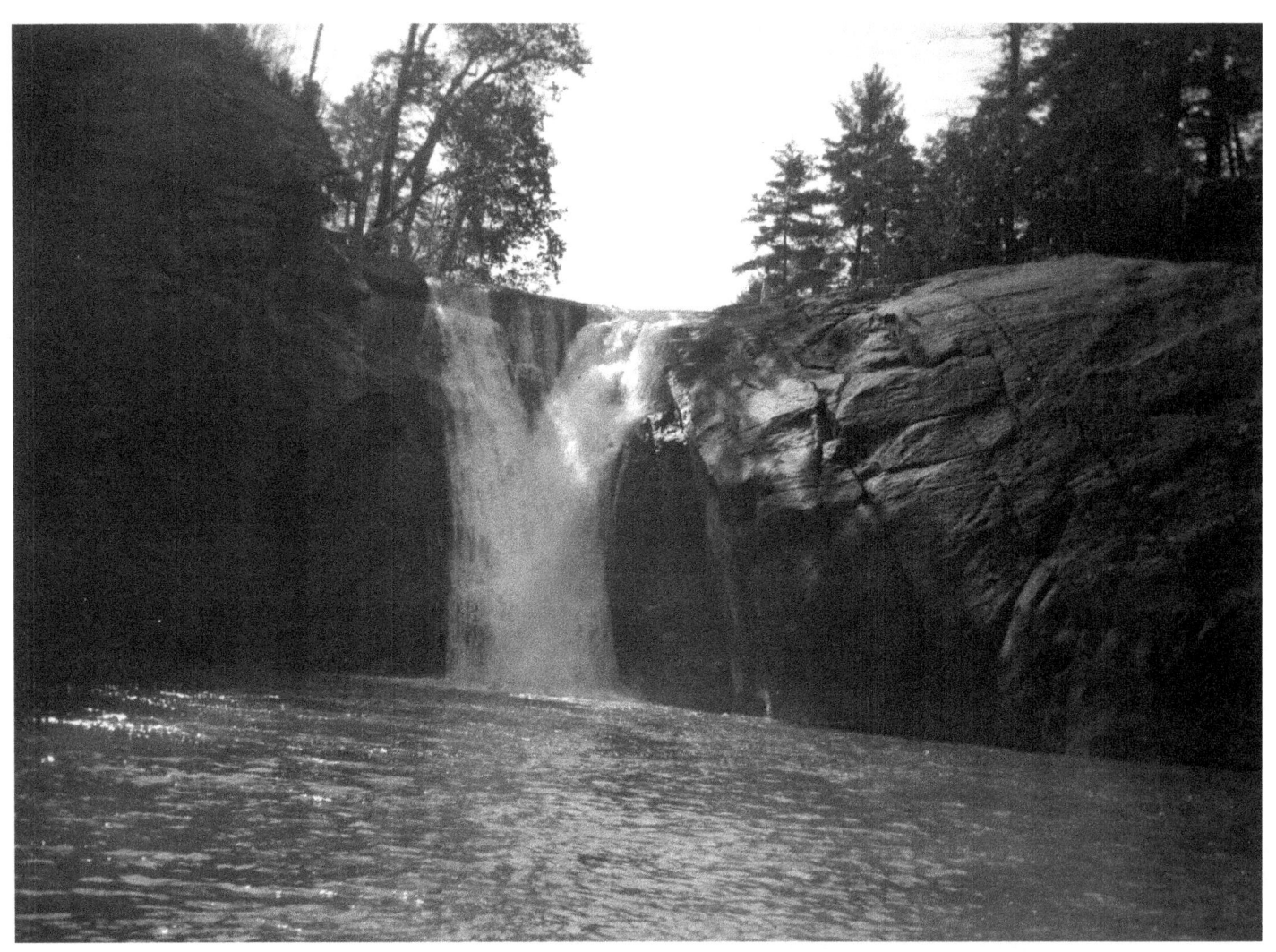

An Appalachian mountain waterfall feeds a natural swimming hole.

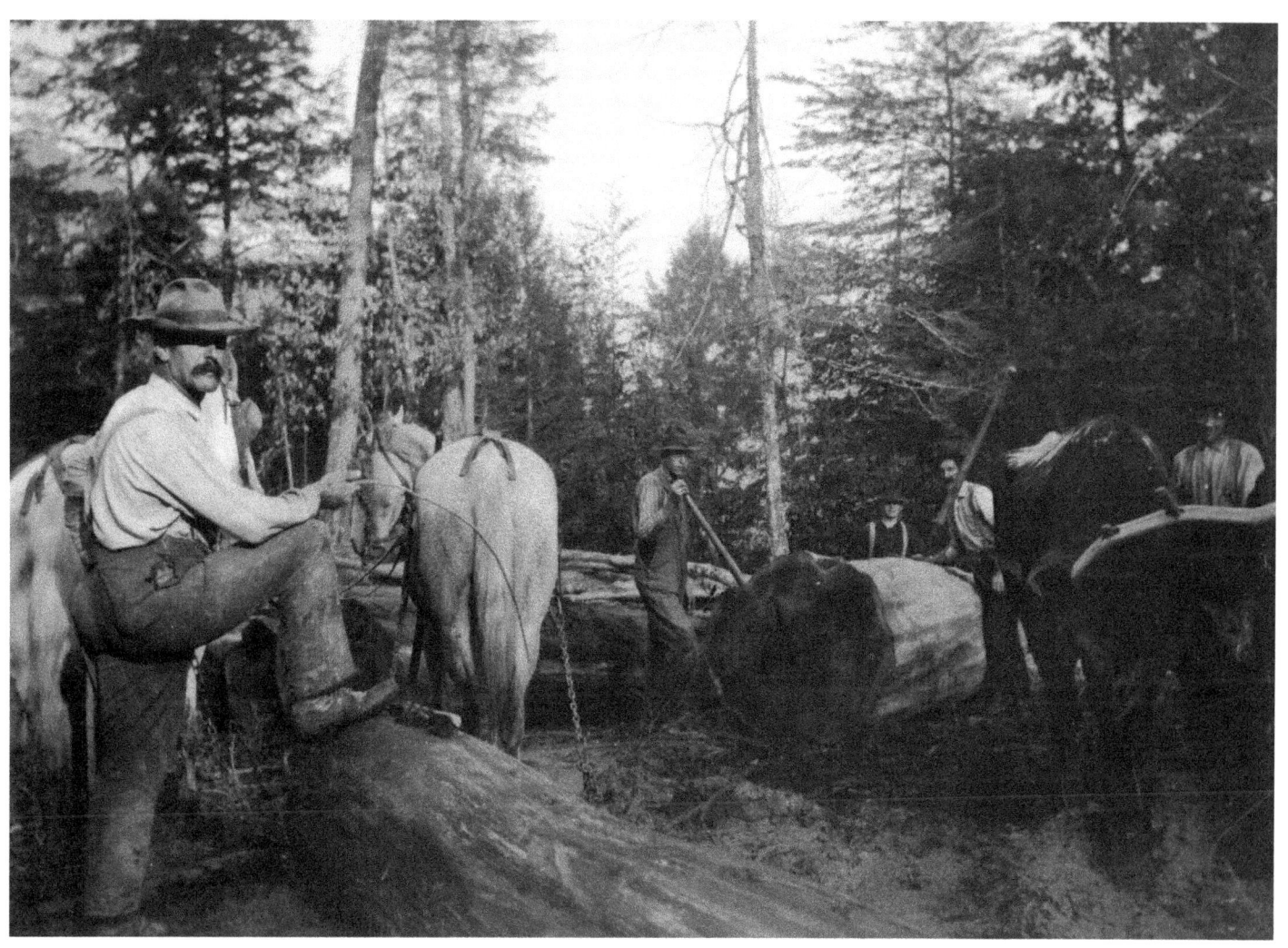

Even in the era of industrial logging (1880–1920), when Appalachian logging operations were dominated by steam-powered equipment, some commercial logging was done with horses and oxen.

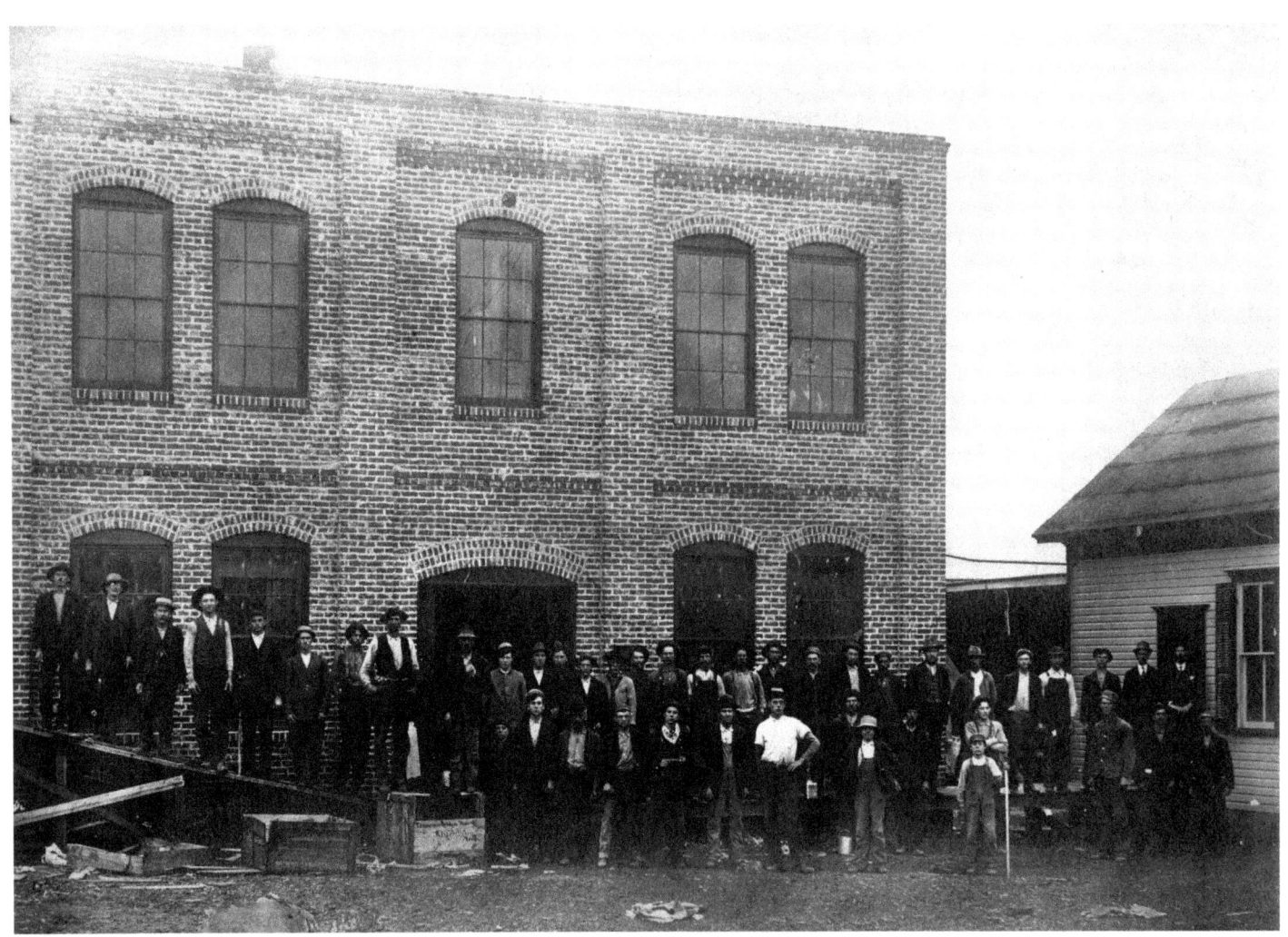

Workers pose in front of the old Johnson City Foundry and Machine Works building, around 1905. Around the turn of the century, such industrial operations drew workers from afar to Appalachia. Describing another Johnson City furnace operation in 1890, the *Comet*, a local newspaper, reported that a "number of Italians with all their worldly good arrived on railcar No. 4 Sunday and were put to work on Monday on the furnace."

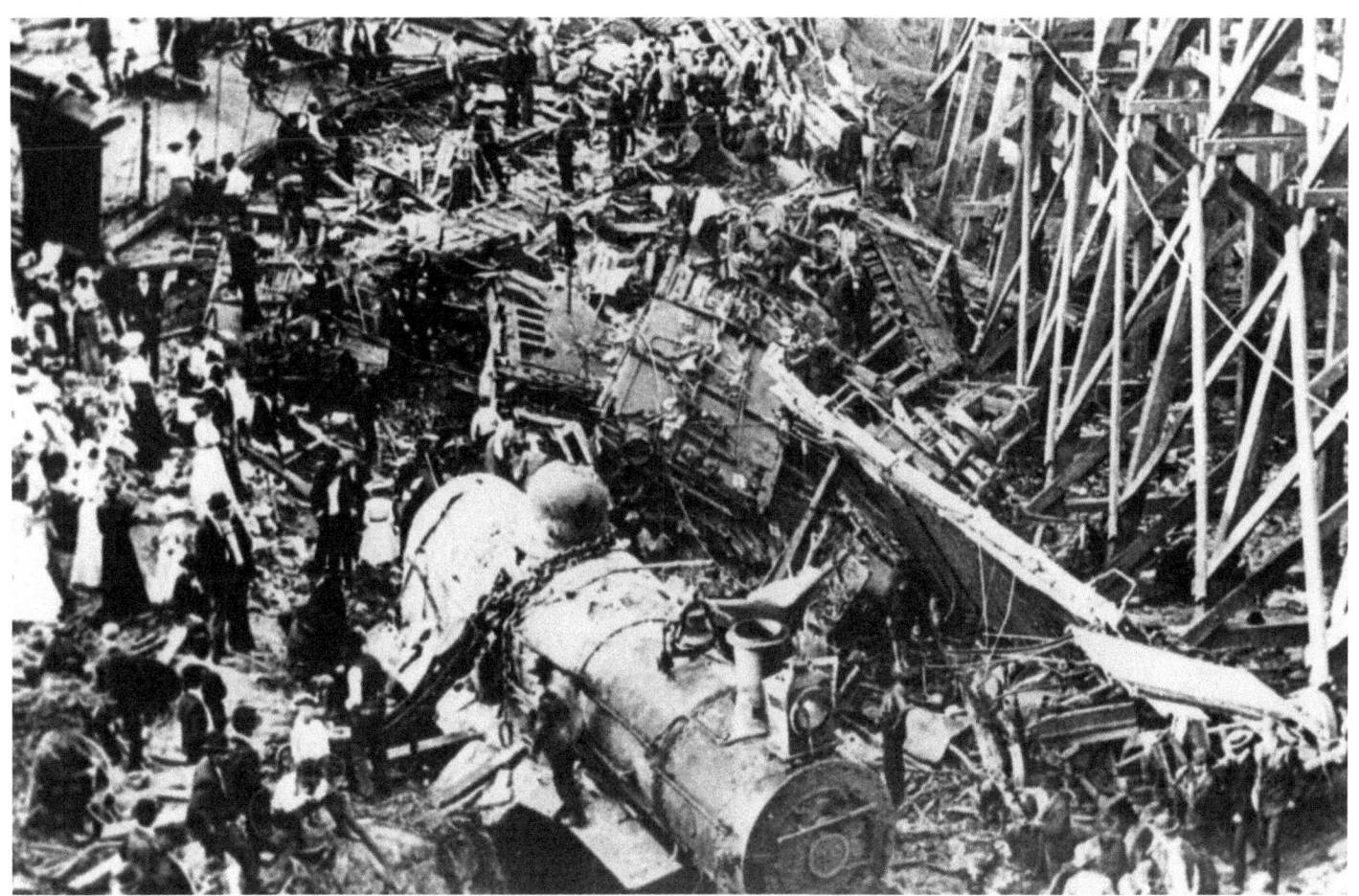

On September 27, 1903, a Southern Express ("Fast Mail") train crashed near Danville, Virginia, killing nine people, as it attempted to make up lost time. The event inspired the famous ballad "The Wreck of the Old 97." The train was moving too fast as it came into a curve at the bottom of the grade approaching this 75-foot-tall trestle. This well-known image is believed to have been recorded a few days after the wreck, after the locomotive was righted.

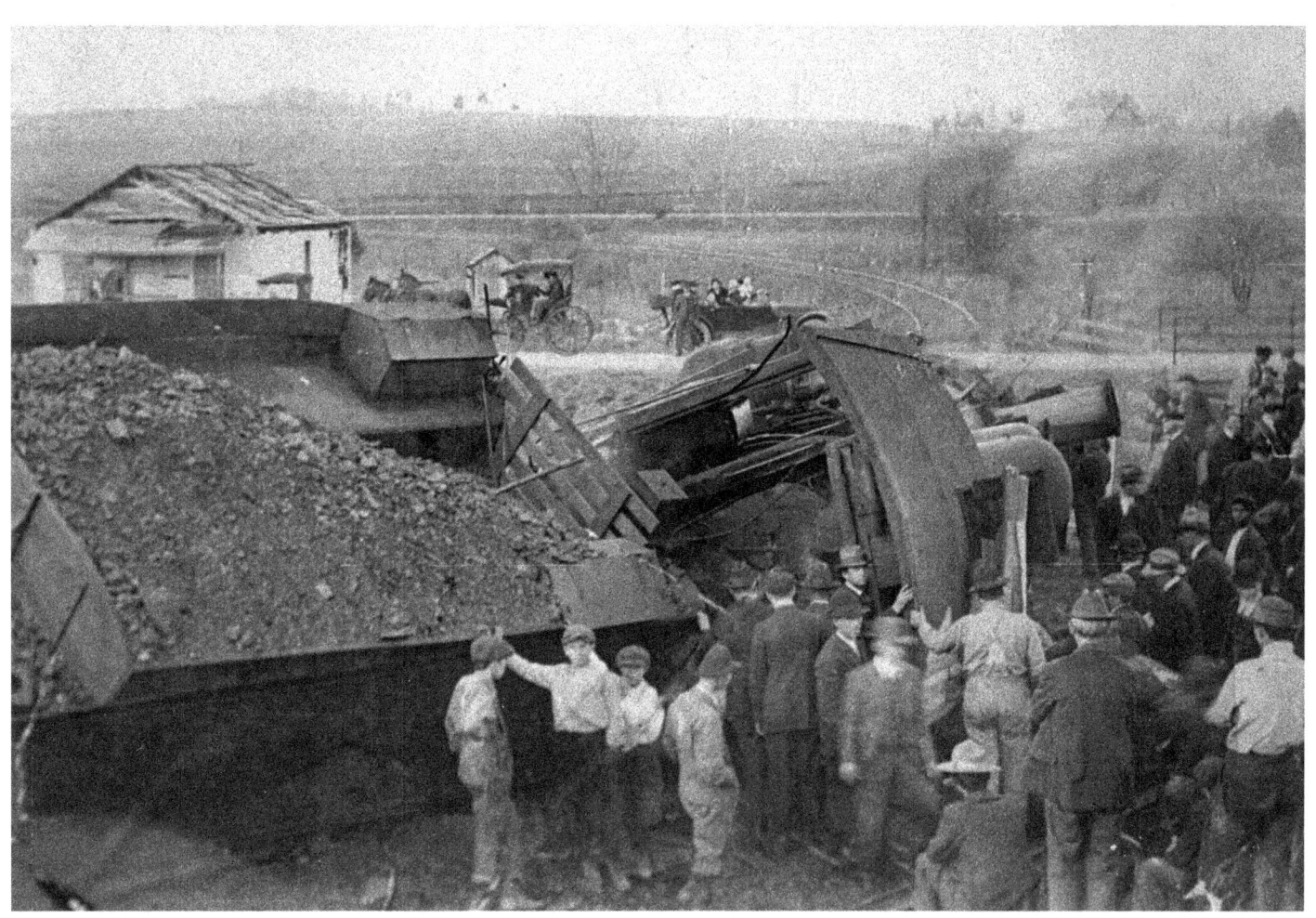

A crowd gathers around a wrecked steam engine, its tender loaded with coal, as "motorists" slow to a stop in the distance. The origins of the phenomenon of "rubbernecking" are clearly much older than today's superhighways.

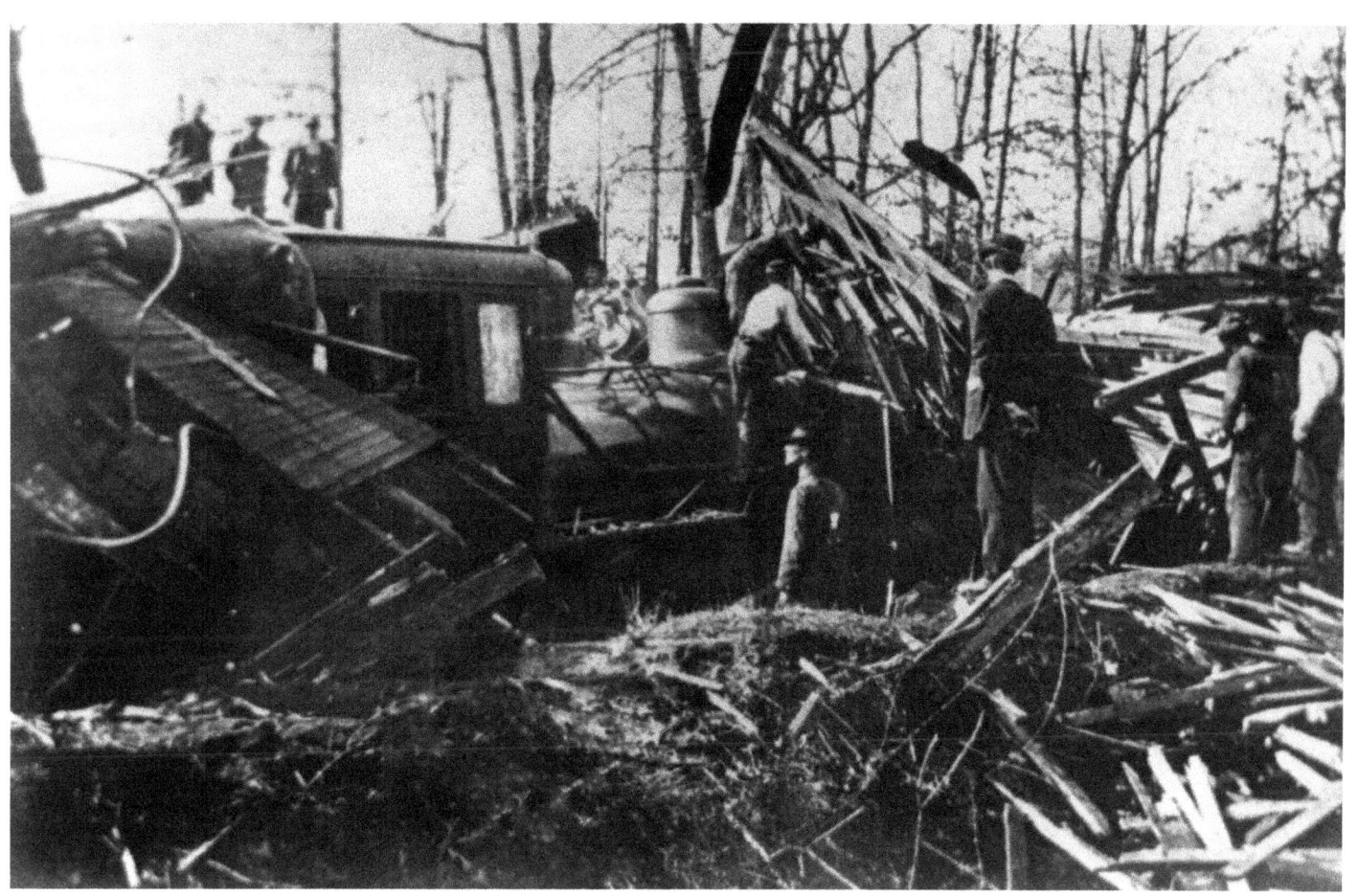

This East Tennessee & Western North Carolina Railroad wreck was photographed east of the railroad shops, near Miller's Road Crossing, in Johnson City, Tennessee. A hand-written note on the original photograph states that "Fireman 'Turkey' Hughes lost his toes in this wreck."

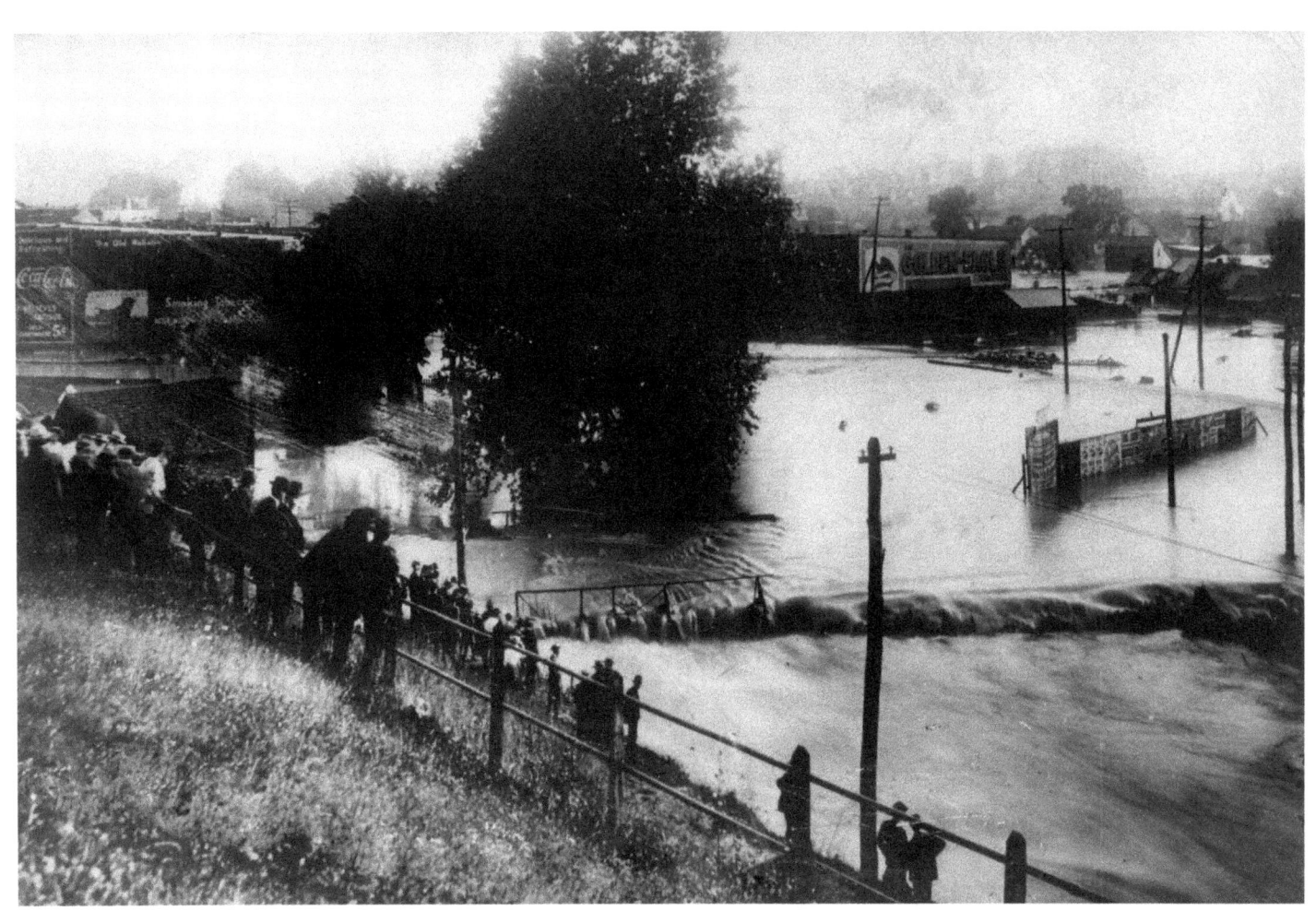

This picture shows floodwaters rushing through the town of Johnson City in the great flood of May 29, 1908. Spring flooding has always been a problem in Appalachia, because of the terrain, and because of the high rainfall the region receives. Heavy logging at the end of the nineteenth century exacerbated flooding, since trees had helped the mountains absorb water.

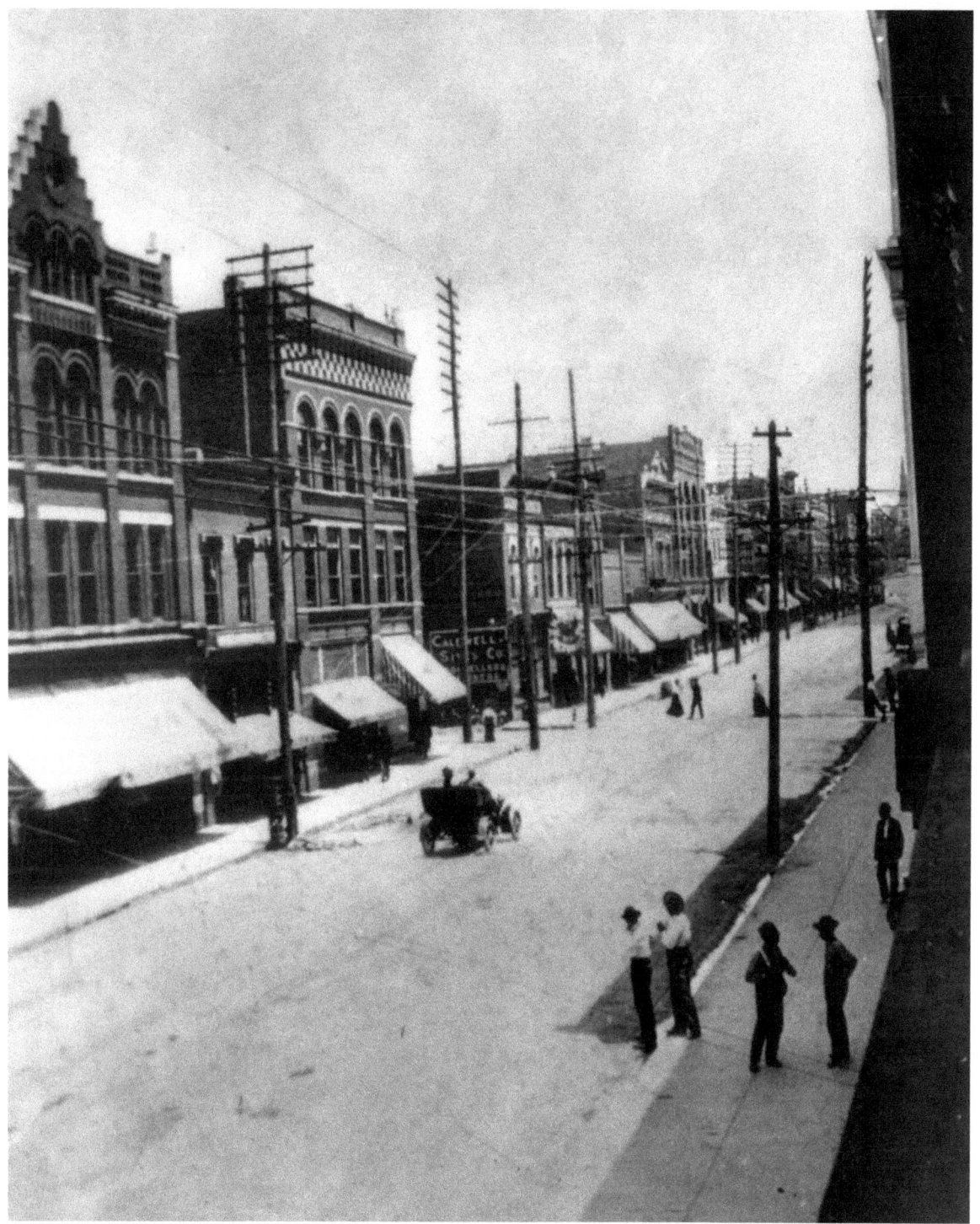

This 1905 photograph of State Street in Bristol, Tennessee, shows what was surely one of the first automobiles in the region. Large-scale manufacture of affordable automobiles was begun by Oldsmobile in 1902.

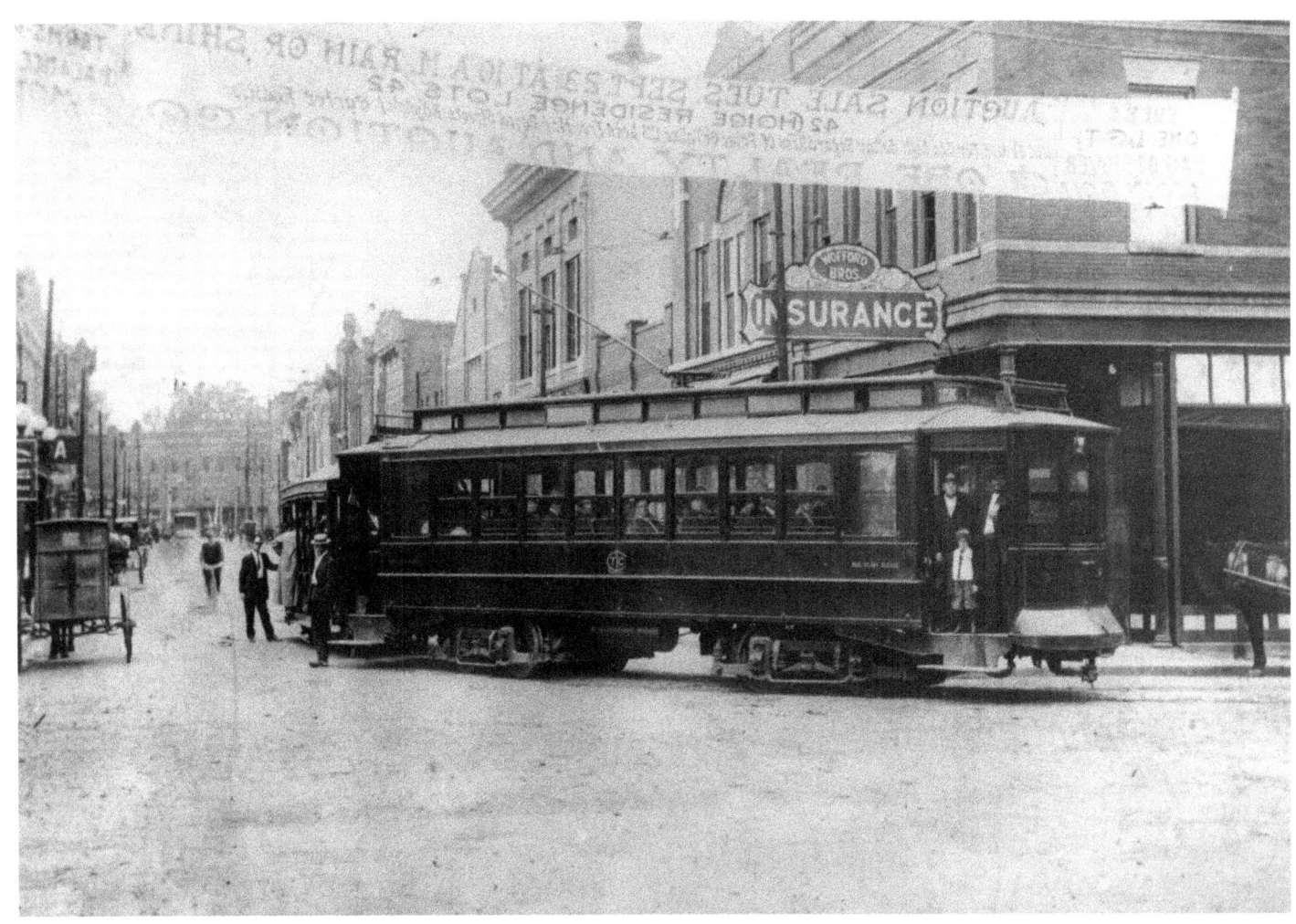

A trolley carries passengers along Main Street in Johnson City, Tennessee. Electric trolley service had begun in the 1890s and continued until the 1930s, when it was replaced by buses. Regional historian Bob Cox quotes a local resident who remembers that a trolley ride once cost a nickel. "Many people walked rather than ride because a nickel was a lot of money in those days."

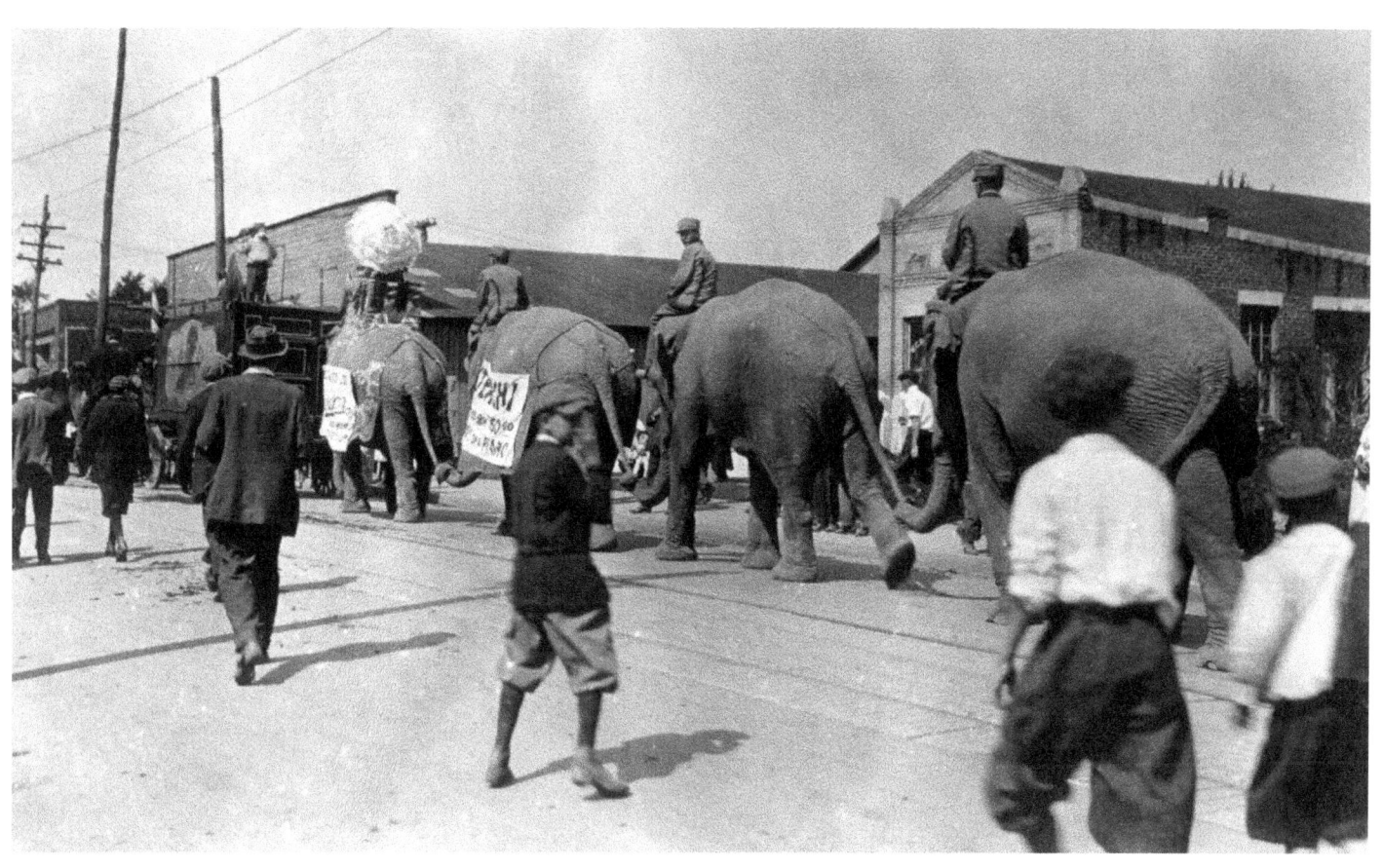

Traveling circuses entertained cities and towns throughout Appalachia in the nineteenth and early twentieth centuries. A troupe of circus elephants on West Main Street, in Johnson City, Tennessee, in the early twentieth century, creates publicity for the show.

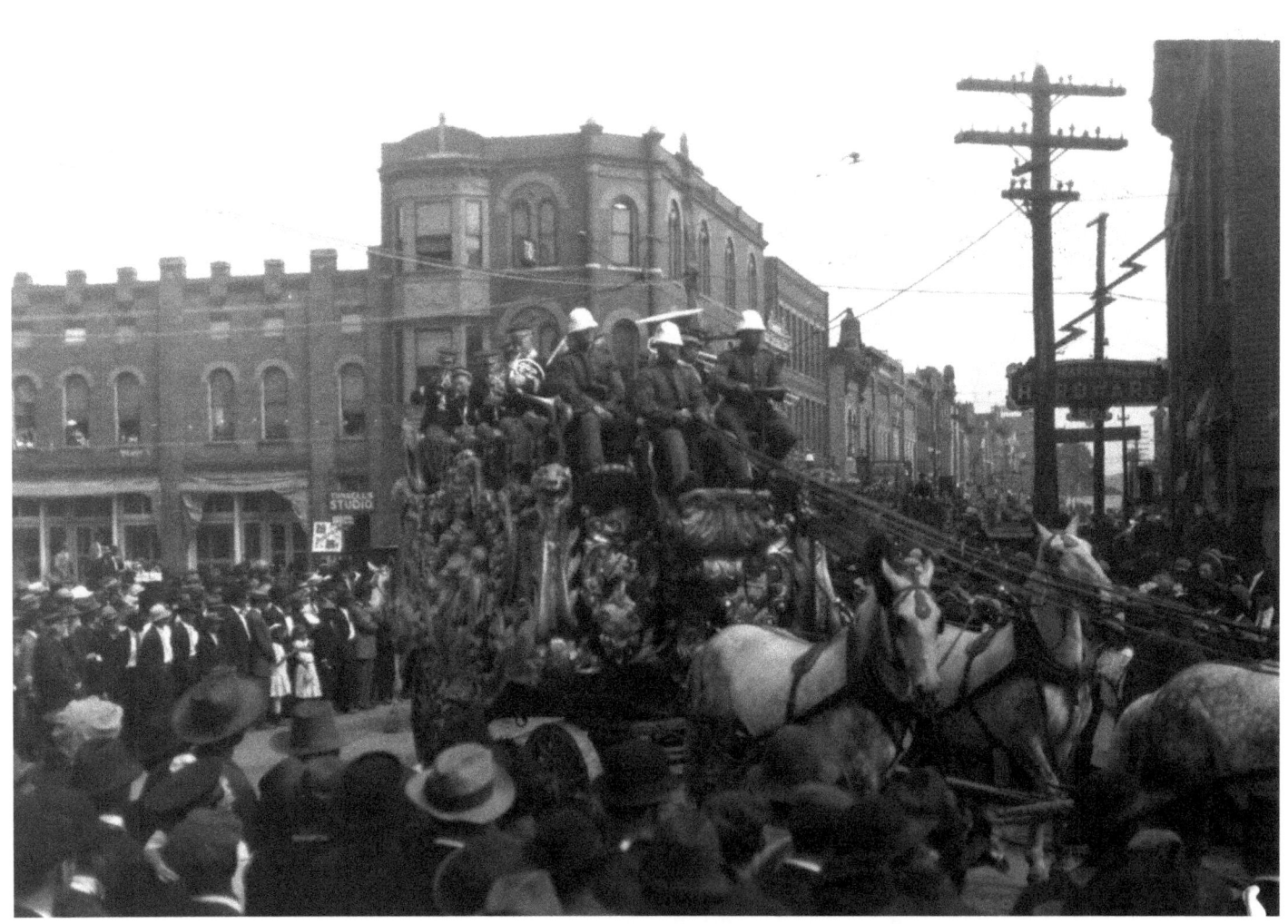

The circus wagon is a center of attention as a circus parade proceeds through the center of downtown Johnson City.

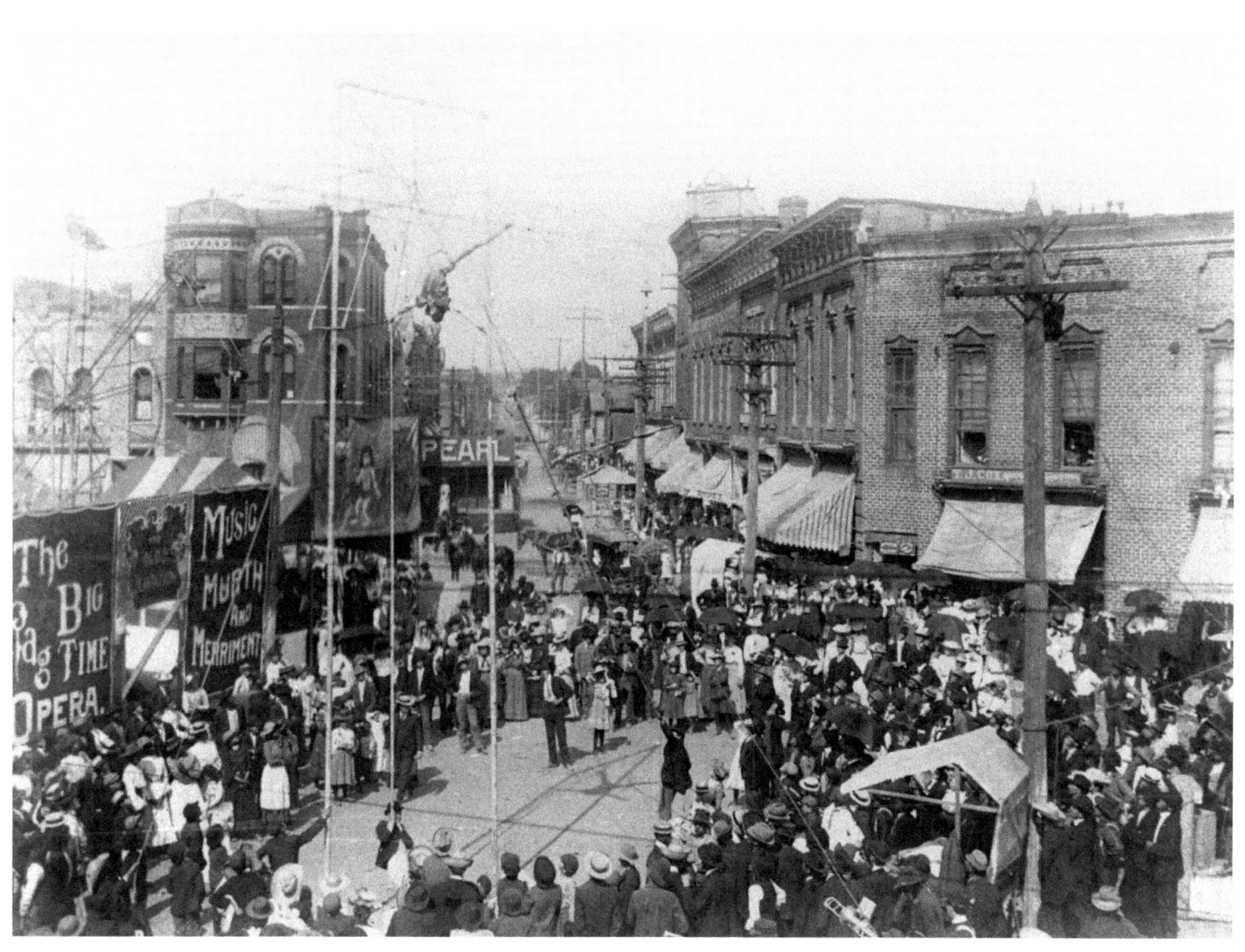

A trapeze artist performs at a street fair in the early twentieth century. Behind the sign which says "Music Murth and Merriment," a Ferris wheel at upper-left gives sightseers a lift.

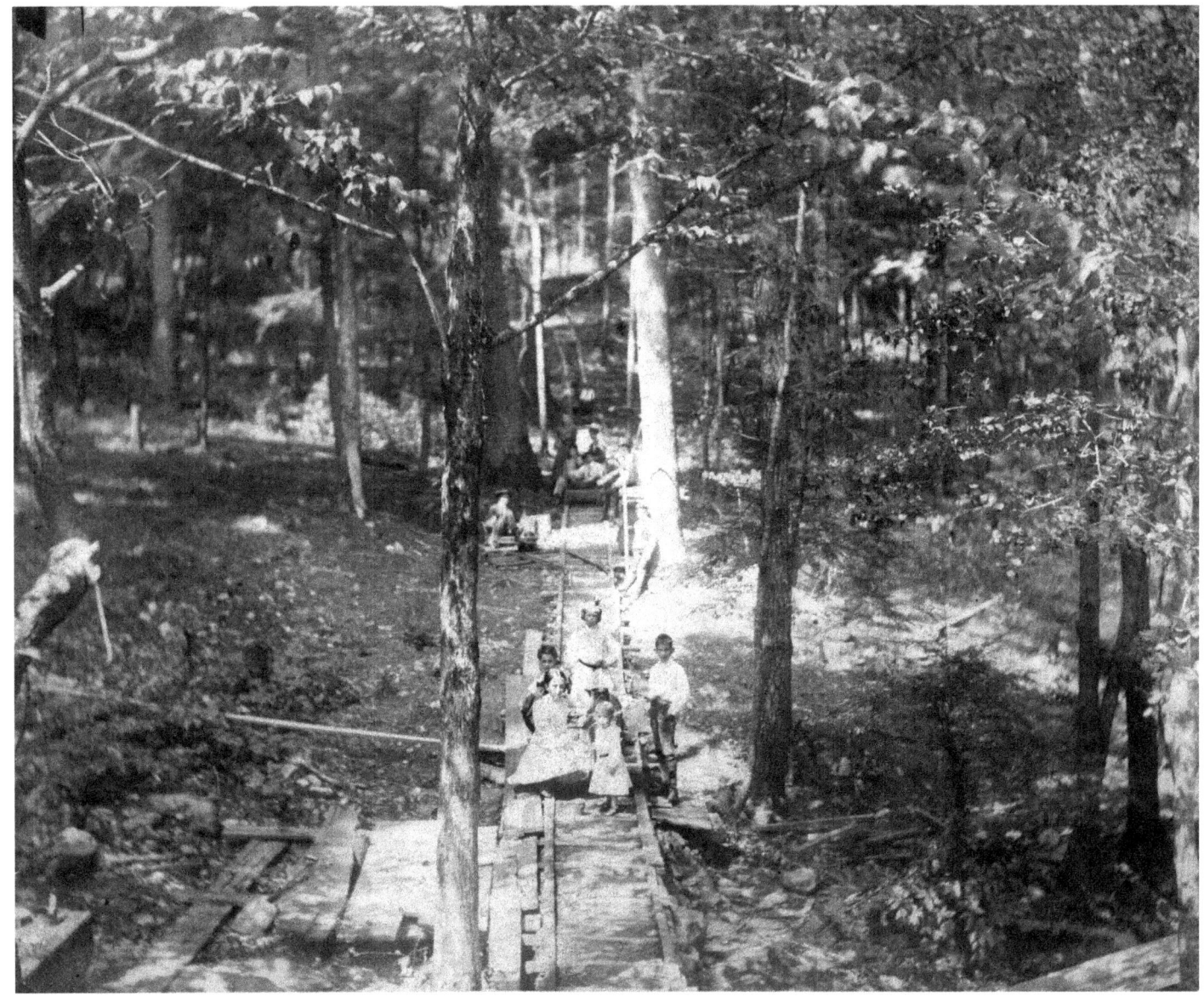

A family enjoys a mountain vacation at Unaka Springs resort, in Unicoi County, Tennessee, posing on what are conjectured to be wooden handcars along a wooden track. The site was near the Clinchfield Railroad. Today, the Appalachian National Scenic Trail crosses this spot, near the Unicoi County end of the Nolichucky River gorge.

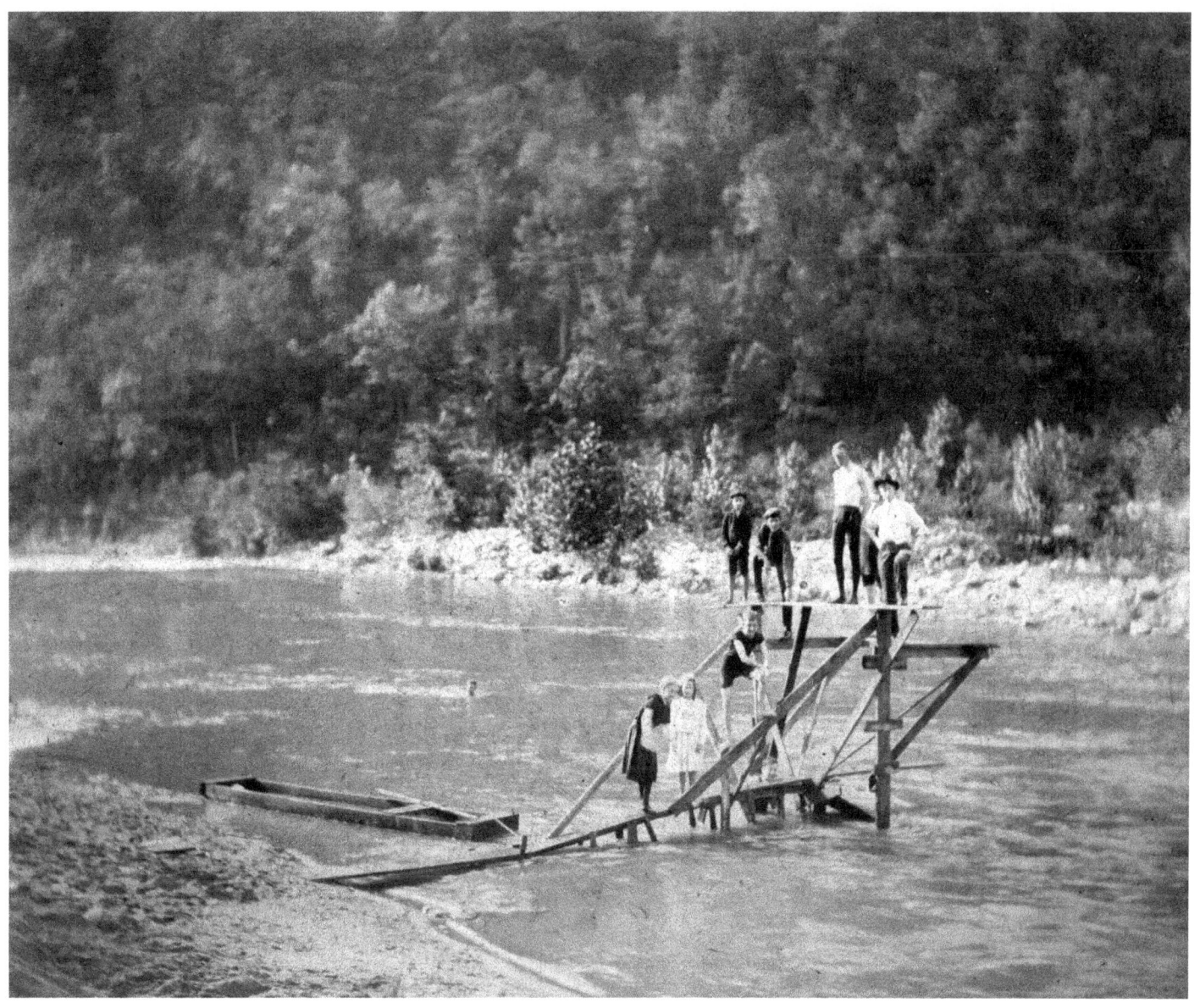

This scene shows a swimming platform at Unaka Springs, on the Nolichucky River. Not long afterward, a railroad bridge was built at this site to carry the tracks of the Clinchfield Railroad through the Nolichucky gorge.

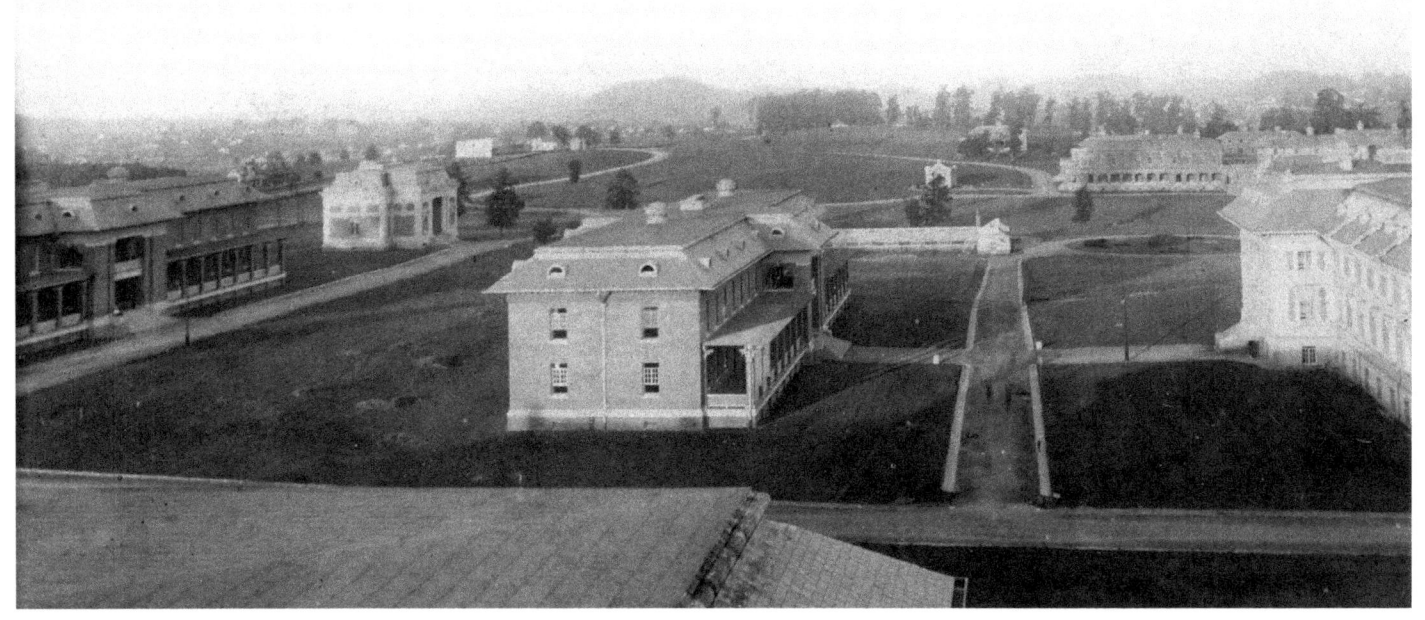

The "Mountain Branch of the National Homes for Disabled Volunteer Soldiers" came to be known as "Mountain Home," or the "Old Soldiers Home." Established by Congress in 1901, this "city within a city," in Johnson City, supplied its own heat, light, and water, and had its own farm, bakery, ice house, and shops. Today the campus is known for its magnificent trees; the photograph shows how the grounds looked when the trees and shrubs had just been planted.

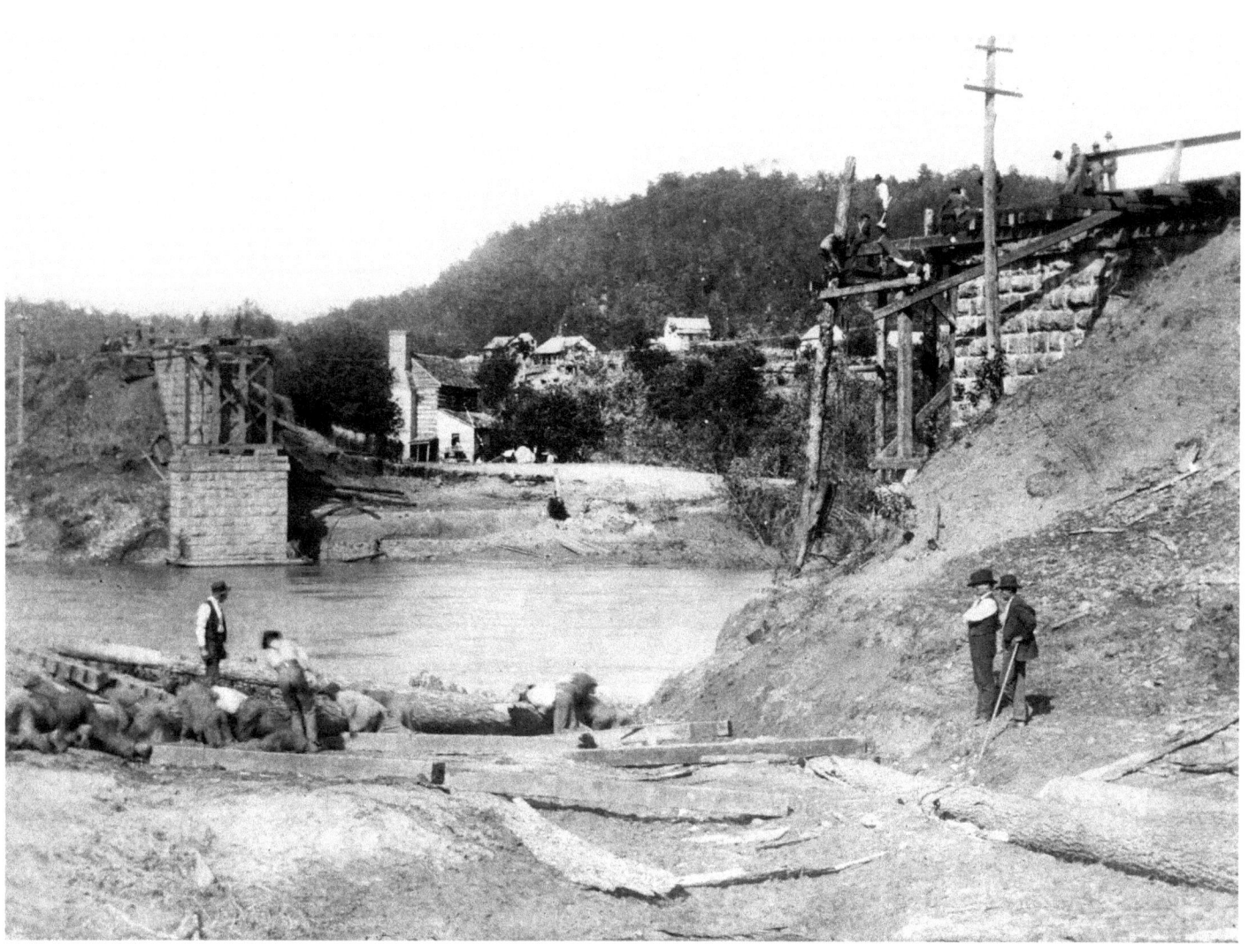

The Southern Railroad bridge over the Watauga River, in Washington County, Tennessee, is shown after it was destroyed by early-twentieth-century flooding. An epidemic of floods in Appalachia in the early twentieth century helped provide the rationale for the Tennessee Valley Authority (TVA), which would be created in the 1930s primarily as a flood control measure.

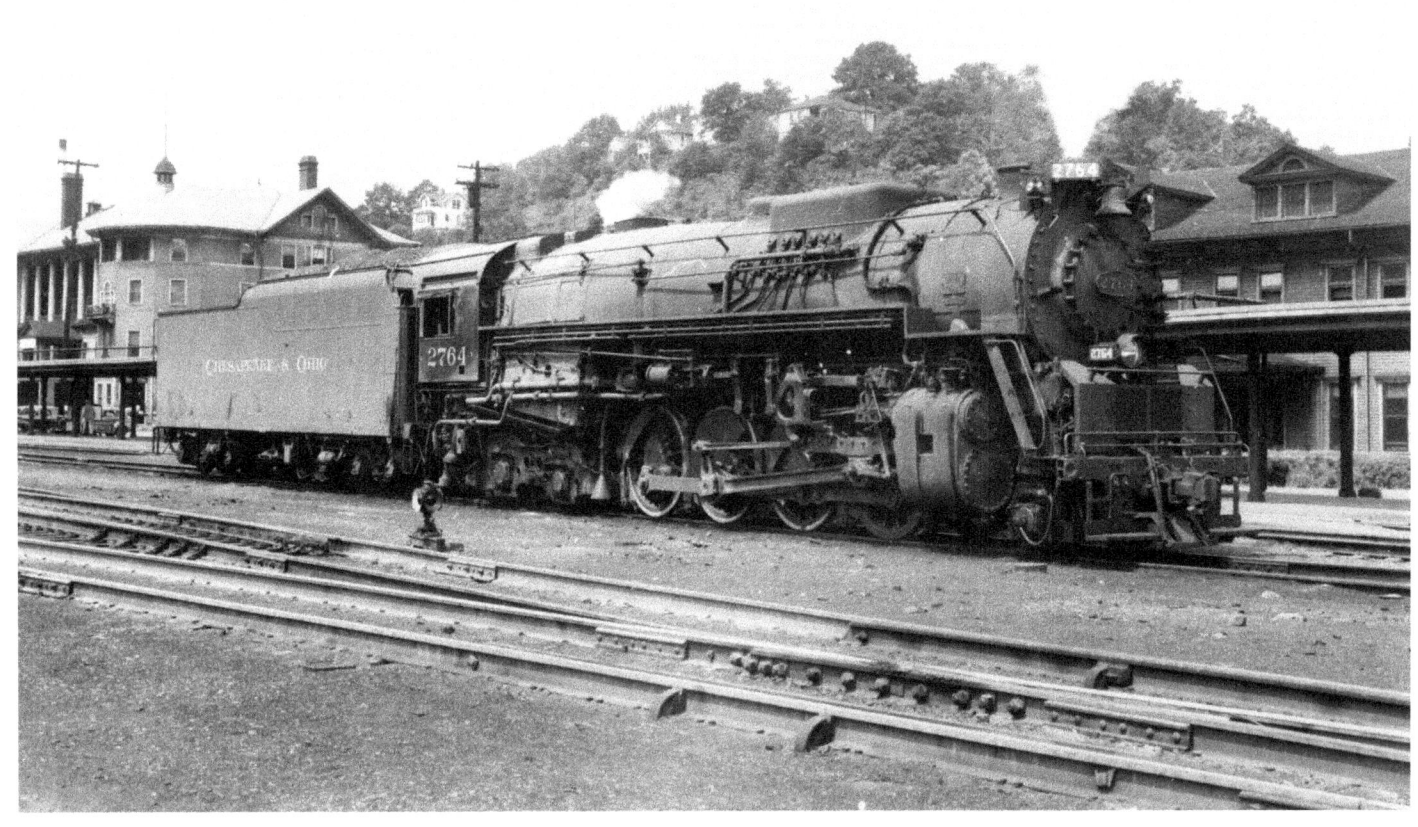

A modern, early-twentieth-century, standard-gauge steam engine and tender sit on the Chesapeake and Ohio Railroad lines, in front of the Y.M.C.A. in Clifton Forge, near Roanoke, Virginia. The C&O, part of the Chessie Railway system, is now operated by CSX Transportation.

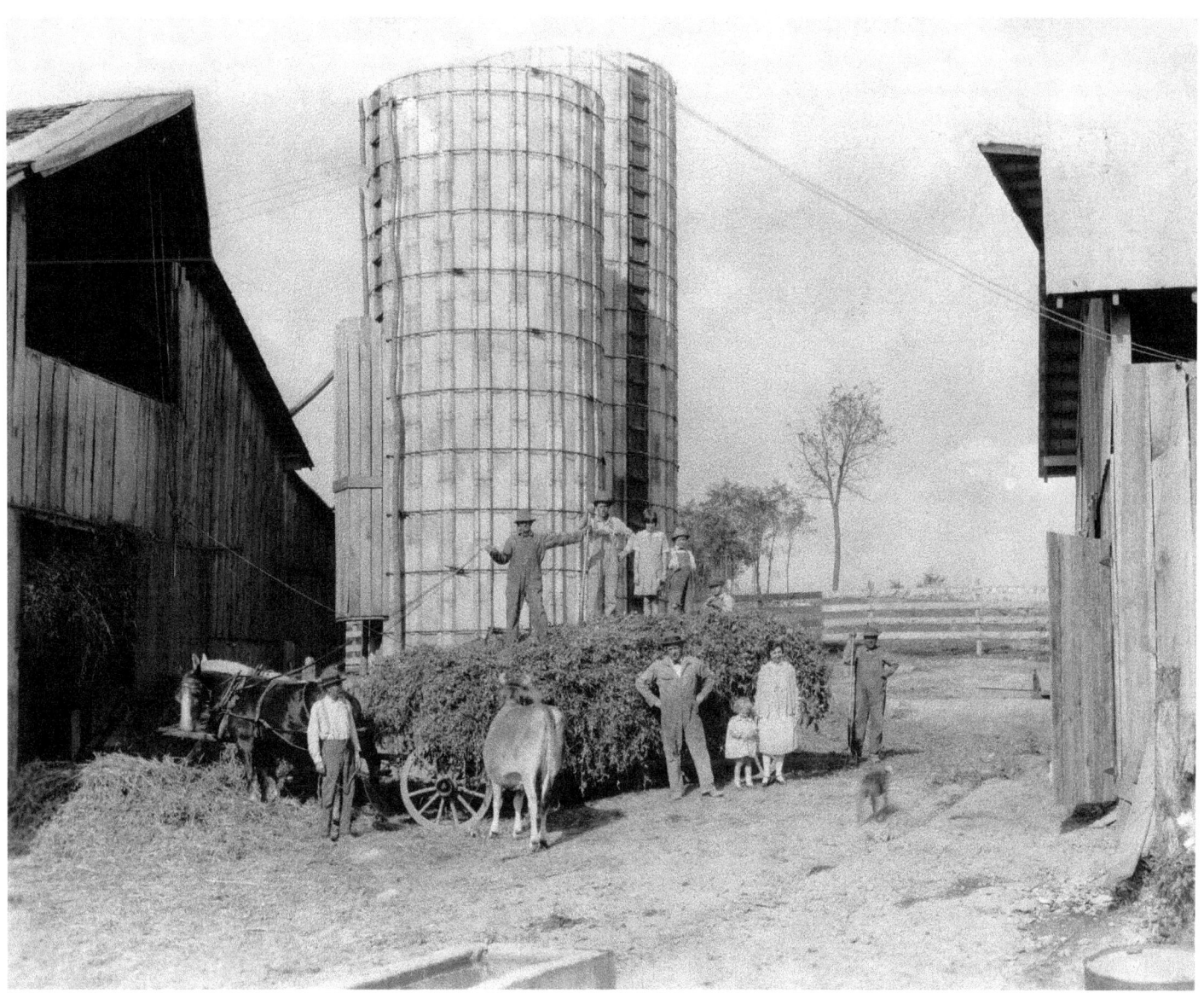

This 1910 Appalachian scene shows a farm family atop a wagonload of what appears to be buckwheat. Buckwheat is neither wheat nor grain. It is related to rhubarb, and its seed is ground into buckwheat flour. For a long time, it was a crop staple in central Appalachia, because it is hardy and resists insects.

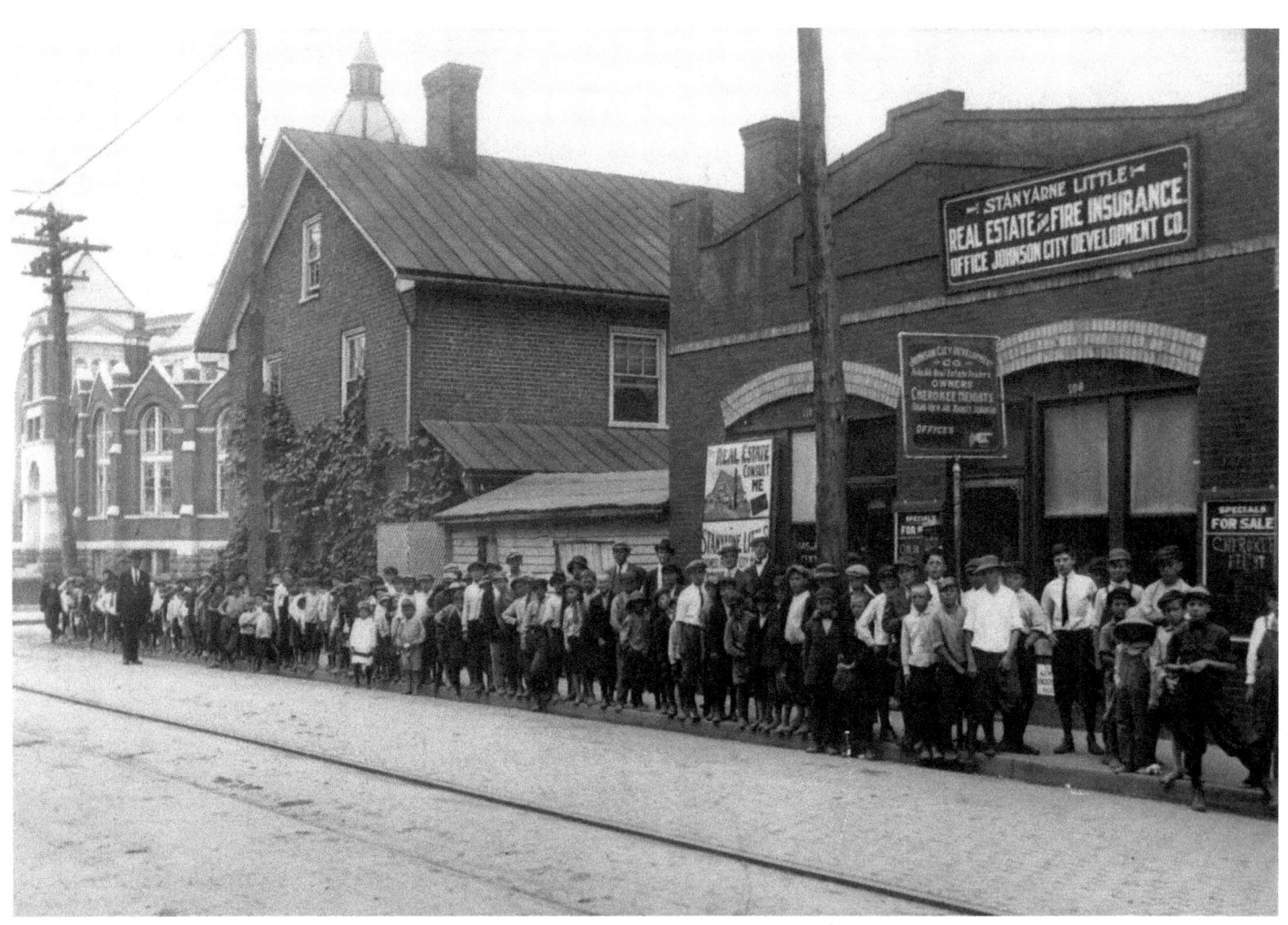

An expectant crowd waits for a parade, along Roan Street, between Market and Main streets, in Johnson City, Tennessee.

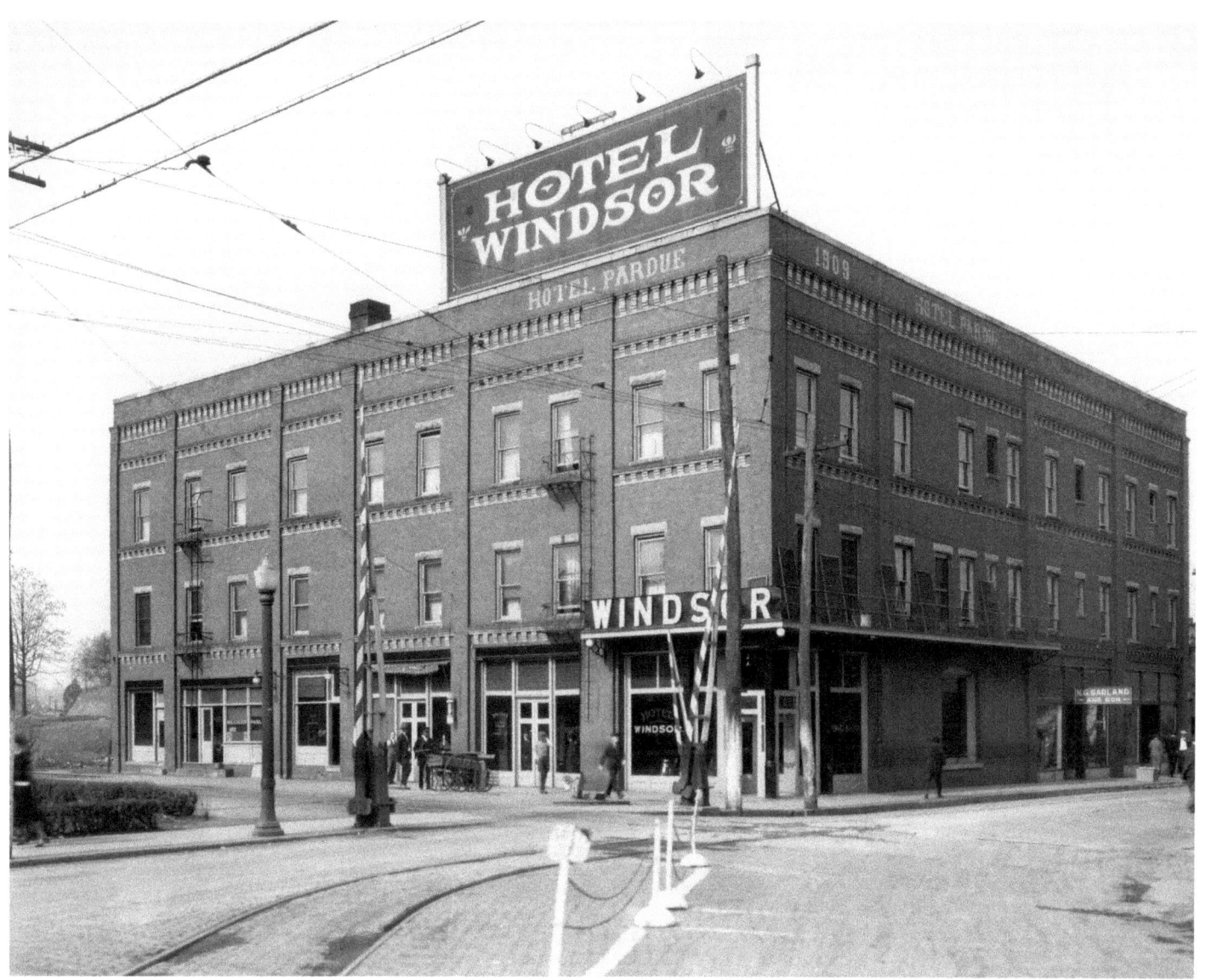

The Hotel Windsor was built in Johnson City in 1909 as the Hotel Pardue, after the man who built it, and was renamed Windsor in 1912. The hotel enjoyed its heyday in the 1920s and was razed in 1971. Hand-lettered advertisements for the Hotel Windsor are still visible on some barns along old U.S. highways in the mountains of East Tennessee and Western North Carolina.

Bystanders examine the wreckage of an automobile hit by a train near Glade Spring, Virginia, in 1916. The caption accompanying the original photograph said "4 killed."

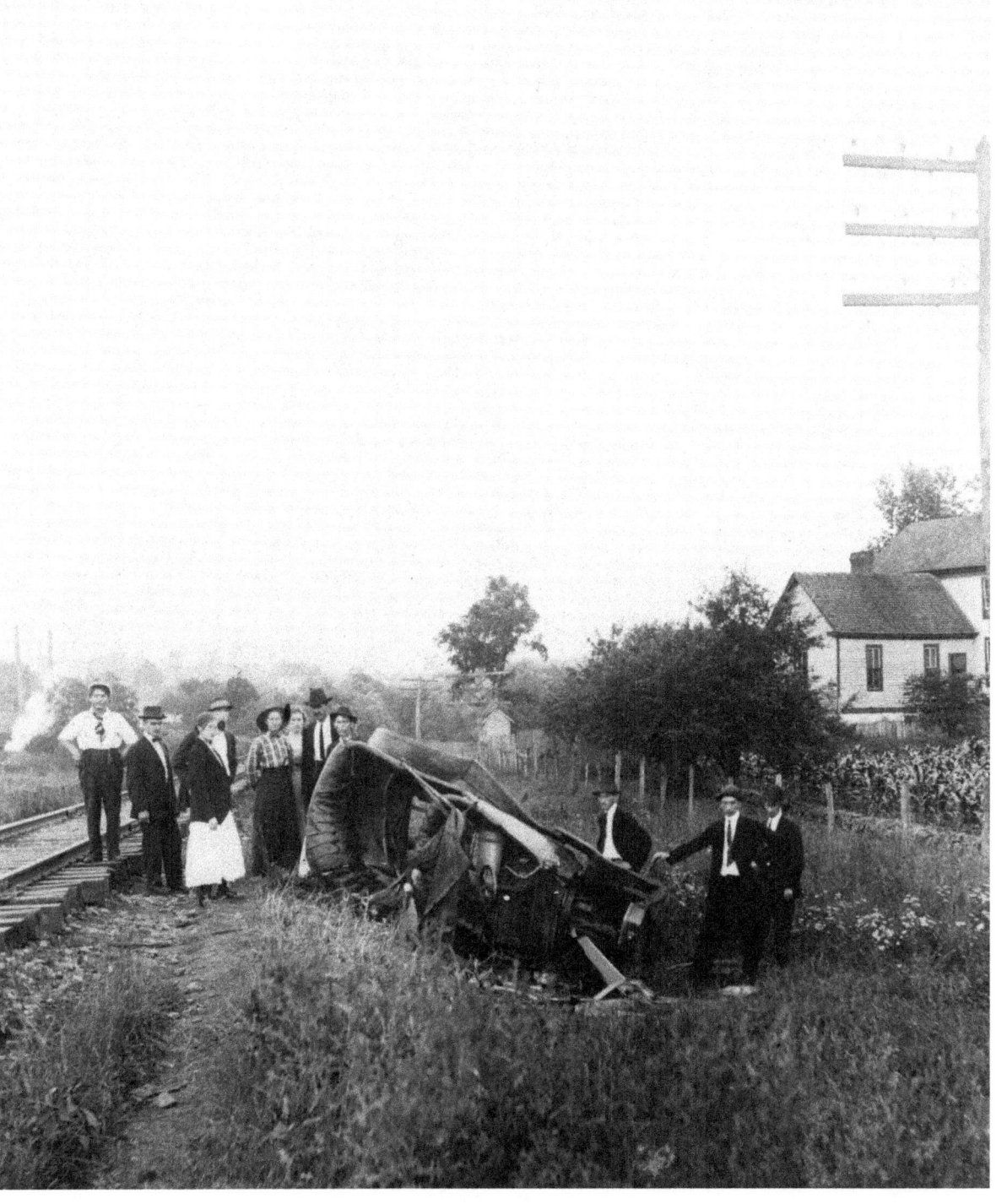

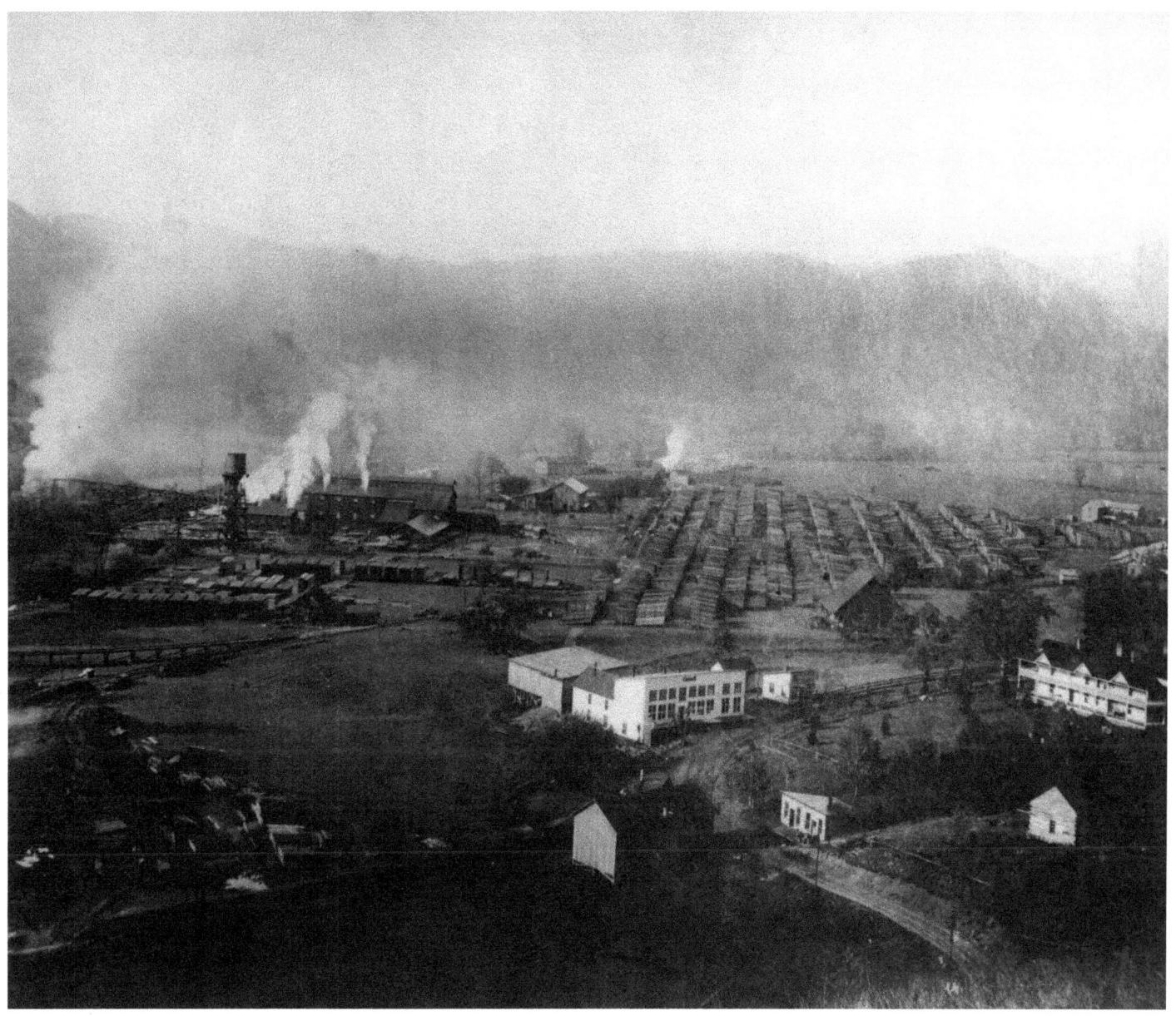

In 1915, the Whiting Lumber Company selected Shulls Mill, North Carolina, in Watauga County, as the location for a high-speed band mill. The town grew from 25 residents in 1910 to a thousand by 1917. By 1918, the company had clear-cut more than 1,463 acres in the area. By the 1920s, all the valuable timber had been cut, and the company moved its operations. In 1940, a flood destroyed most of the buildings that remained.

This view of the Delaware Water Gap—
from a stereograph titled "View at
Promontory"—shows how the railroad
and carriage road are squeezed in along
the river, through the gap. The point at
which the Delaware River cuts through
the Appalachian ridges, in Pennsylvania,
near the New Jersey border, is taken by
some to mark the northern boundary
of central Appalachia. The classic view
was a popular subject of paintings and
engravings in the nineteenth century.

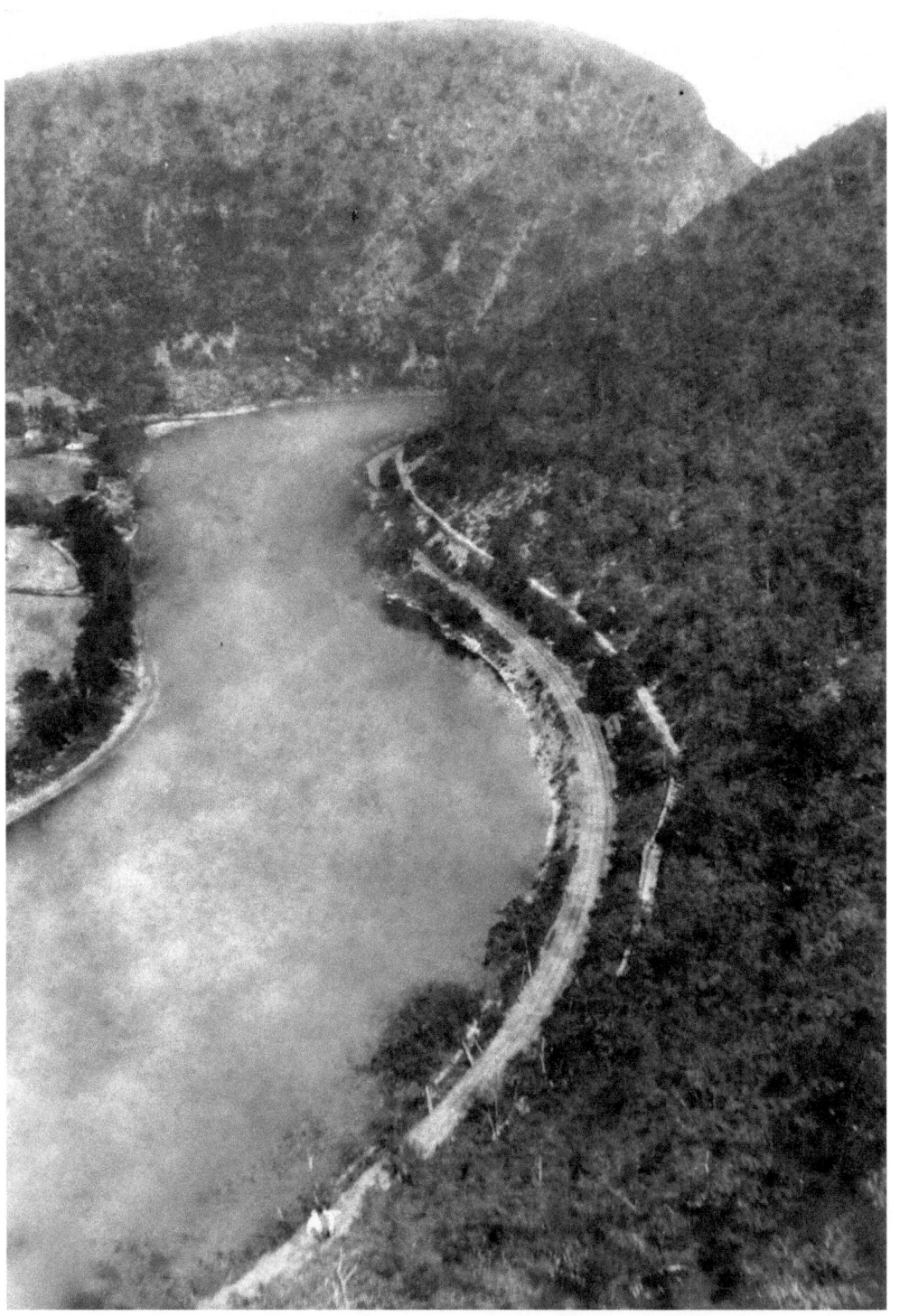

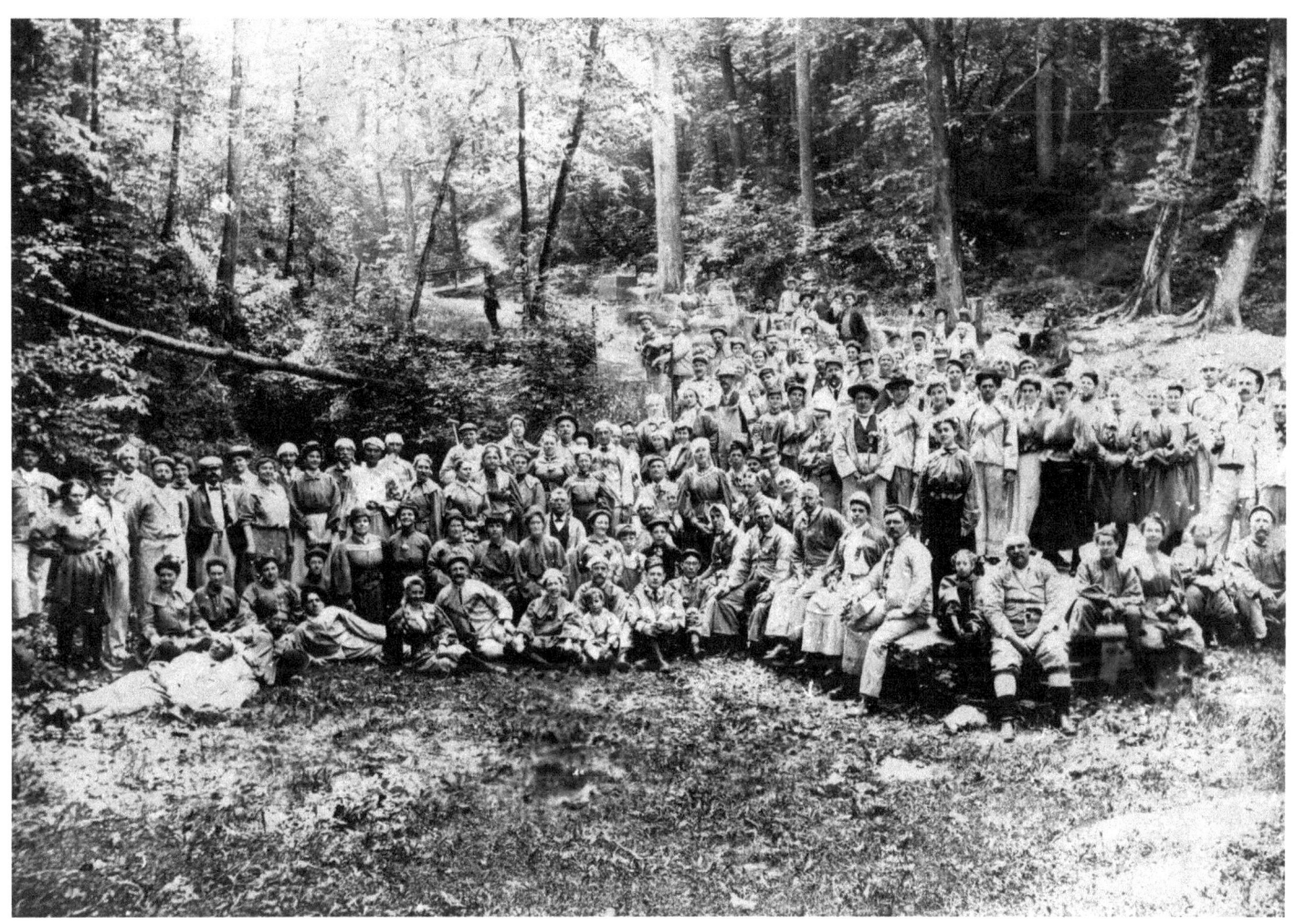

This photograph shows a fraternal society gathering at a forest retreat, probably in Smyth County, Virginia, in the early twentieth century.

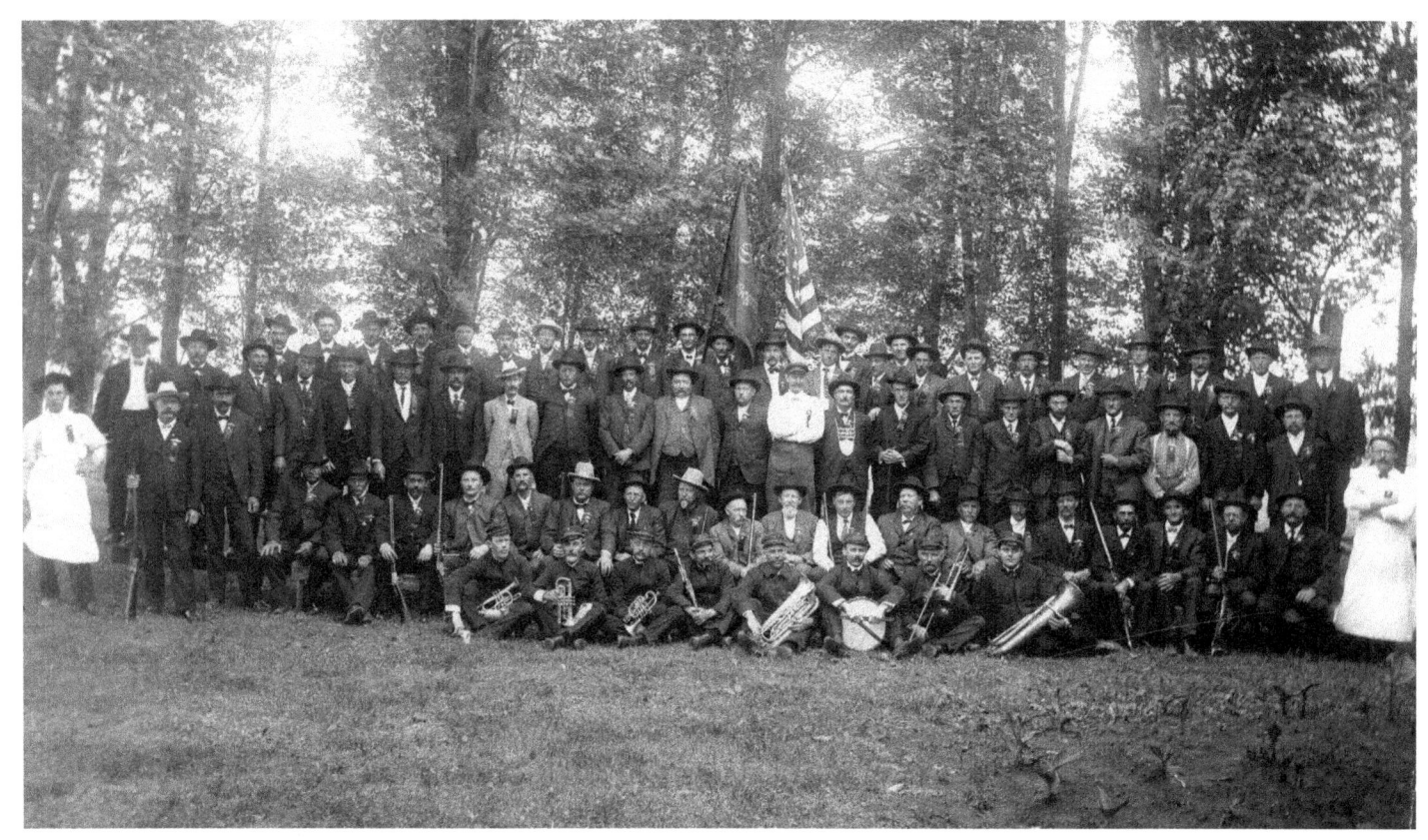

Members of a German Fraternal Order gather in Appalachia in the early twentieth century. With the great southern migration of the mid-1700s, German settlers moved down the valley of Virginia into the western Carolinas, becoming a significant portion of early European immigrants to Appalachia. In the year 2000, Americans of German descent made up 13 percent of the population of the region.

BOOM, BUST, AND DAMS

(1920–1939)

After World War I, the economic boom of the Roaring Twenties enjoyed by much of the nation took hold in Appalachia. Business and industry thrived and real estate values rose sharply. Of singular importance for the region, the recording industry made regional music available nationwide, leading to increasing attention to the "hillbilly music" of Appalachia.

The Great Depression hit Appalachia especially hard. By 1930, most of the valuable, old timber was cut over. Iron ore veins rich with promise at the turn of the century were mostly played out. Commercial agriculture was weakened because it could not compete with the large-scale, industrialized agriculture that had emerged in the grain belt of the Midwest. Nonetheless, pockets of bustling economic activity continued apace. The coal industry, for example, did increasing business during the depression years. After a period of labor unrest, coal miners' unions won victories in the early 1930s that helped improve stability and increase production in the Appalachian coal fields, along with unanticipated benefits to mine owners. Towns such as Bristol, on the Tennessee-Virginia state line, where coal-mine owners lived and shopped, thrived as a result.

FDR's "New Deal" programs funded with tax dollars reached far into Appalachia. The Civilian Conservation Corps set up camps in the Great Smoky Mountains in 1934, in order to build the infrastructure for the new national park that would officially be dedicated by FDR in 1940. The Tennessee Valley Authority was created with the power to move people off their land in order to pursue large-scale projects, including hydroelectric power projects requiring the construction of dams—without having to be accountable to those people's representatives in Congress. The TVA caused widespread upheaval and dislocation, but it created enormous benefits as well. Initially established primarily for flood control, it improved river navigability and provided hydroelectric power, both of which provided an economic boost to the region.

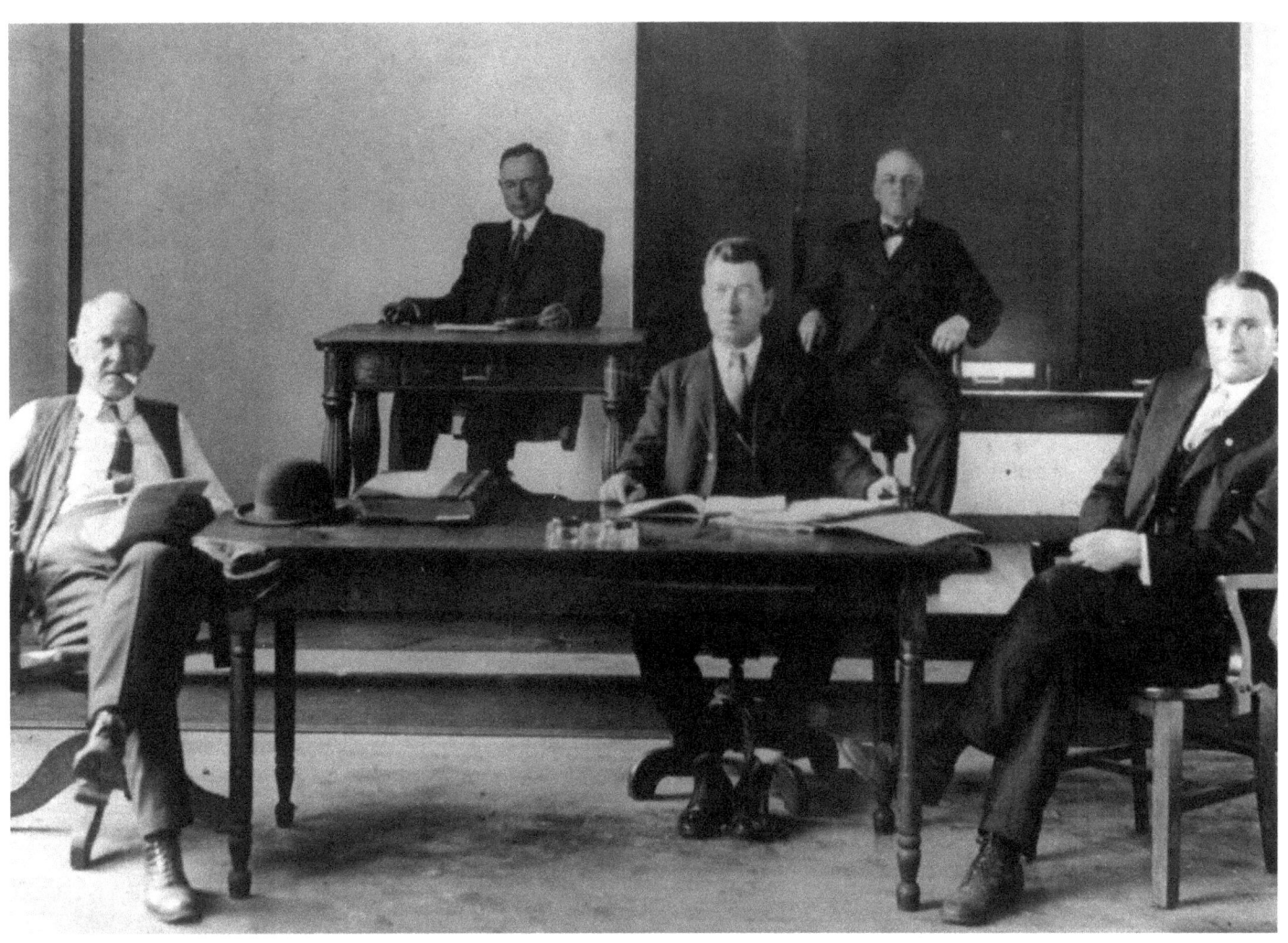

A city commission meeting in Johnson City, Tennessee, is in progress around 1920. According to a handwritten note on the back of the original photograph, pictured are William B. Ellison, P. F. McDonald, Robert Warren, a Mr. Pierce, and W. O. Dyer.

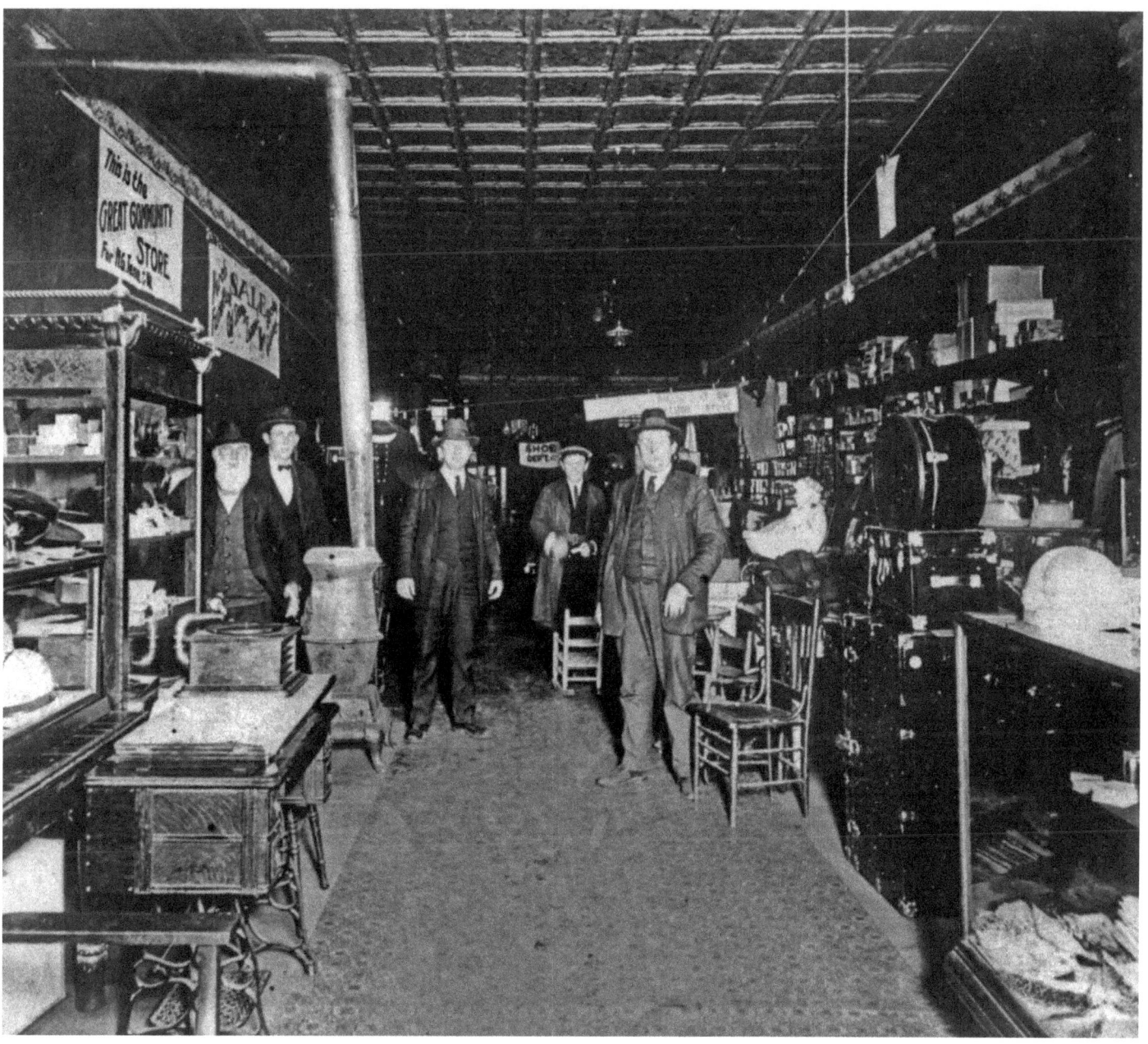

This scene shows an interior of the "Great Community Store" in Johnson City, Tennessee, in the 1920s. The man to the right is identified as Mr. Wilson. The department store carried many products for women, including the sewing machines and hats shown here, but store clerks at that time were always men.

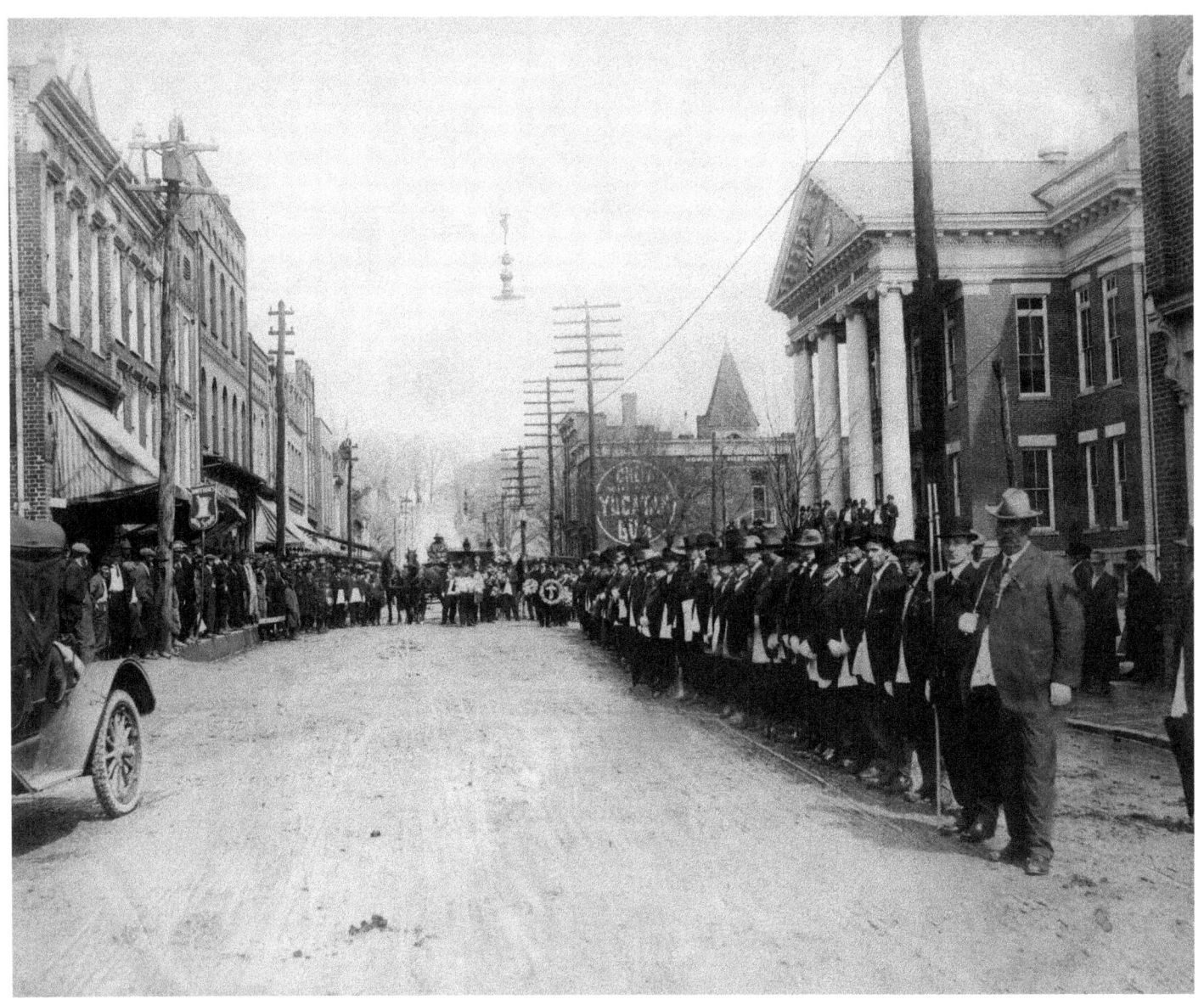

Members of a fraternal organization, perhaps Freemasons, attend a funeral in downtown Jonesborough, Tennessee. The new courthouse, built in 1913, is visible at right, and at center an early streetlight hangs where later a more modern traffic signal would be installed.

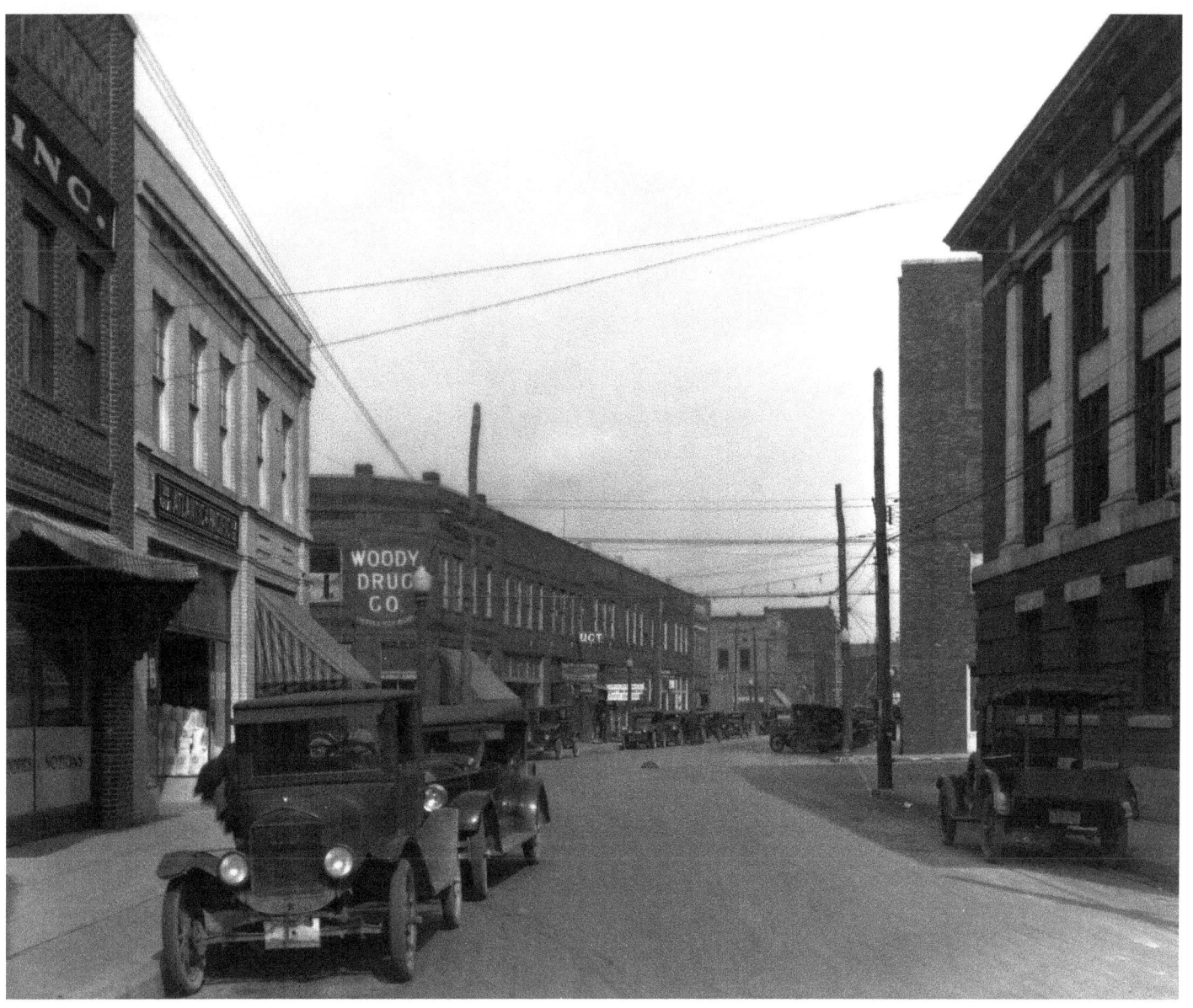

Johnson City's Spring Street, facing south from the intersection with Main Street, in the 1920s. Asphalt paving had replaced brick to provide a smoother ride for automobiles, and the small hump just visible in the intersection, known as a "turtle," marked lanes in the days before painted stripes became commonplace.

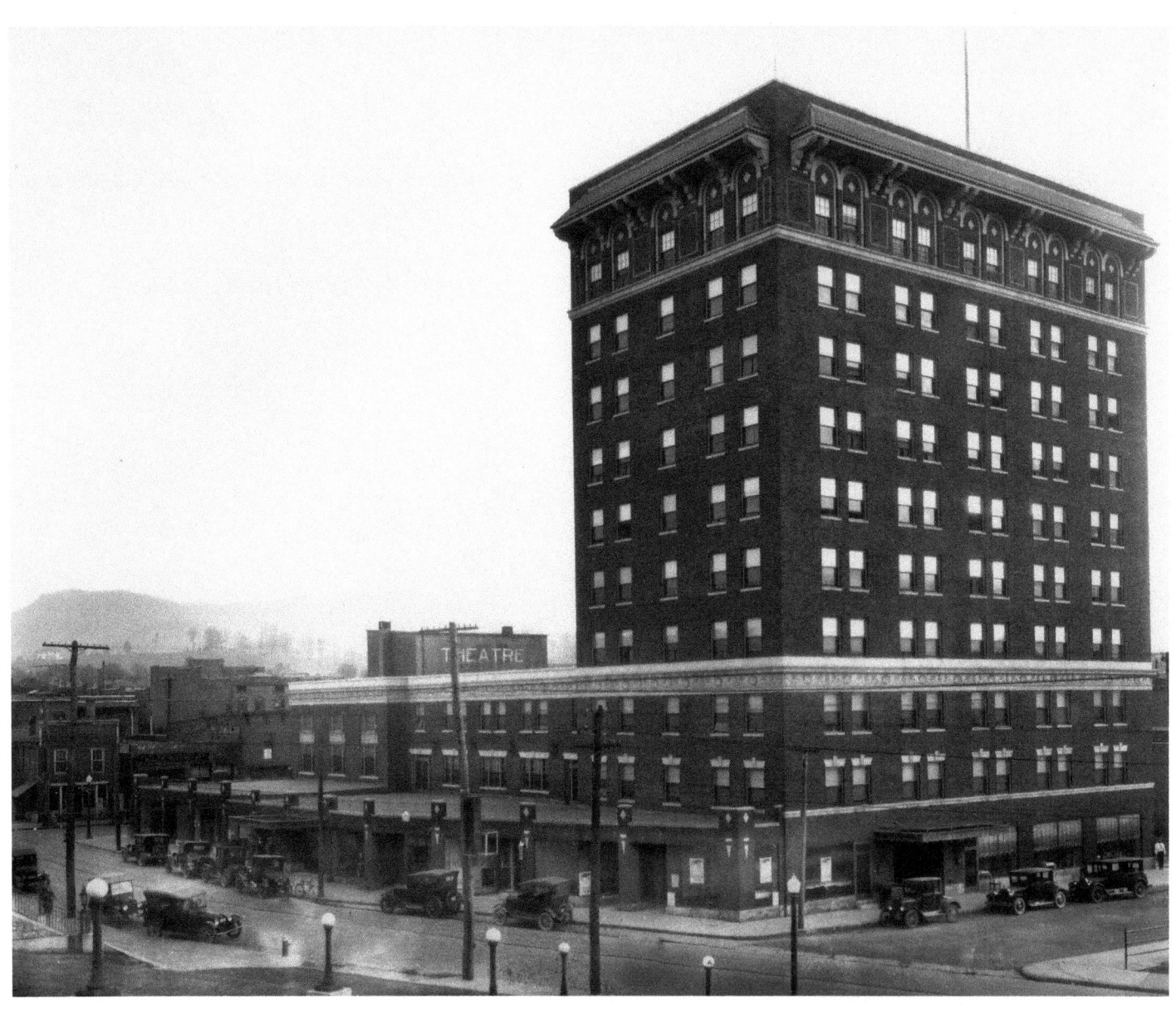

The John Sevier Hotel, in Johnson City, was constructed as the tallest building in the city in 1924. This photograph was taken before a large addition was constructed in 1929. A third addition was planned but never built because of the Great Depression.

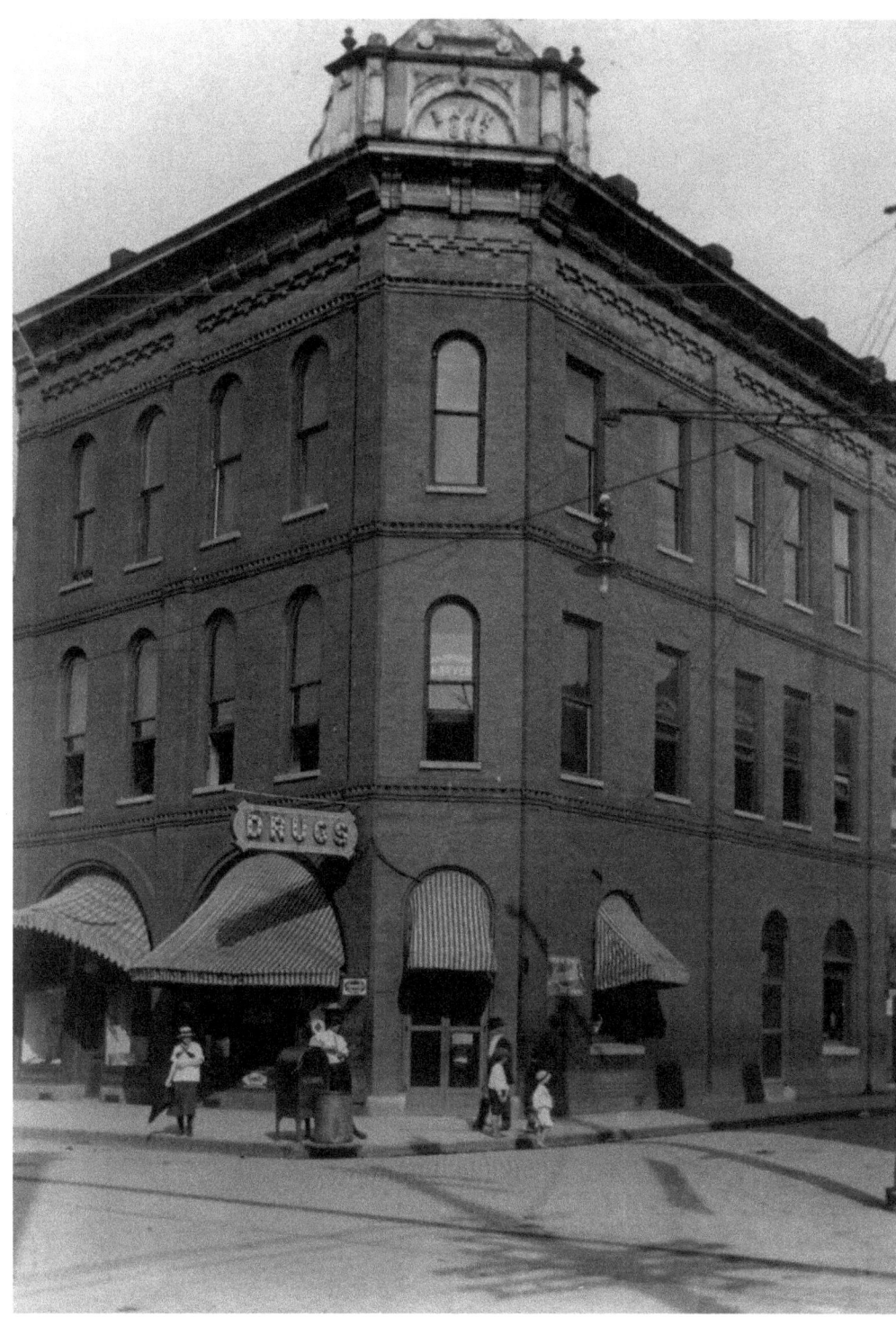

The Jobe Building, at the corner of Spring and Main streets (the present site of the Hamilton Bank Building), in Johnson City, is shown here around 1920. In the days before the widescale availability of air conditioning, elaborate awnings helped shade businesses and homes from the sun, serving as a complementary architectural component to the structure as well.

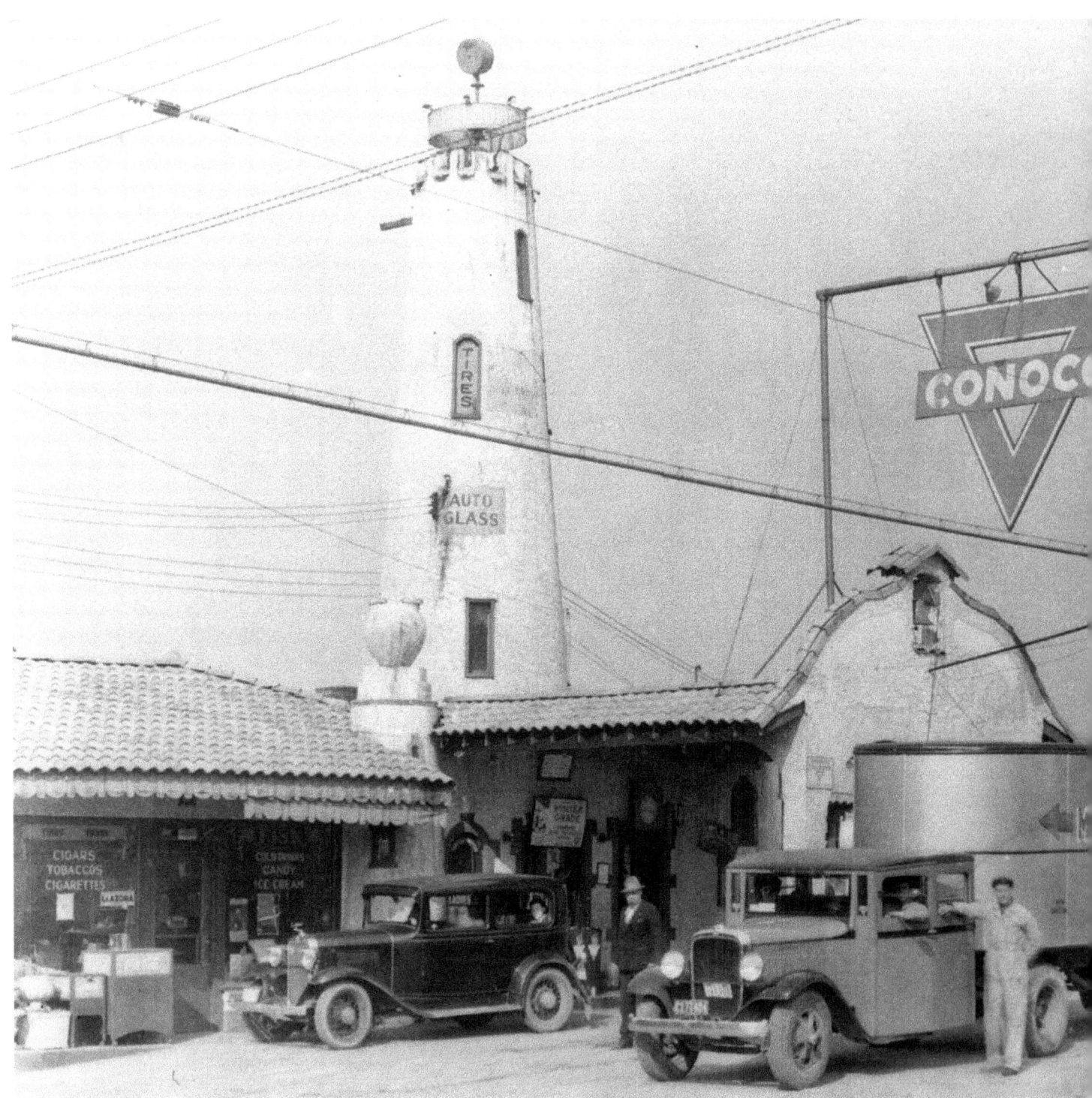

CONOCO

TIRES

AUTO
GLASS

CIGARS
TOBACCOS
CIGARETTES

112

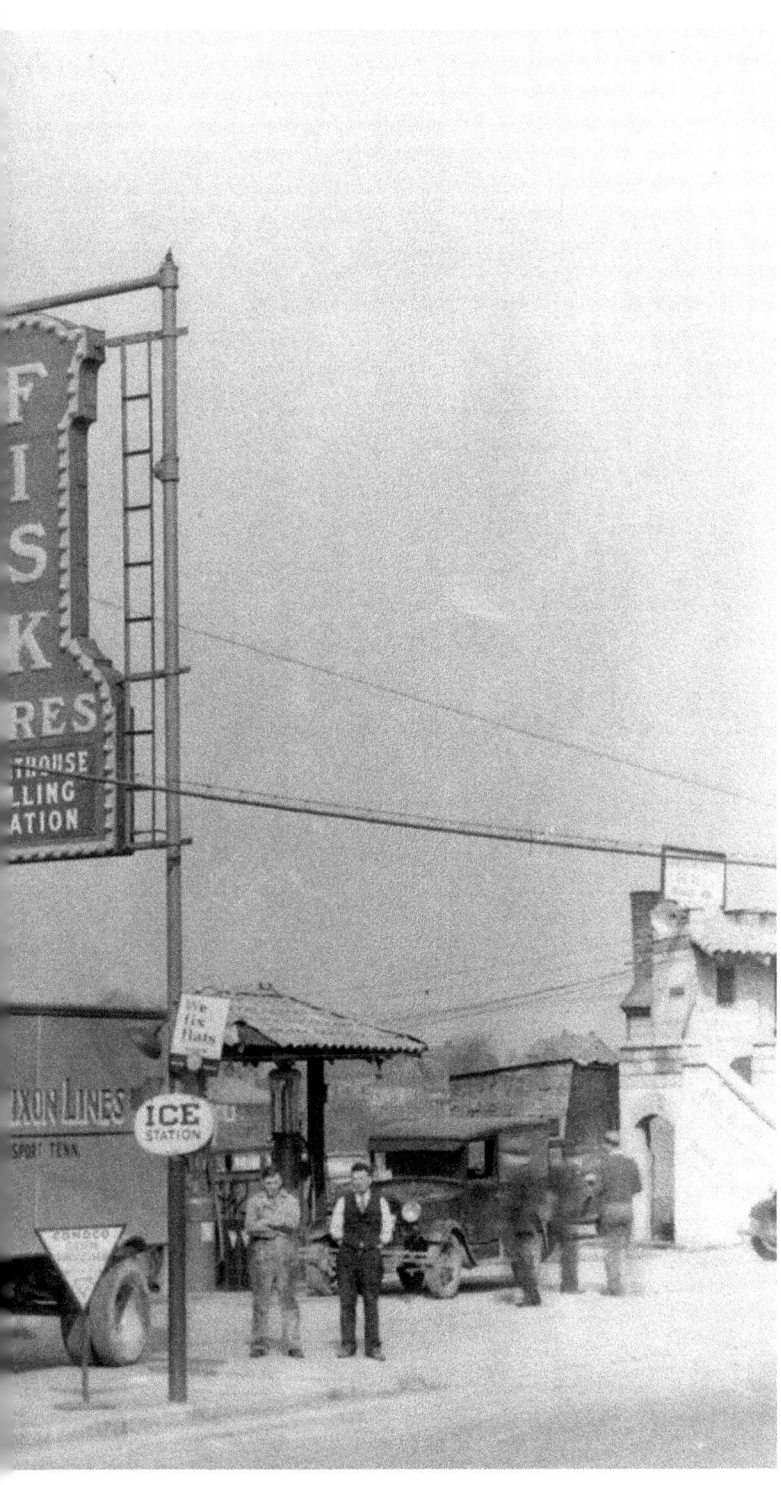

The Lighthouse Oil and Gas filling station, on Pierce Street (now Morrison Boulevard) in Bristol, Tennessee, was built to resemble a lighthouse. Early filling stations across America often featured whimsical architecture, which frequently included terra cotta roofing, as here. A Mason & Dixon Lines transport vehicle idles at front as the driver and several other folks pose for the photographer.

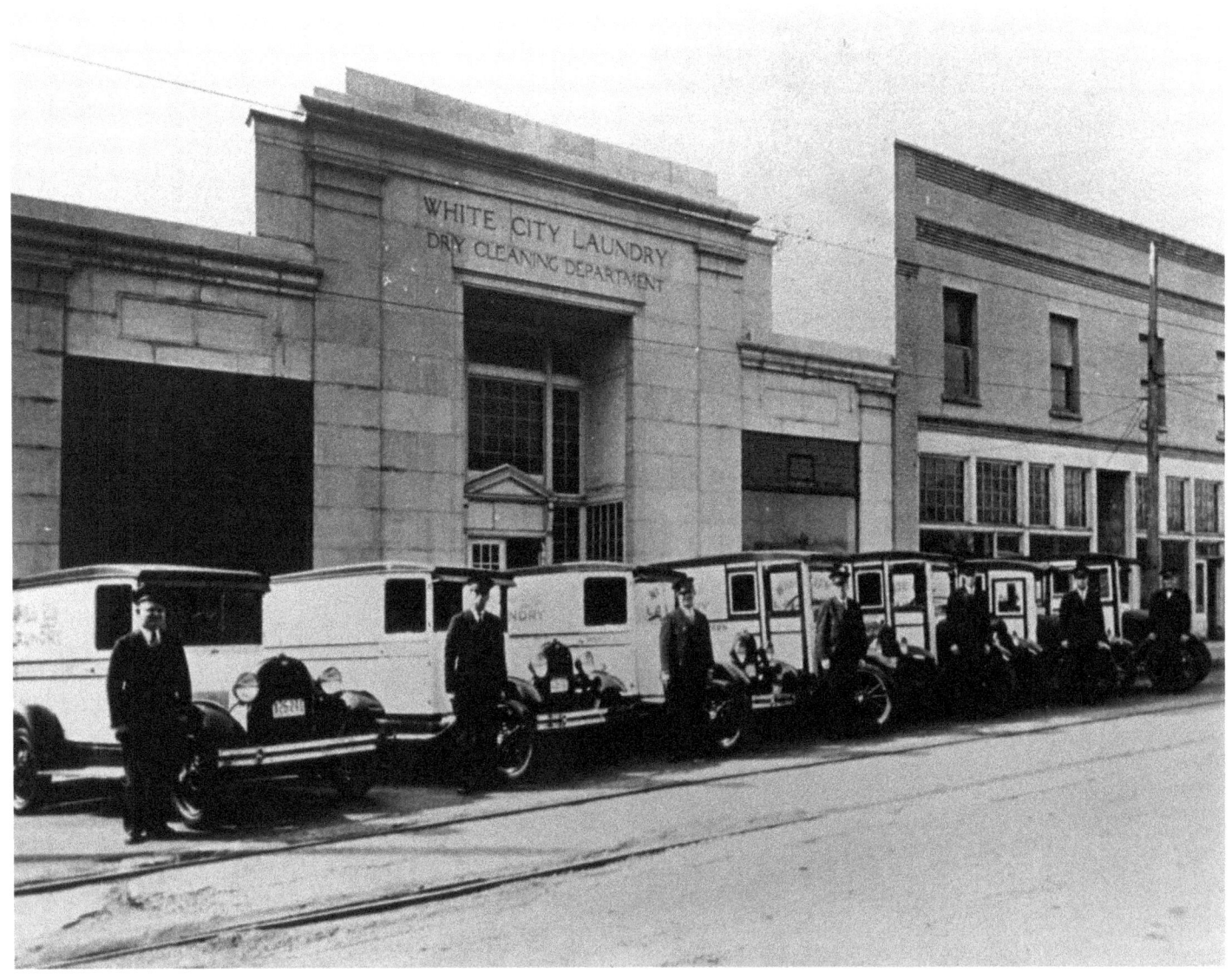

The dry-cleaning department of the White City Laundry, owned by J. H. Miller, in Johnson City, Tennessee, provided for home pickup and delivery in the 1920s. Commercial laundry service for the home boomed during that decade, relieving those who could afford it of a great burden on wash day. After washing machines for the home became available, most commercial services went out of business.

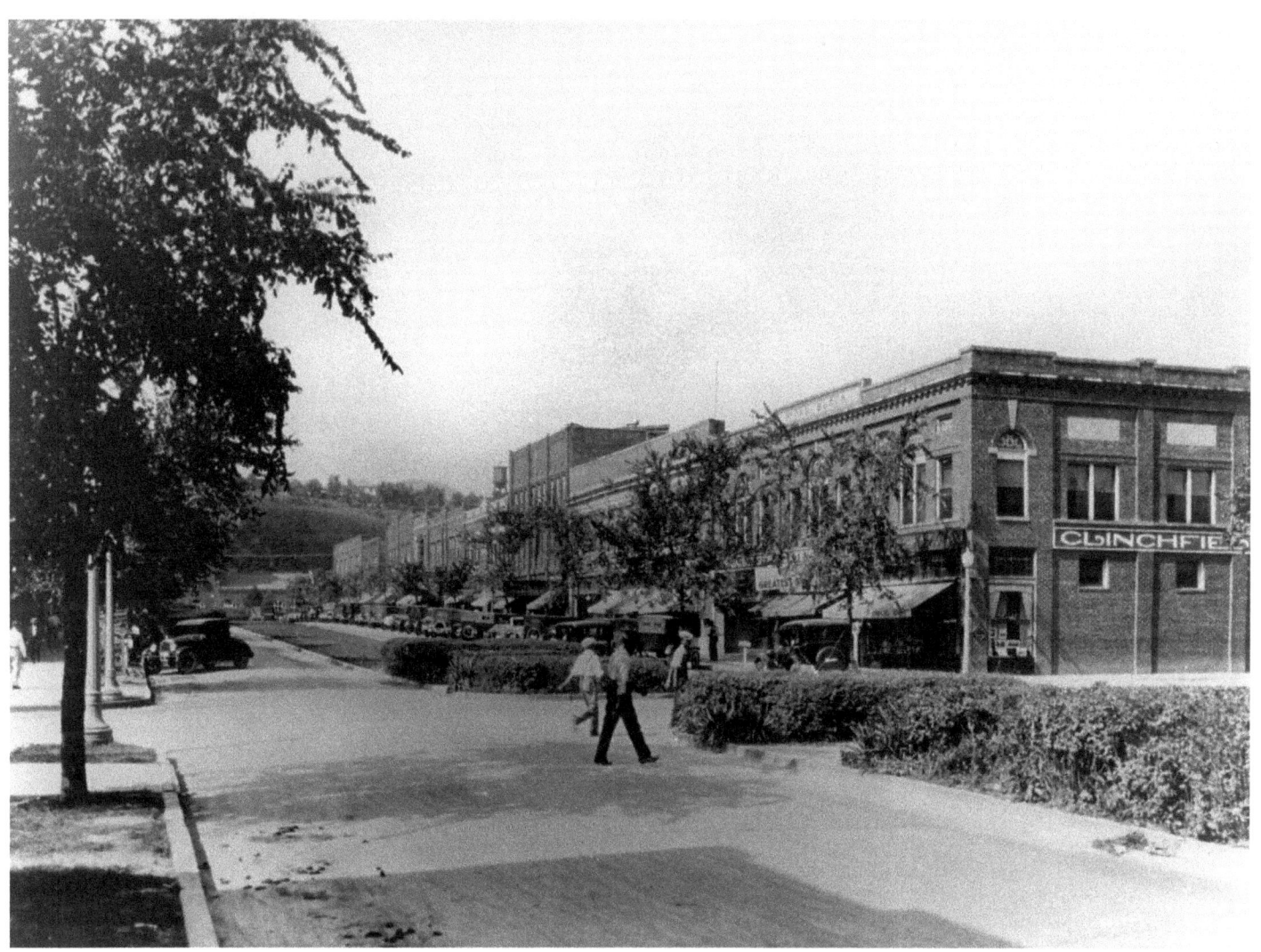

Kingsport, Tennessee, near the Clinchfield (Carolina, Clinchfield & Ohio) Railroad offices on Broad Street, around the late 1920s. The Clinchfield contributed greatly to the development of Kingsport, running from the coalfields in the Clinch River region of southwest Virginia to the textile mills of South Carolina. Today CSX Transportation owns the route.

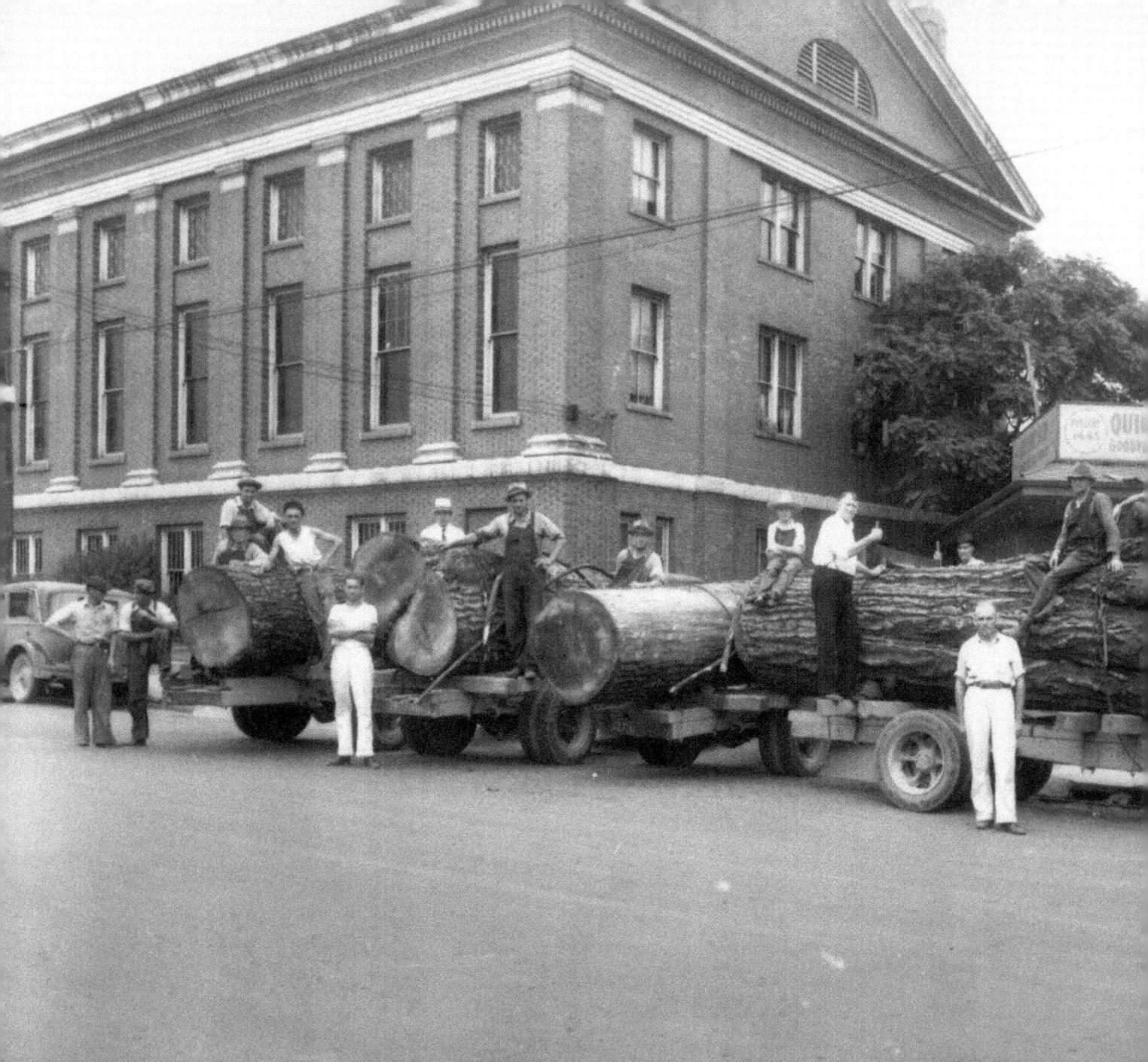

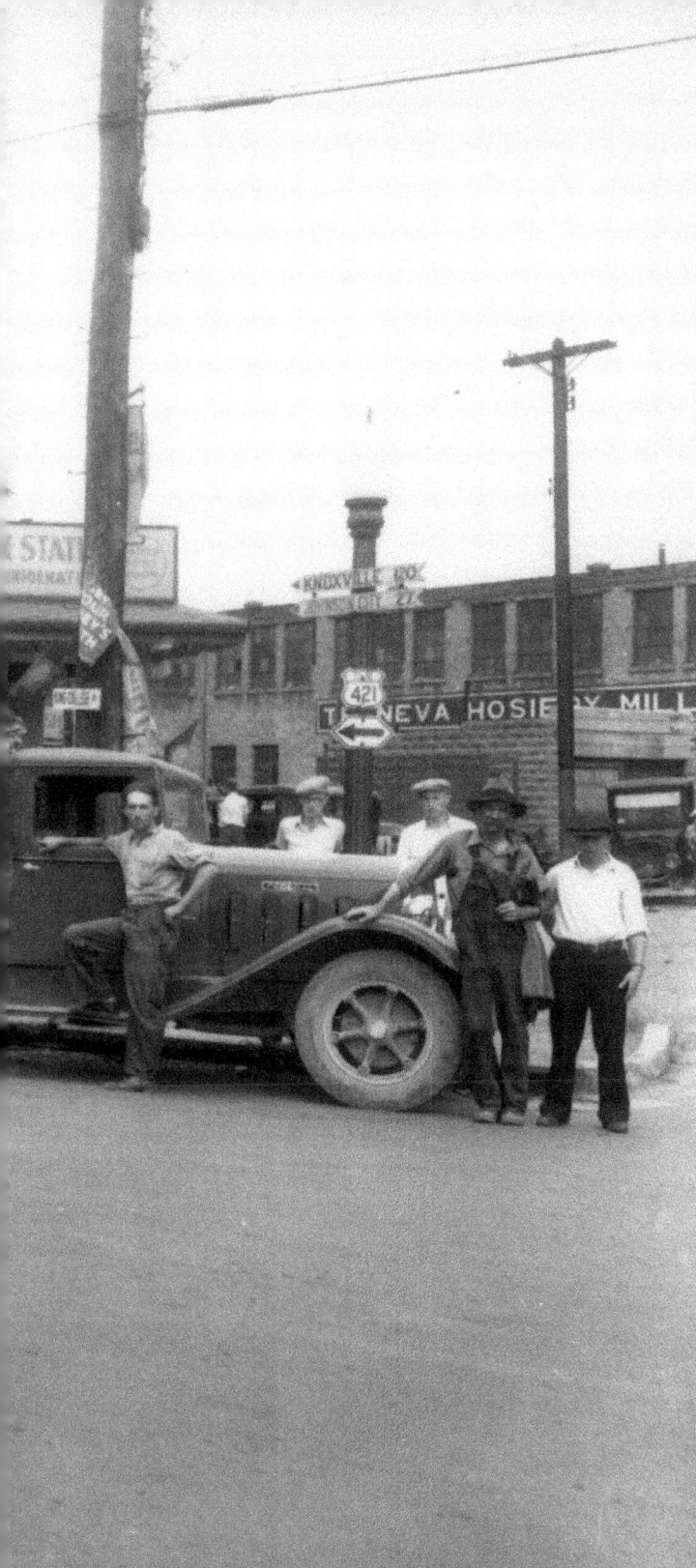

By the 1920s, gasoline-powered trucks were being used for logging operations. This truck is shown in the town of Bristol, Tennessee.

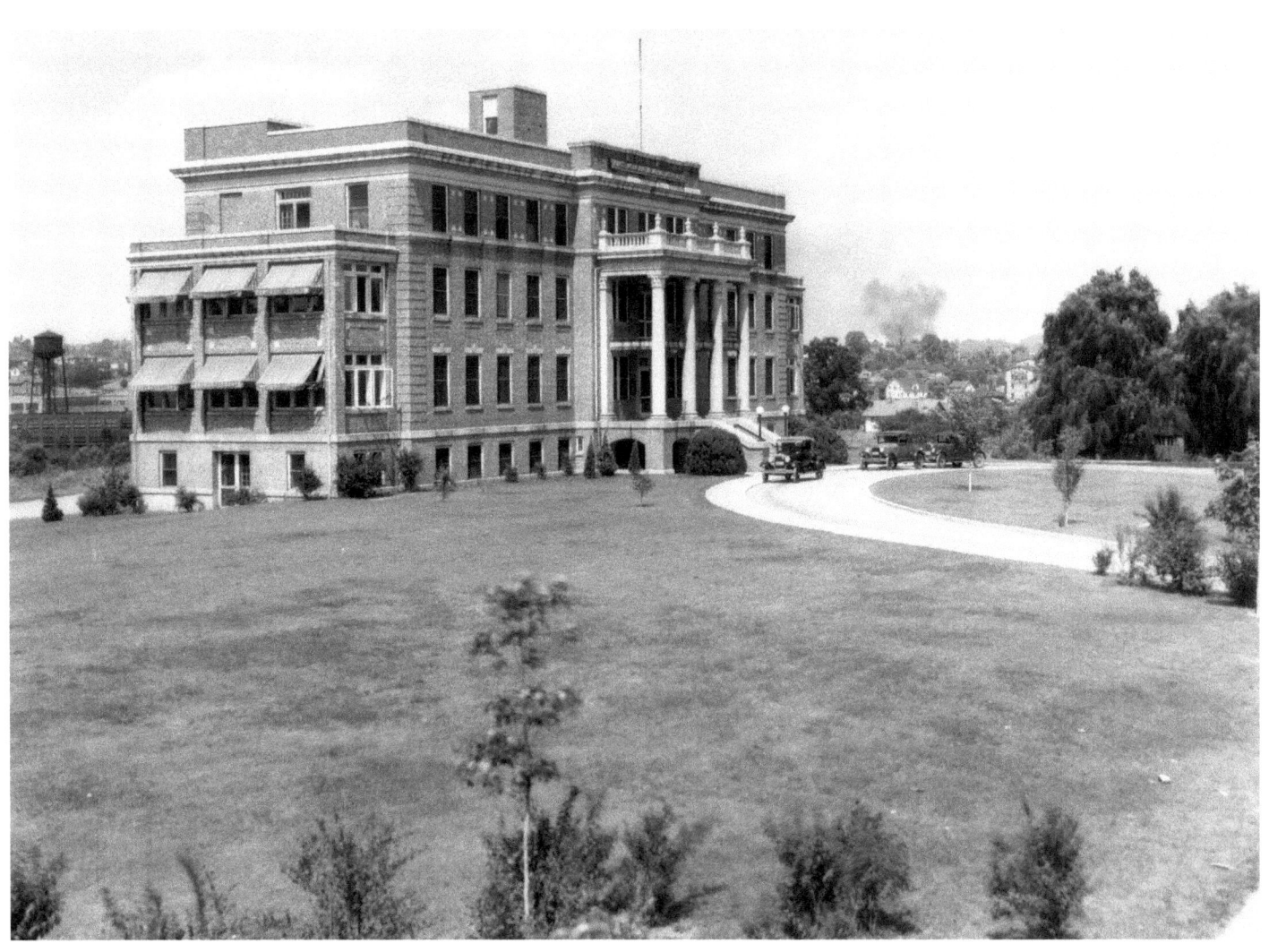

King's Mountain Hospital served the people of Bristol, Tennessee, from 1925 until 1953. The building stood vacant for almost half a century before being torn down in 2008.

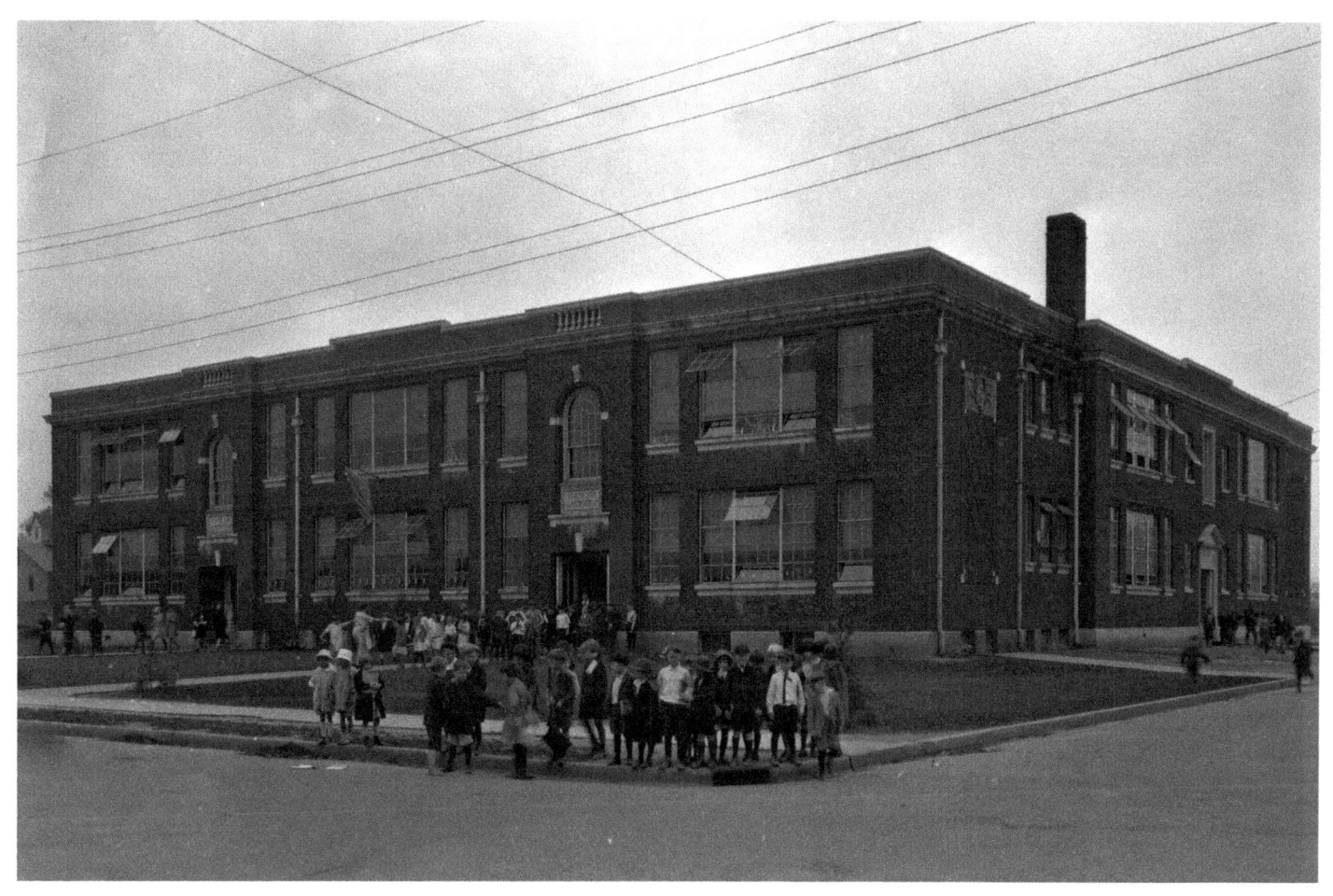

Students stand in front of North Junior High School, on North Roan Street, in Johnson City, Tennessee, in the 1920s. North Side Elementary is now located on the site.

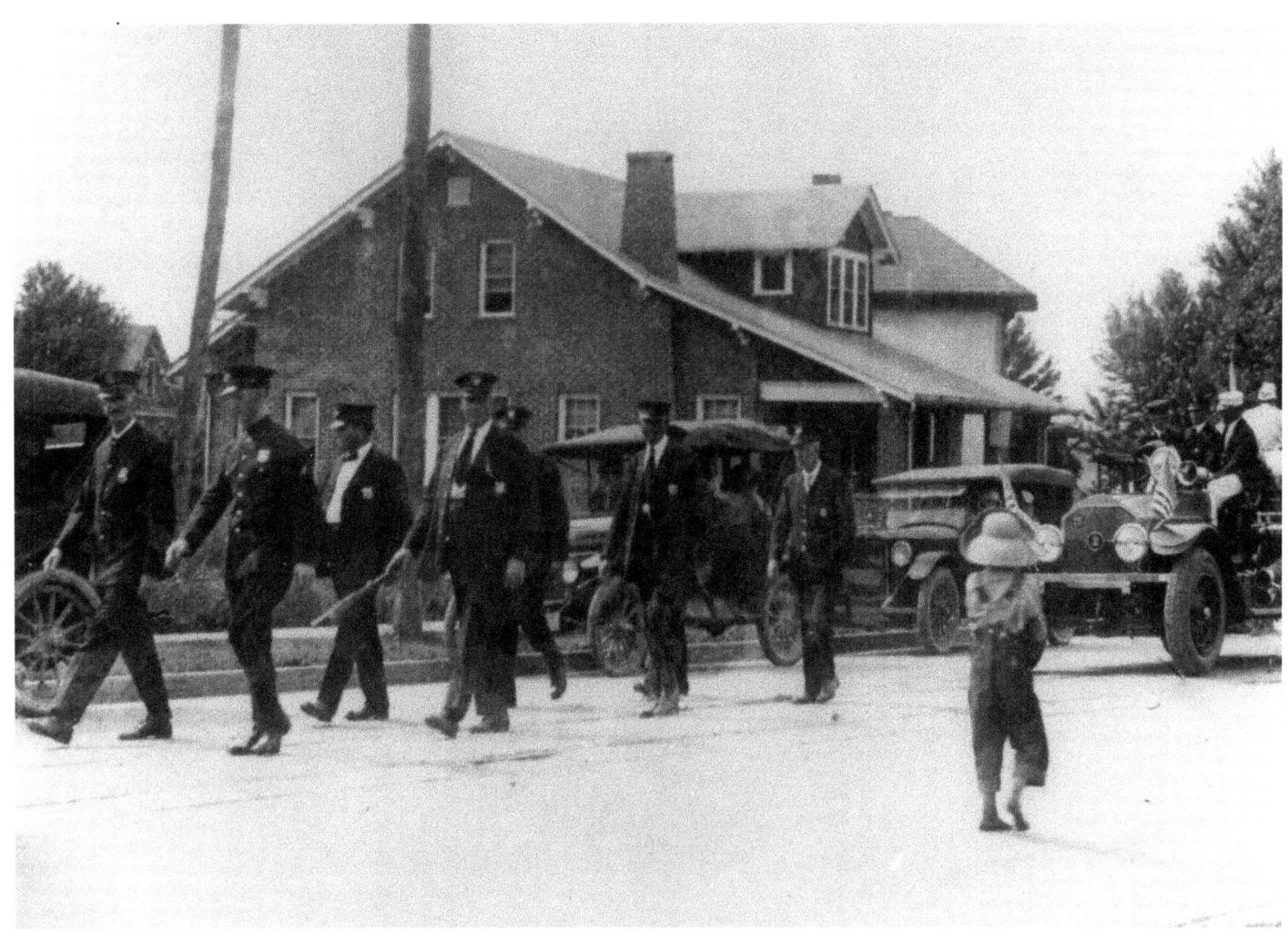

A Johnson City Police and Fire Department parade provides a spectacle for young and old alike. This barefooted youngster takes in the performance wearing overalls and a straw hat. Behind the group stands a bungalow, with wide front porch and long gabled roofline, one of the most popular and distinctive housing styles of the era.

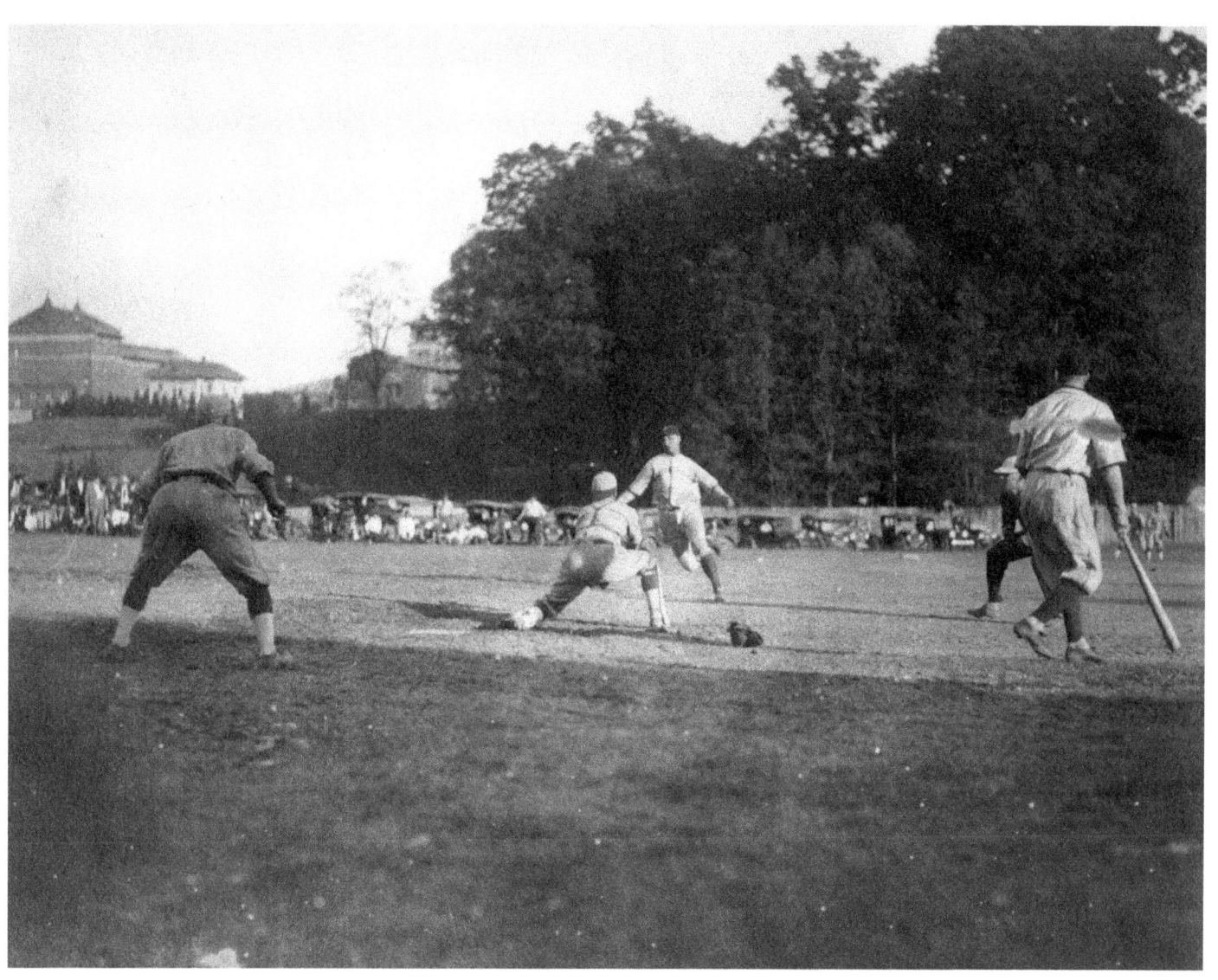

A baseball game is under way in the 1920s, in an early incarnation of the Appalachian League. Beginning in 1937 and continuing to this day, the Appalachian League is a Rookie class minor league for the Major League Baseball system. In the 1920s, the Appalachian League operated at the "Class D" level.

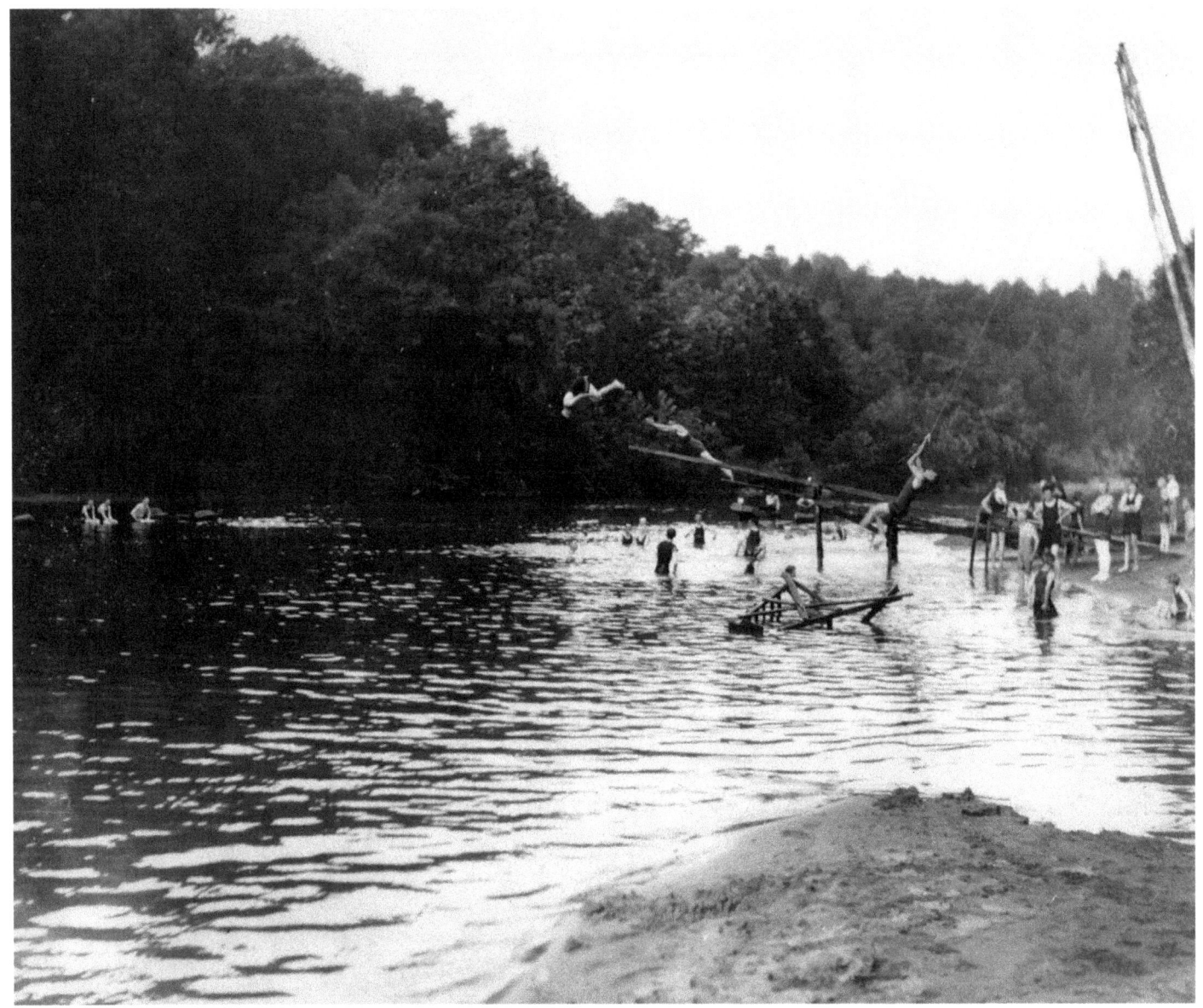

This spot on the Nolichucky River, in Unicoi County, Tennessee, was a popular swimming hole in the 1920s.

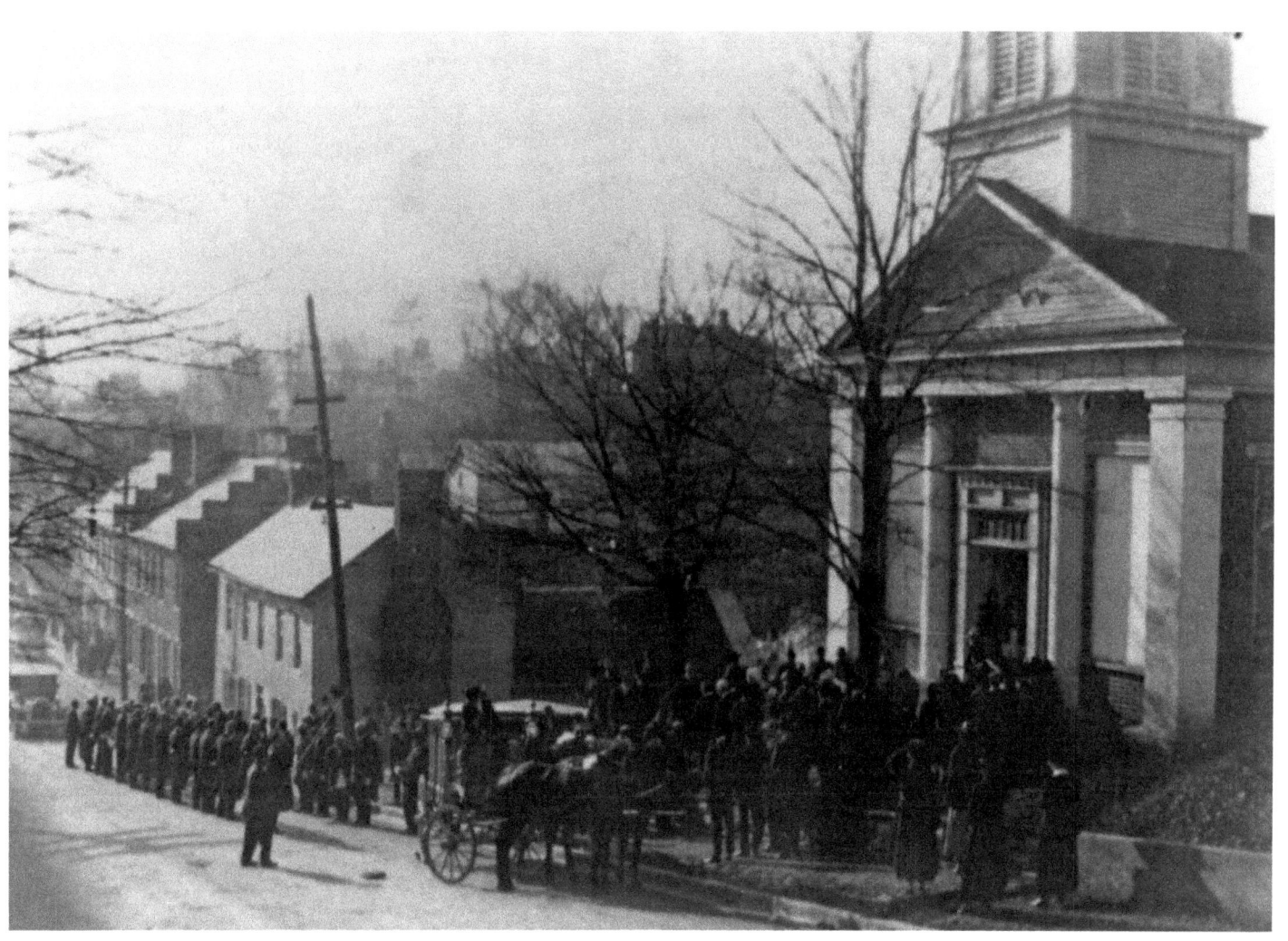

Appalachia in wintertime in the 1920s. A procession of mourners assembles for a funeral in front of the First Baptist Church in Jonesborough, Tennessee.

Although automation, pesticides, and artificial fertilizers produced with fossil fuels did not sweep American agriculture until after 1945, farm automation was under way across the nation and in Appalachia in the 1920s. Here a crew poses with a steam-powered tractor and harvesting implement.

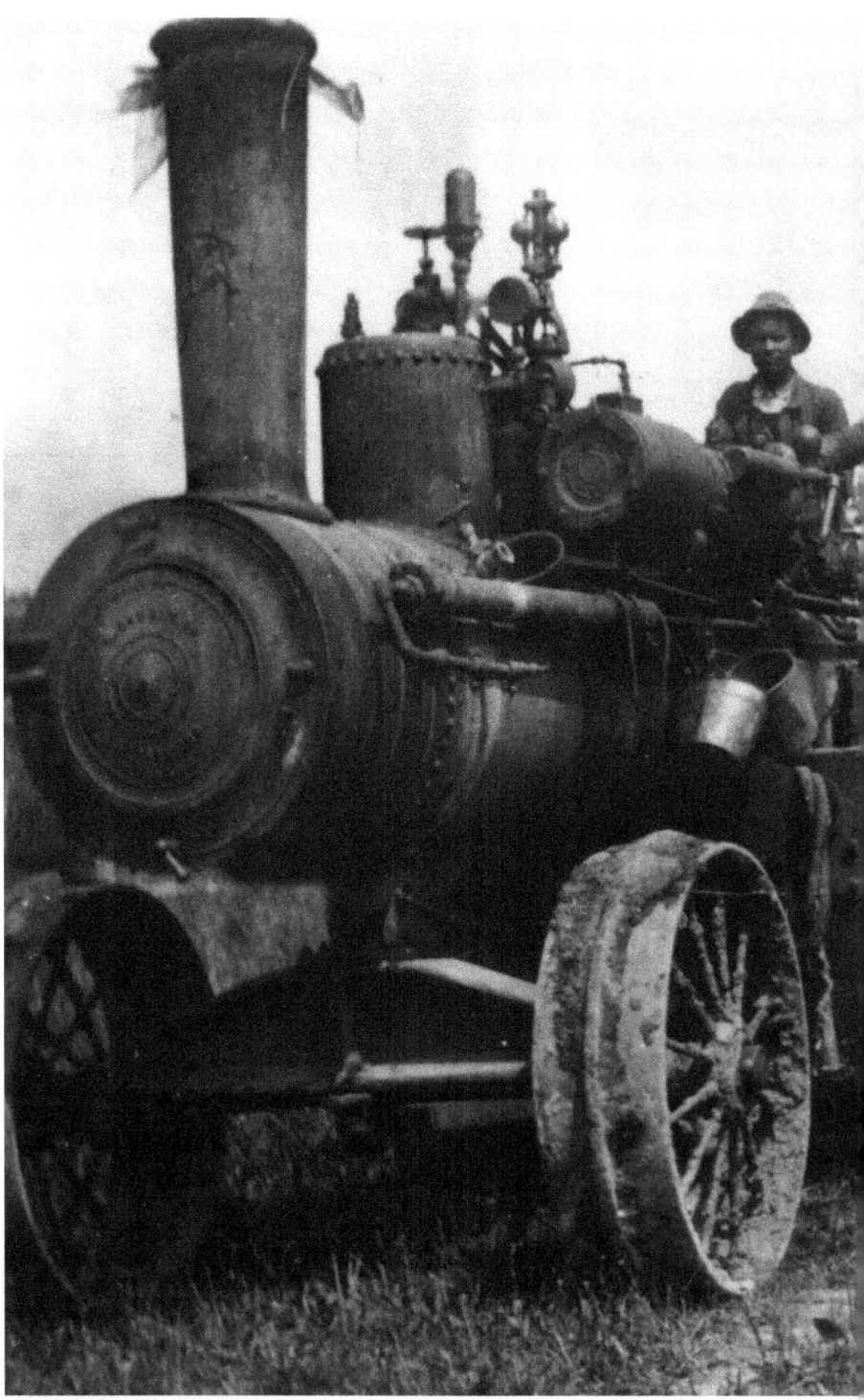

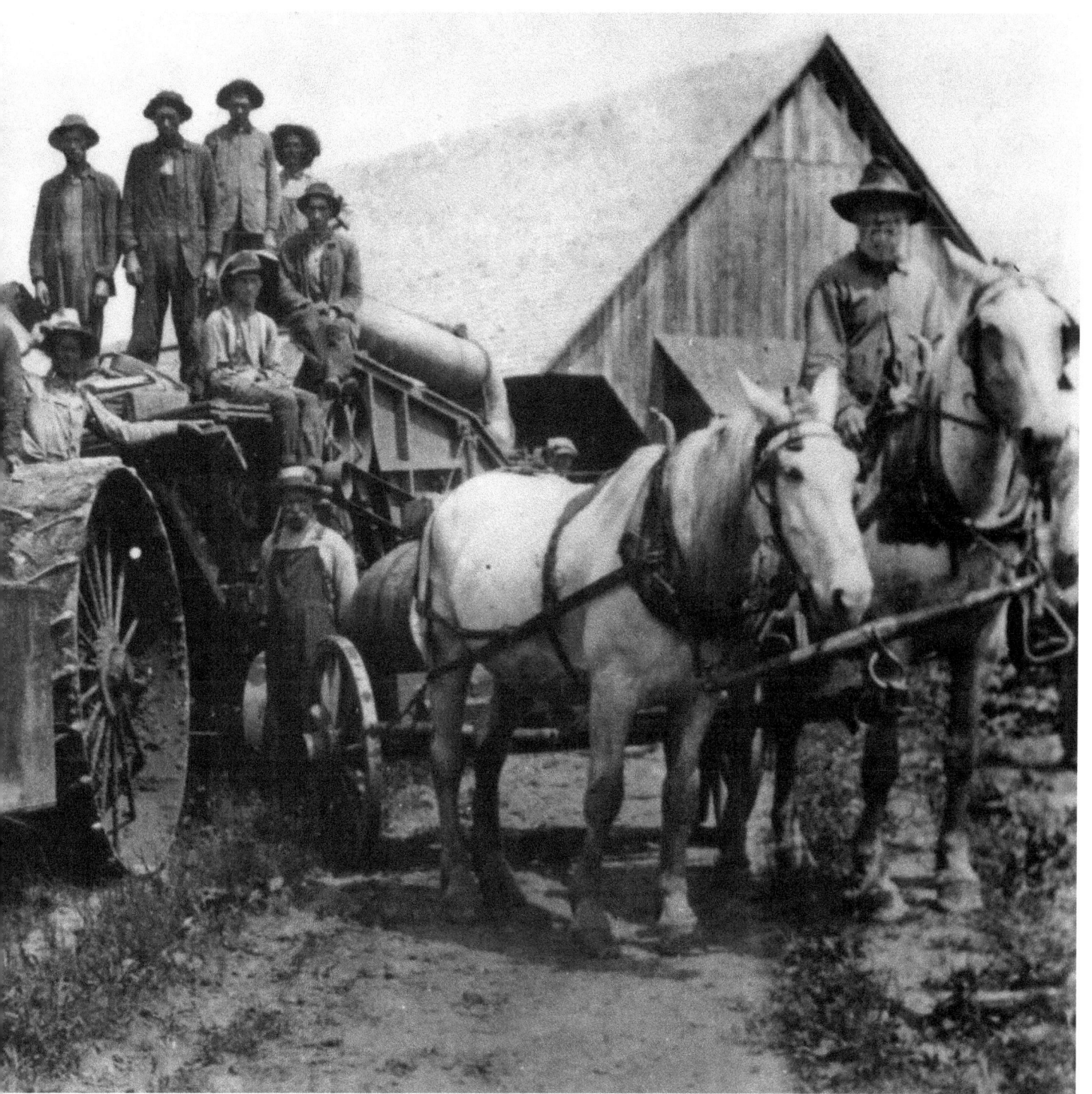

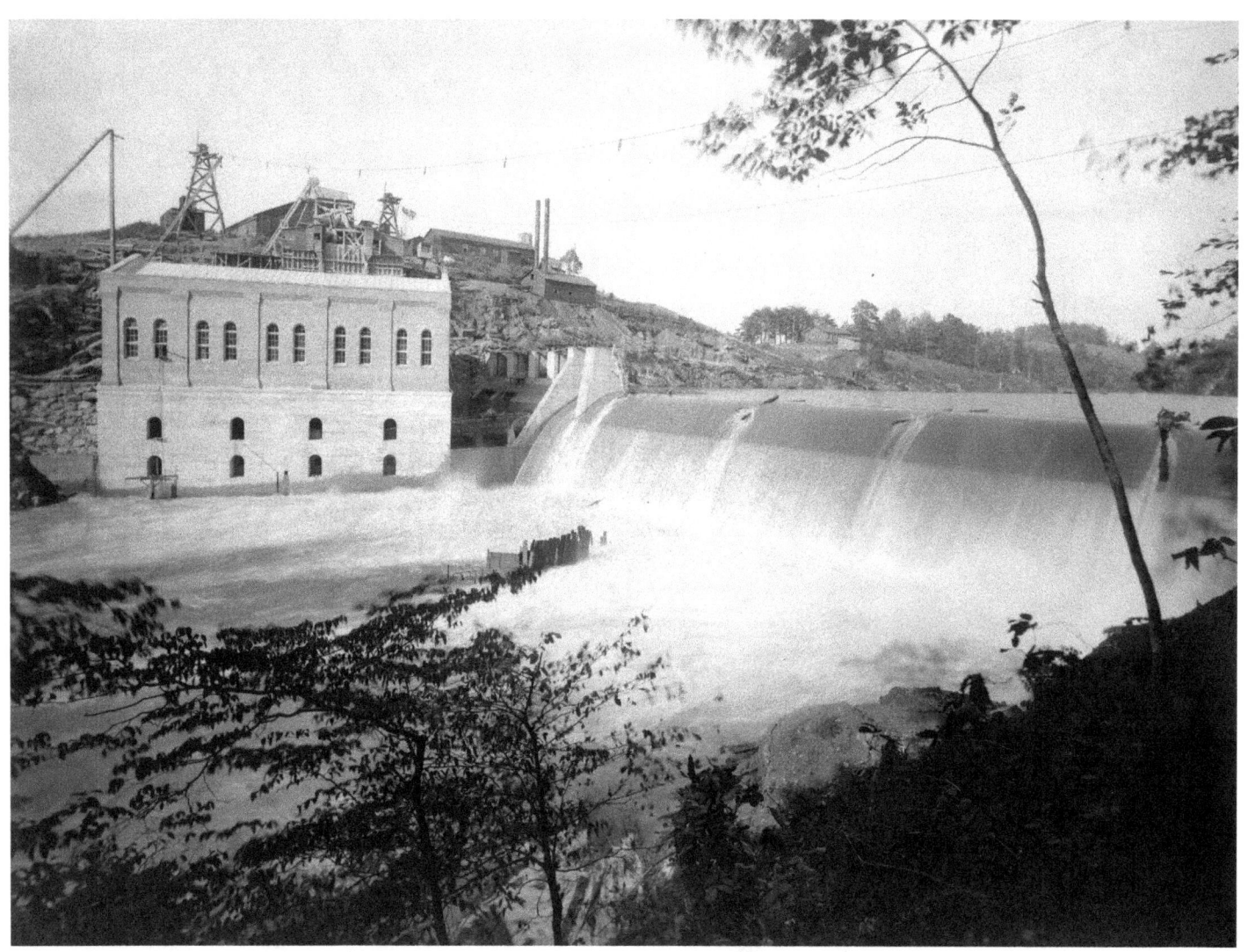

Between 1912 and 1925, the Tennessee Eastern Electric Company hydroelectric plant, on the Nolichucky River, near Greeneville, Tennessee, supplied power to Johnson City. For the most part, rural areas did not have access to electricity at that time. Two generating units at this plant produced a total capacity of 5,000 kilowatts. Hydroelectric power was supplemented by a coal-burning steam reserve plant in Johnson City.

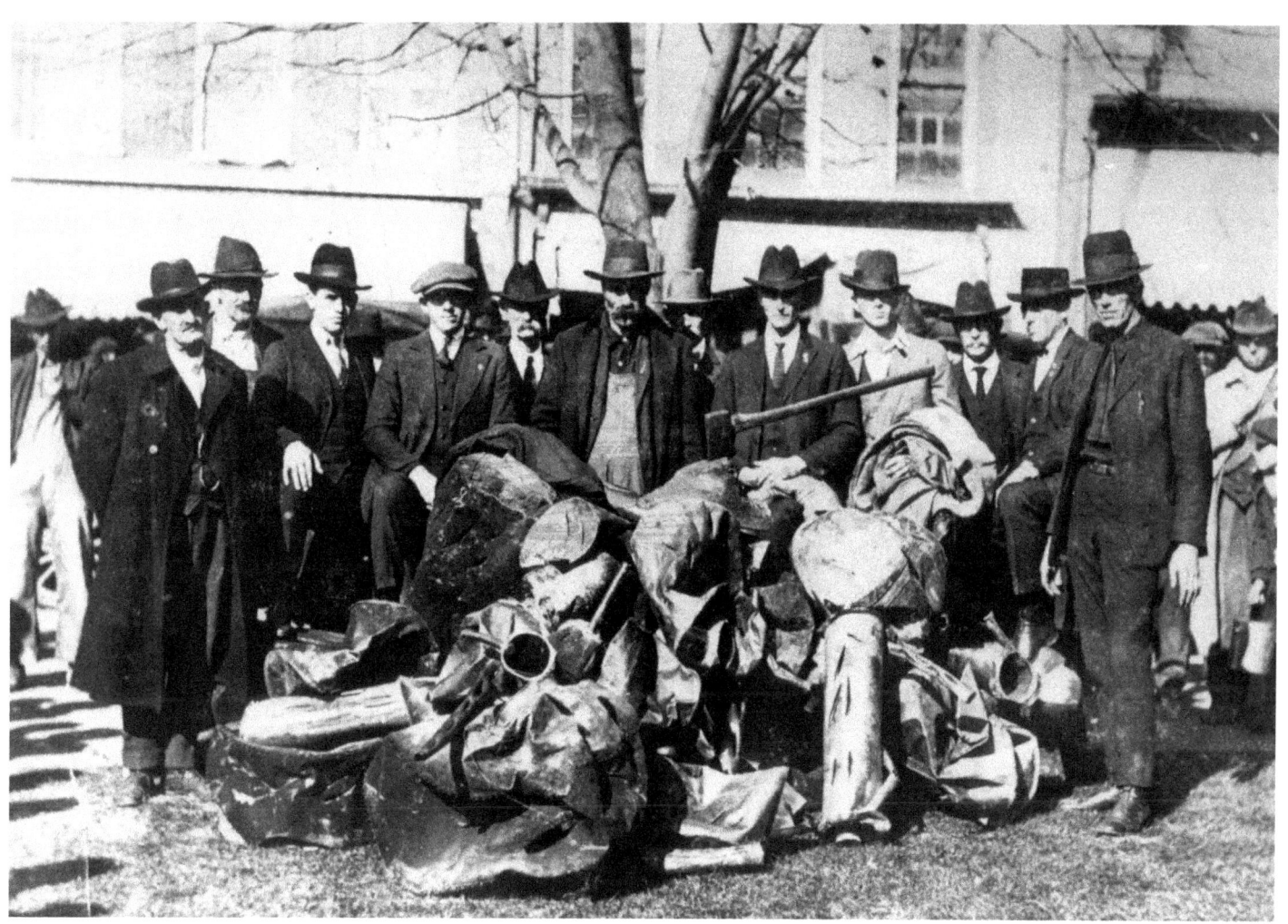

This photograph shows law enforcement agents with a destroyed still. Demand for illicit liquor increased in the United States under Prohibition (1920–1933). Appalachian moonshining traditions developed in the nineteenth century, in part, as a way of converting corn into a product that could be transported to market over bad roads.

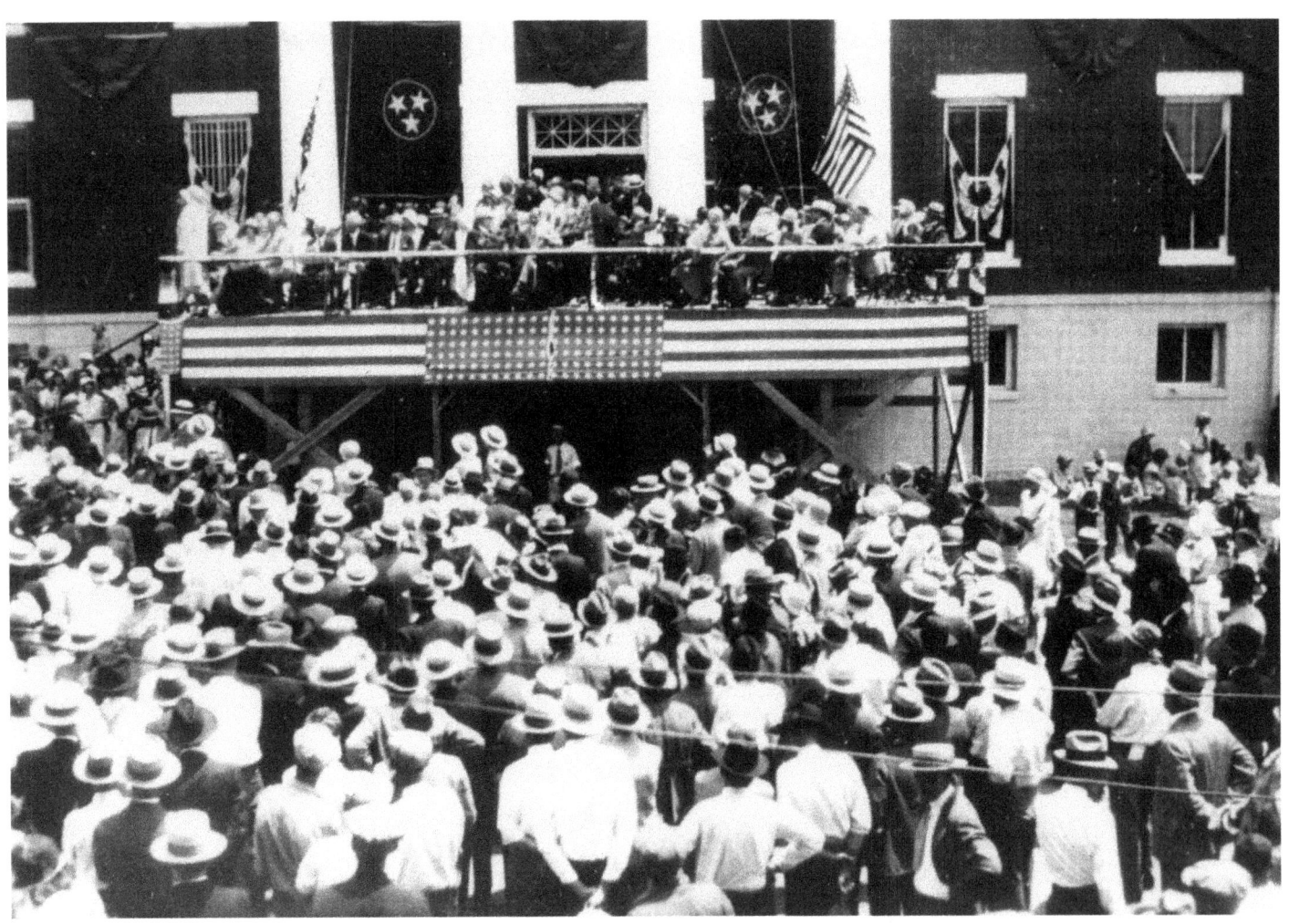

A crowd gathers for an Independence Day celebration in Jonesborough, Tennessee, on July 4, 1930. Alf Taylor (1848–1931), a colorful public figure from Carter County, Tennessee, who was a Congressman (1889–1895) and later Tennessee governor (1921–1923), is shown giving a speech. Taylor's speeches were said to be humorous, moralizing, and crowd-pleasing.

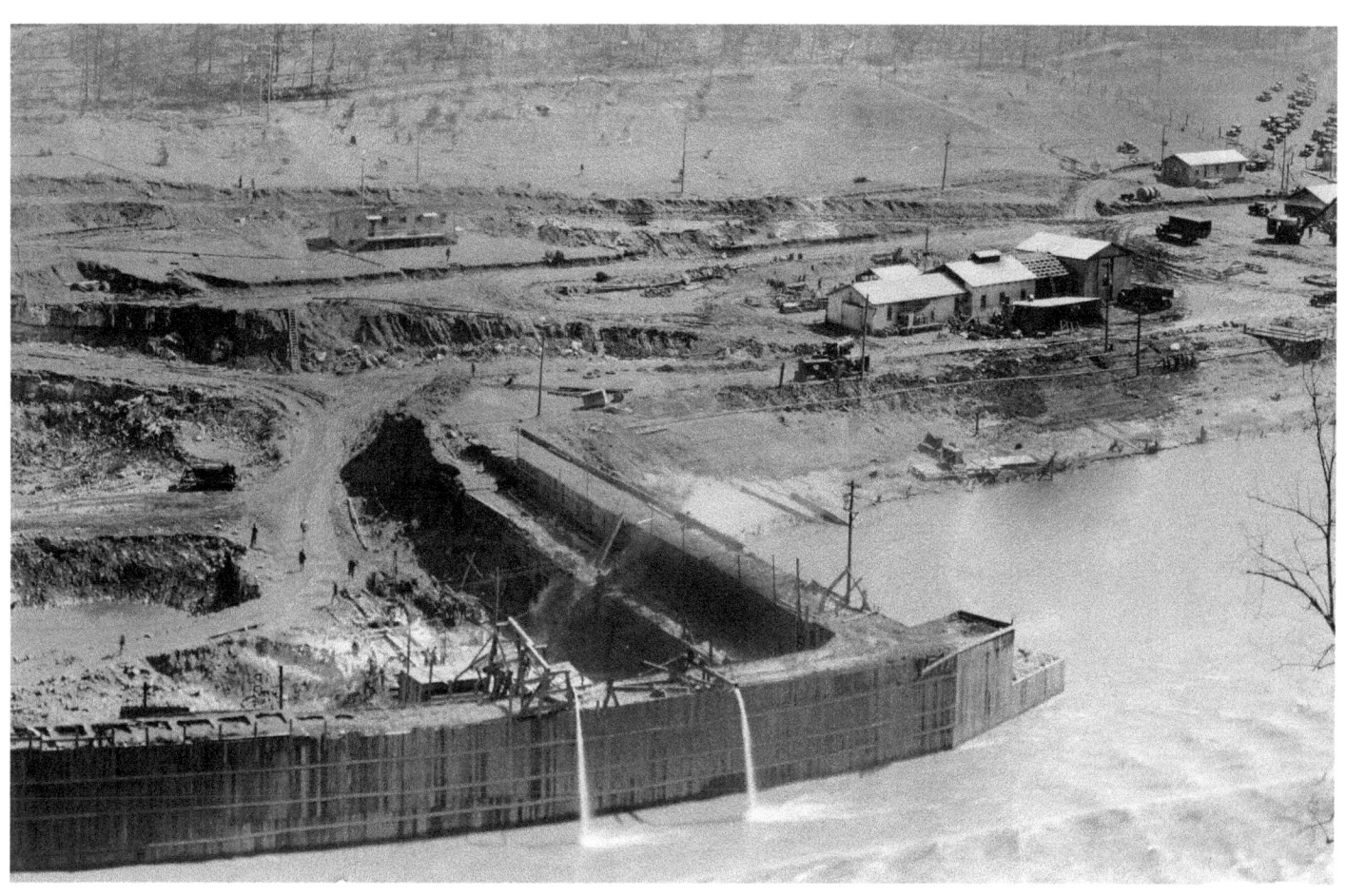

Located on the Clinch River, in Cove Creek, Tennessee, Norris Dam—shown here under construction in 1934—was one of TVA's earliest dams. It is named for Nebraska senator George Norris, a longtime supporter of the TVA. The lands surrounding the reservoir created by the dam are now run as a Tennessee state park.

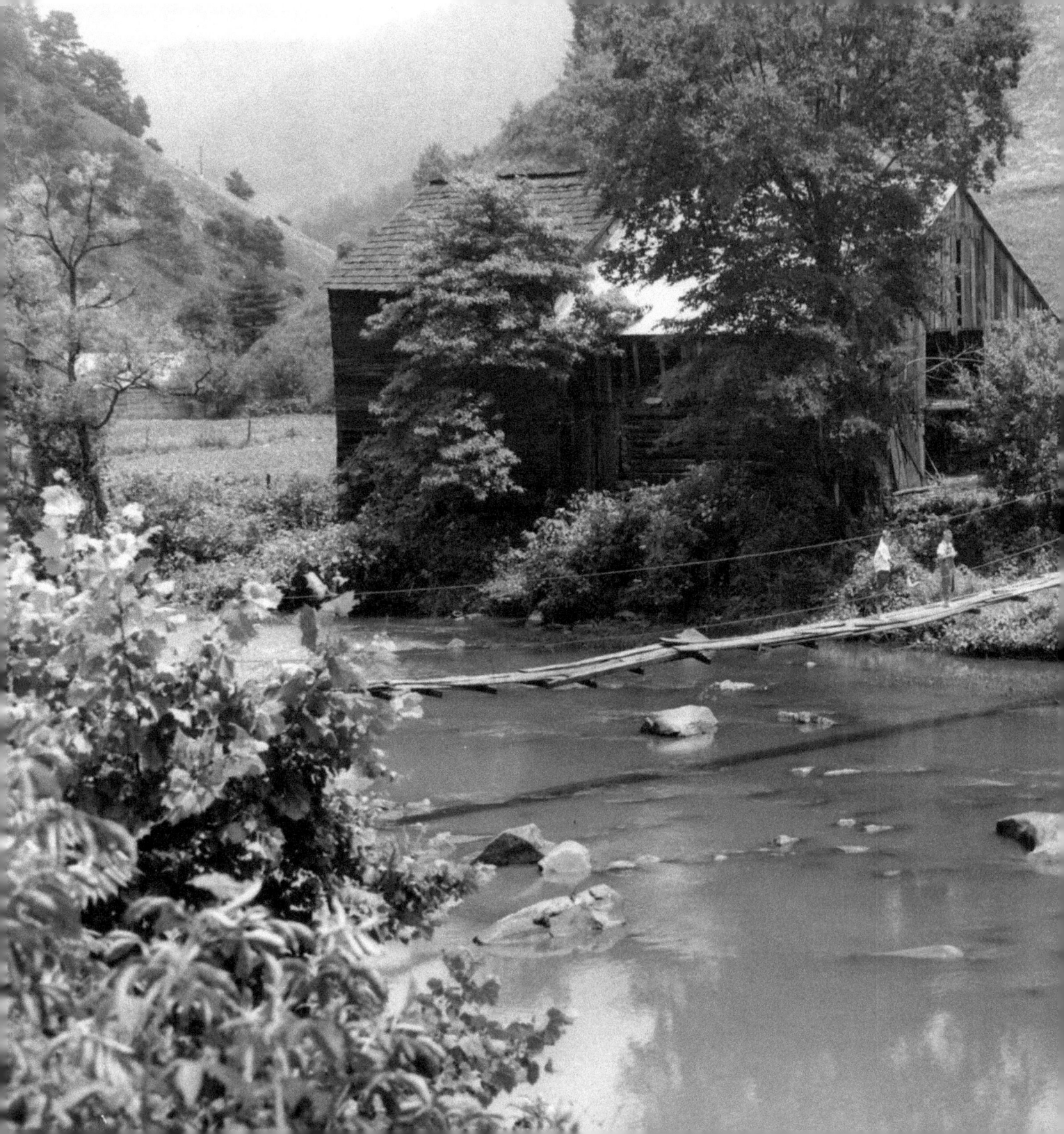

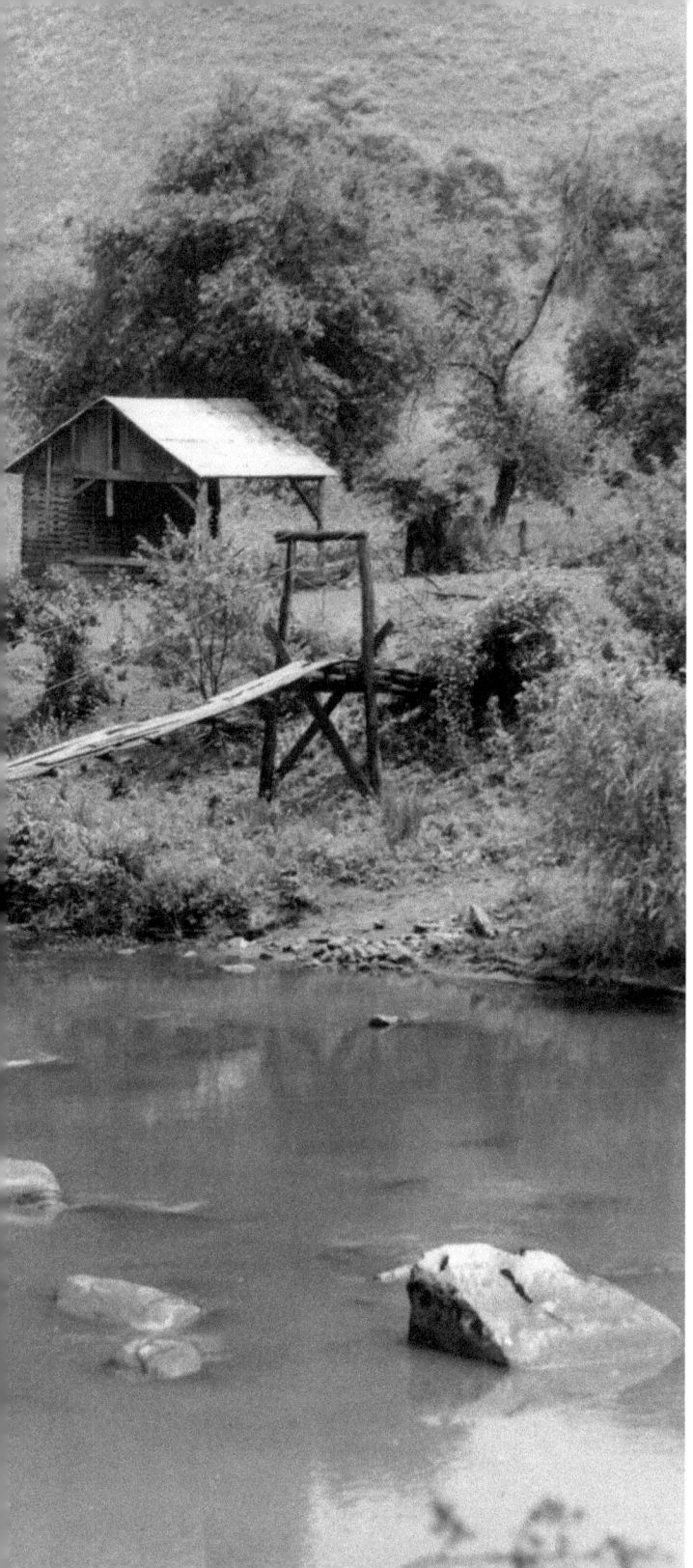

In the mountainous regions of Appalachia, flat bottomland has always been prized. Often the best farmland shares a bottom with a river and a road. So it is not uncommon to see this sort of arrangement: the road on one side of a river, farms and buildings on the other, and a suspension bridge in between. In the Toe River country of Yancey County, North Carolina, suspension bridges are still common today.

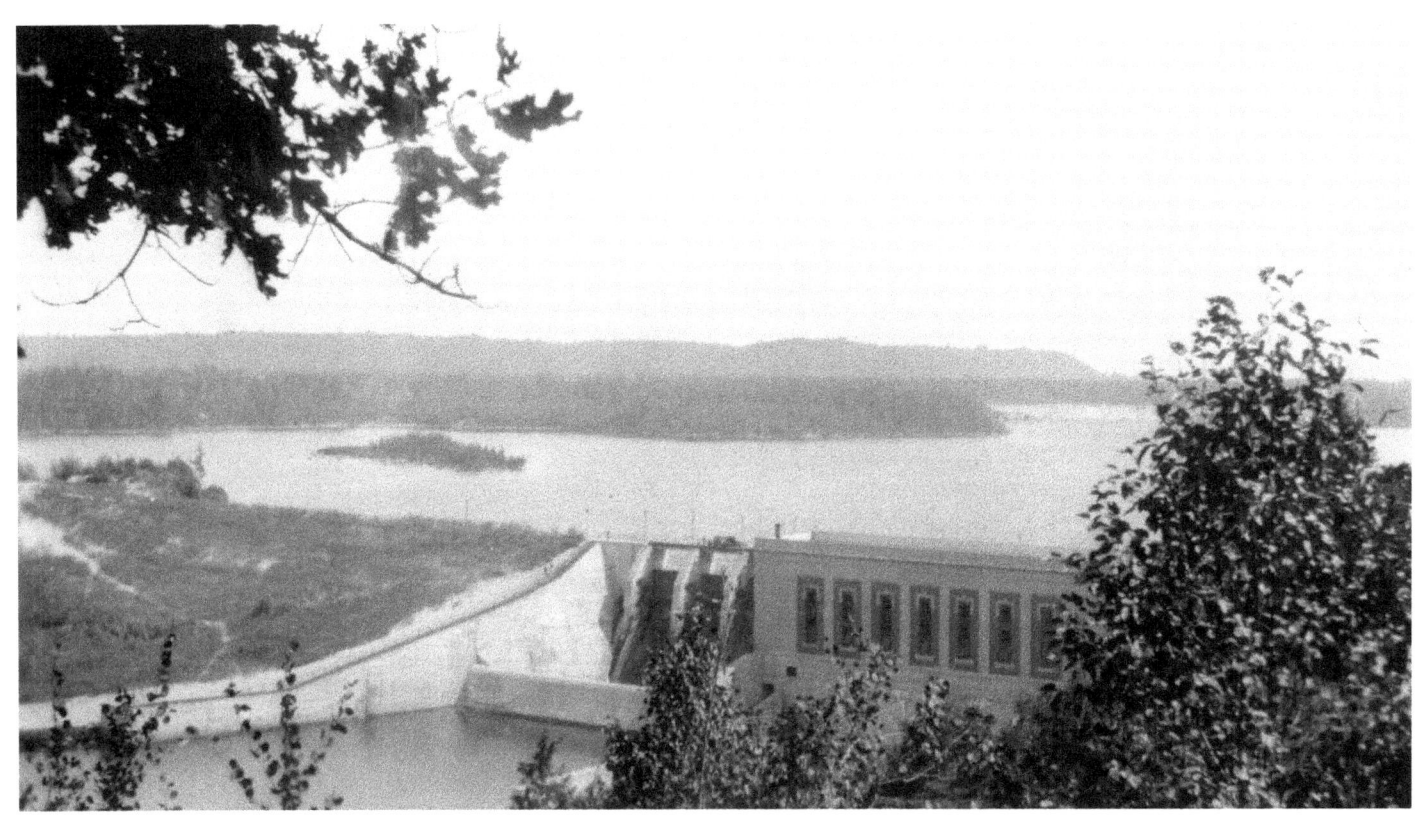

One of the Tennessee Valley Authority's many dams. The TVA was formed in the 1930s to "tame" the Tennessee river system, in order to provide flood control, increase navigability, and create hydroelectric power.

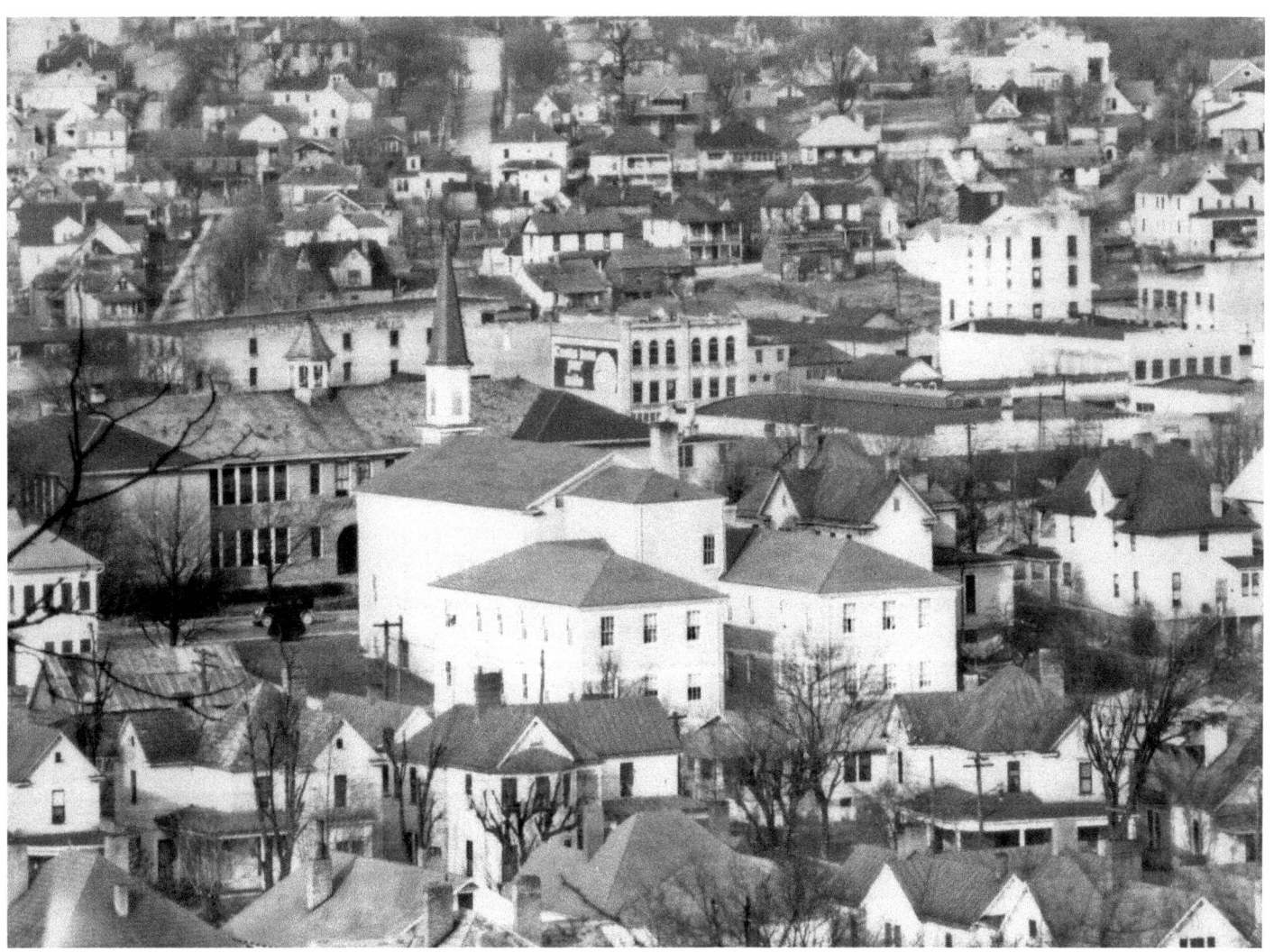

Anderson Street Methodist Church rises amid homes and businesses in Bristol in the 1930s. Bristol, Tennessee, and Bristol, Virginia (the town sits astride the state line), thrived in the early twentieth century, as owners and managers of mining operations in the coalfields farther north moved to town.

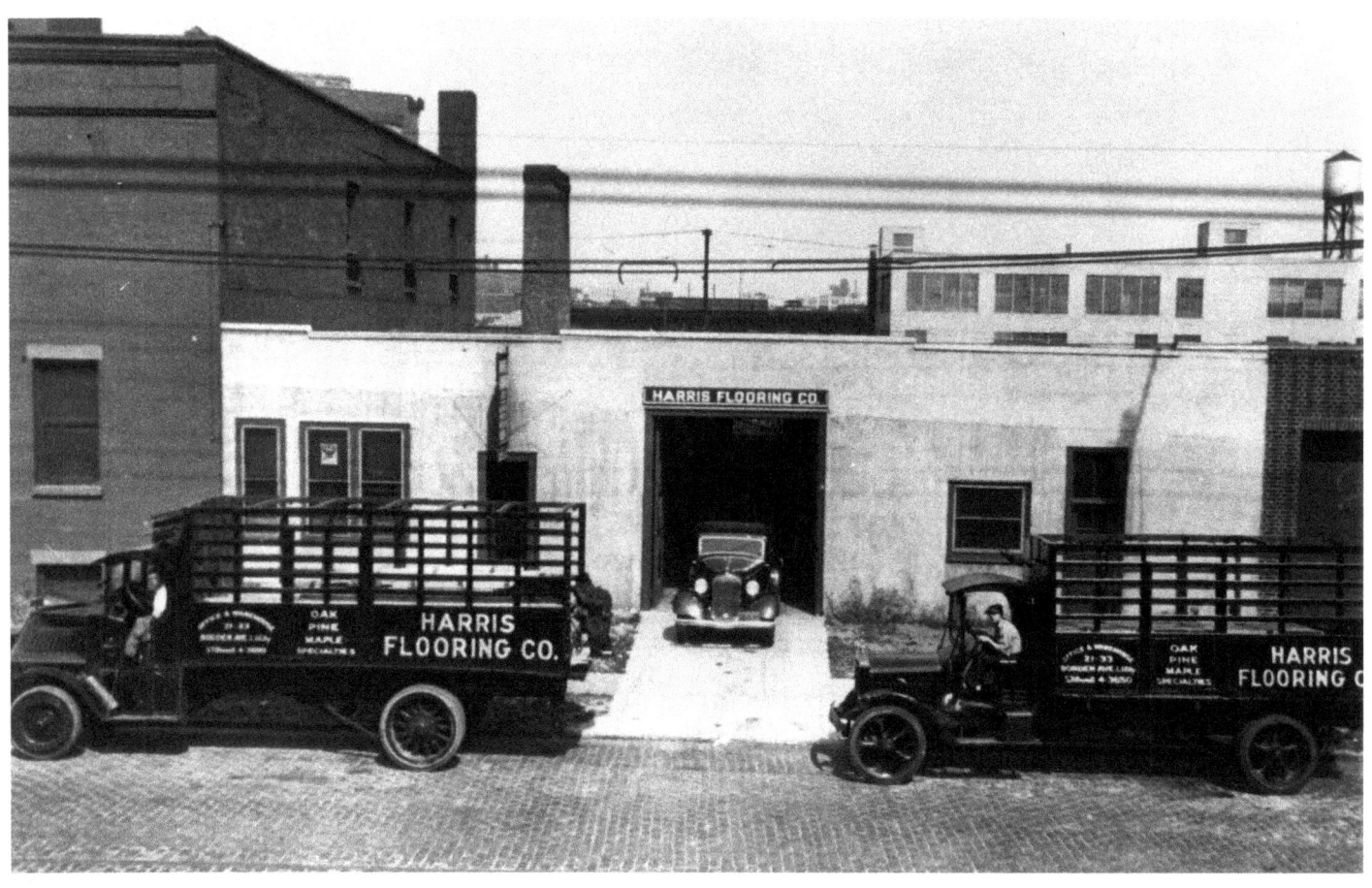

Harris Flooring Company, of Johnson City, Tennessee, built a reputation in the 1930s for its pre-finished wood flooring. This image shows the old plant on East Maple Street. At the beginning of World War II, a few years after this picture was taken, the demand for standard flooring products collapsed. The company converted to the manufacture of war products at all its plants, and then converted back to wood flooring after the war.

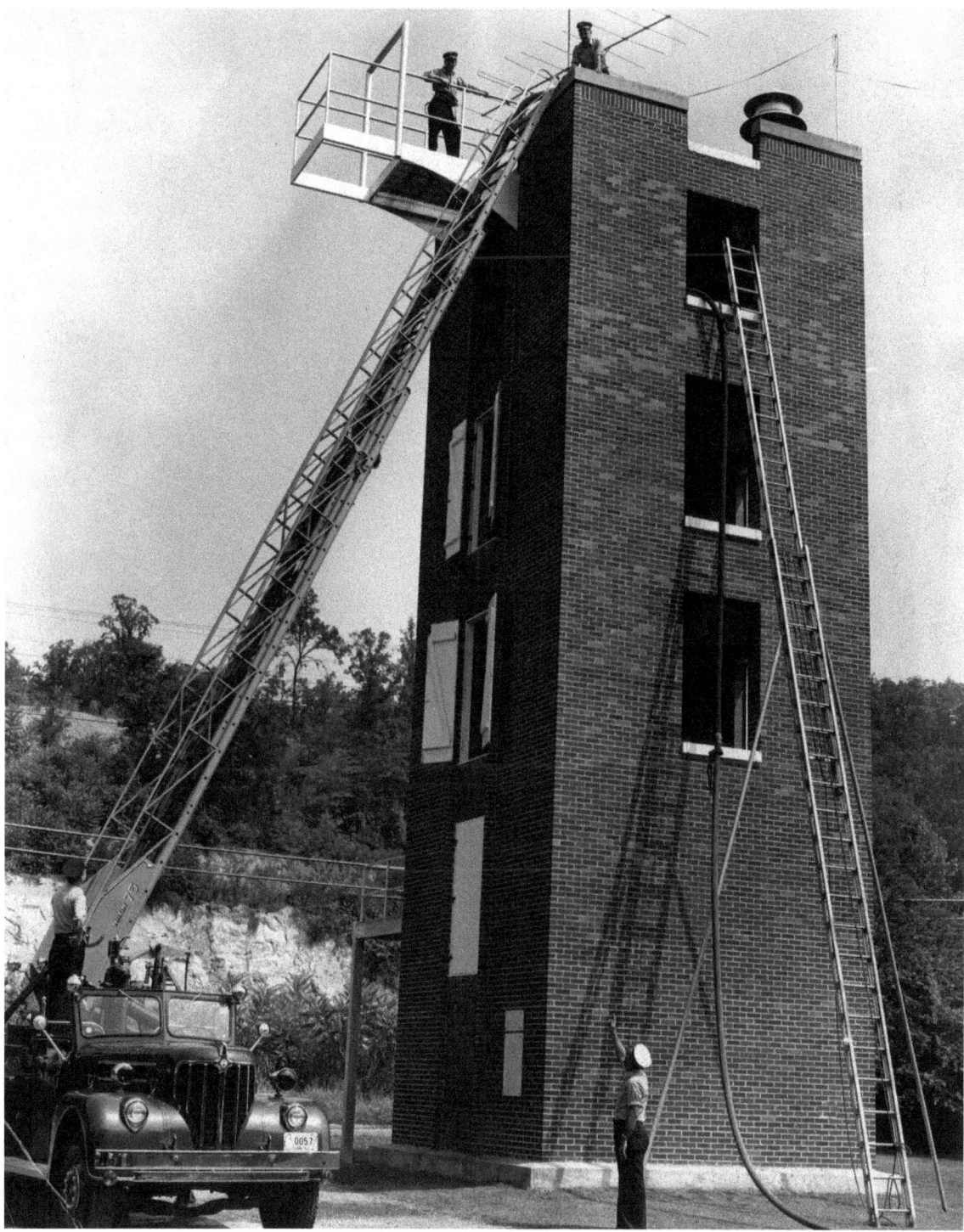

Johnson City fire
fighters train on this
training tower in the
1930s.

Abraham Lincoln selected Andrew Johnson as his running mate in 1864 as a gesture of reconciliation toward the South. Following Lincoln's assassination, Johnson became president. When Johnson died in 1875, he was buried in his hometown of Greeneville, Tennessee, where this memorial obelisk was erected a few years later. In 1942, the National Park Service became custodian of the site and now manages it as a National Cemetery.

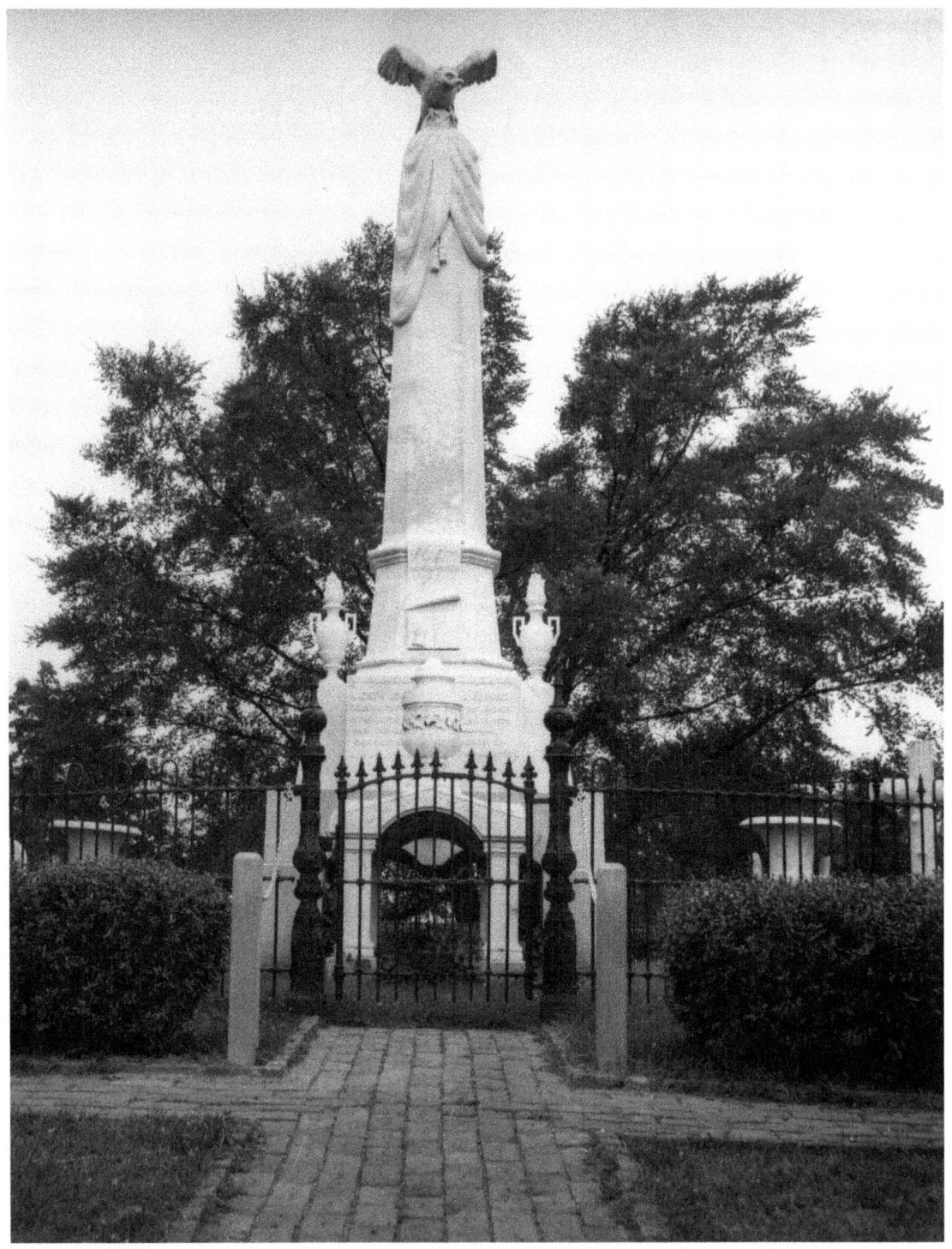

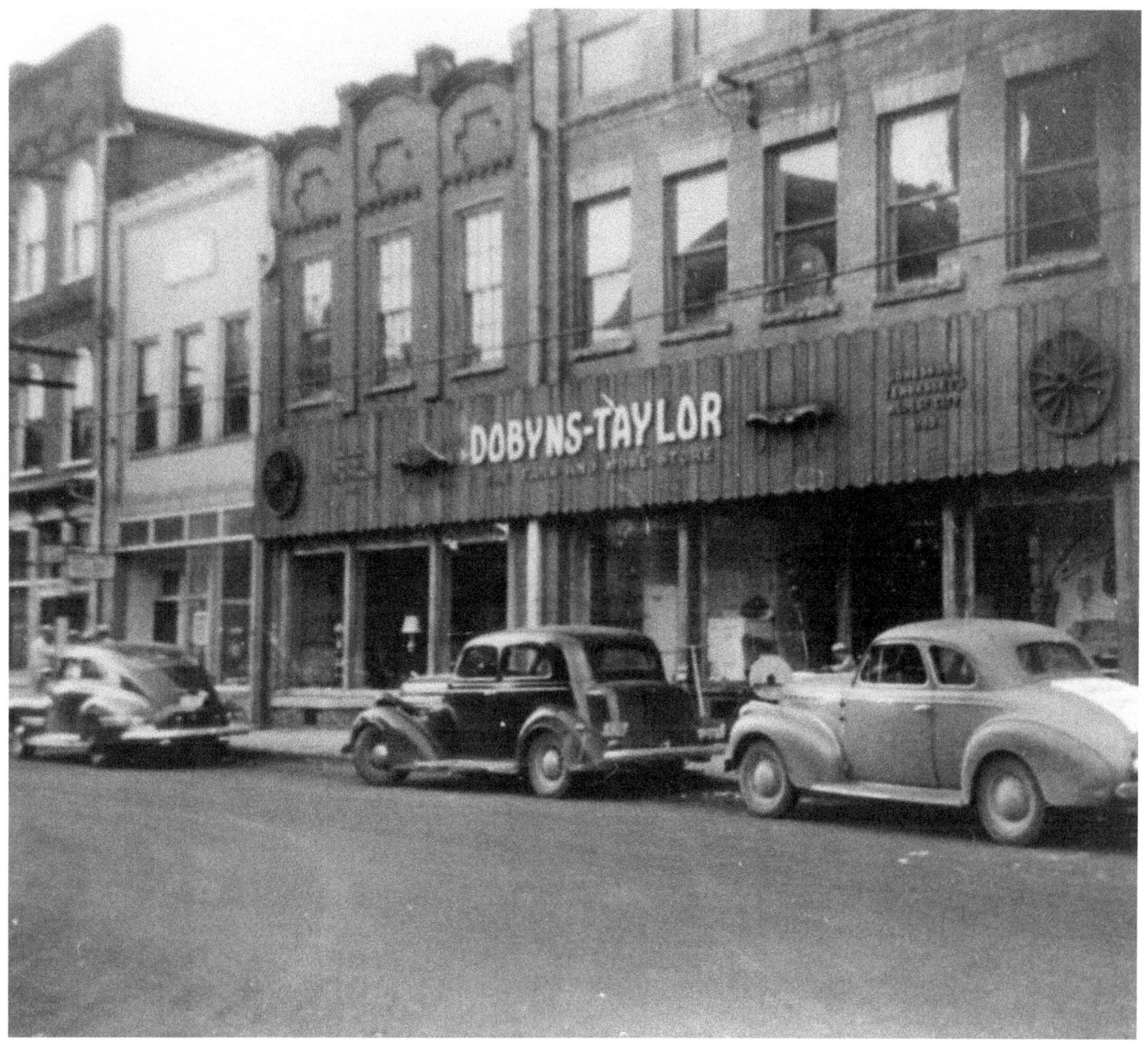

Dobyns-Taylor Farm and Home Store, in Jonesborough, Tennessee, is open for business here in the 1930s.

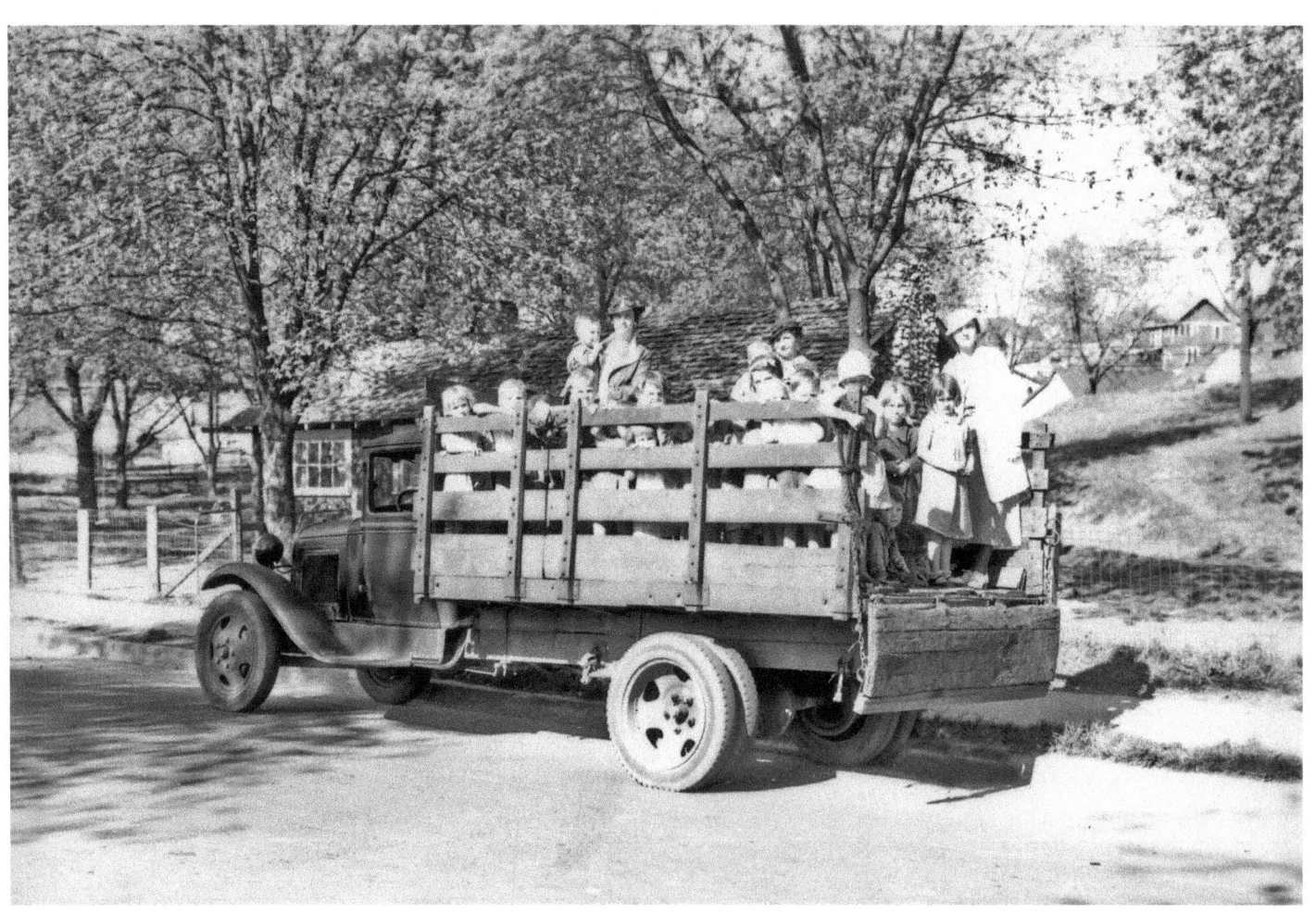

A truckload of children is shown on Piedmont Street, in Bristol, Tennessee, in the 1930s, en route to a T. B. Camp. Tuberculosis summer camps were common in the early decades of the twentieth century, with the goal of providing sick children with fresh air and sunshine.

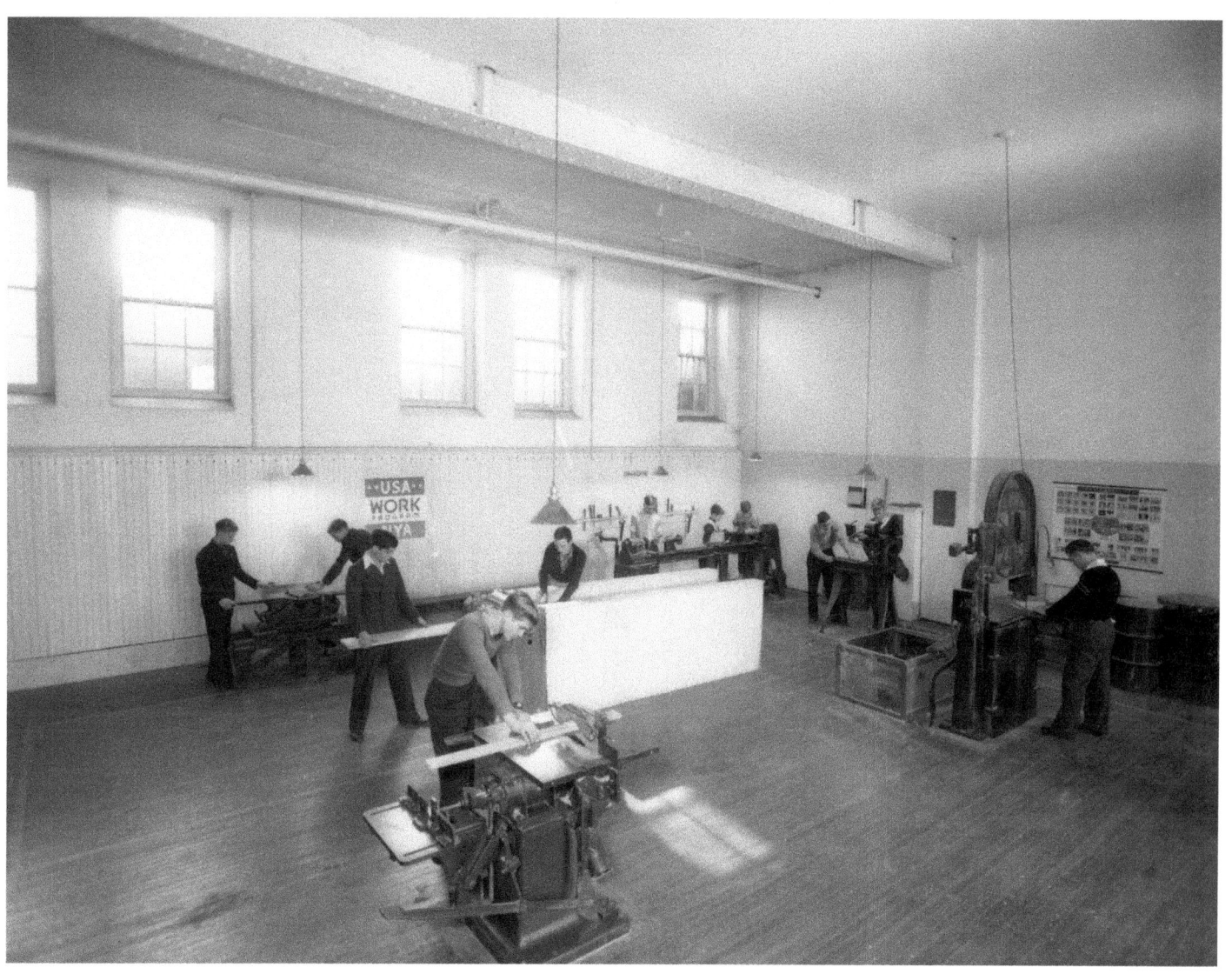

As part of FDR's Depression-era "New Deal" policies, the National Youth Administration was formed to provide "work-study" projects for high-schoolers. This image depicts boys in an NYA woodworking program in Bristol, Tennessee.

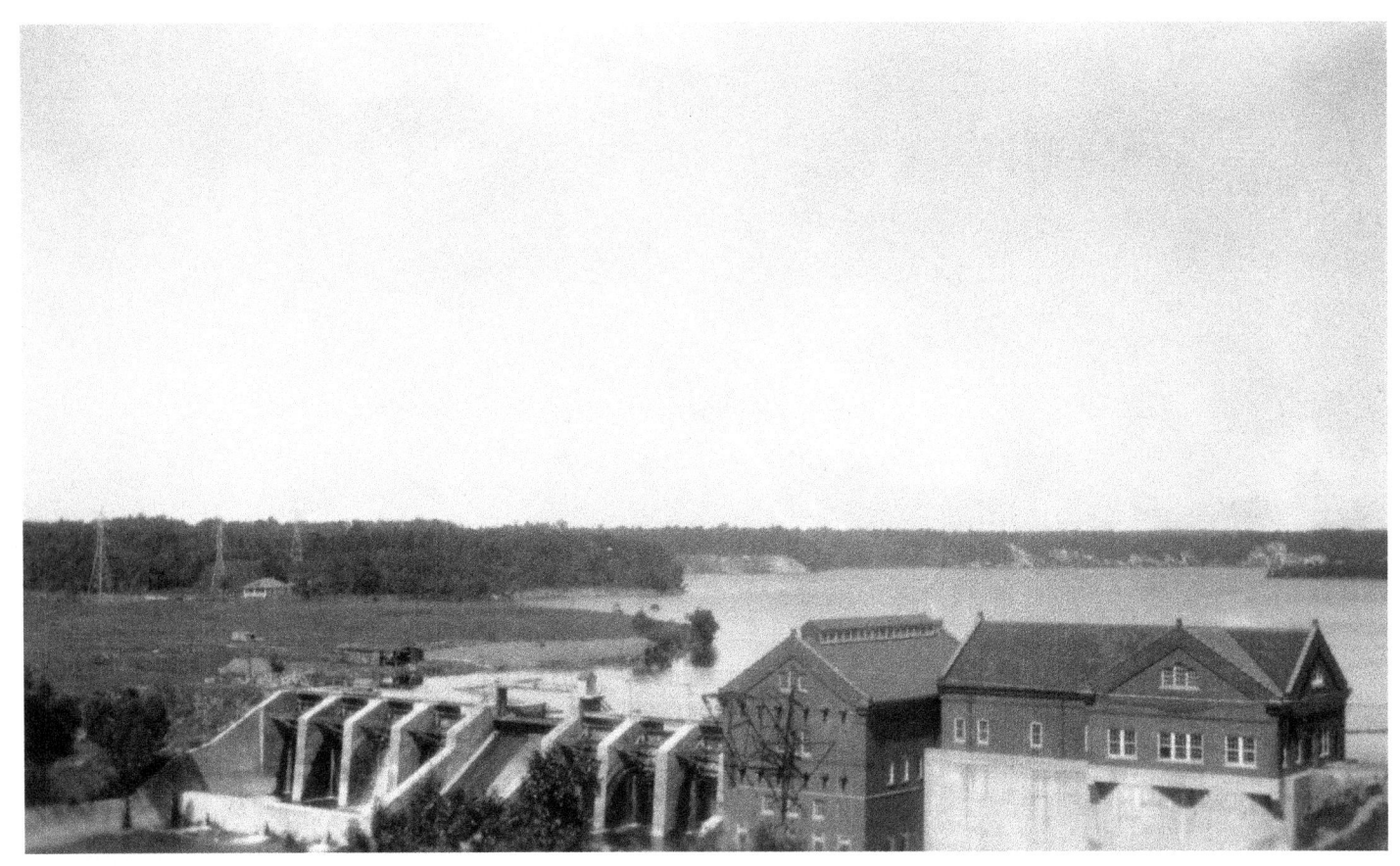

The Tennessee Valley Authority was formed in the 1930s to "tame" the Tennessee river system, in order to provide flood control, increase navigability, and create hydroelectric power. This dam is one of many in the TVA network.

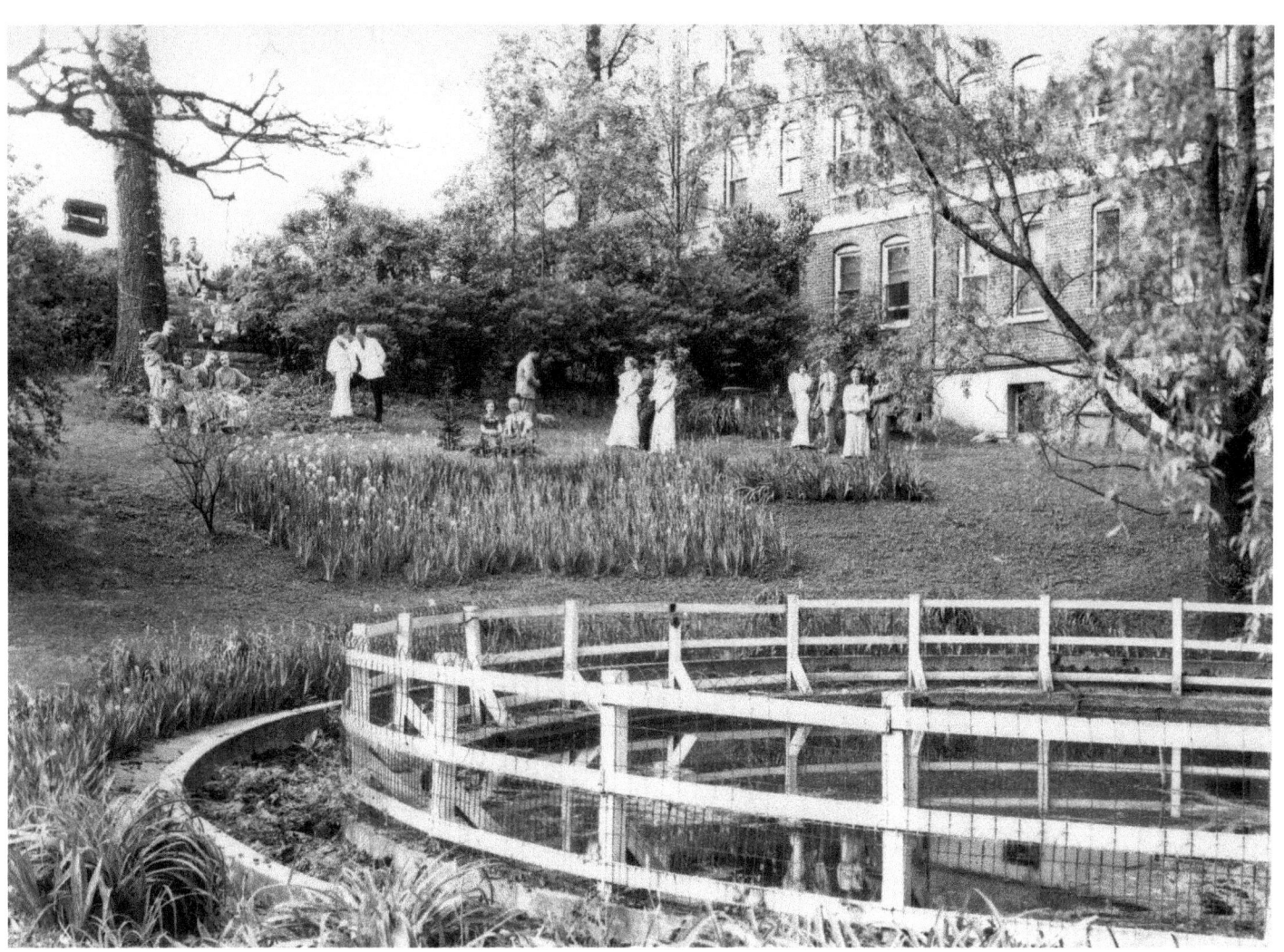

Students pose in formal dress in a flower garden at Sullins College, in Bristol, Virginia, in May 1935. Sullins College for women was founded in 1870 and included a grammar school and high school as well as the college. The original buildings, on James Street near downtown, burned in a fire in 1915. The college reopened as a junior college for girls in 1917. Financial straits forced it to close in 1976.

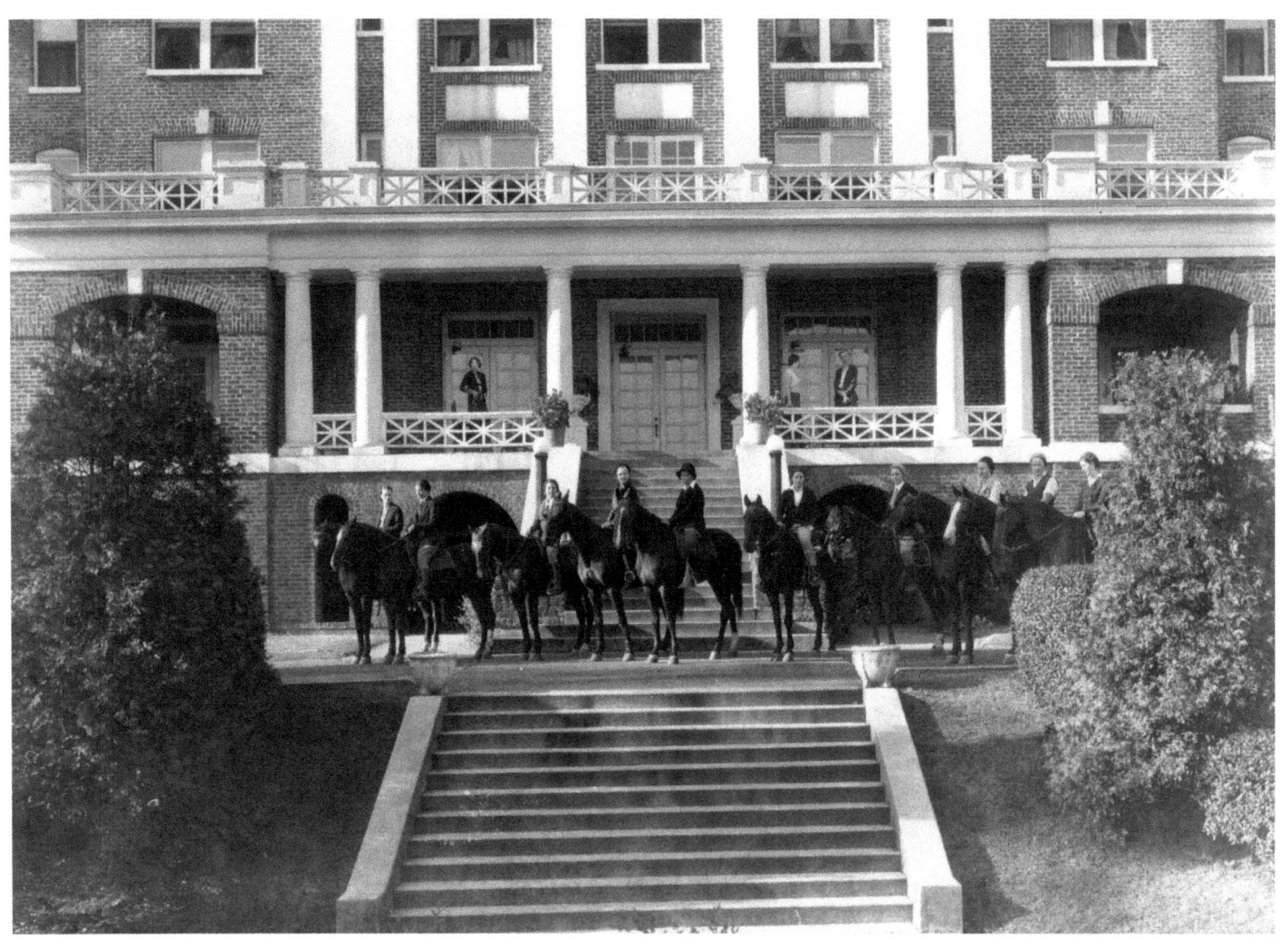

Students at Sullins College display their equestrian skills.

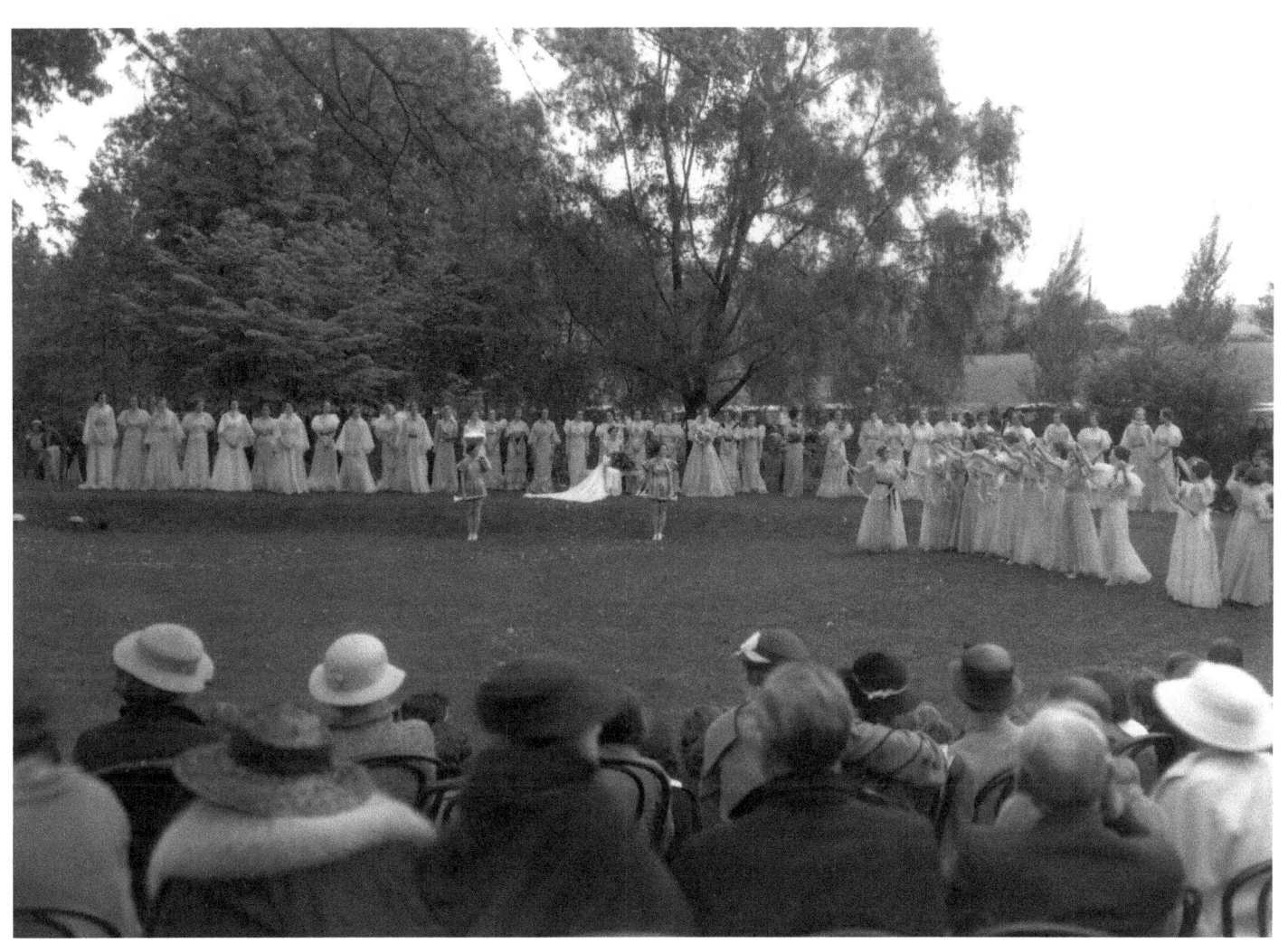

Celebration of May Day 1935 is under way at Sullins College.

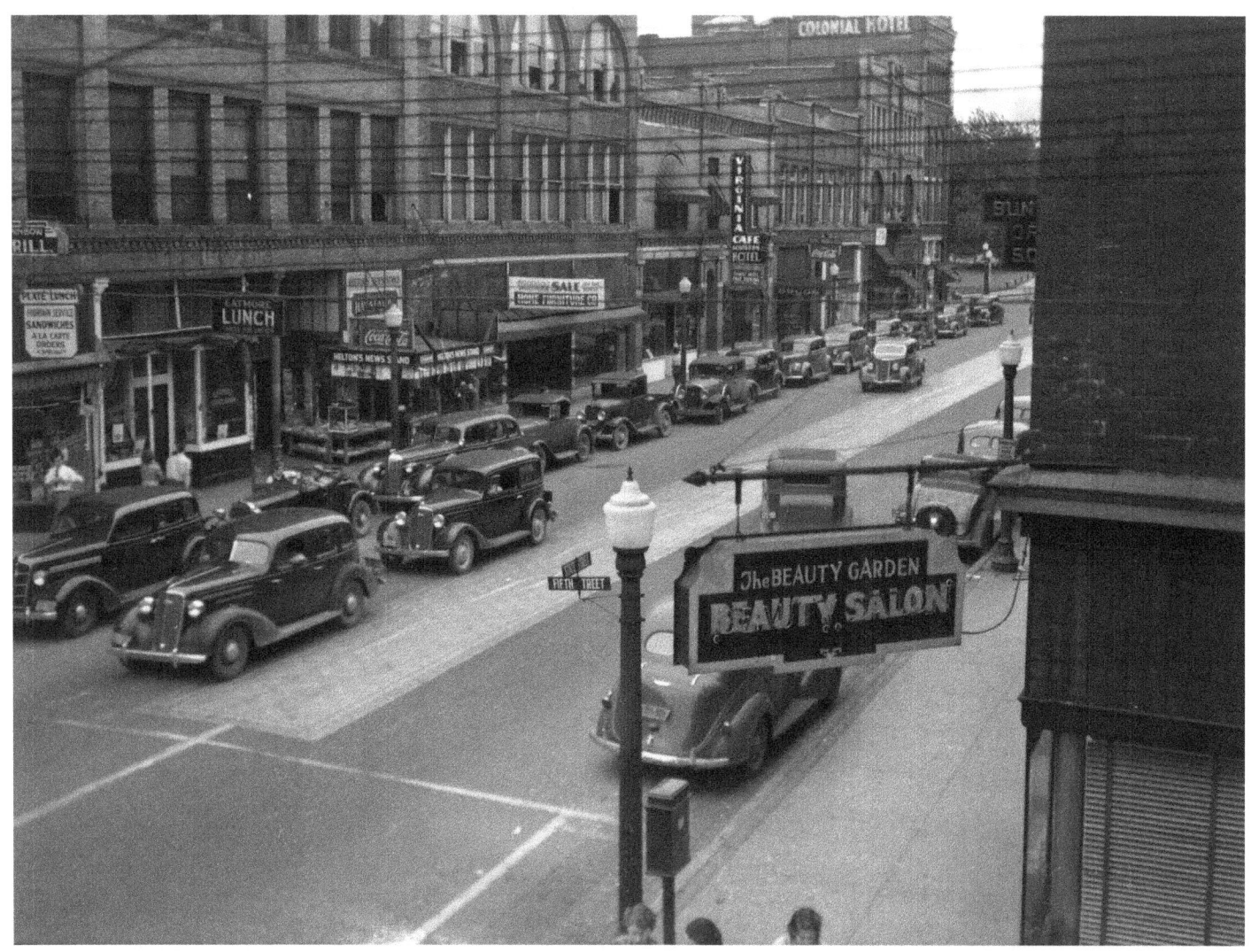

Coal profits fueled the economy of Bristol, Tennessee-Virginia, even as the Great Depression caused widespread hardship. State Street bustles with automobiles in this view from the corner of Fifth and State.

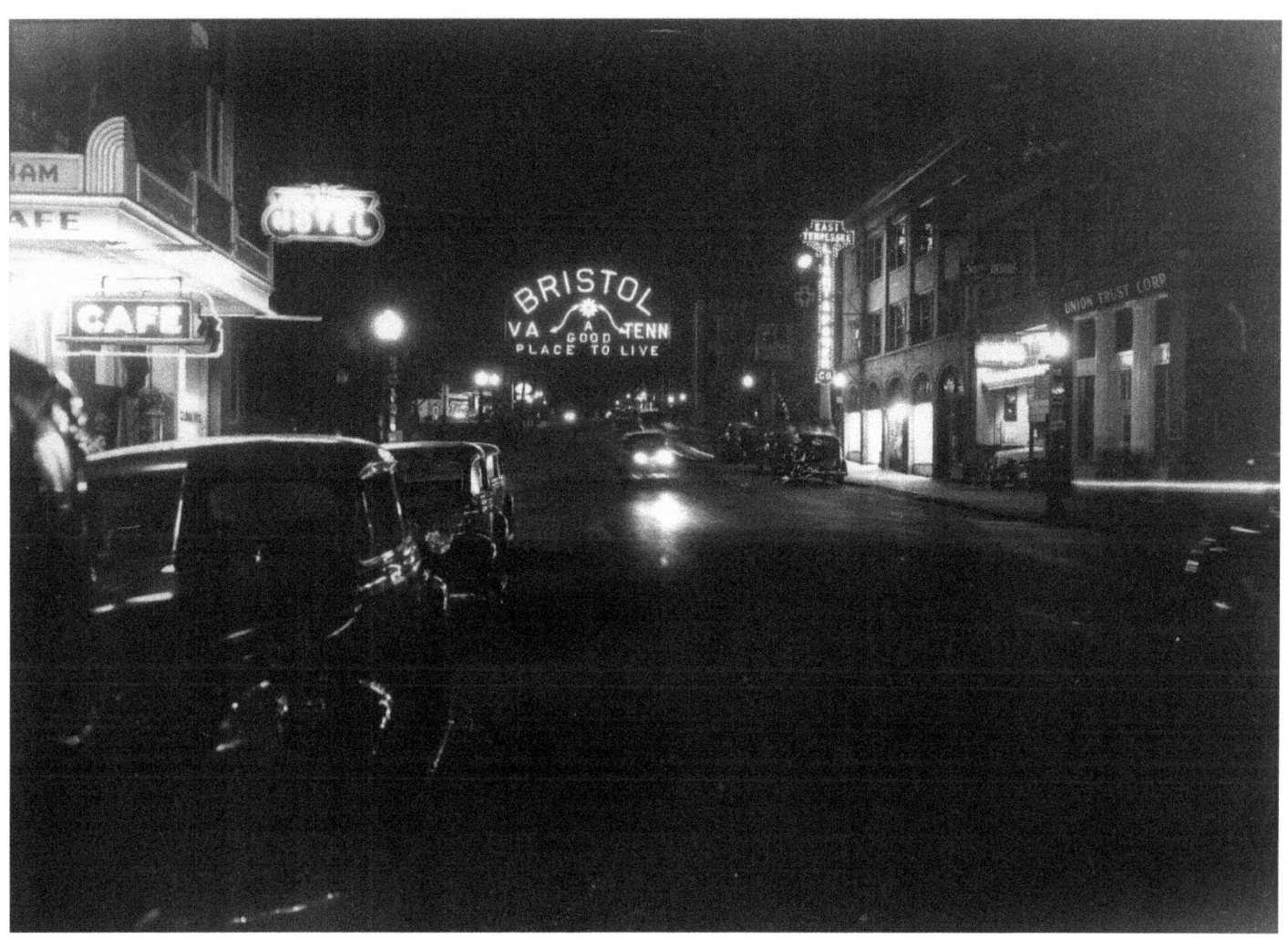

This night view of State Street, in downtown Bristol, Tennessee-Virginia, shows the landmark sign that is still in place today. First erected in 1910 atop a hardware company building at Third and State, the sign was moved to its present location over the street in 1915, and the slogan was changed to the current one in the 1920s. The official state line between Tennessee and Virginia runs beneath the sign, down the middle of State Street.

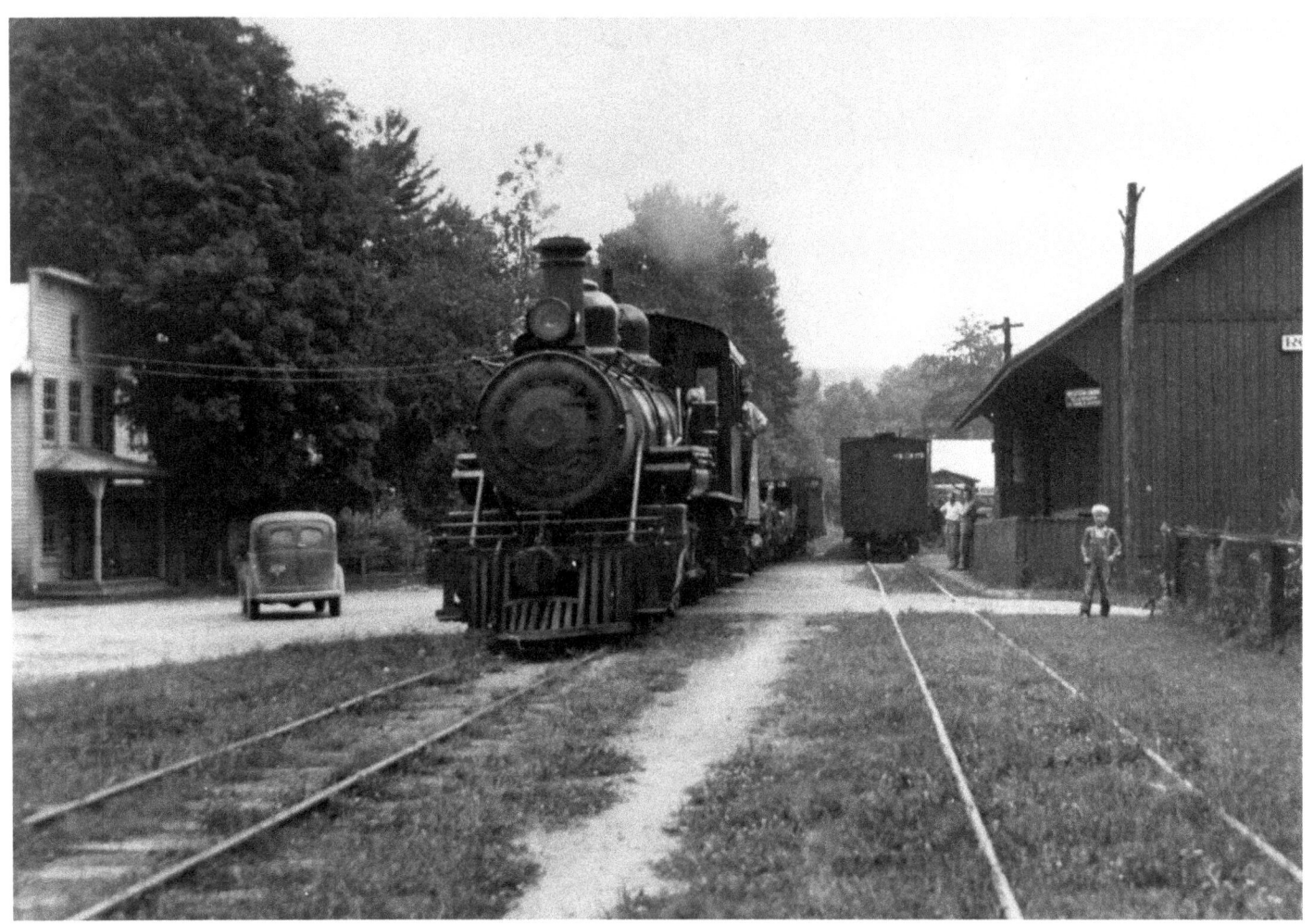

An East Tennessee & Western North Carolina (Tweetsie) "mixed train"—a train transporting both passengers and freight—pulls out of Roan Mountain station in the late 1930s near the Tennessee–North Carolina border. The railroad ceased operations in 1950. The community of Roan Mountain is situated below the summit of the mountain, which tops out at 6,285 feet and features the catawba rhododendron and flame azalea, a natural floral display that continues to draw visitors today. The Appalachian Trail runs through the area.

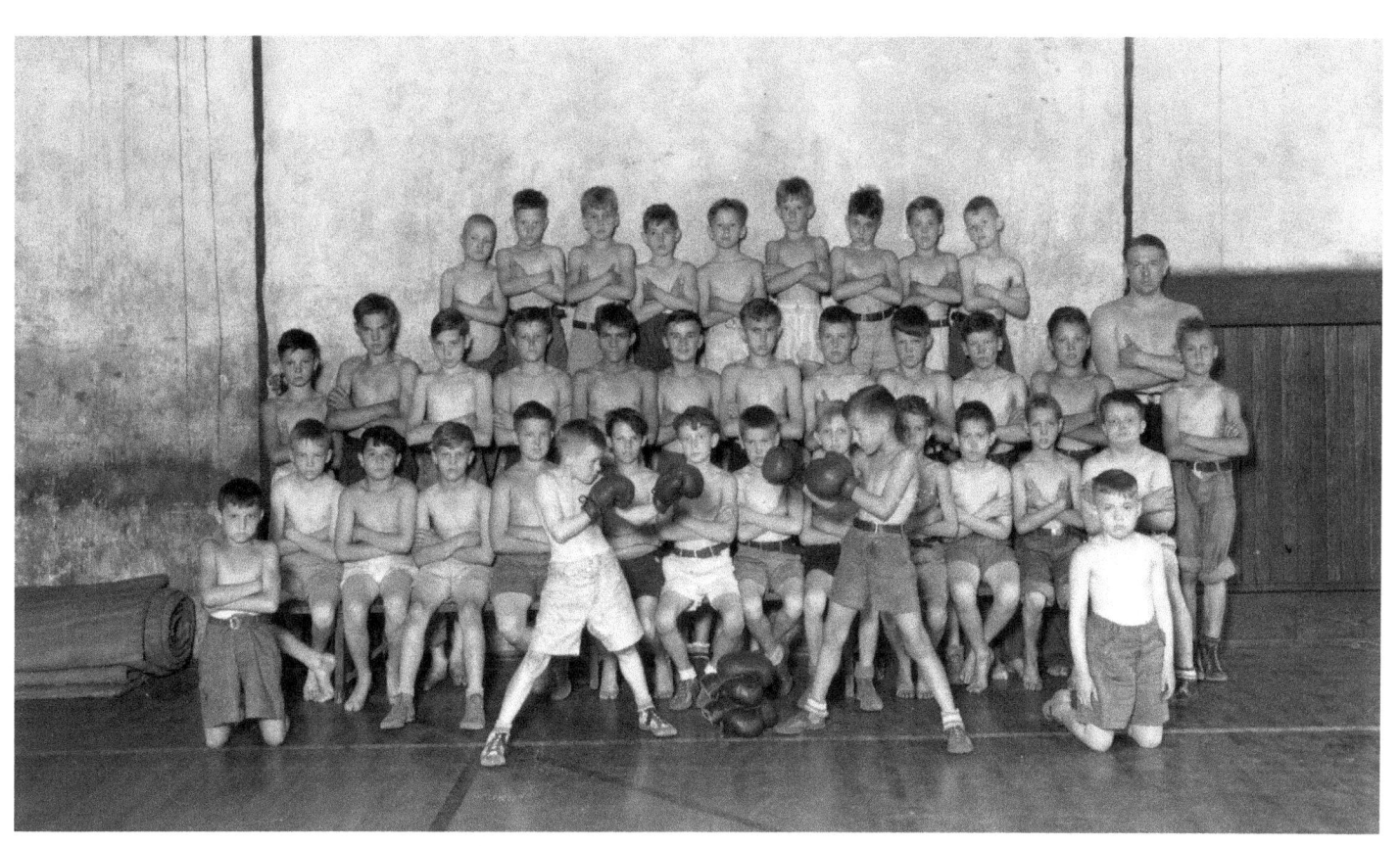

Members of the "Midgets," the Y.M.C.A. boy's boxing class in Bristol, strike poses for the camera.

Royal Crown Cola heads the menu at the Dixie Cafe in Bristol in 1939. Local patrons and staff pause briefly to let the photographer capture this moment in time.

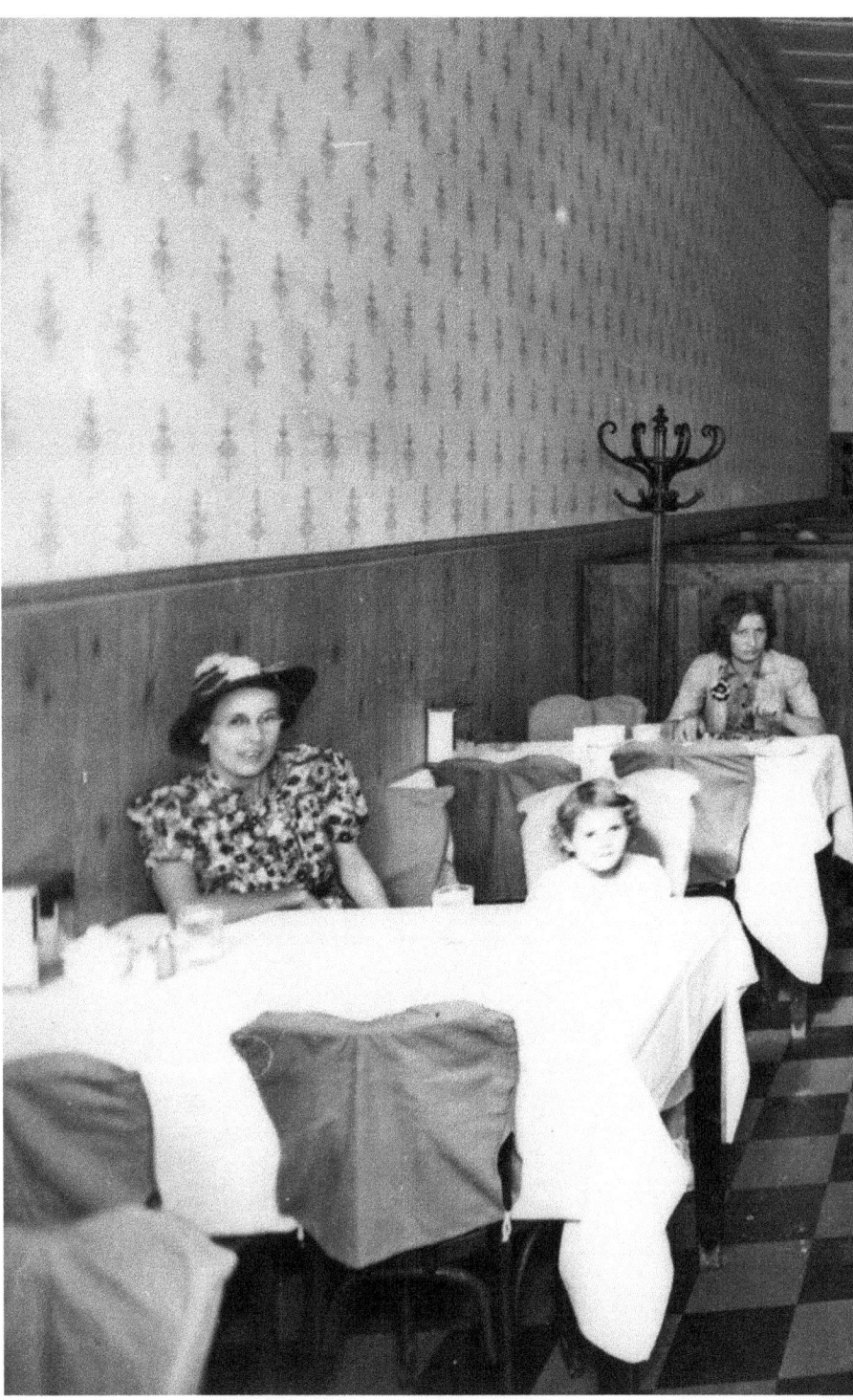

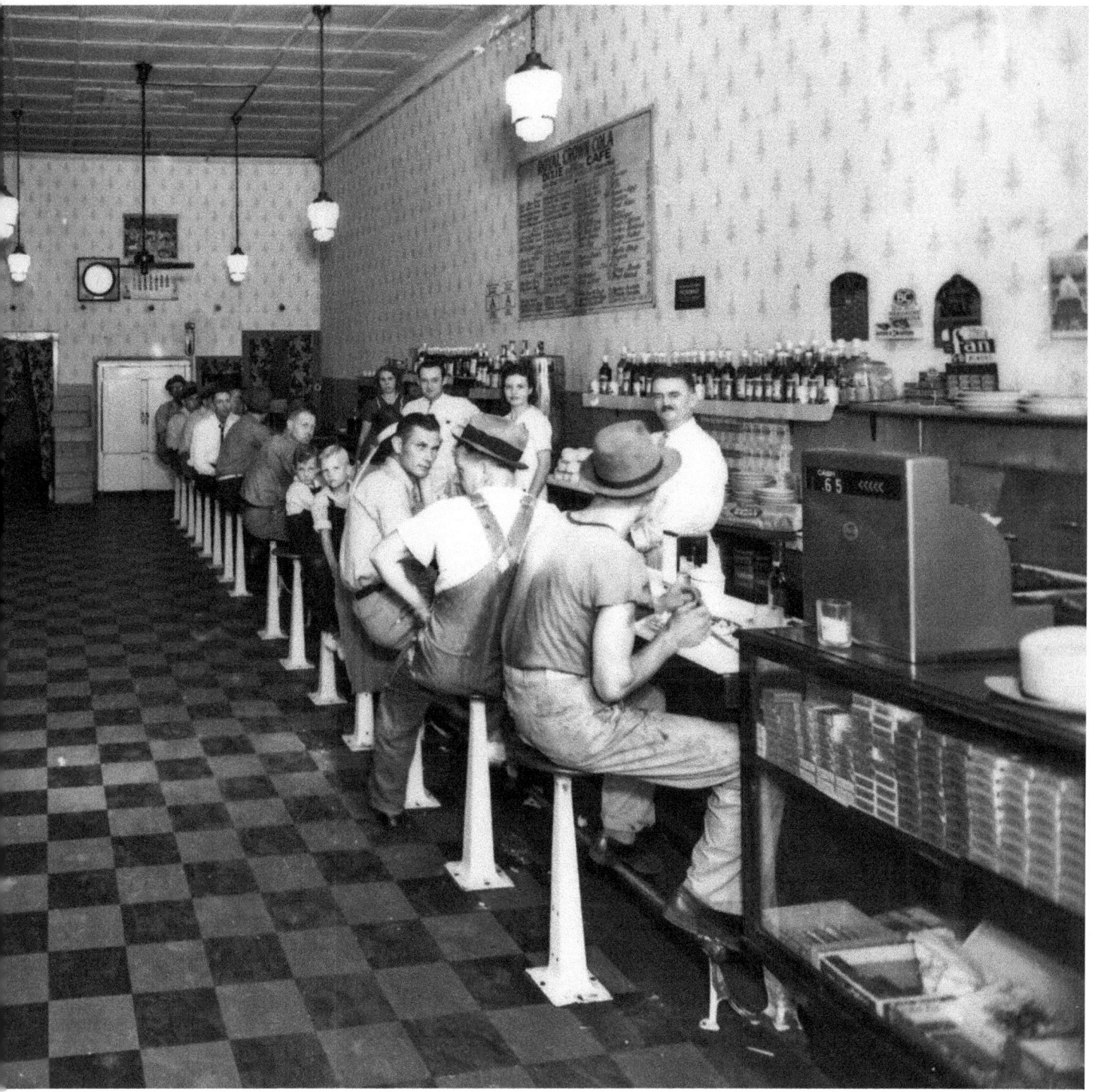

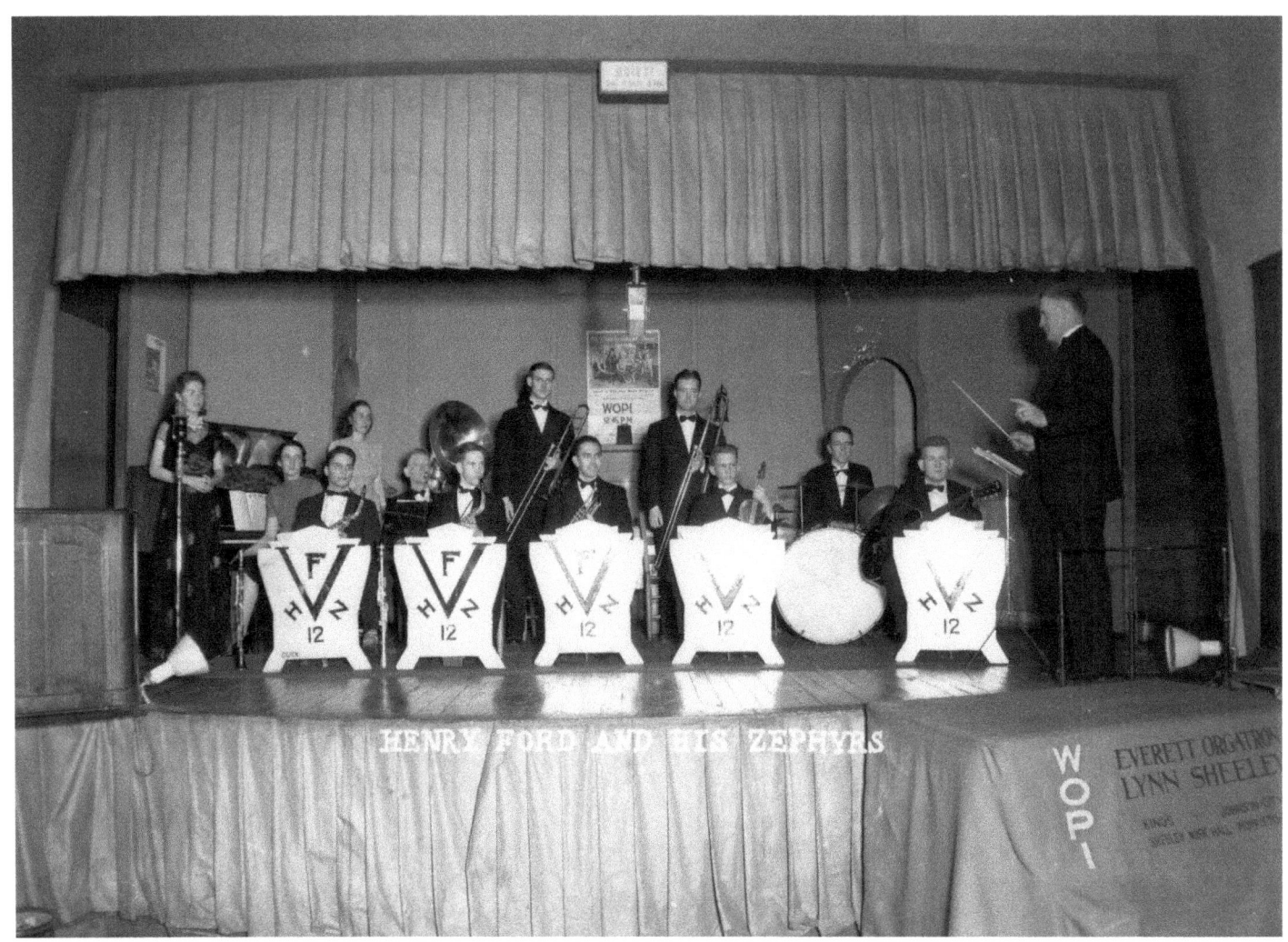

Radio station WOPI first began broadcasting in 1929 from a combined studio and transmitter site at State and 22nd streets in Bristol, Tennessee. At the time, it was the only radio station between Roanoke, Virginia, and Knoxville, Tennessee. Musicians performed live for broadcast. Pictured here are Henry Ford and His Zephyrs, poised to perform.

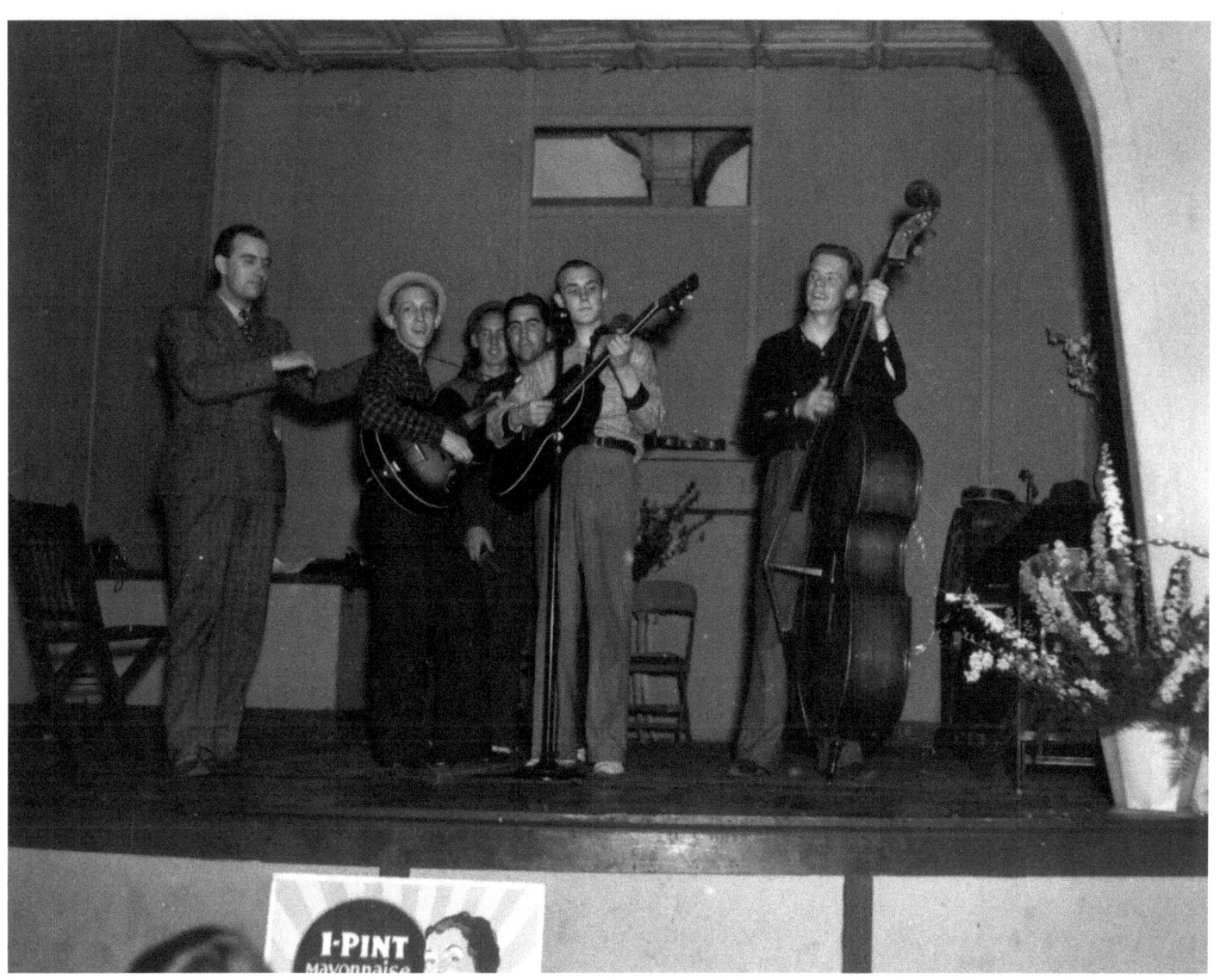

A group performs live on the radio at WOPI in Bristol on May 3, 1938. Bristol still bills itself as the "birthplace of country music." In 1927, Ralph Peer, a producer for the Victor recording label, went to Bristol and held a series of recording sessions which have subsequently been dubbed "the Big Bang of country music." Out of those sessions came the first commercial recordings of Jimmie Rodgers, the Carter Family, and others.

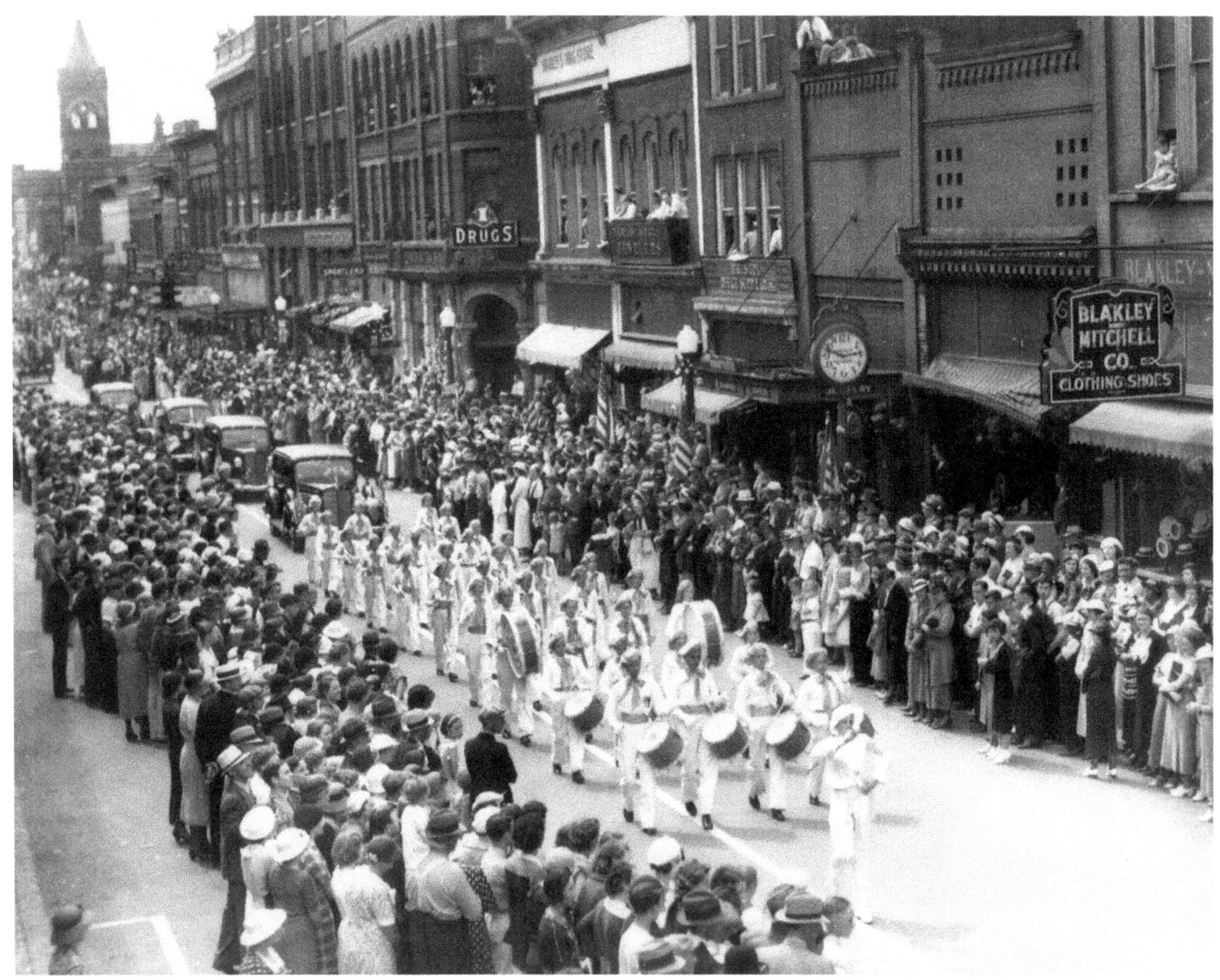

Americans in every region of the nation have always loved a parade. This lively parade marches along State Street, in Bristol, in the 1930s.

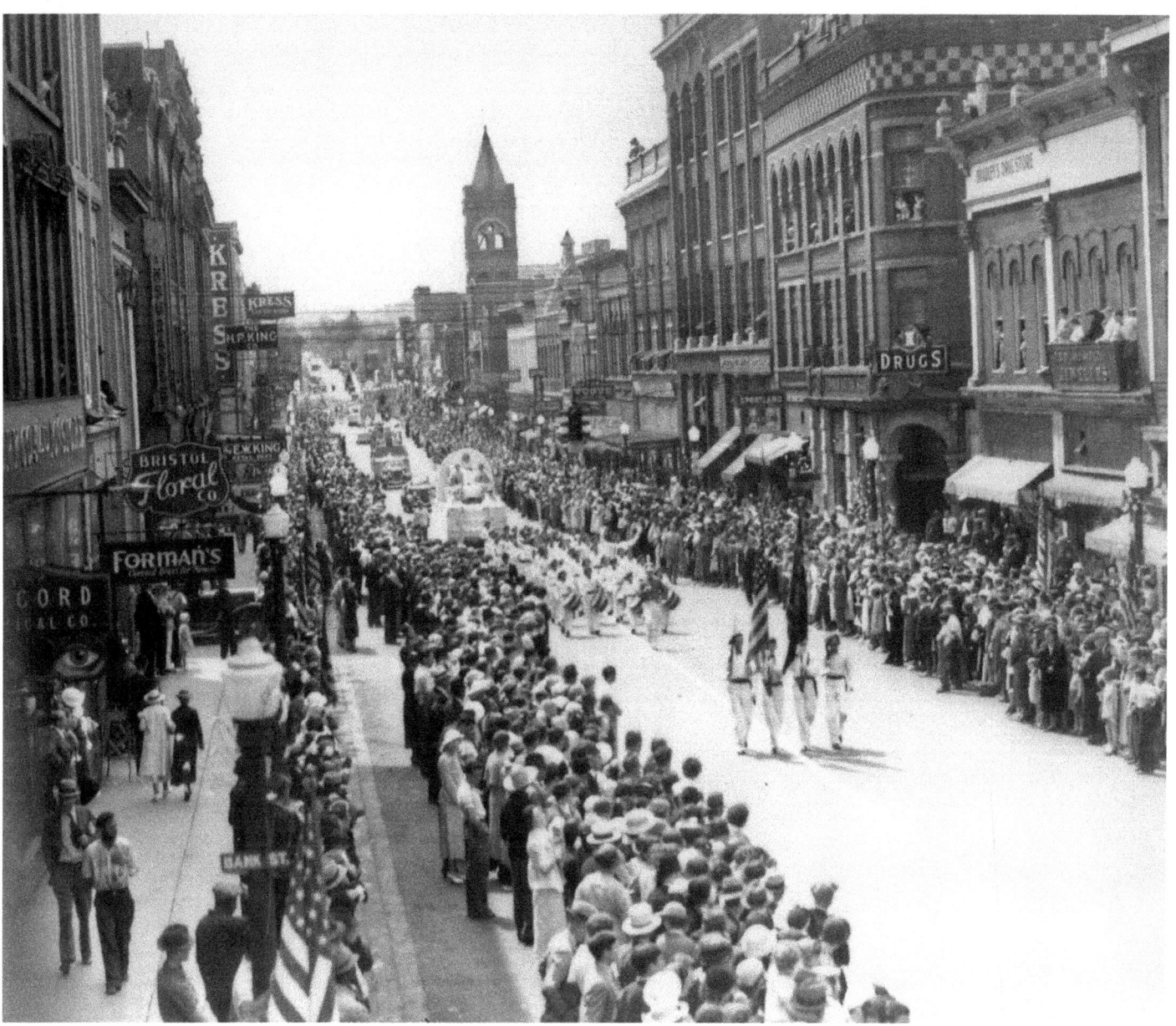

The parade marches on. Local businesses often used parades as a means of advertising. Among the merchants in view here are the Bristol Floral Company, Forman's Correct Dress for Women, and the Kress 5-10-and-25-cent store, a chain of five and dimes popular across the nation and noted for its distinctive storefront architecture.

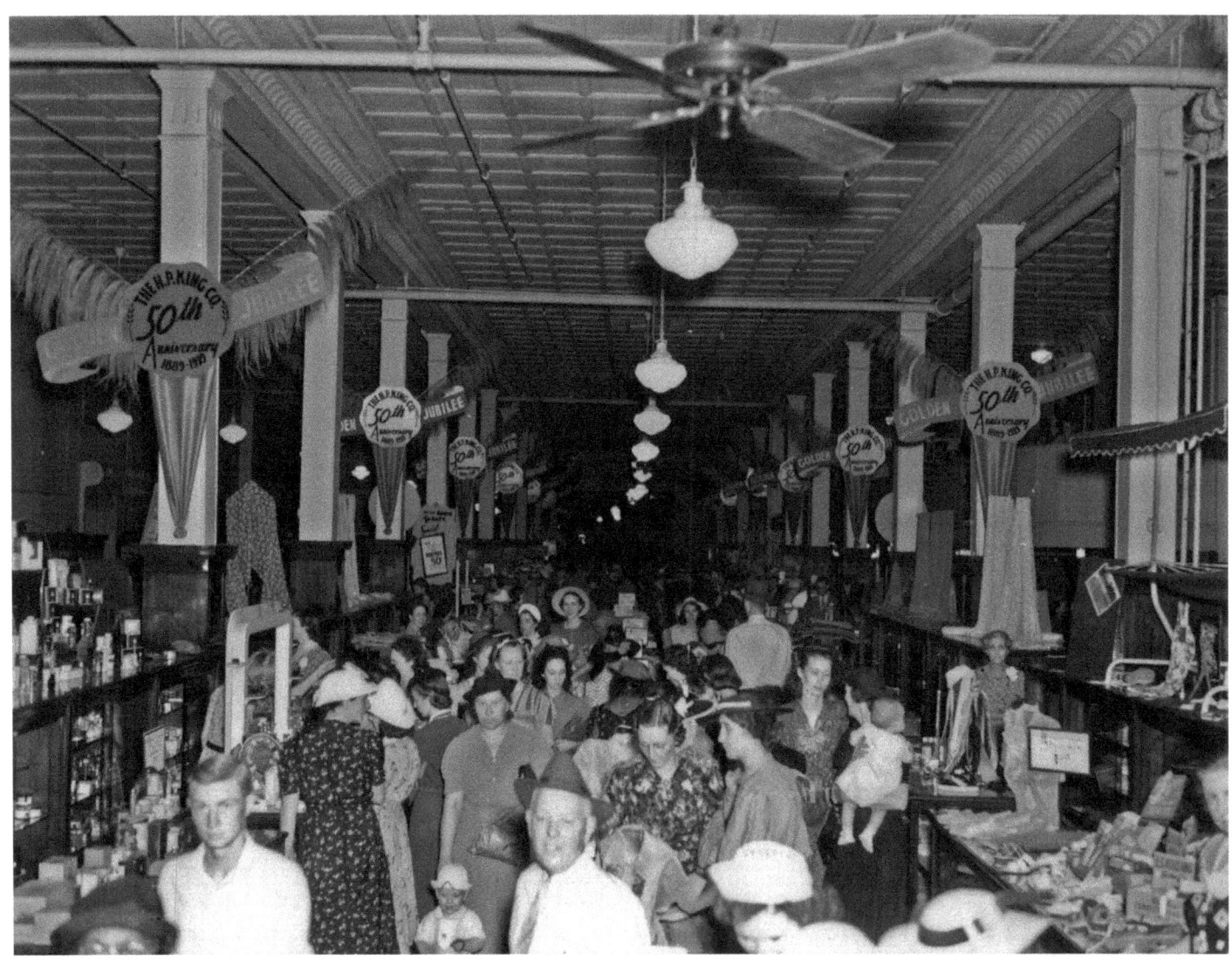

Shoppers crowd the H. P. King Company department store in 1939 on the occasion of its 50th anniversary, in Bristol, Tennessee. The store had multiple locations in the region over the years, and at one time accepted scrip from coal mining companies, in lieu of cash.

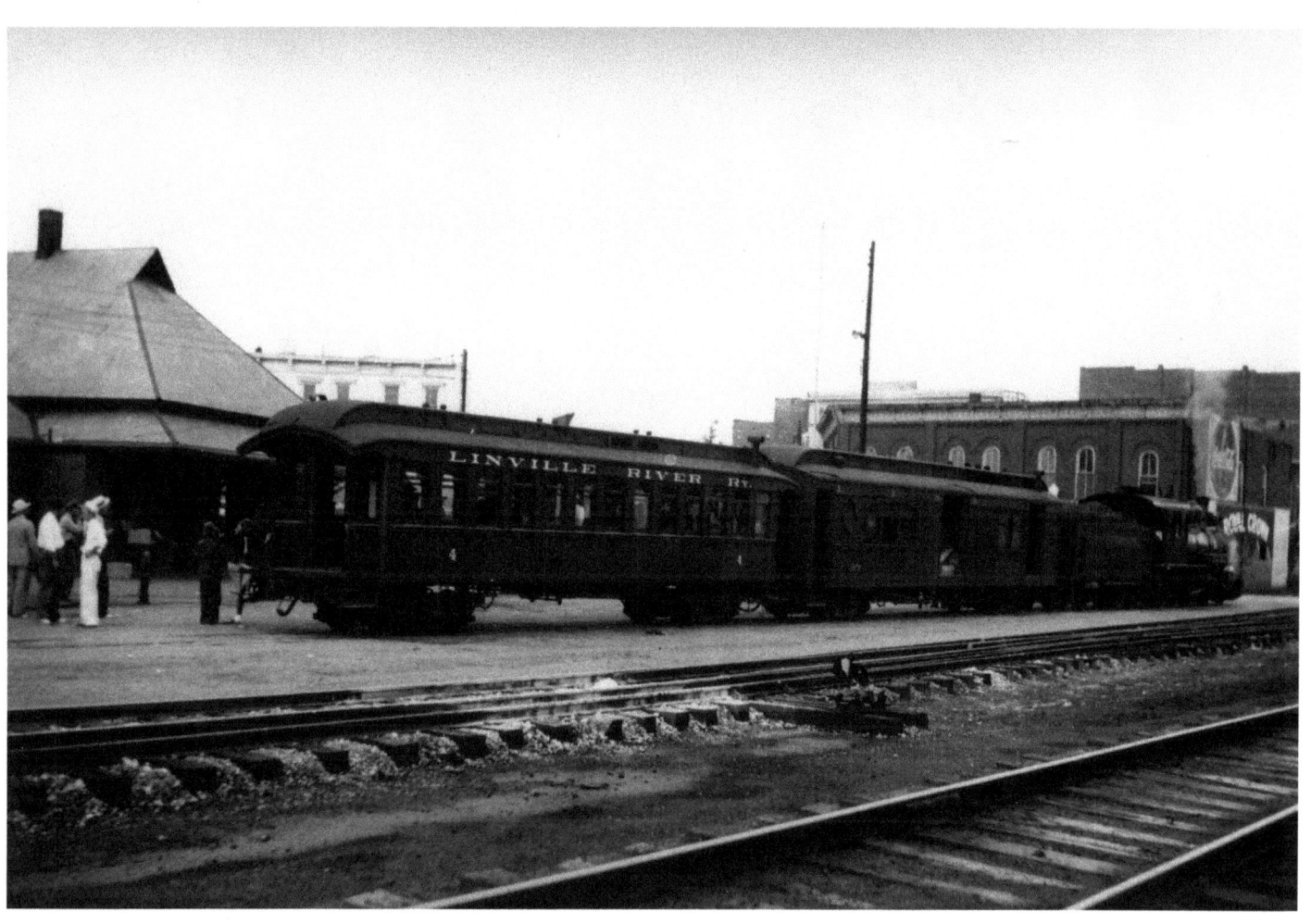

A passenger train for the Linville River Railway waits on the track in the 1930s. The railroad was formed to transport timber from the region around Pineola, North Carolina. By the time this photograph was taken, the railroad's heyday was over. Most of the timber in the region was cut, and the railroad was being used more for passenger service and excursions than for freight. These cars and the engine exemplify designs in service in the late nineteenth century and had evidently weathered many decades on the rails.

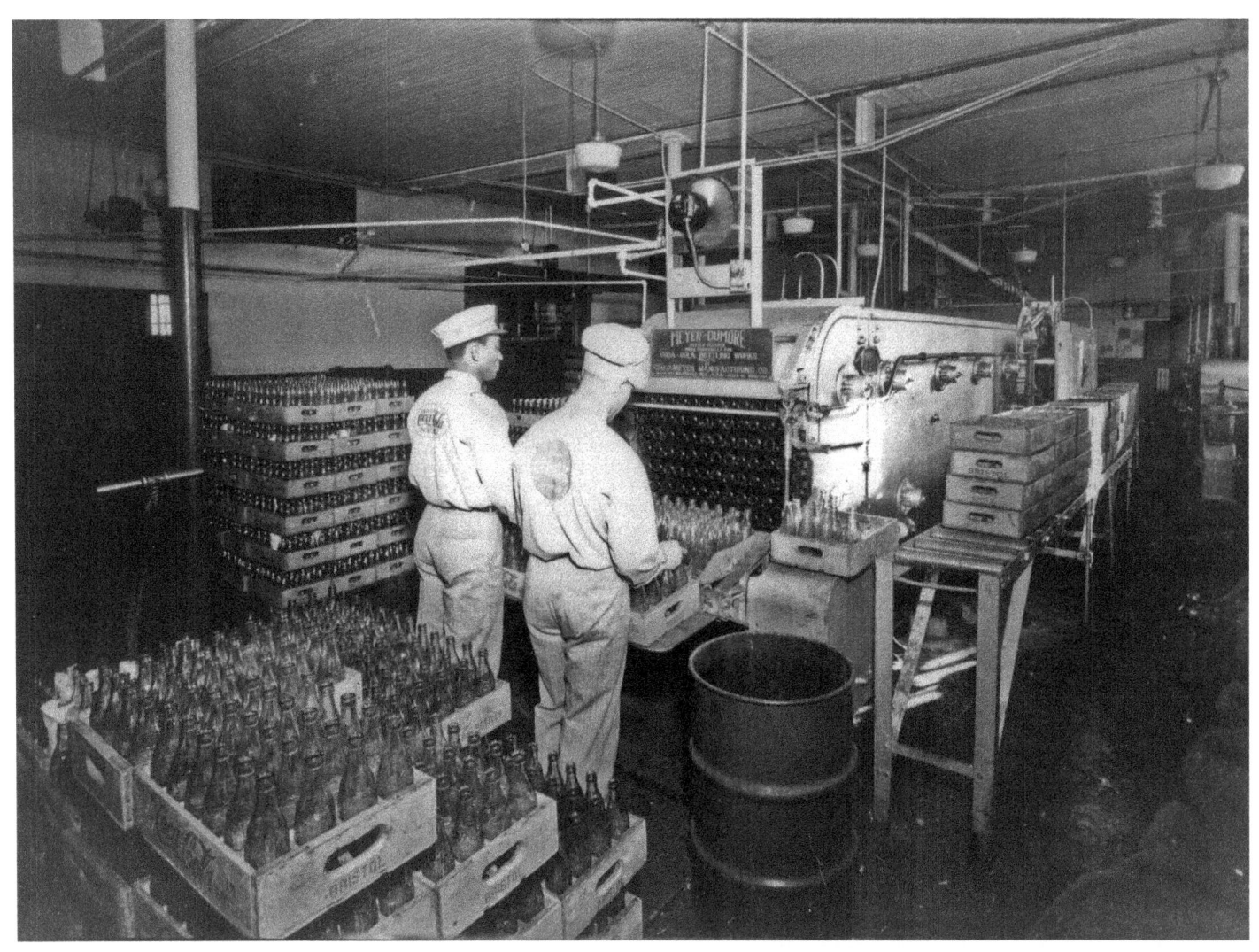

Dixie Bottling Works, located at the corner of Lee and Sycamore streets in Bristol, Virginia, is a busy place here in 1939. For many decades, soft drinks were available in glass bottles only, which were cleaned for reuse in machines like this one. Deliverymen transported Coca-Cola, bottled at the plant, to drugstores where it was sold. Before 1914, the works were at the corner of Washington and Buford streets. Around the turn of the century, before it had a contract with Coca-Cola, the old plant bottled ginger ale, vinegar, soda water, mineral water, and beer.

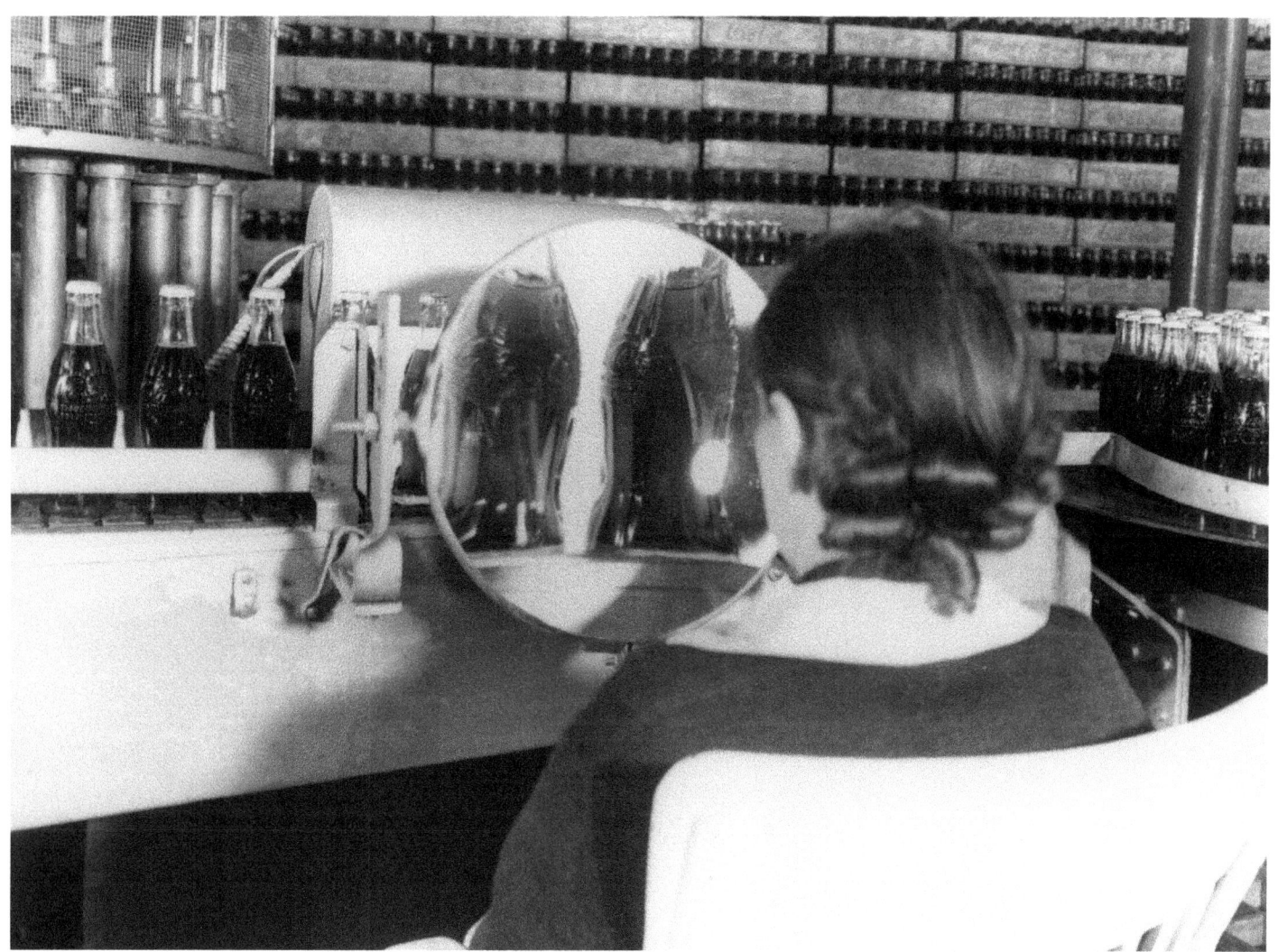

An inspector for quality control scrutinizes the bottling line at the Dixie Bottling Works in Bristol. Years later, in 1950, a new plant would be built on West State Street.

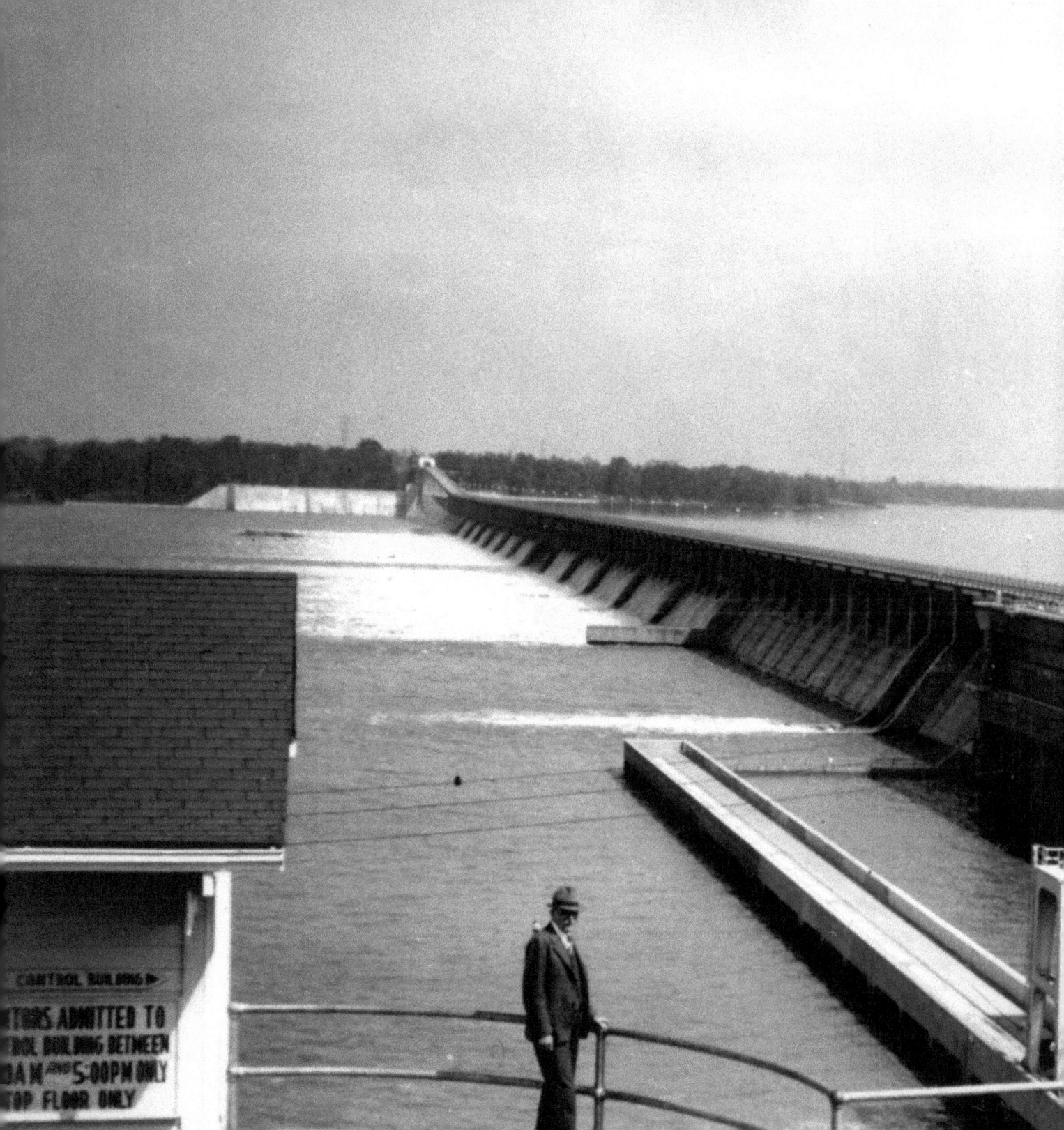

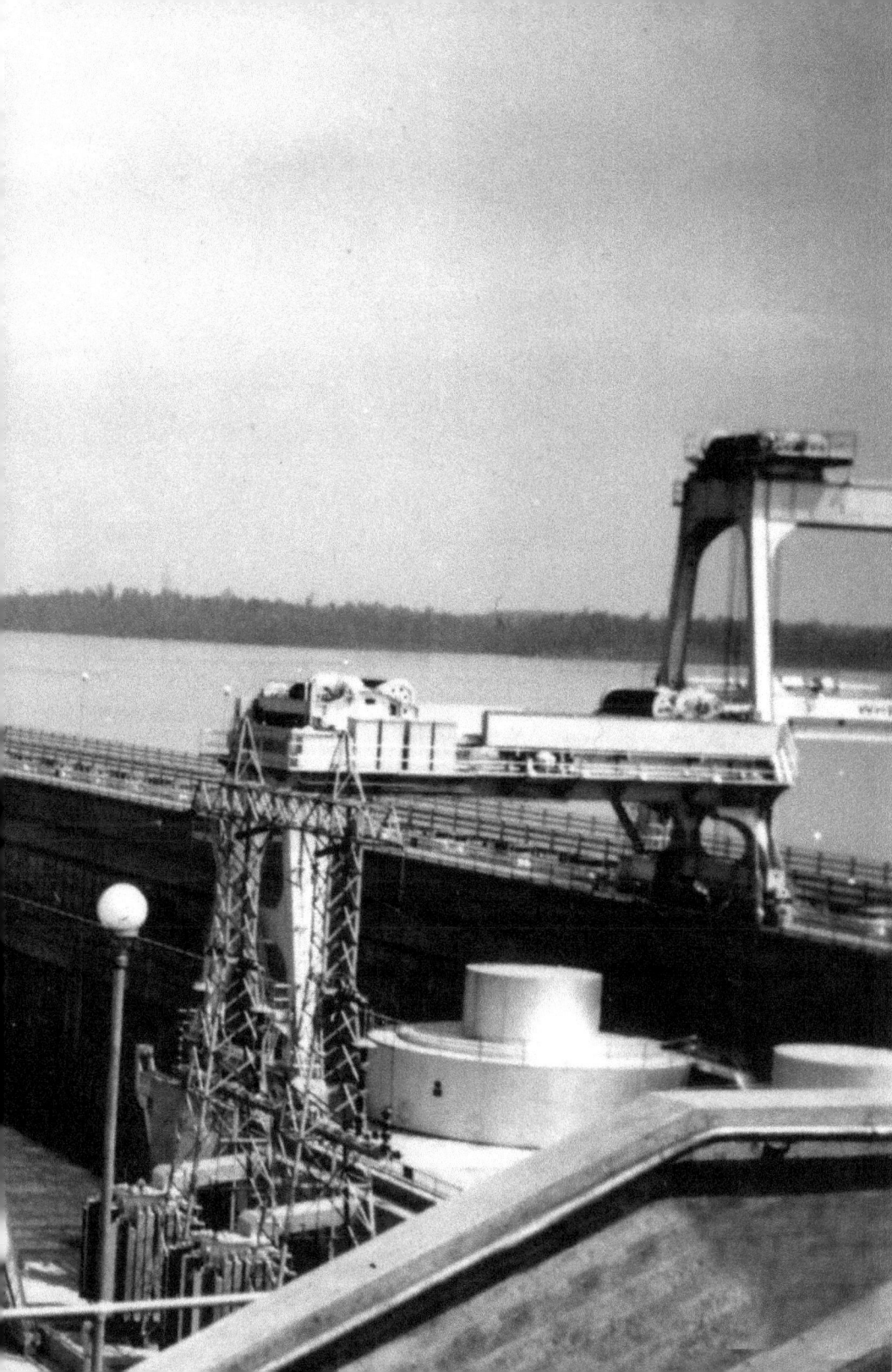

Wheeler Dam, on the Tennessee River, in Lauderdale County, Alabama, is one of nine hydroelectric dams operated on the river by the Tennessee Valley Authority. The Authority was established in the 1930s as a "New Deal" initiative, to provide flood control and hydroelectric power, and to improve navigation on the river. The photo shows Wheeler Lock in the foreground as it appeared in April 1938.

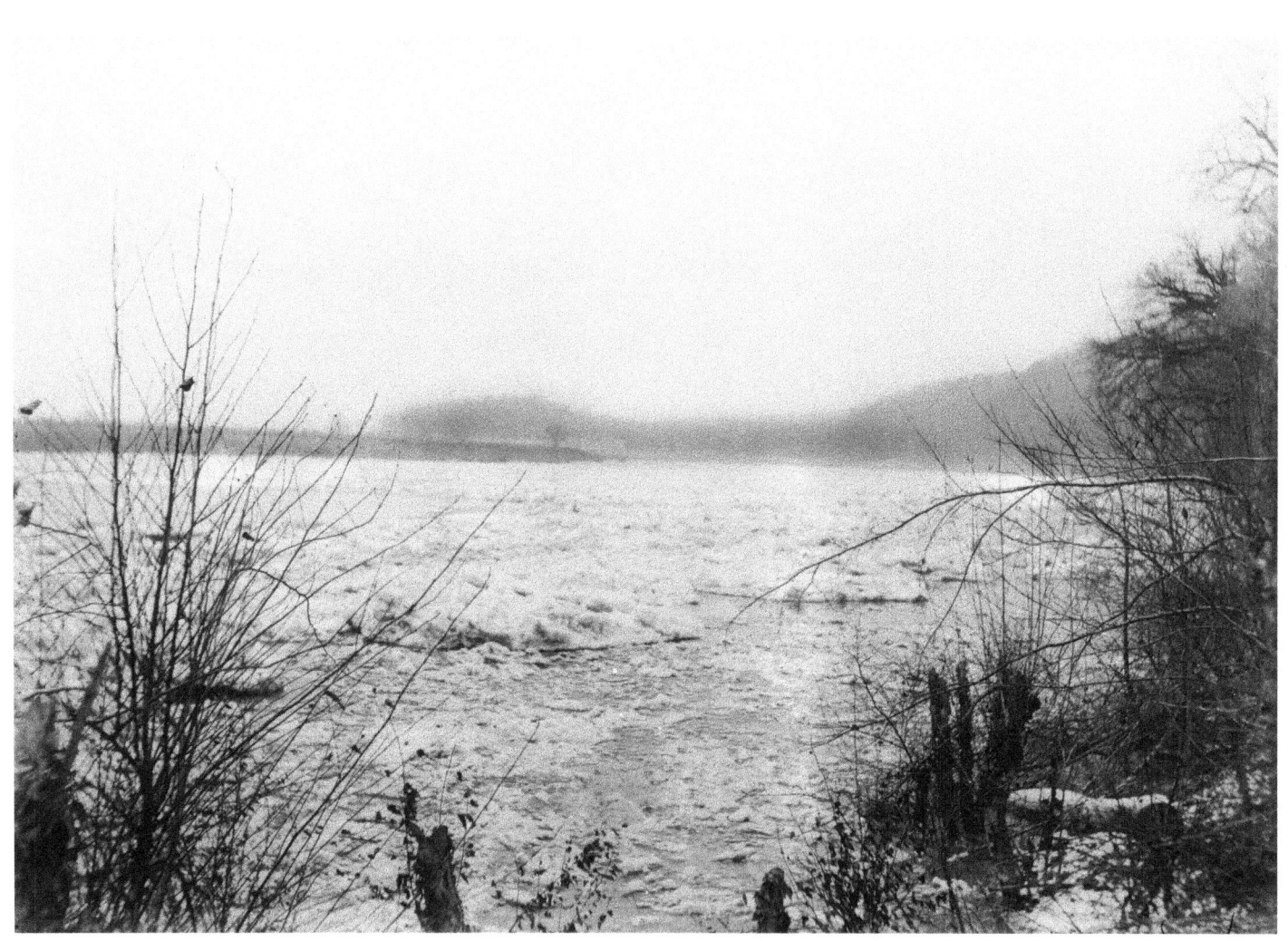

In 1916, portions of southern Appalachia experienced severe flooding, from early spring into midsummer. The flooding hit Ashe County, North Carolina, where this photograph was taken, especially hard. Ashe County, in the upper western portion of the state, was sometimes known as the "Lost Province," because of its bad roads and isolation. The flooding severely damaged the tracks of the Watauga and Yadkin River Railway, which was built to haul timber out of the county.

HIGHWAYS, REVIVALISM, AND COAL-COUNTRY POVERTY

(1940–1970)

With World War II and its aftermath came increased economic development, including the steady improvement of the U.S. Highway system and, later, the development of the Eisenhower National System of Interstate and Defense Highways, as the Interstate highway system was officially known. Likewise, improved designs and wider availability of automobiles in the years after the war changed the character of Appalachia.

Yet even as luxury hotels and automobile destination resorts sprang up, and as the old ways slipped into the past, there was, paradoxically, a growing interest in preserving or reviving the folk culture of the region. The folk music revival movement in America, which began in the 1940s and hit full steam in the 1960s, led to growing interest in Appalachian musical traditions that had been preserved in the mountains. Likewise, the back-to-the-land movement of the 1960s led more Americans to value scenic, rural Appalachia, and the traditions preserved there: small-scale farming, the making of apple butter and molasses, and even moonshining. Ways that had once been belittled as backward came to be cherished.

Meanwhile, the poverty that persisted in some rugged, isolated areas of Appalachia, especially in the coal regions of West Virginia and eastern Kentucky, drew national attention. In 1964, President Lyndon B. Johnson announced a set of federal initiatives called the "War on Poverty," to address persistent poverty in certain regions of the United States, including Appalachia. In February 1968, not long before announcing his candidacy for the presidency and four months before he was assassinated, Robert F. Kennedy visited eastern Kentucky for three days, in order to assess how well that war was going. Kennedy concluded that hunger and poverty remained serious problems.

Residents of Appalachian coal communities are sometimes offended by images of regional poverty. "Where are the pictures of the clean, well-parented children?" they ask. Not every child in the coal camps has subsisted on welfare, of course. And images of Appalachian poverty can lead to careless stereotyping. Nevertheless, coal country poverty remains as real today as it was in the late 1960s, when the more recent of these images was recorded.

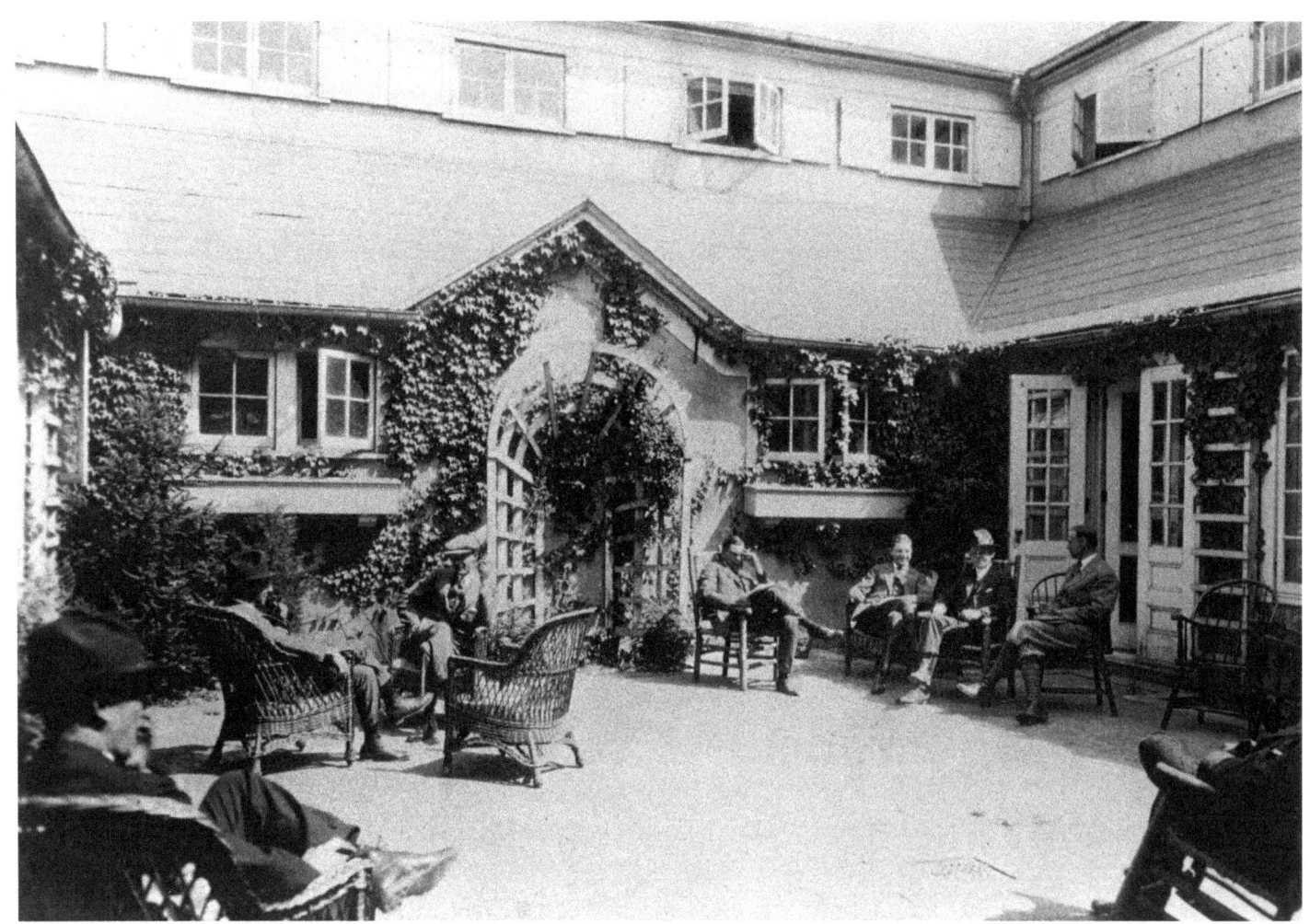

Visitors relax in the courtyard of the Old Kingsport Inn, in downtown Kingsport, Tennessee, on Broad Street, near Church Circle. The inn opened in the spring of 1917 and became known as a stopping place for travelers between New York or Chicago and points south. By the 1940s it had fallen into disrepair, and it was razed around 1960.

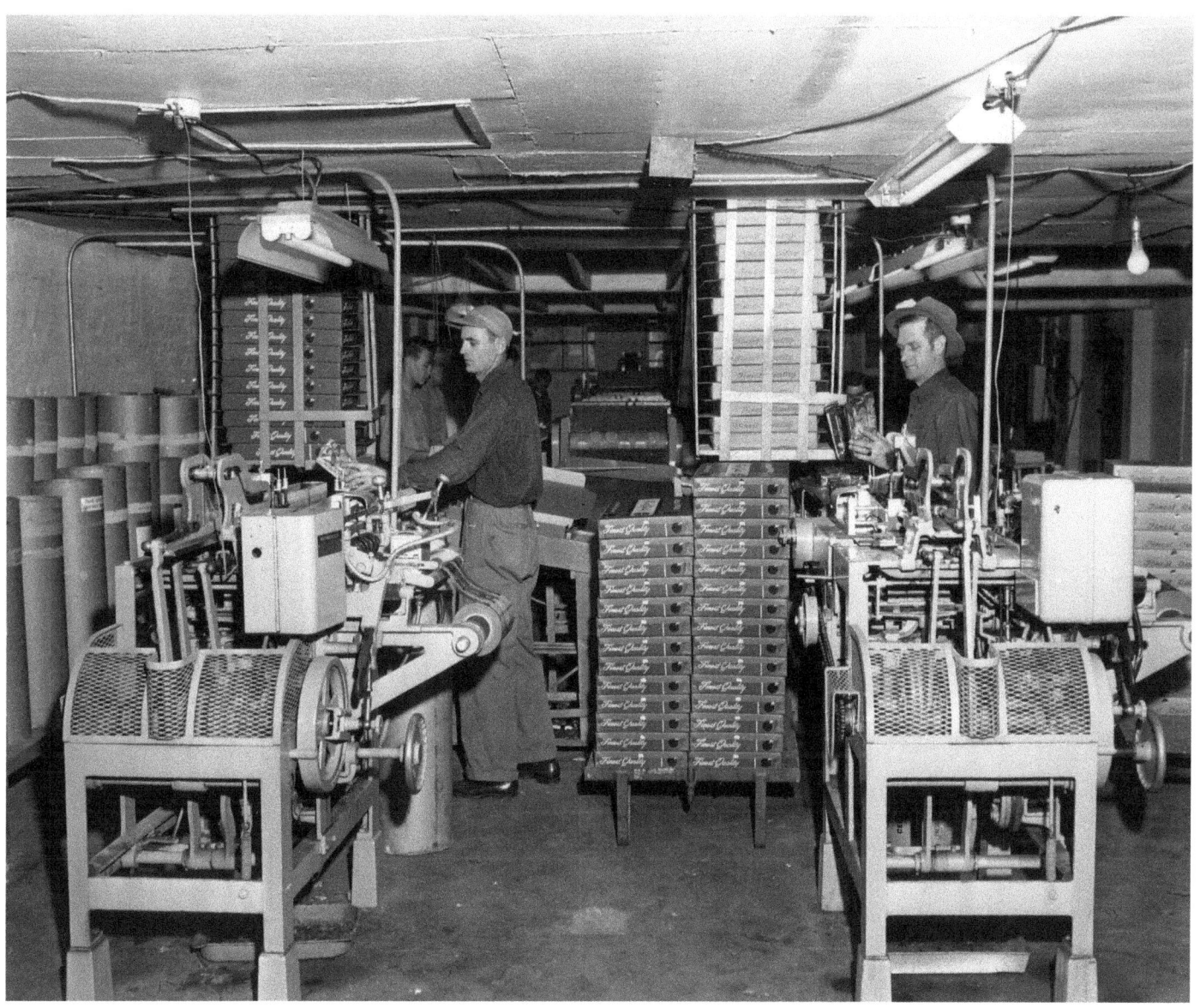

Work is in progress at Hicks Produce Company, in Johnson City, Tennessee, in the 1940s. Earl Hicks ran the company as a "repack operation," buying tomatoes in California, trucking them to Appalachia, and sorting and packing them for sale to local grocery stores and stands. The operation shut down every year between July 4 and September 15, when locally grown tomatoes were available.

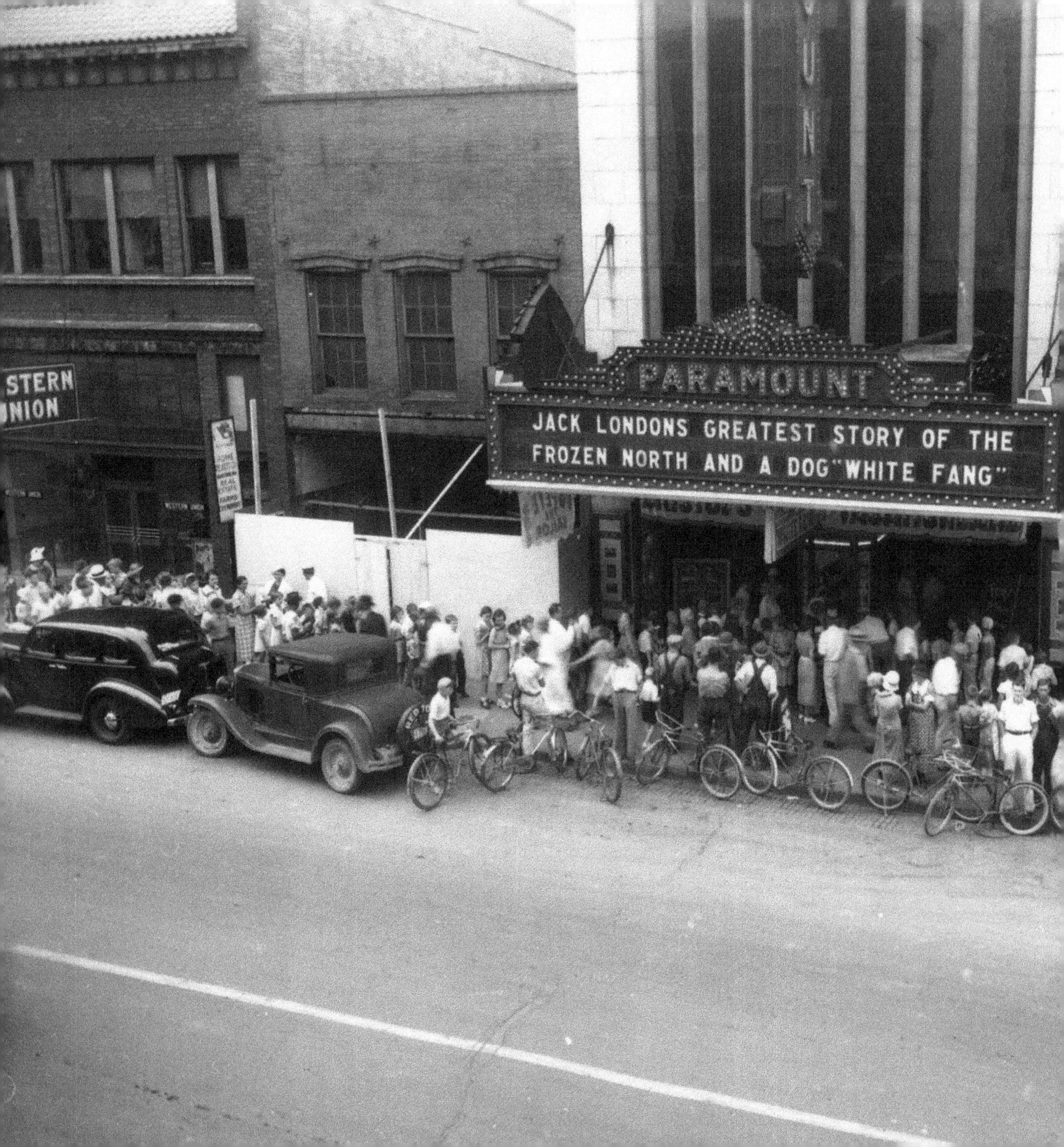
PARAMOUNT
JACK LONDONS GREATEST STORY OF THE
FROZEN NORTH AND A DOG "WHITE FANG"

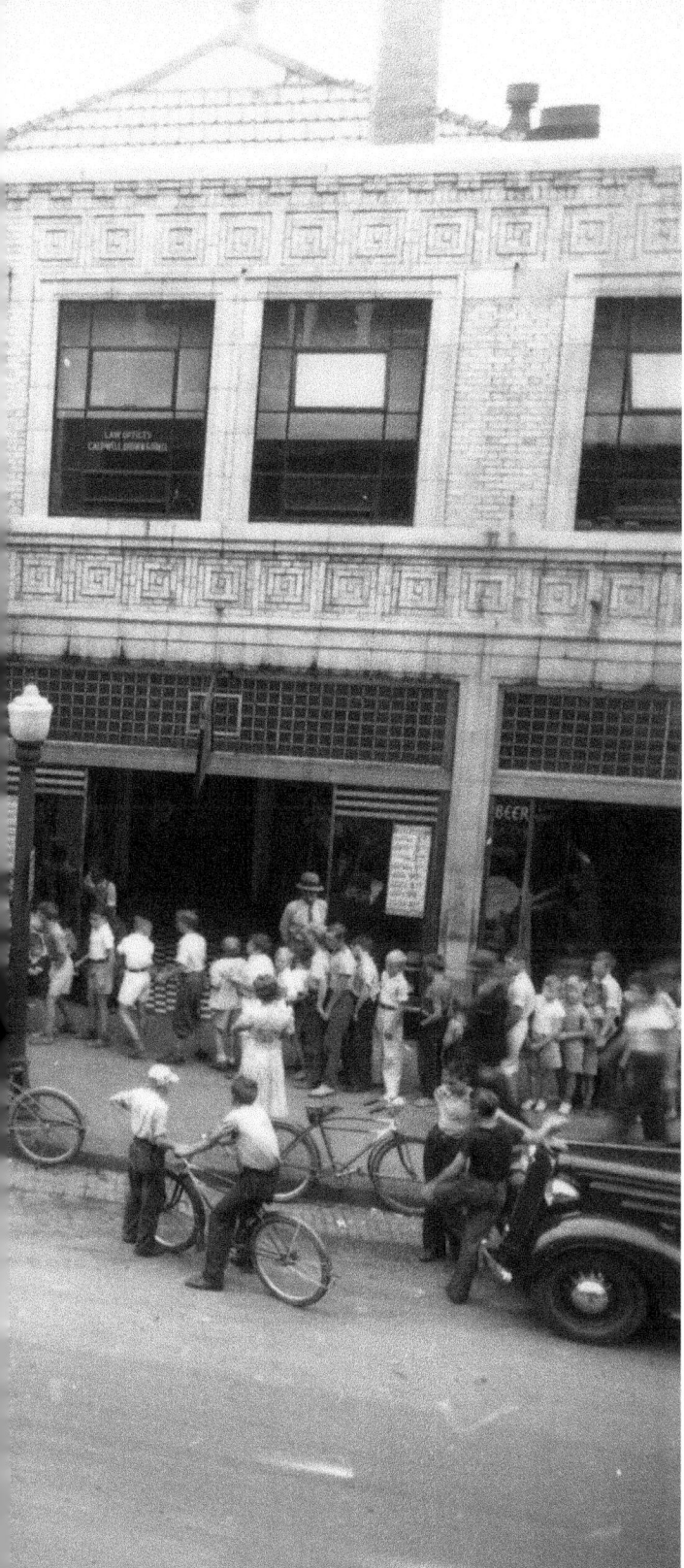

The Paramount Theater, on the Tennessee side of State Street in downtown Bristol, is shown here in 1940. The theater was constructed in the midst of the Great Depression and at the time was regarded as one of the finest theaters in the South. The theater was restored in the 1980s. Now called "Paramount Center for the Arts," it hosts a variety of live performance events.

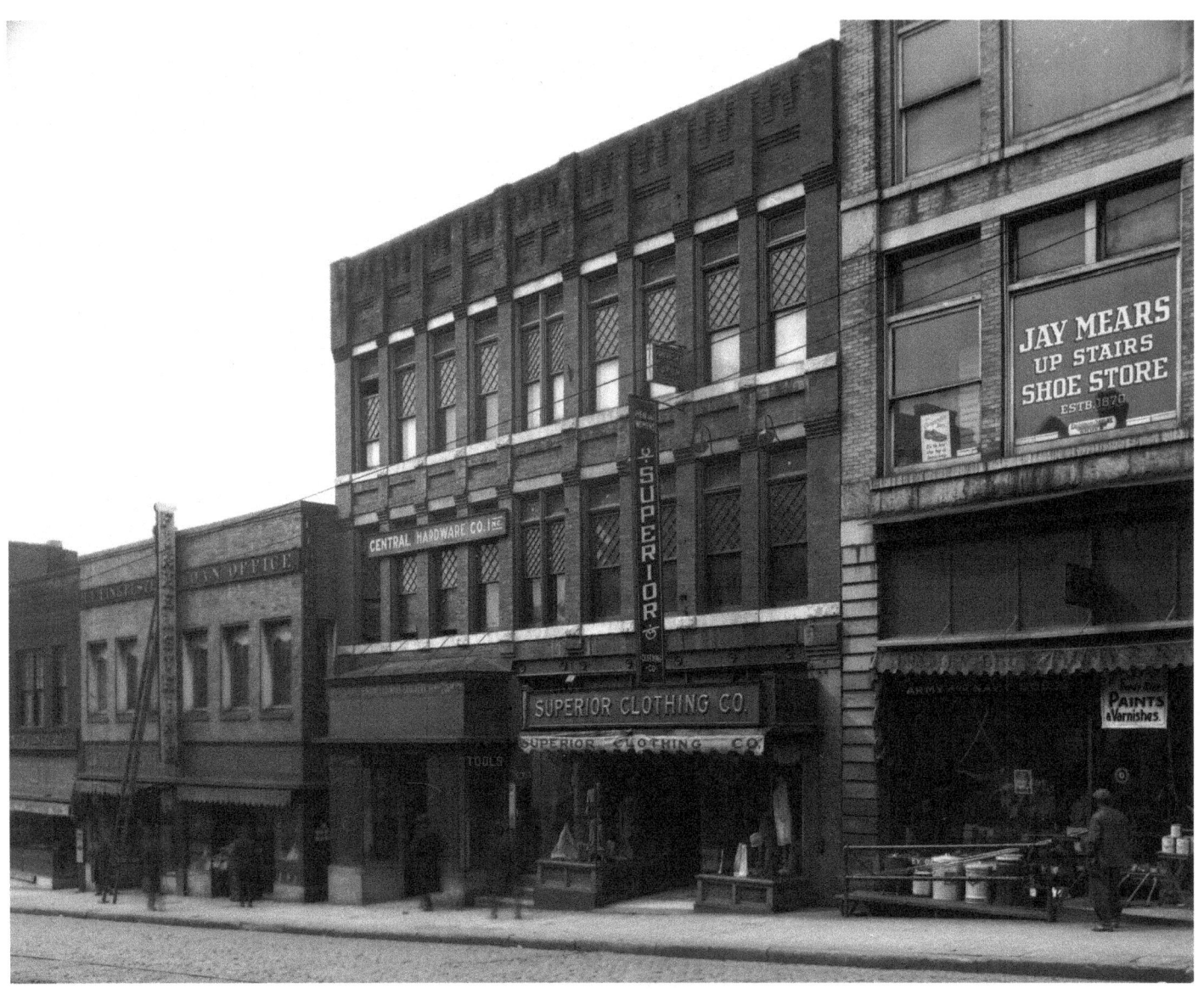

Pack Square, in Asheville, North Carolina, is today on the National Register of Historic Places. This view of the southwest side of the square, recorded in the 1940s, shows buildings erected in the 1890s that still stand today. Perhaps best-known of Asheville's historic places is the Biltmore Estate, just outside the city, built by George W. Vanderbilt in 1895 as a summer retreat and reputedly America's largest mansion.

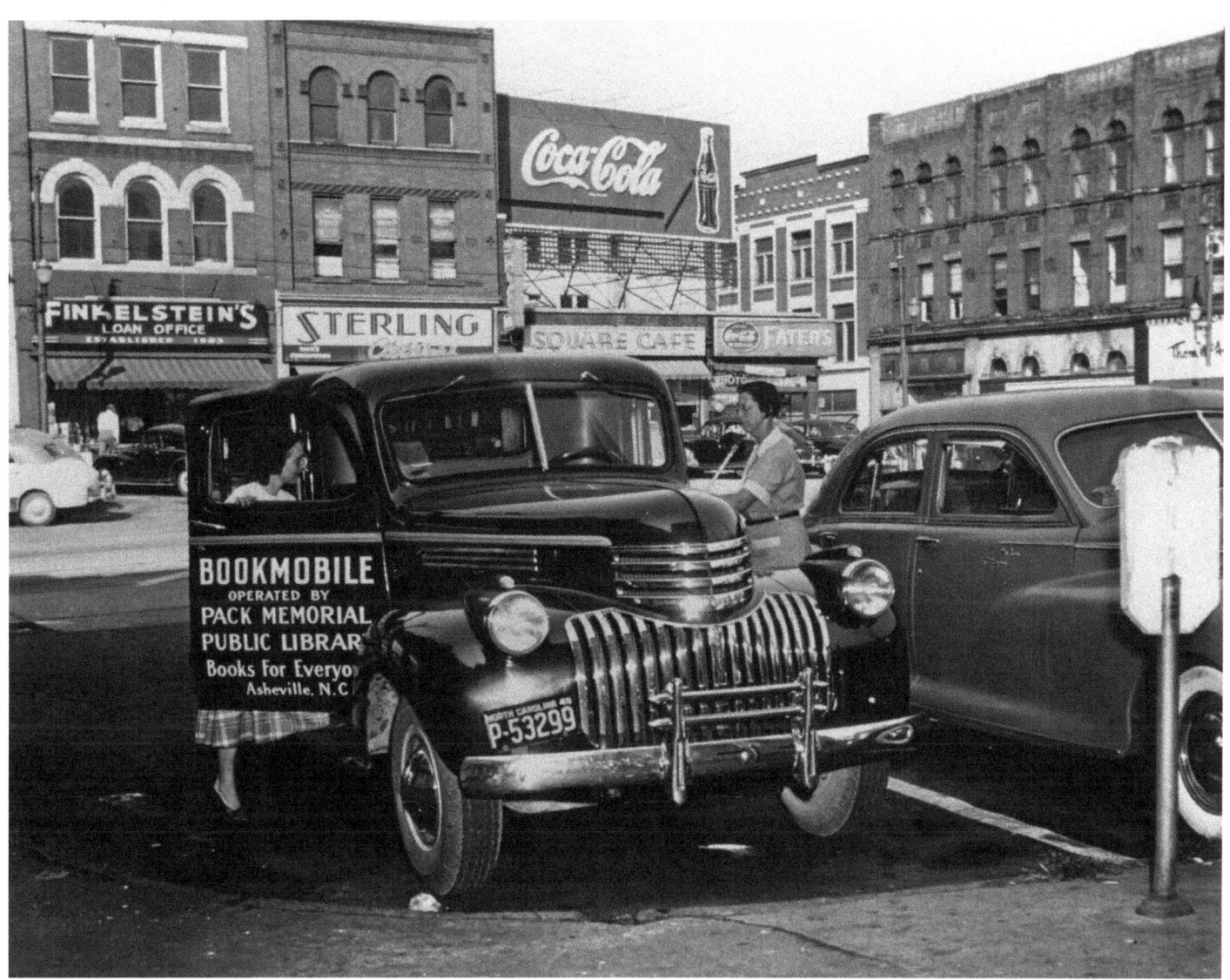

Here in the 1940s, Asheville's Pack Square reveals tidy shops and storefronts and a close-up look at the local bookmobile. This library on wheels could have written a book—on chrome.

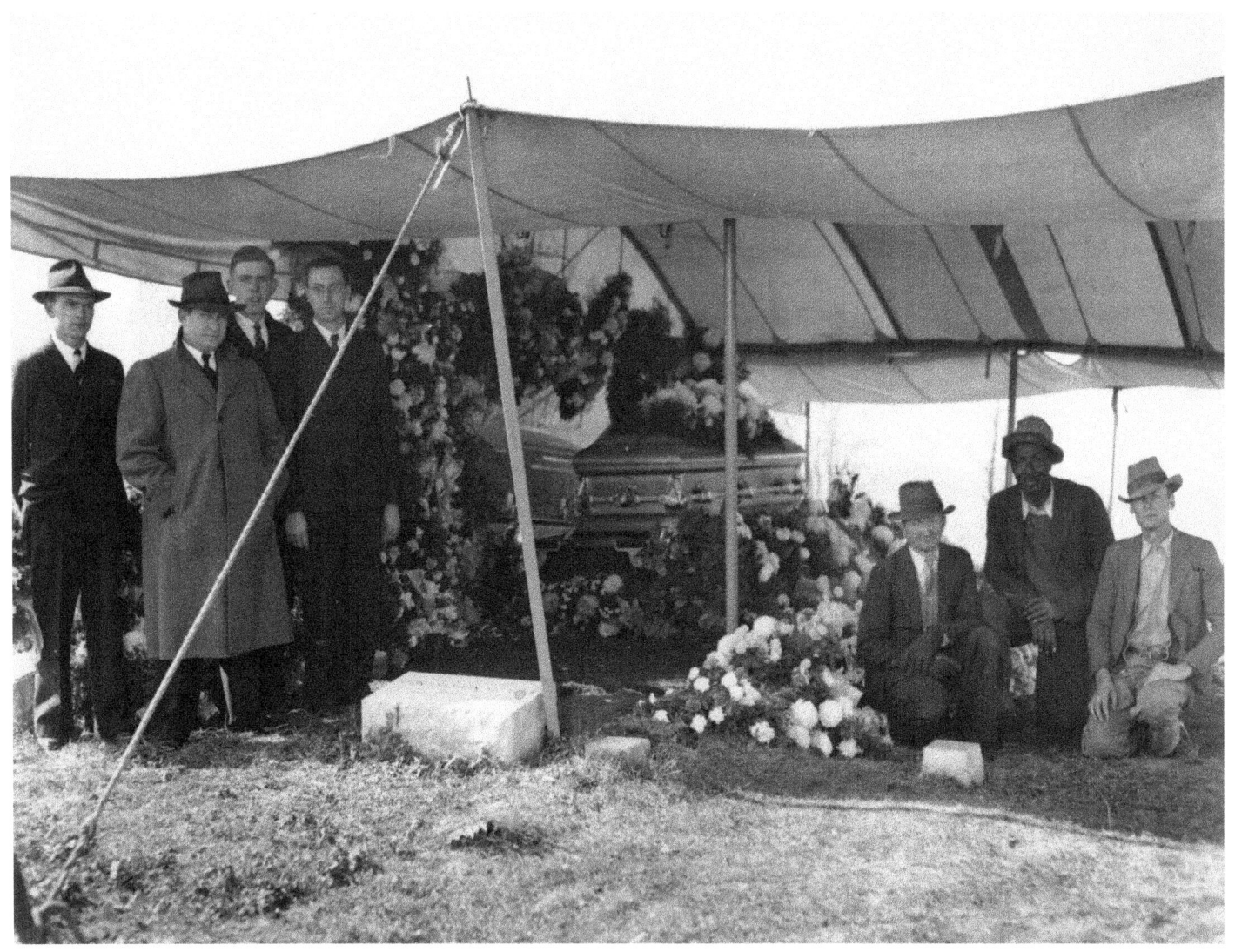

This burial scene is from an archive of photographs depicting Smyth County, Virginia.

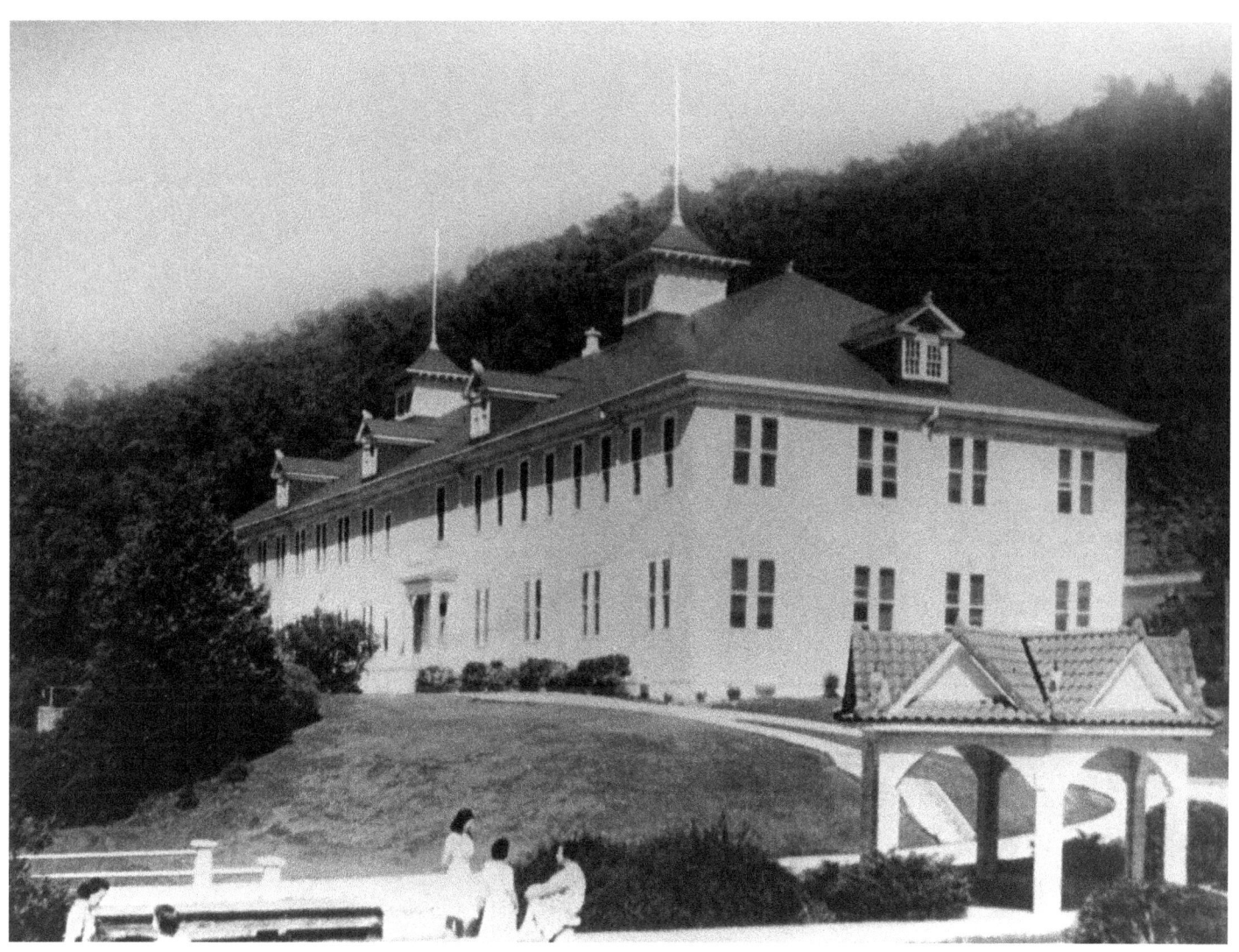

The Pressman's Home—established in 1911 by the International Printing Pressmen and Assistants Union of North America, in Clinch Valley, Hawkins County, Tennessee—included a retirement home and sanitorium, as well as a trade school and headquarters for the union. The facilities also included a hydroelectric power plant. The building in view here housed the first training school and, after 1948, became an administration building.

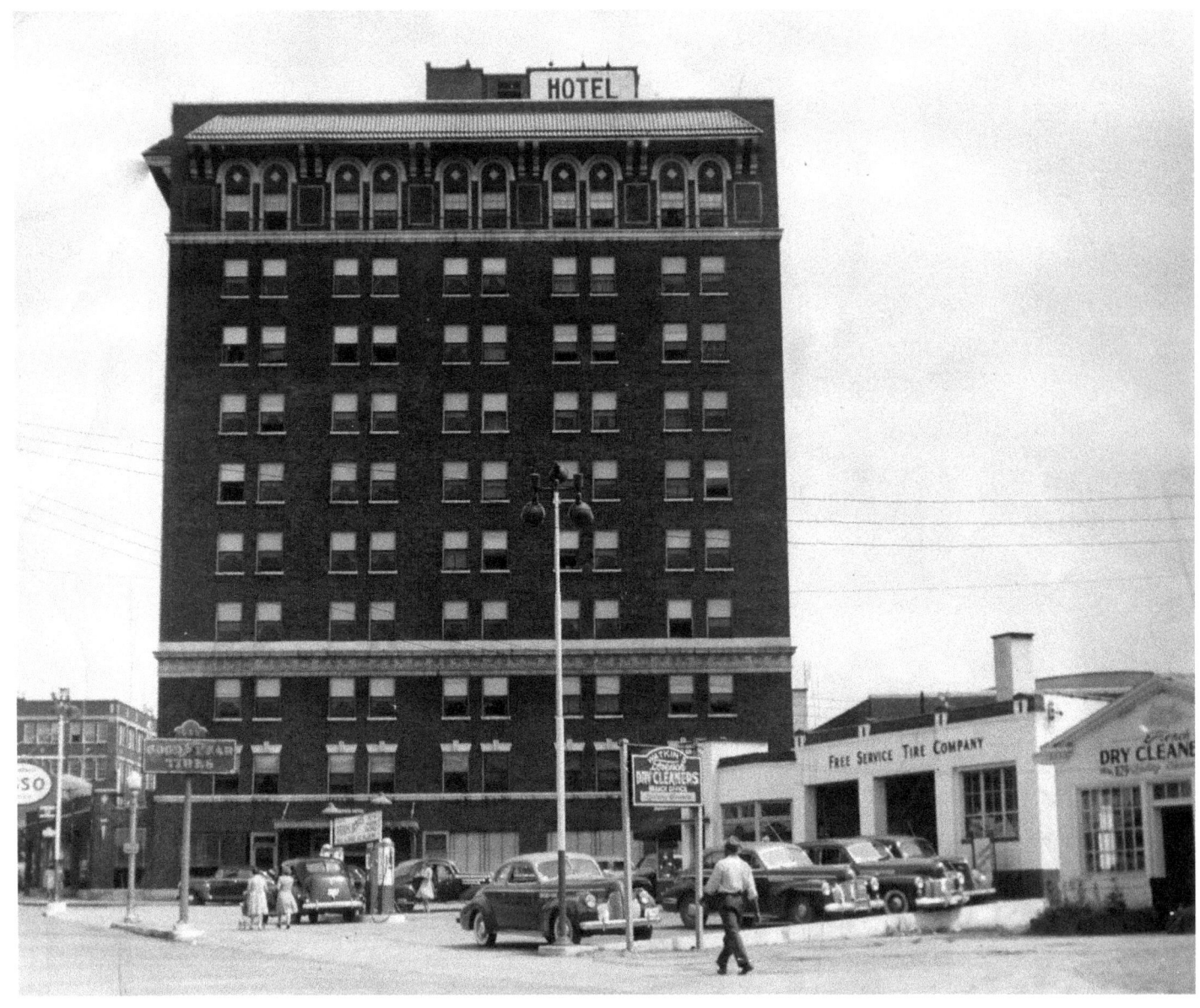

The scene at the John Sevier Hotel, in Johnson City, on a day in the 1940s. The building still stands and is now an apartment complex for lower-income residents.

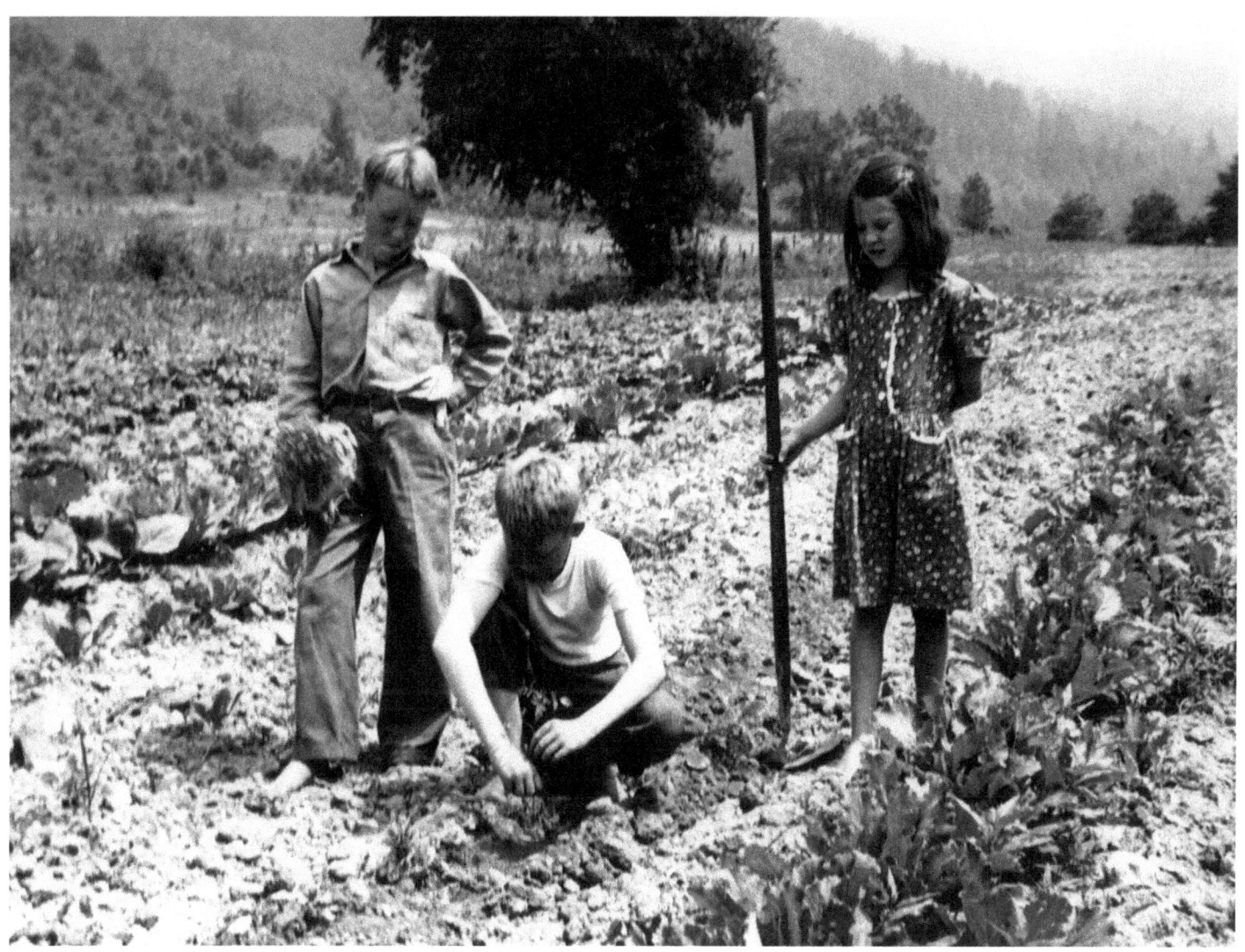

These Appalachian children are tending a Victory garden of mixed vegetables in the summer of 1945. Victory gardens were among the many efforts of citizens on the home front to help win World War II. More food at home meant more food available for the troops fighting overseas.

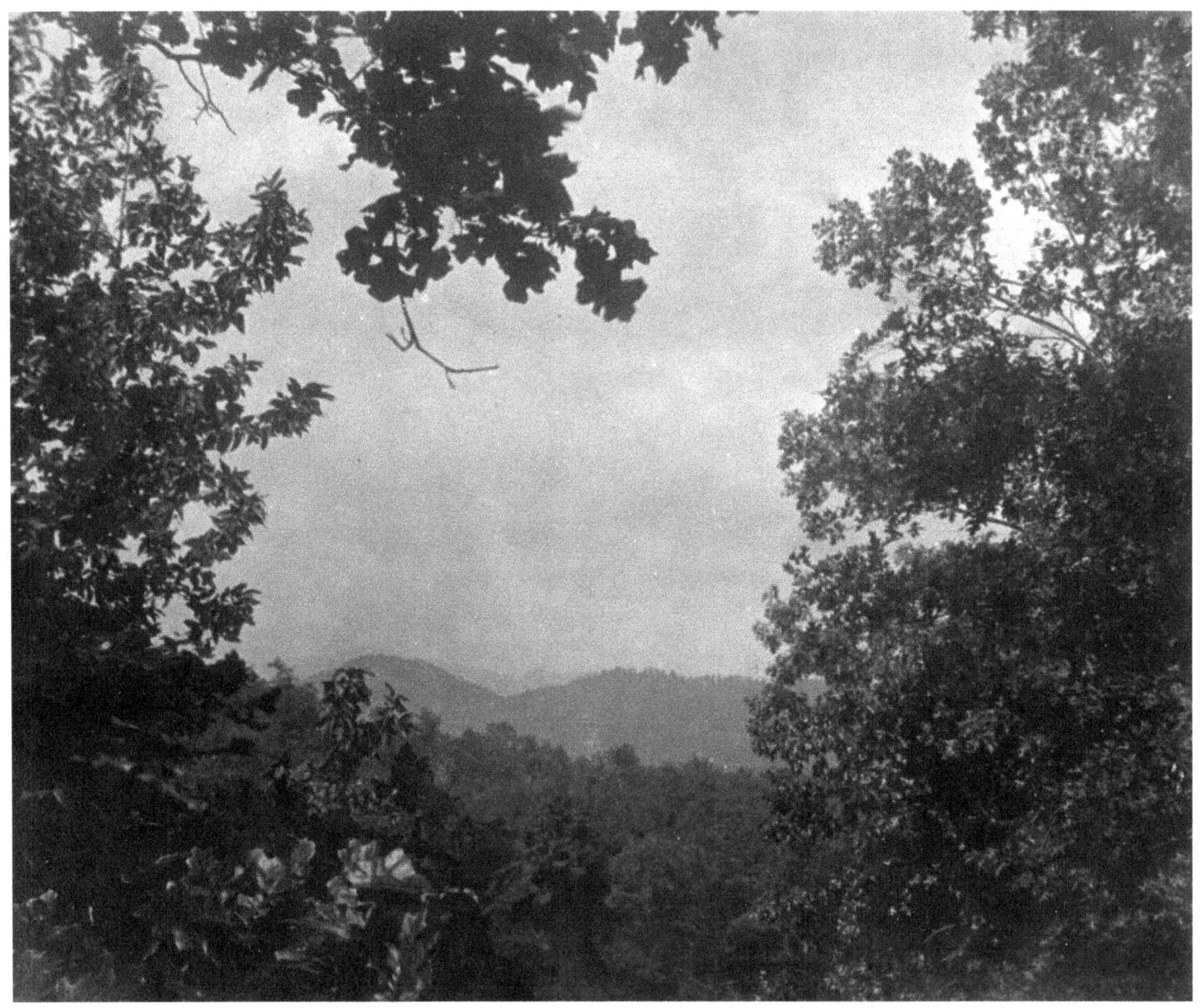

The mountainous regions of Appalachia boast the tallest peaks found anywhere in eastern North America. Among the tallest peaks are North Carolina's Mount Mitchell, at 6,684 feet above sea level, Mount Le Conte, at 6,593 feet, Clingman's Dome, at 6,643 feet, and Mount Guyot, at 6,621 feet above sea level. By other measures, Le Conte is the "tallest," rising 5,301 vertical feet from its base near Gatlinburg, Tennessee.

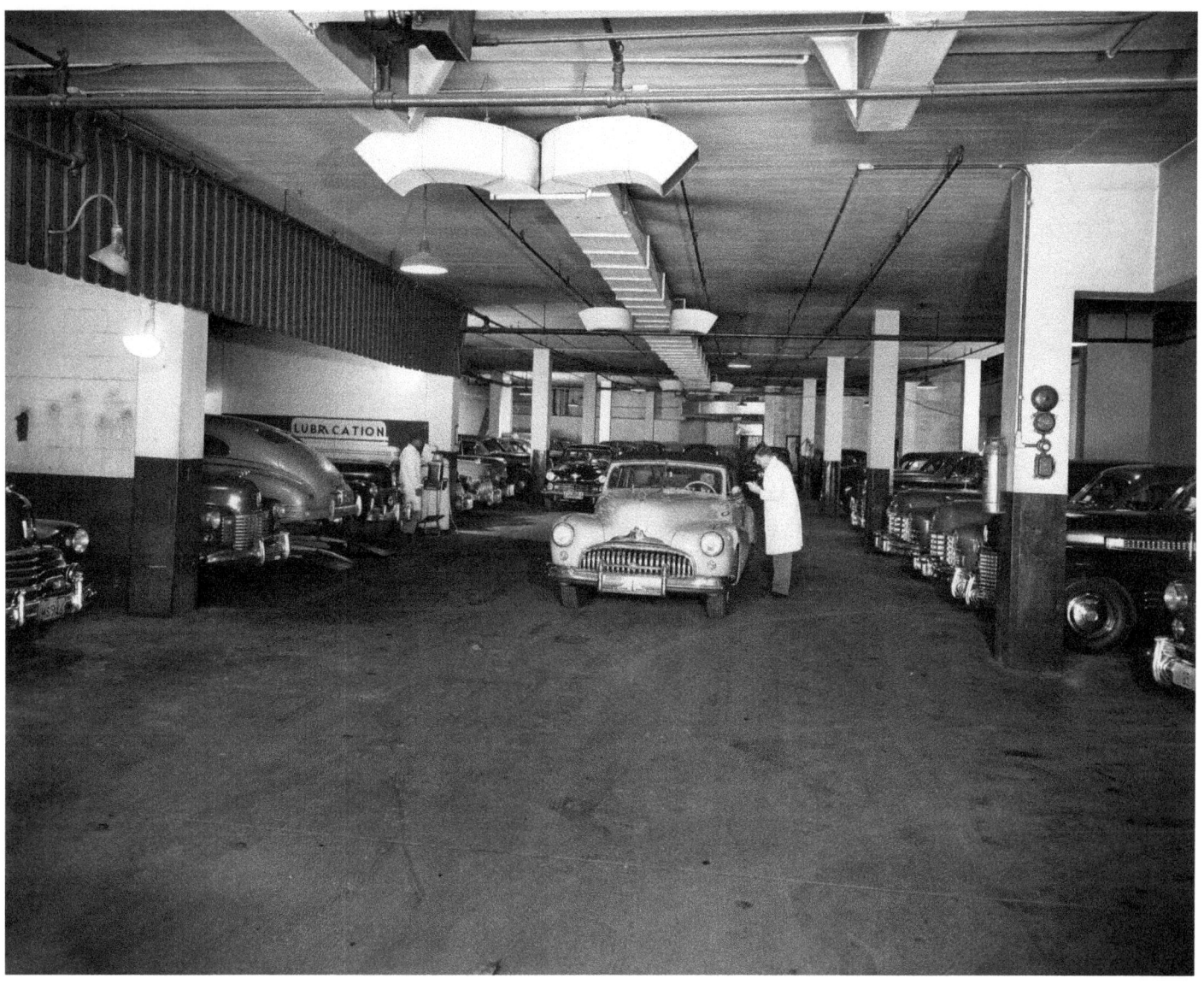

Inside the garage of the luxurious Hotel Roanoke, in the 1950s. The hotel was originally built by the Norfolk and Western Railway in the 1880s and has undergone many renovations. It still operates today and is now owned by Virginia Polytechnic Institute and State University (Virginia Tech).

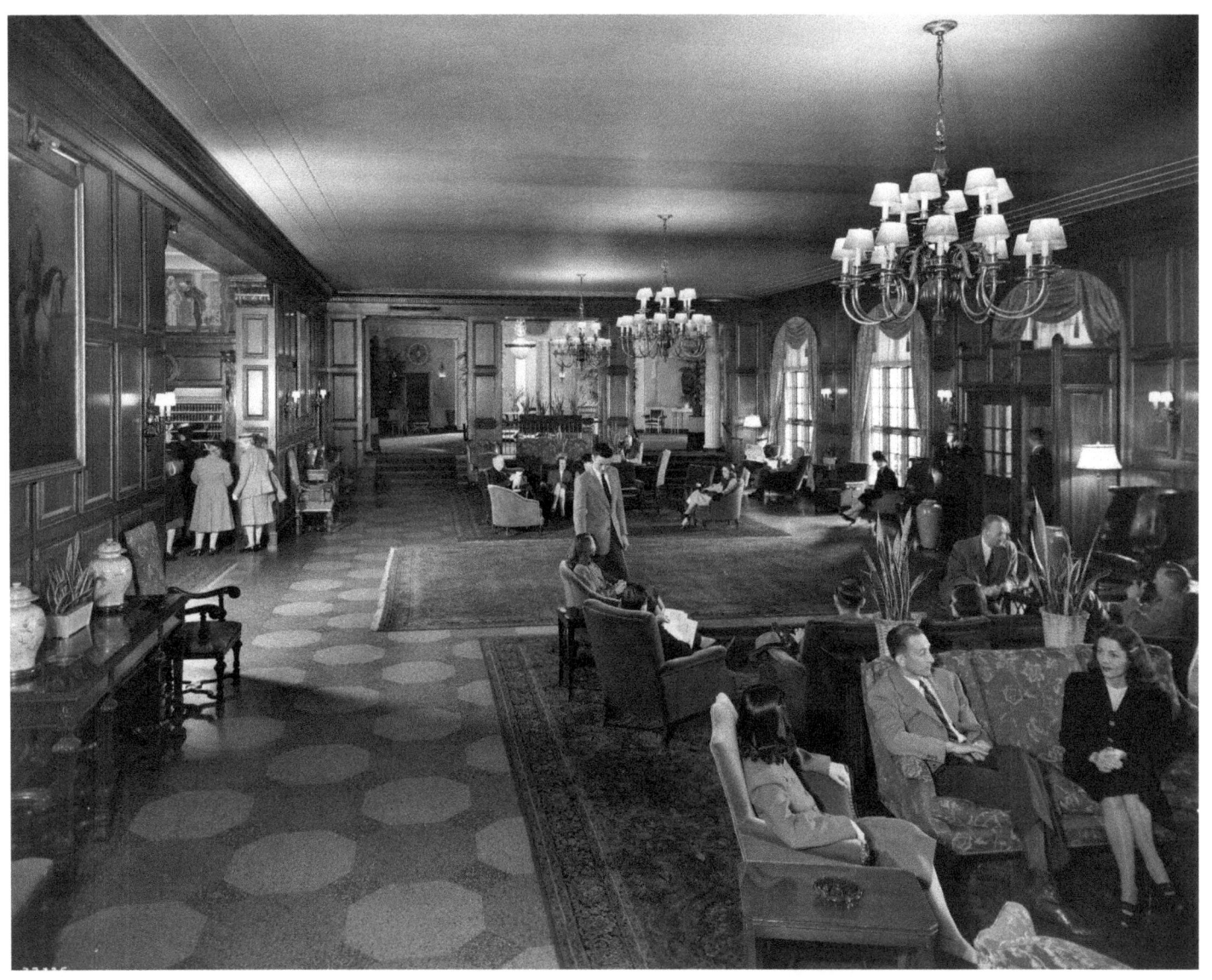

Visitors relax in the lobby of the Hotel Roanoke, a luxurious Appalachian hotel that today is registered as a National Historic Landmark.

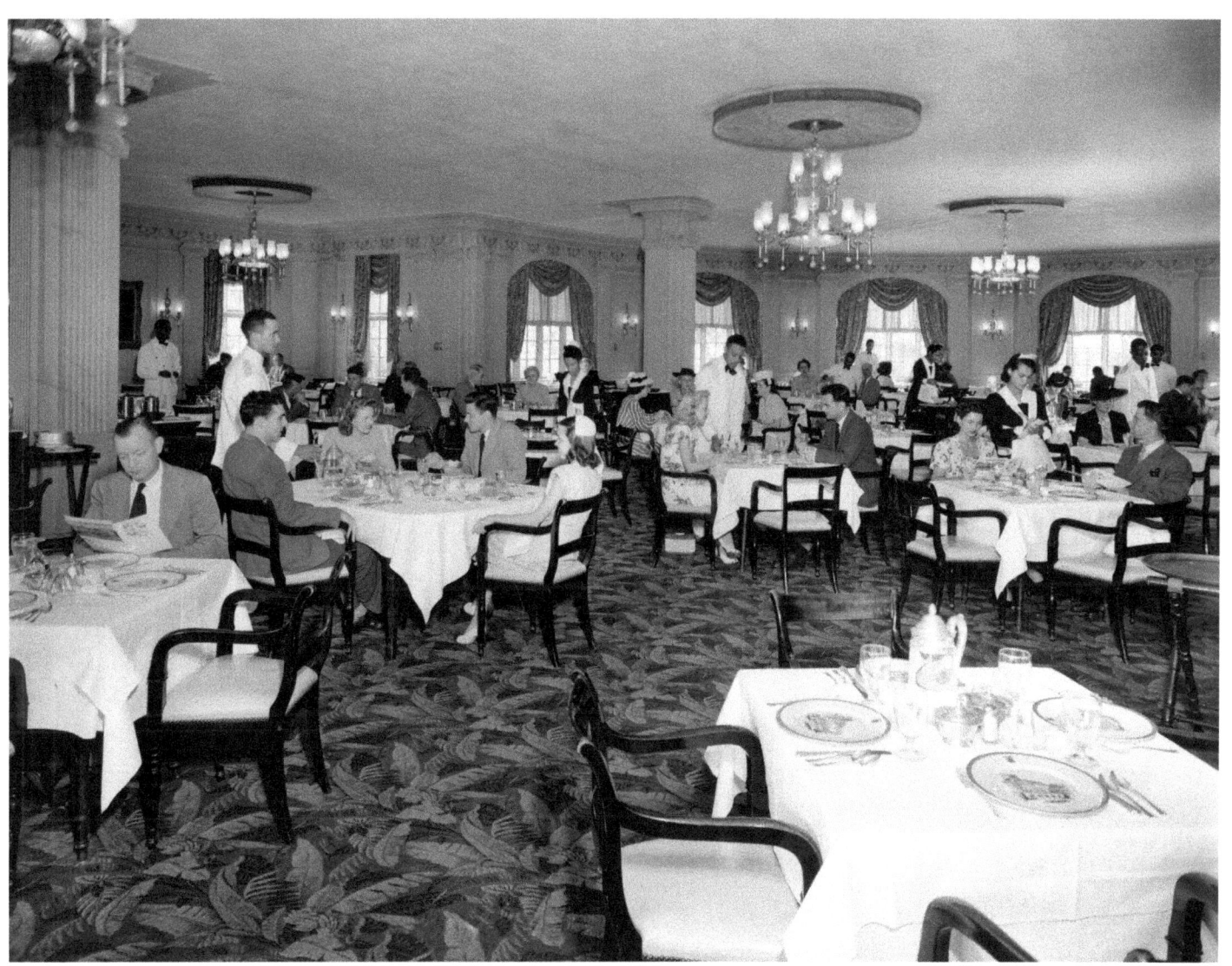

A scene in the main dining room at the Hotel Roanoke.

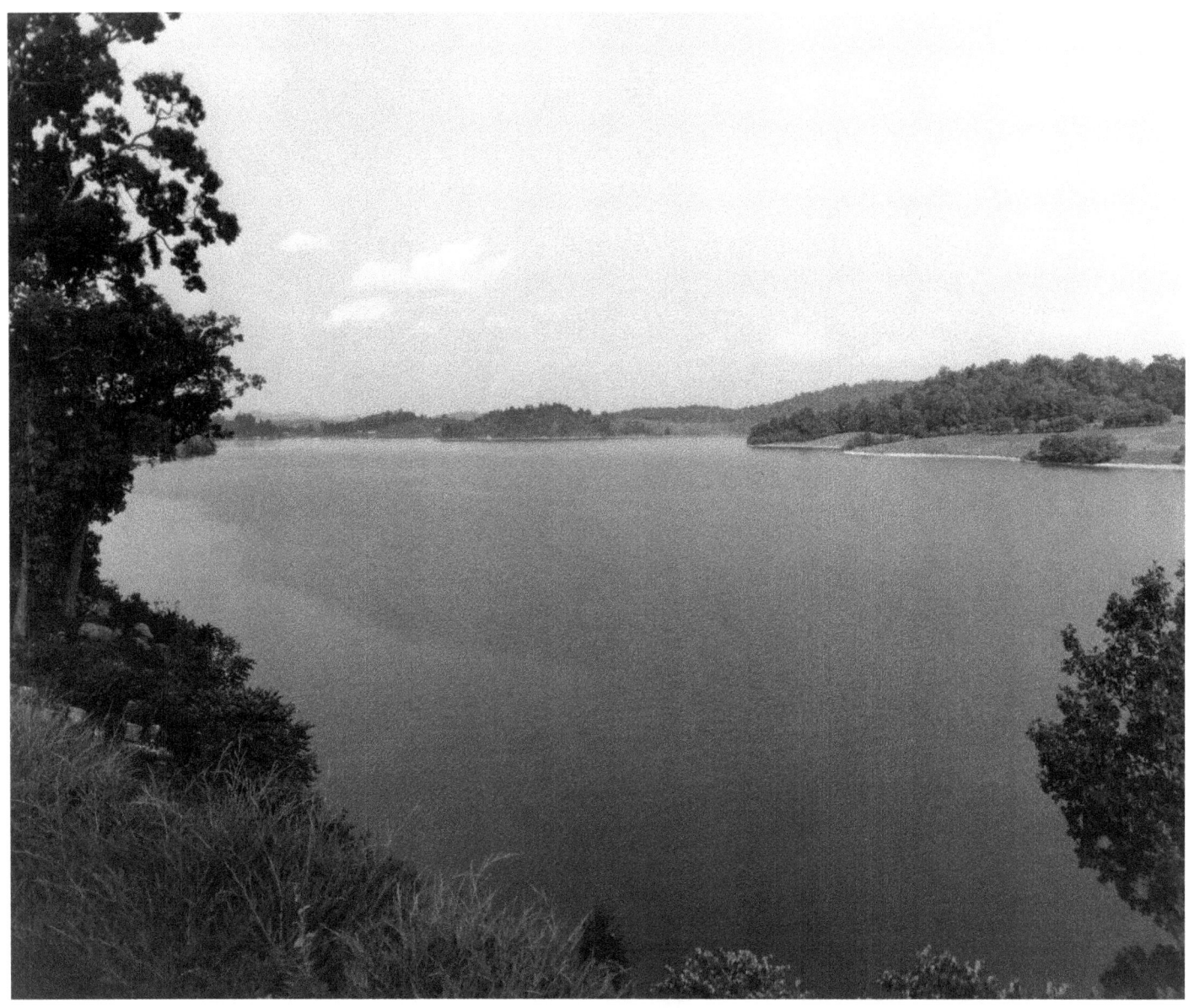

This southern Appalachian lake, seen here in the 1950s, was man-made. Southern Appalachia has almost no natural lakes because it was never glaciated. The Ohio River roughly delineates the farthest southern reach of North American glaciation during the last ice age.

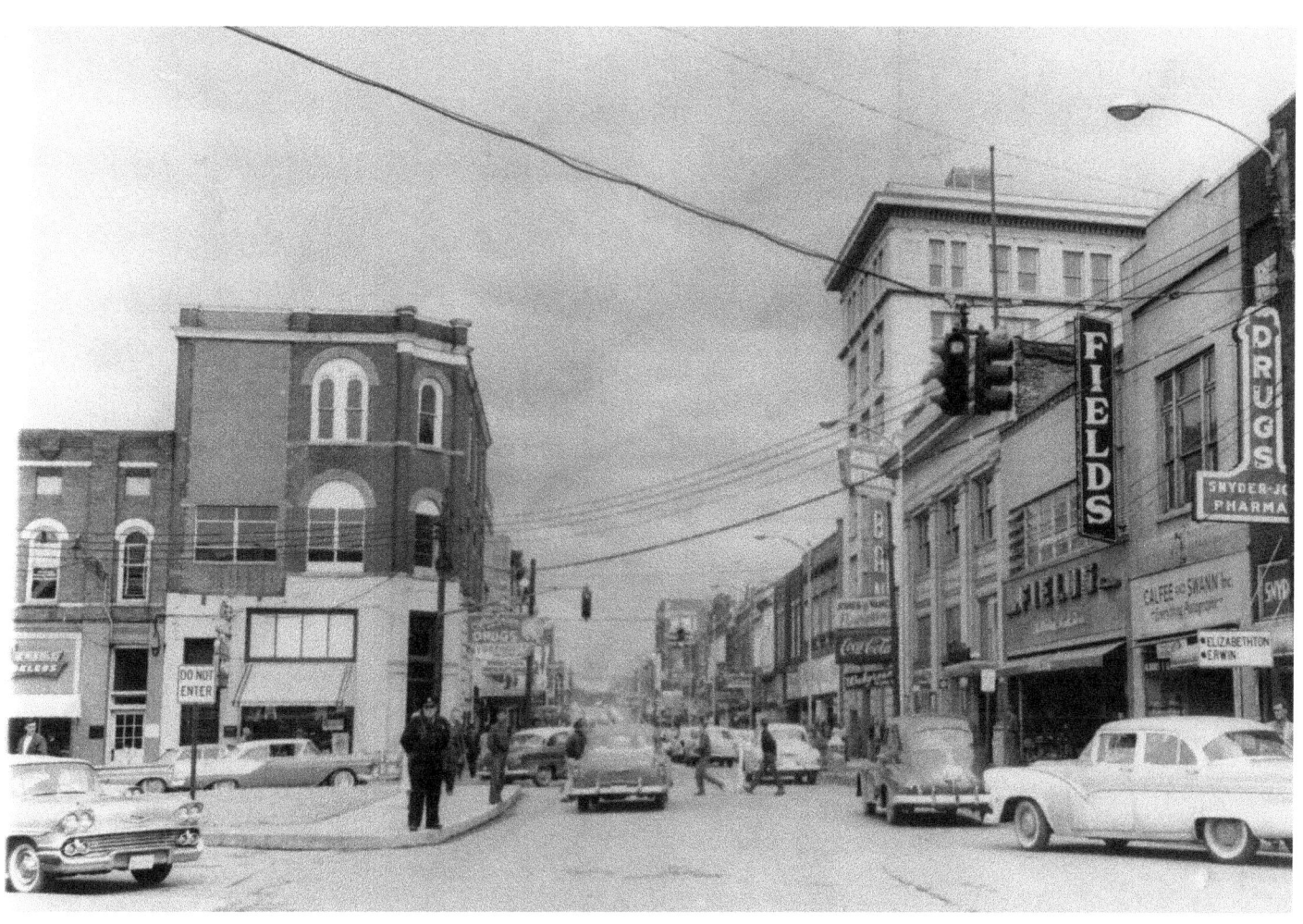

A policeman patrols a corner on Main Street, in downtown Johnson City, Tennessee, in the 1950s.

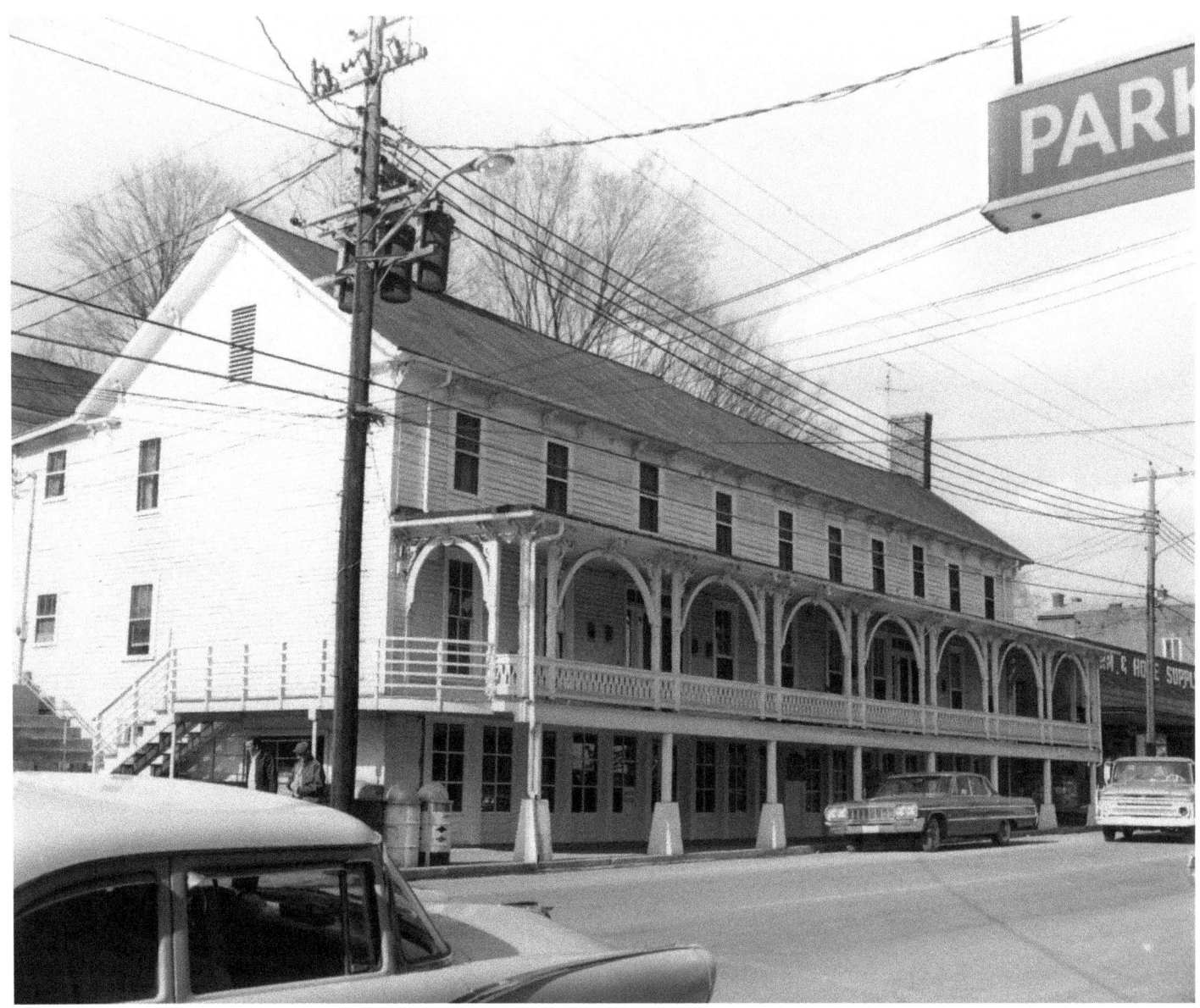

The Chester Inn, in Jonesborough, Tennessee, has been continuously occupied—as an inn, hotel, or apartment building—since it was built in 1797, as an inn on the old stage road that came down into Tennessee from the Great Valley of Virginia. Shown here around 1960, today it is used for events and offices by the National Storytelling Association.

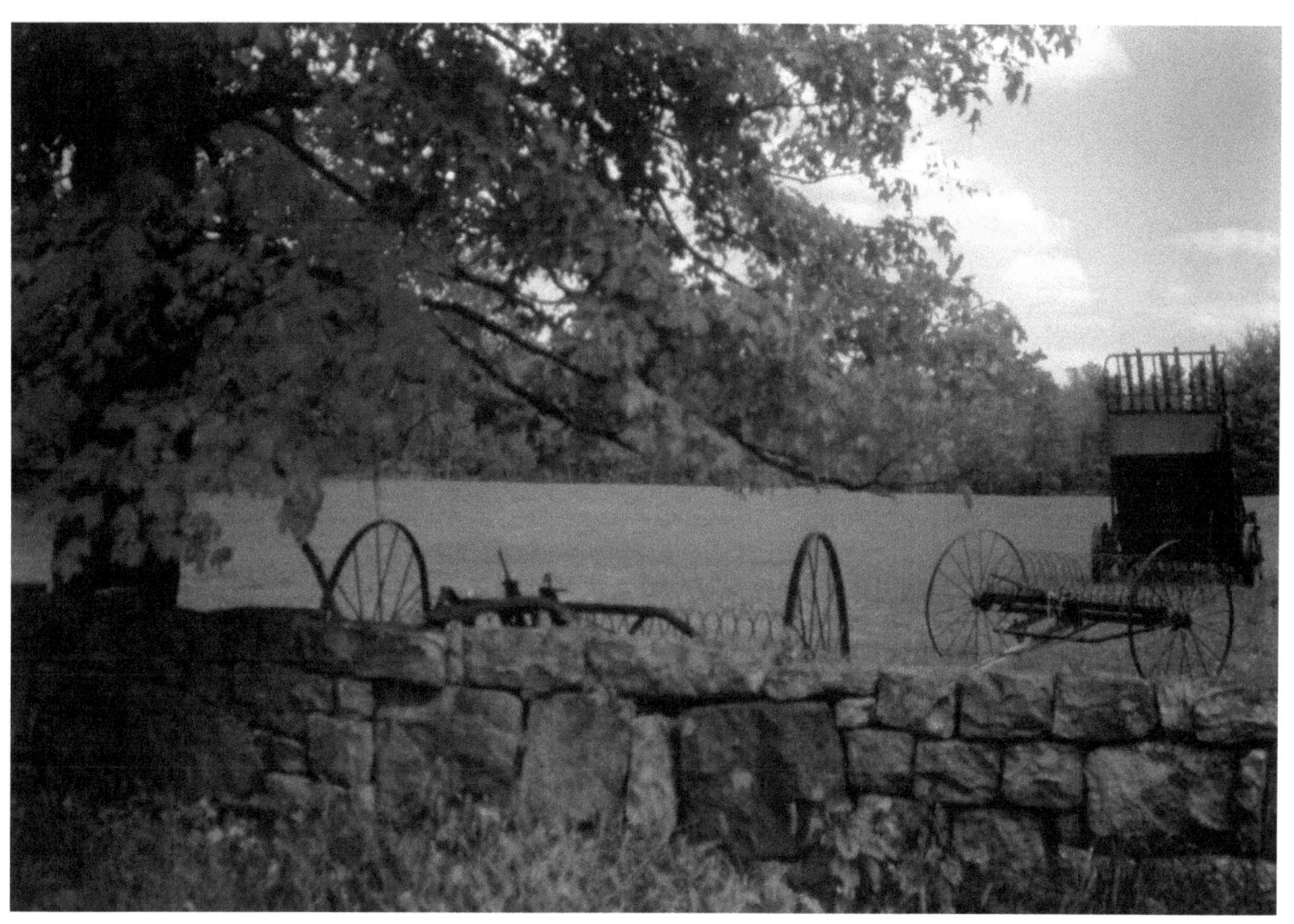

This nostalgic view of a rural Virginia scene in autumn shows archaic farm equipment and a stone wall in the early 1960s.

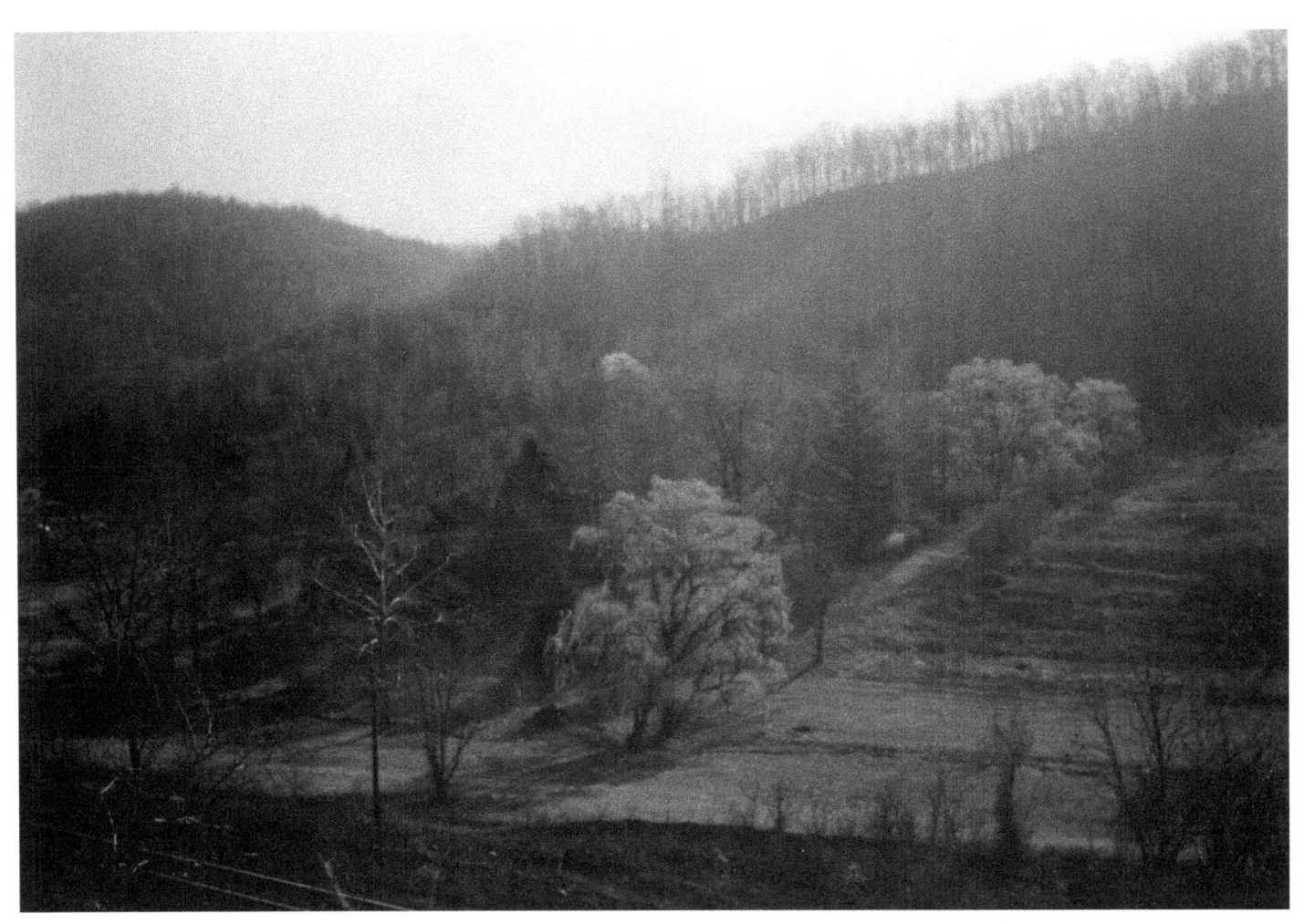

This hillside in Albermarle County, Virginia, is located in the Piedmont region of Appalachia—the hilly region between the high Blue Ridge and the coastal plain of the eastern seaboard.

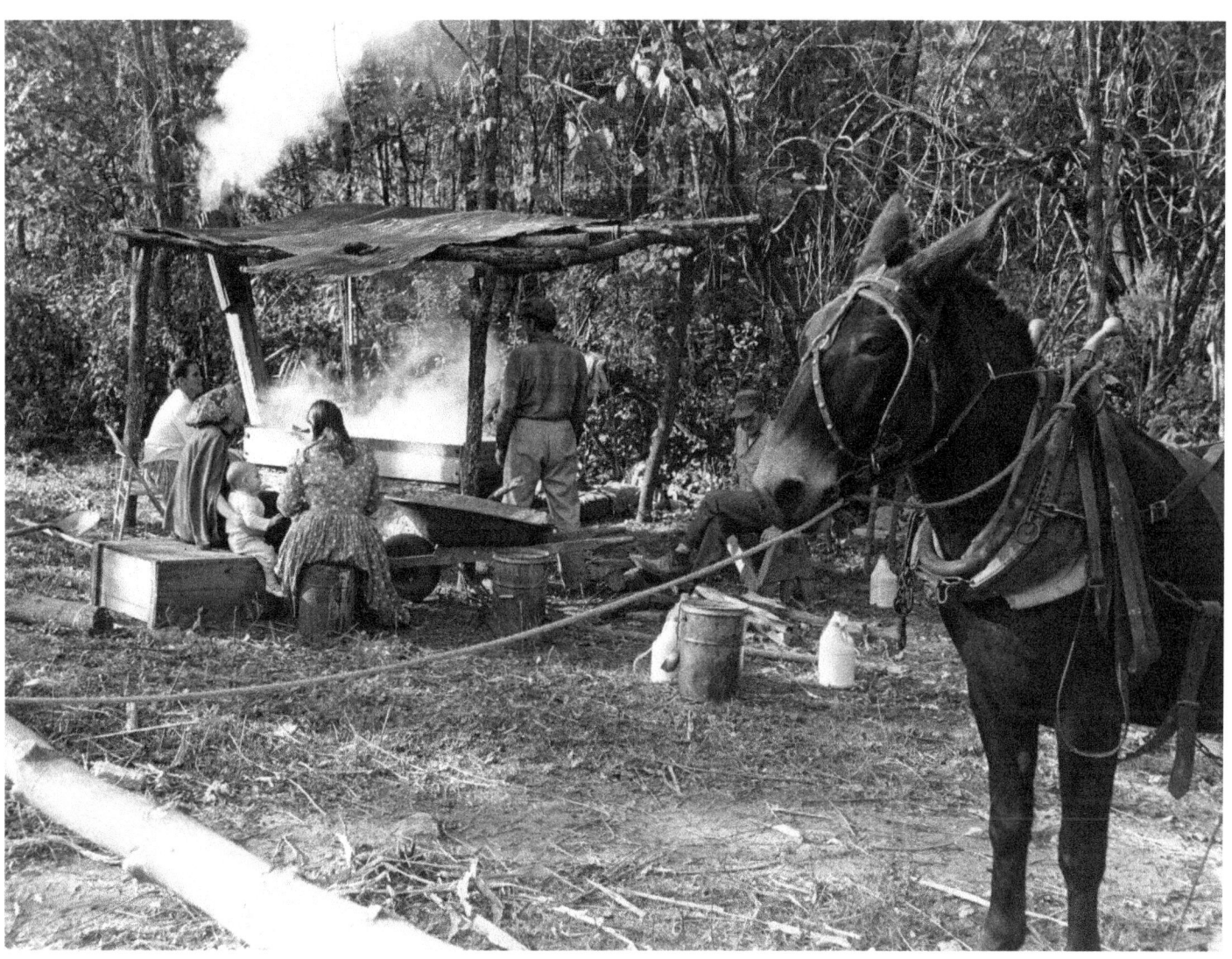

A family makes sorghum cane molasses. In the nineteenth century, mountain residents commonly grew the cane as an important supplement to a diet that usually lacked sweeteners, apart from honey. The cane was cut in the fall, pressed in a mule-powered mill, and then boiled down to produce the sweet sorghum syrup. This photo was taken in the 1960s, when a resurgence of interest in the old ways was taking hold in some quarters.

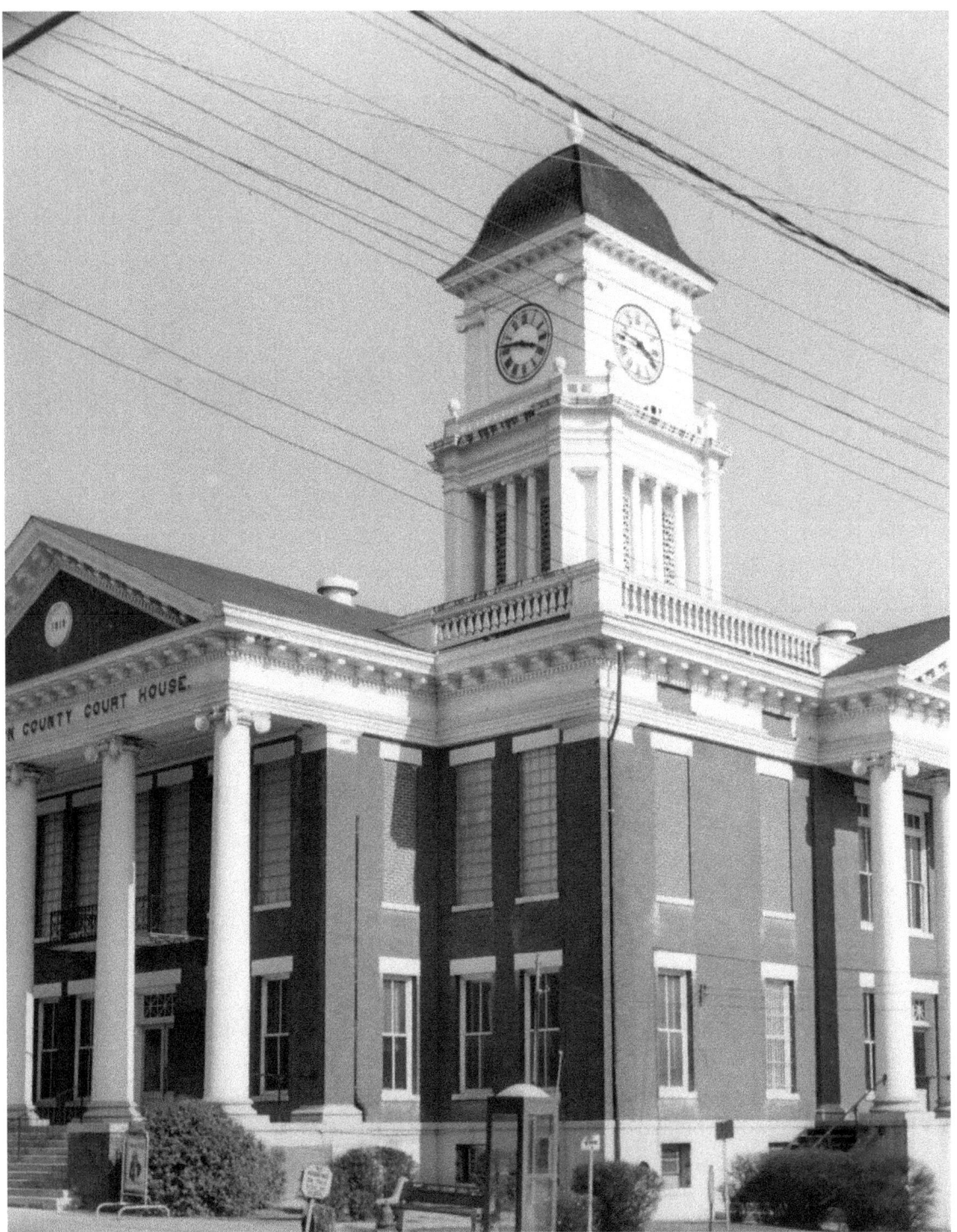

The "new" Washington County Courthouse, in Jonesborough, Tennessee, was built in 1913. It is shown here in the 1960s and is still in use today.

E.T.&W.N.C. (Tweetsie) engine no. 207 runs the rails near Milligan, Tennessee, in the late 1960s. Tweetsie narrow gauge service was discontinued in 1950, but the standard-gauge line between Johnson City and the Bemberg Rayon plant in Elizabethton continued to operate. No. 207 was one of the railroad's last operating steam engines.

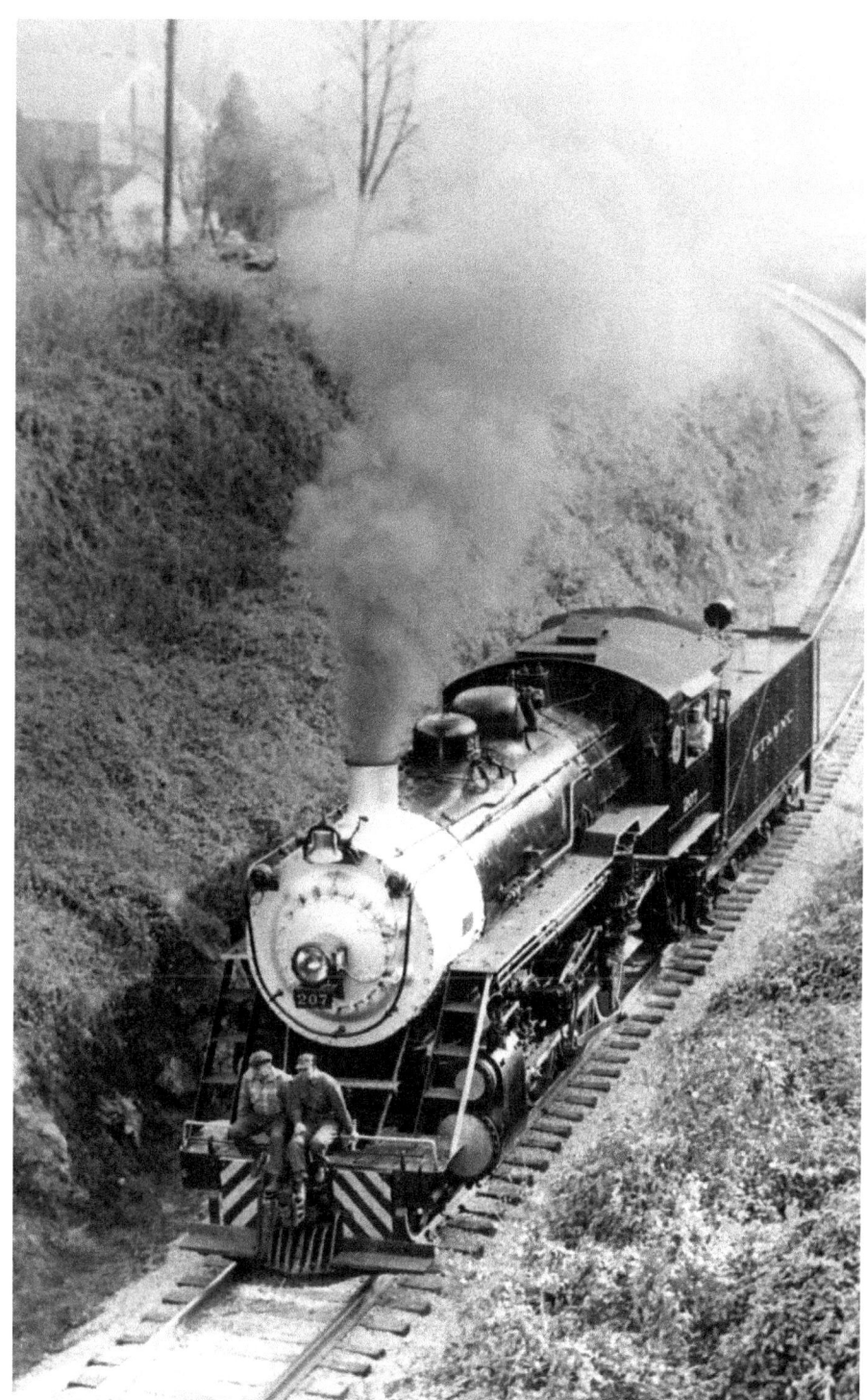

This photograph of Johnson City in December 1958 shows onlookers at a fire or railroad accident. Fire fighters pulling a hose are visible in the left side of the frame, in the middle distance, and smoke is drifting into the frame from the left.

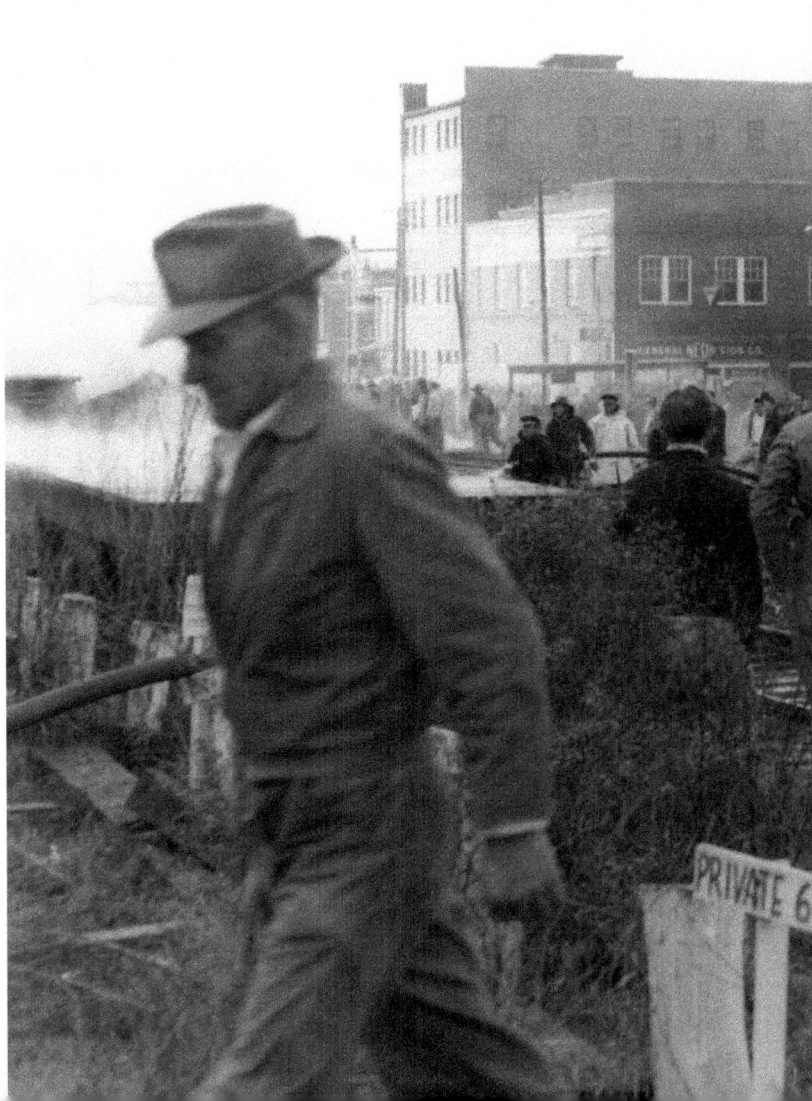

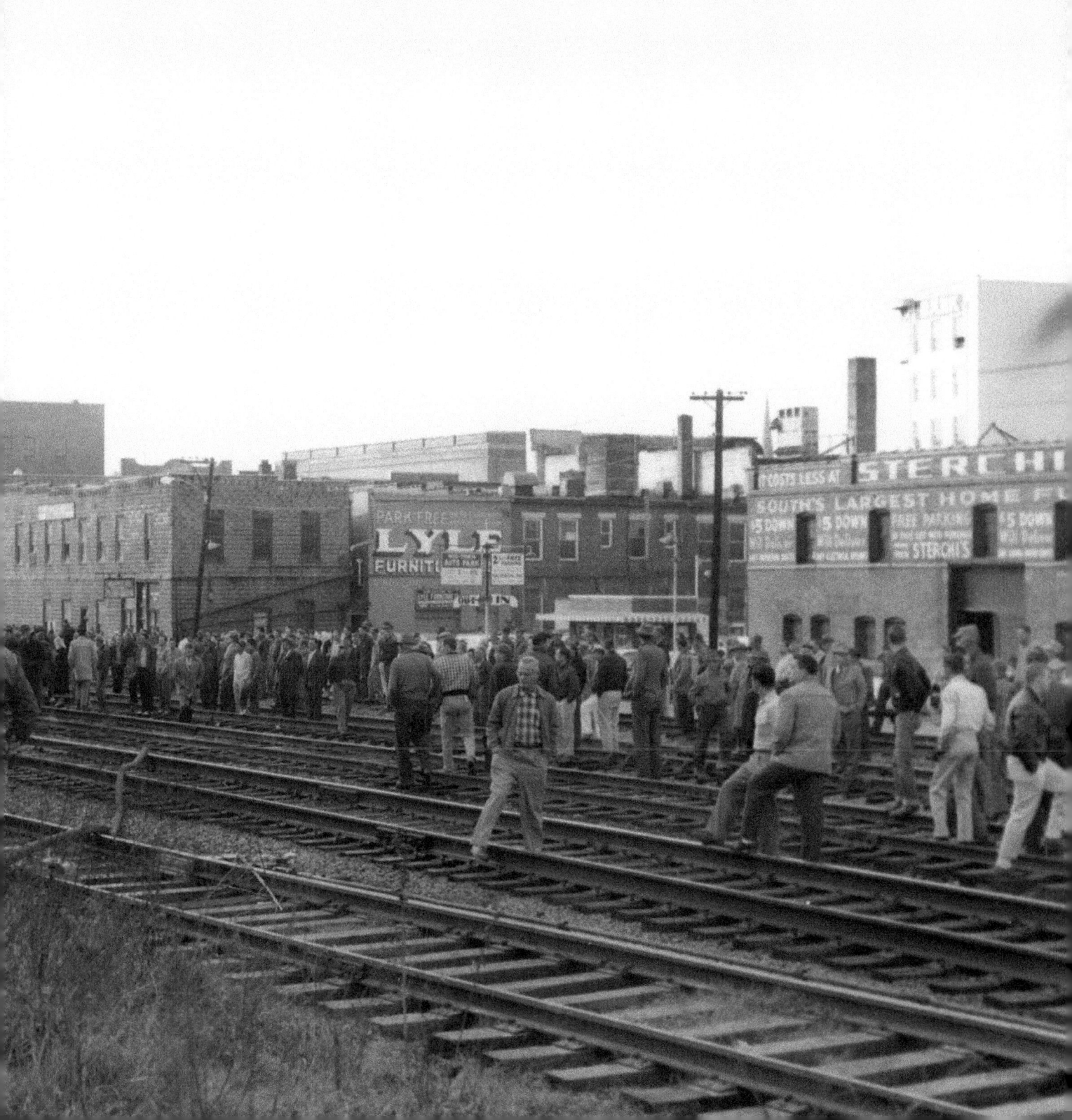

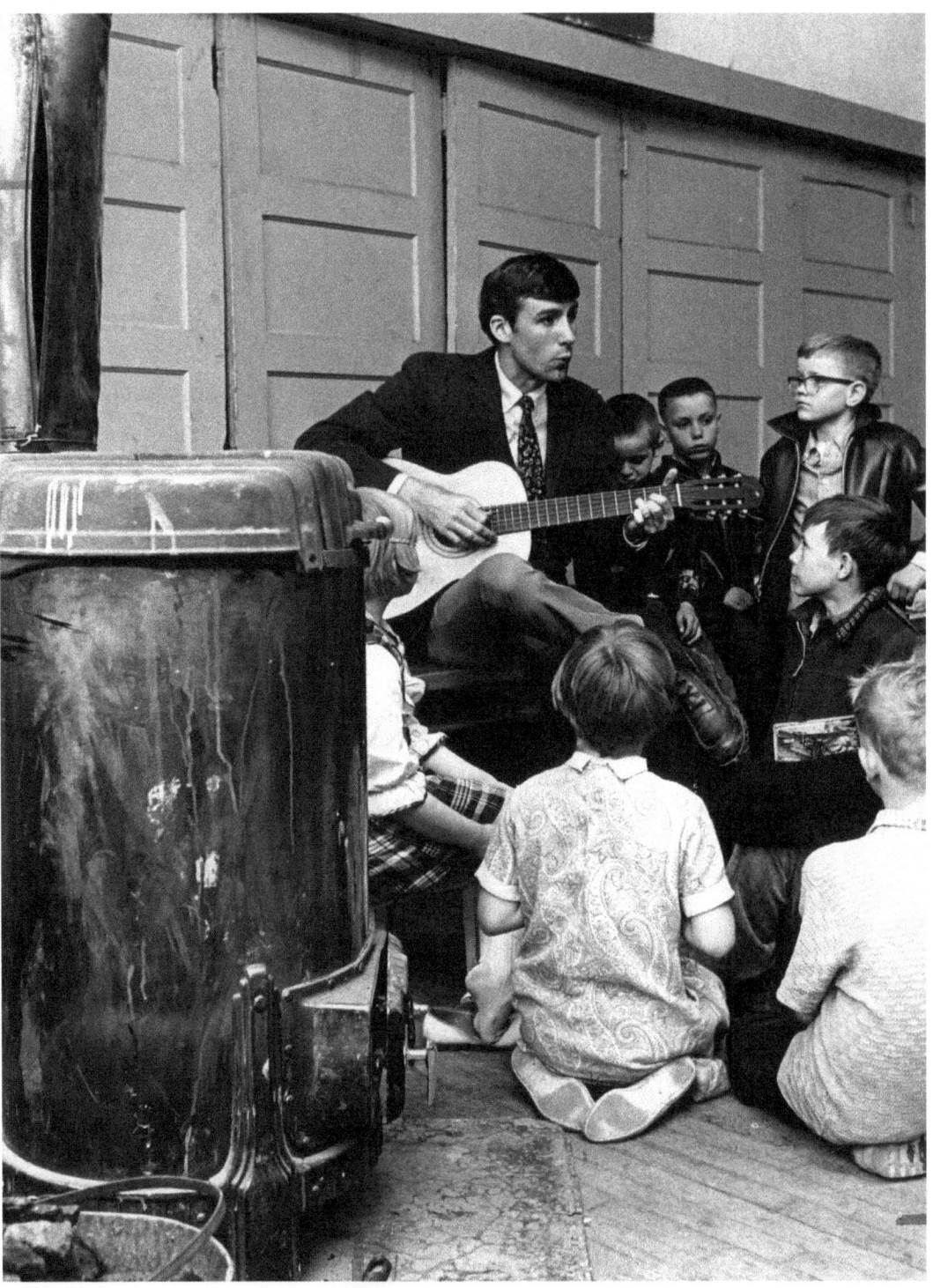

A musician performs for schoolchildren. The revival of folk music in America in the 1950s and 1960s led to new appreciation for Appalachian musical traditions.

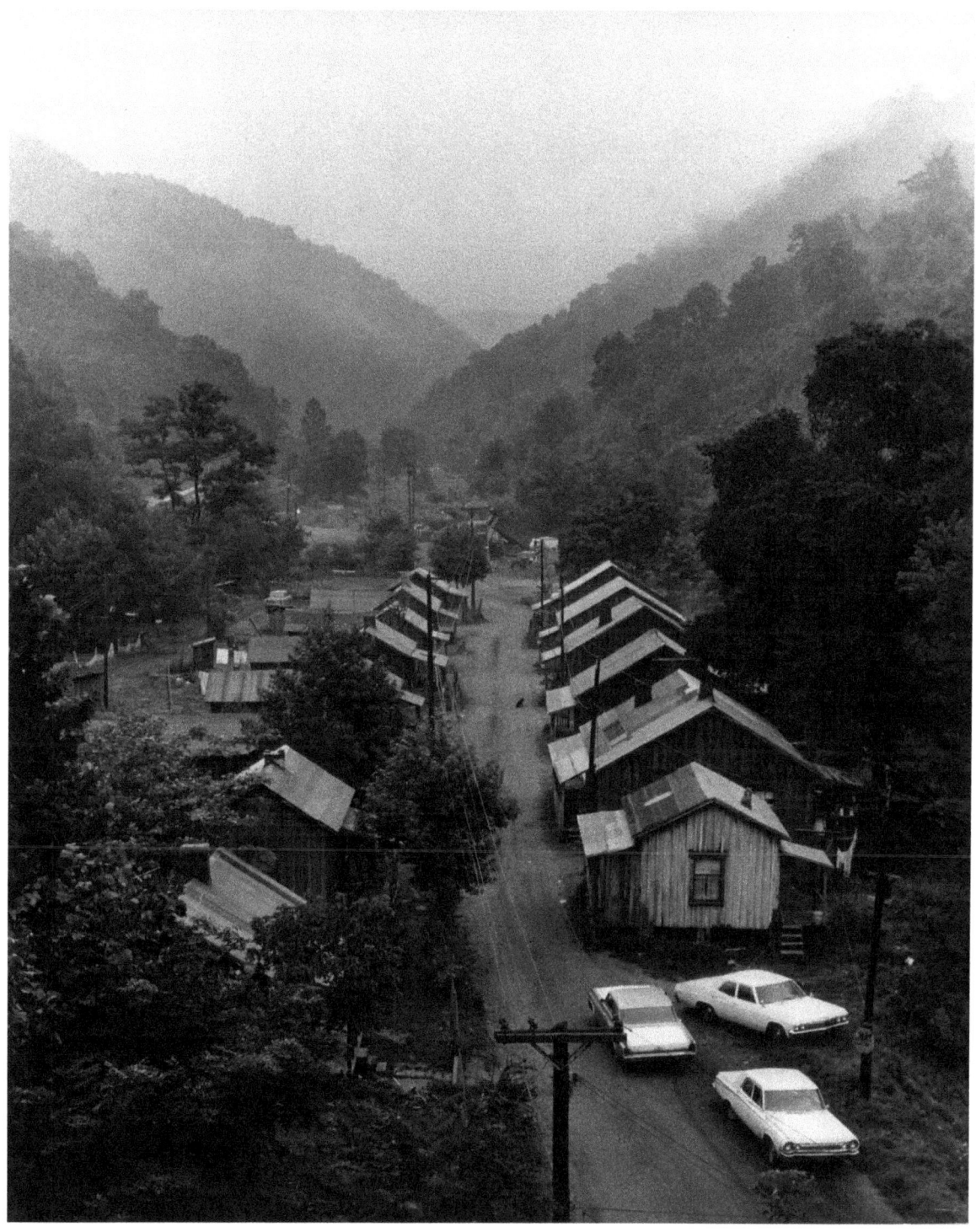

Cabin Creek coal camp, in Ingram Branch, West Virginia, in 1972. By the late 1950s, the robust period of Appalachian coal mining was drawing to a close. Many of the smaller mines had begun to play out, and industry consolidation led to fewer jobs. In 1964, President Lyndon B. Johnson announced a set of federal initiatives called the "War on Poverty," to address the poverty that persisted in some regions of the United States, including Appalachia.

A coal camp in Rita, West Virginia, in the late 1960s. By that time, coal mining was becoming increasingly automated and strip mining more commonplace. These developments dealt a double blow to Appalachia's coal country: the number of available jobs fell and injury to the local environment rose.

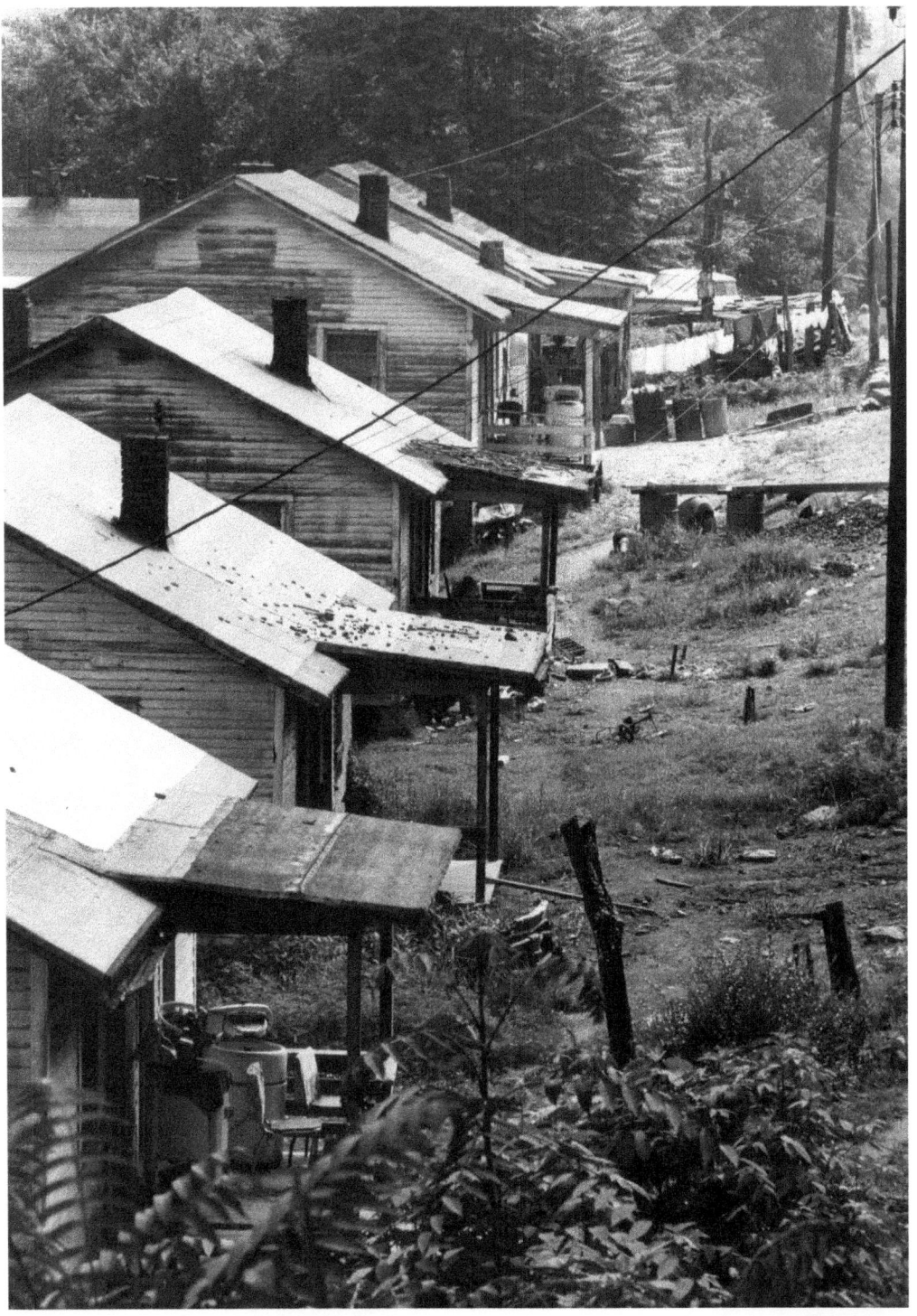

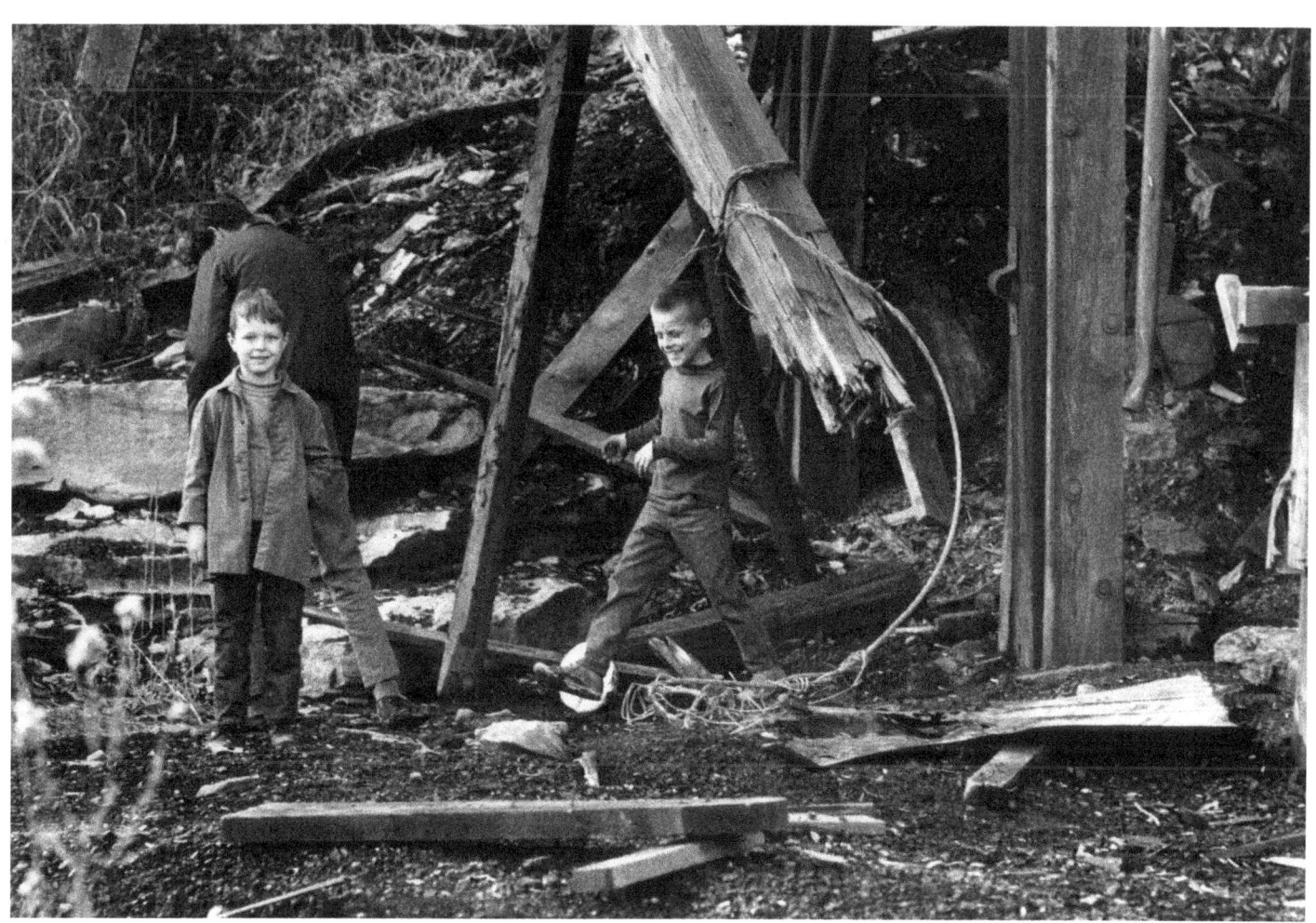

Children play in a West Virginia coal camp in the late 1960s.

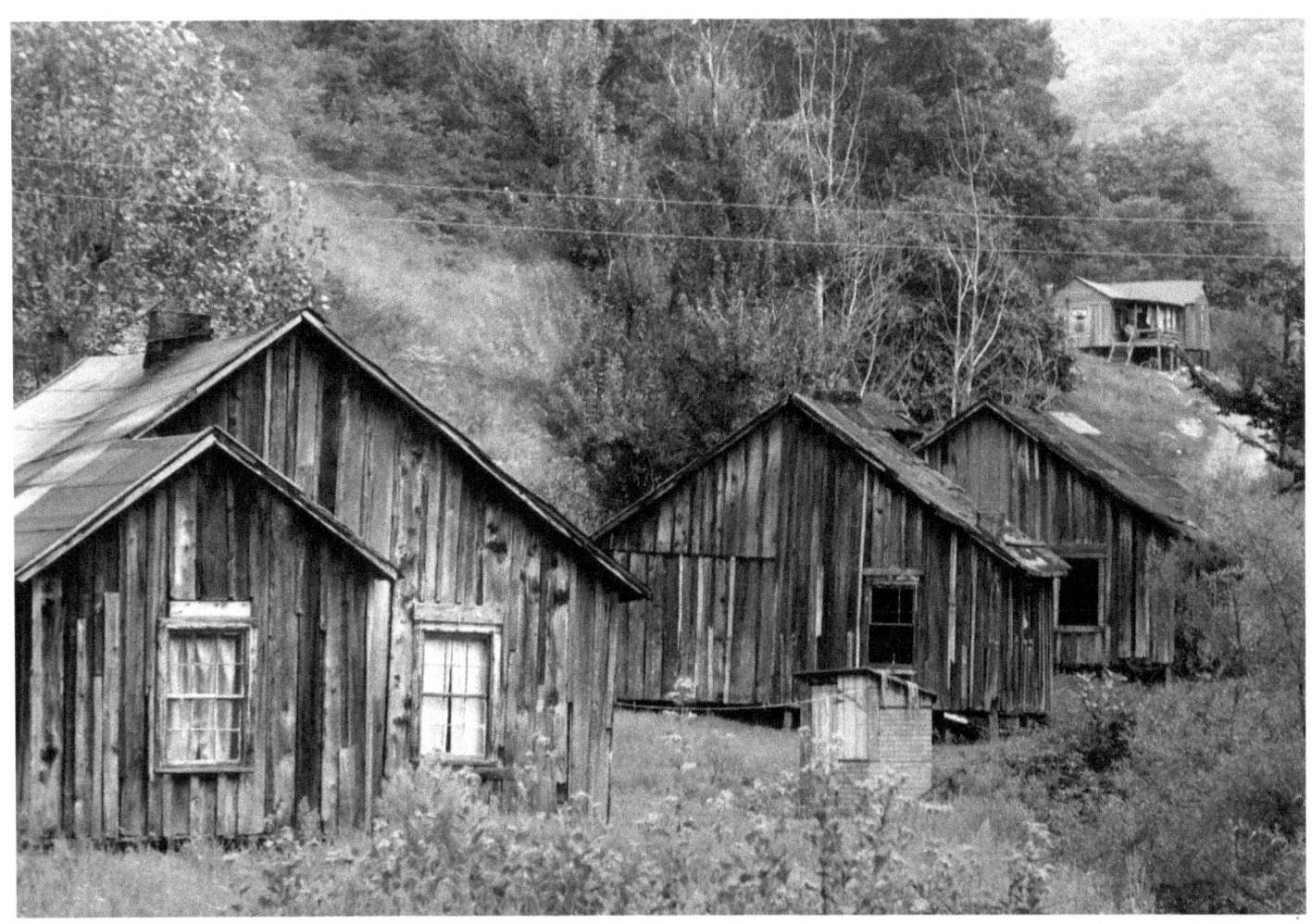

This coal camp was situated in Davy, West Virginia. Residents of coal communities are sometimes offended by images of poverty, which can lead to negative stereotyping. Nevertheless, such images reflect a reality. In 1968, Robert F. Kennedy visited eastern Kentucky and concluded that hunger remained a serious regional problem.

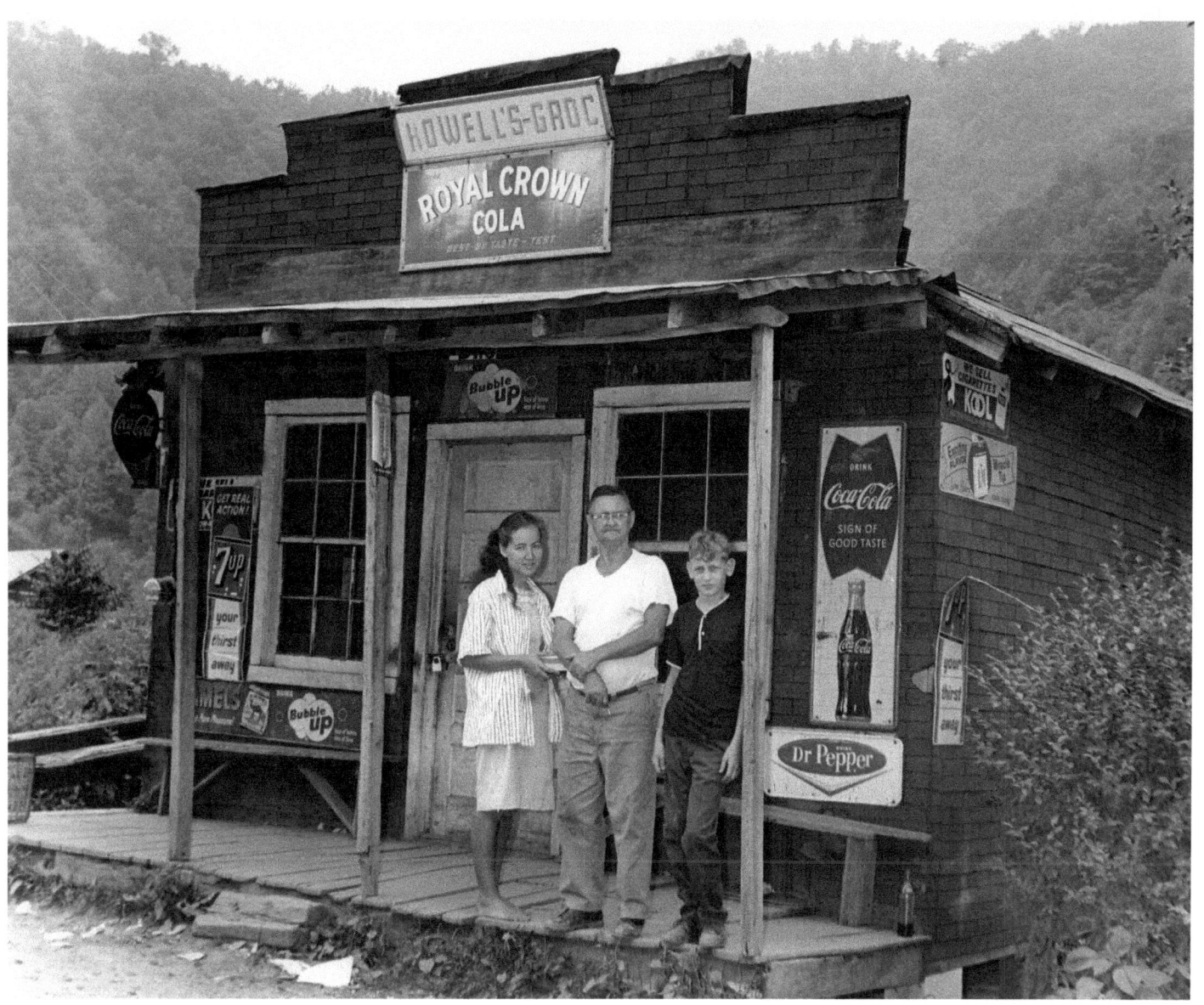

A West Virginia family poses for the photographer in 1967, surrounded by storefront signage for soft drinks that remain popular today.

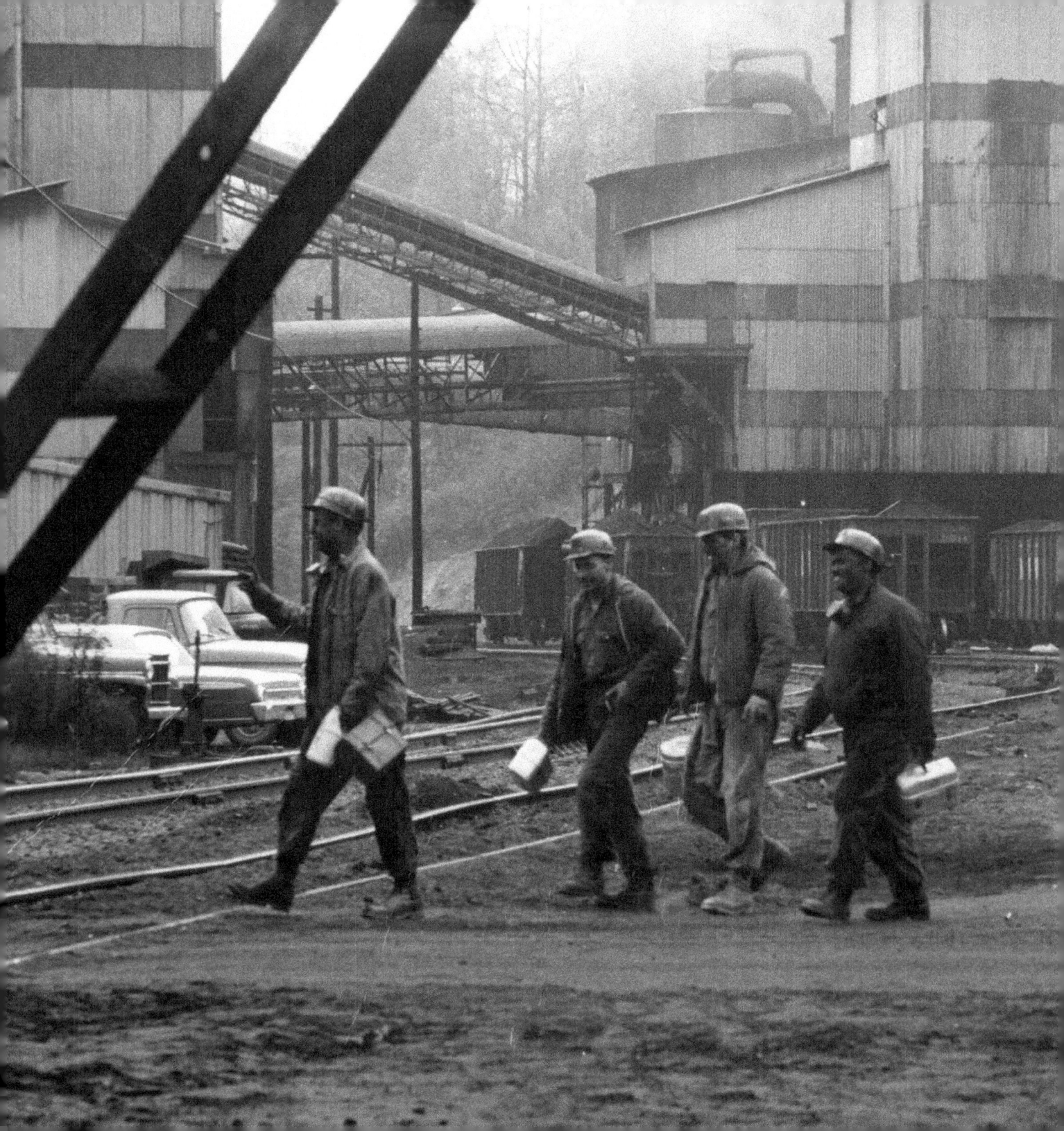

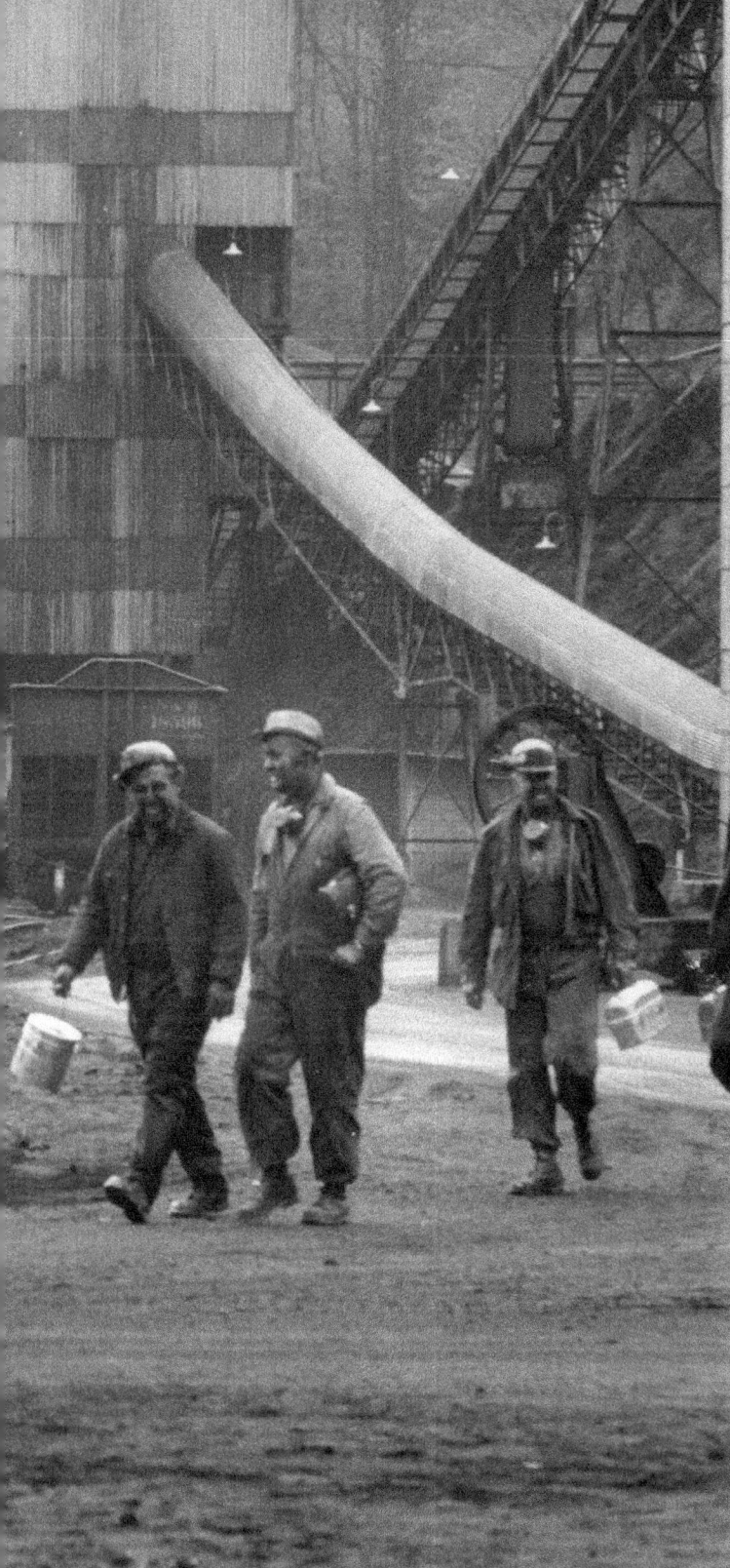

A shift changes at a coal mine in Tams, West Virginia.

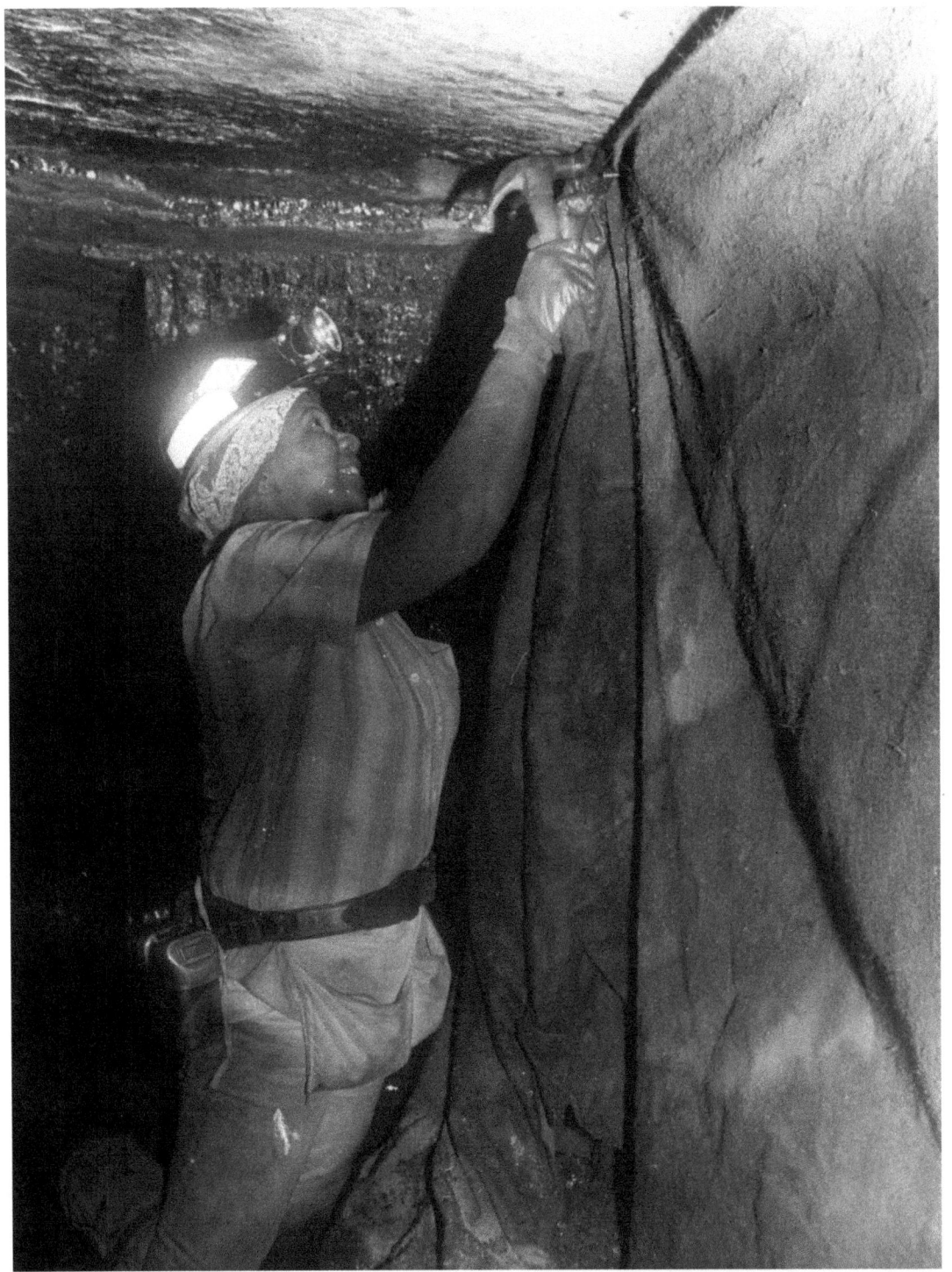

By the early 1970s, more and more women were becoming coal miners, joining other women in the workforce during a time of sweeping change in societal conventions and behavior.

This historical marker in front of the Carter County Courthouse in Elizabethton, Tennessee, commemorates the "Watauga Old Fields," a term that refers to the bottomlands along the historic Watauga River, in the upper Tennessee valley. When European settlers arrived in the region around the mid eighteenth century, they saw signs of cultivation predating the arrival of the Cherokees. The Cherokees themselves referred to the bottoms as "old fields."

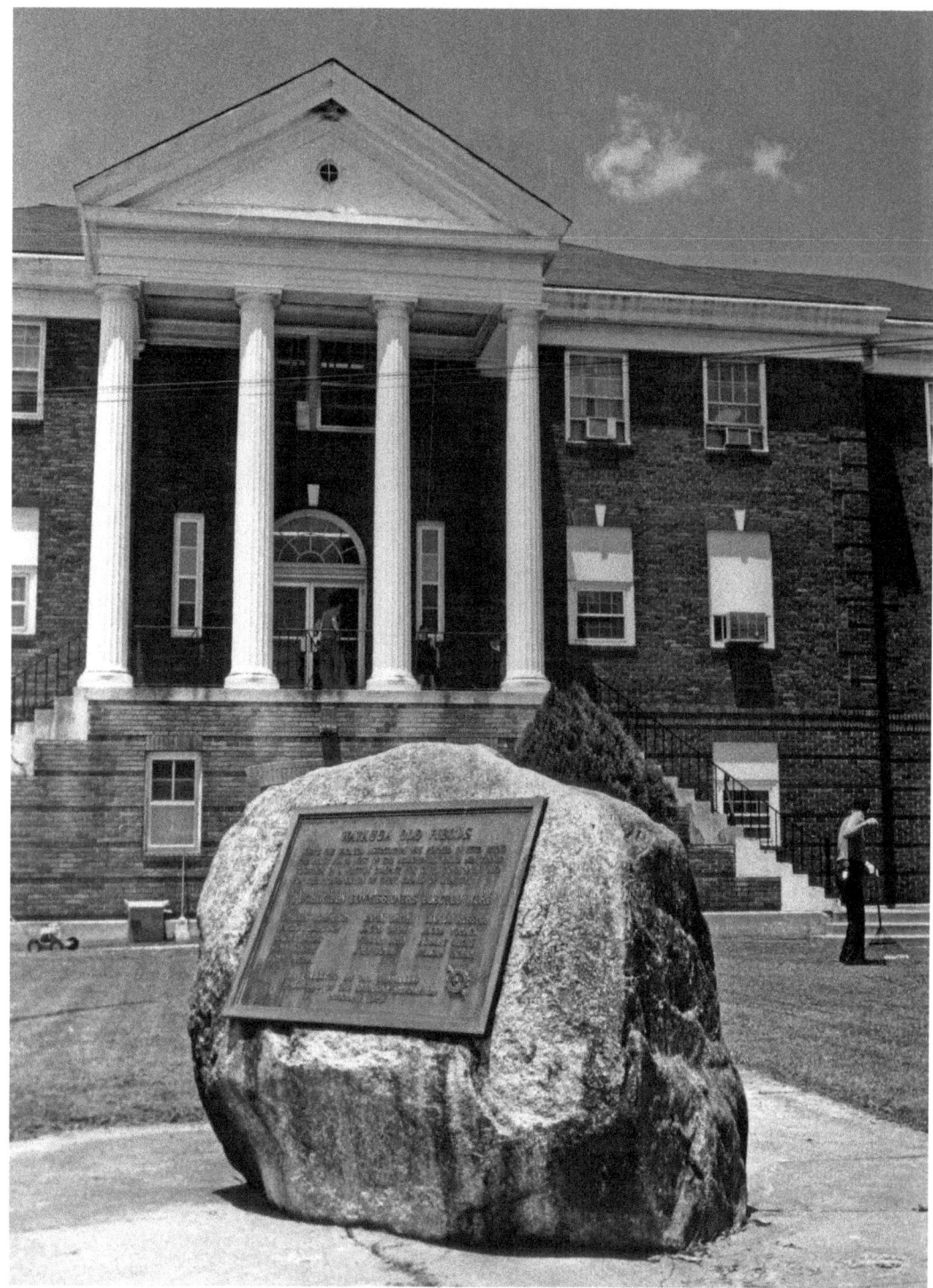

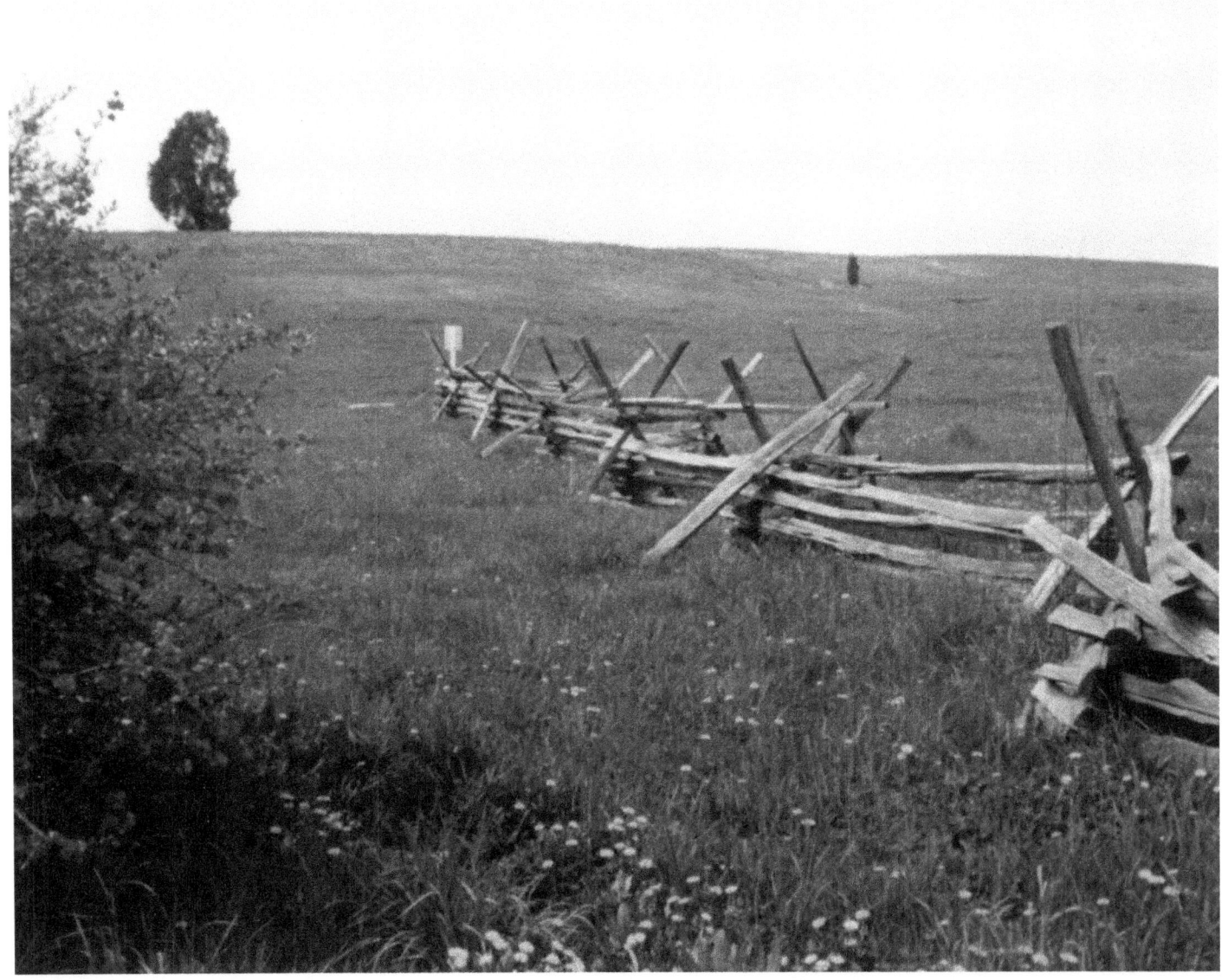

Manassas Battlefield, depicted here in the early 1970s, was the site of two important Civil War battles. The Piedmont region around Manassas, in upper Virginia, was the site of multiple engagements because it lies at the top of the Great Valley of Virginia. During the war, armies tended to travel north and south through the valley, turning the valley's northern exit into strategic geography.

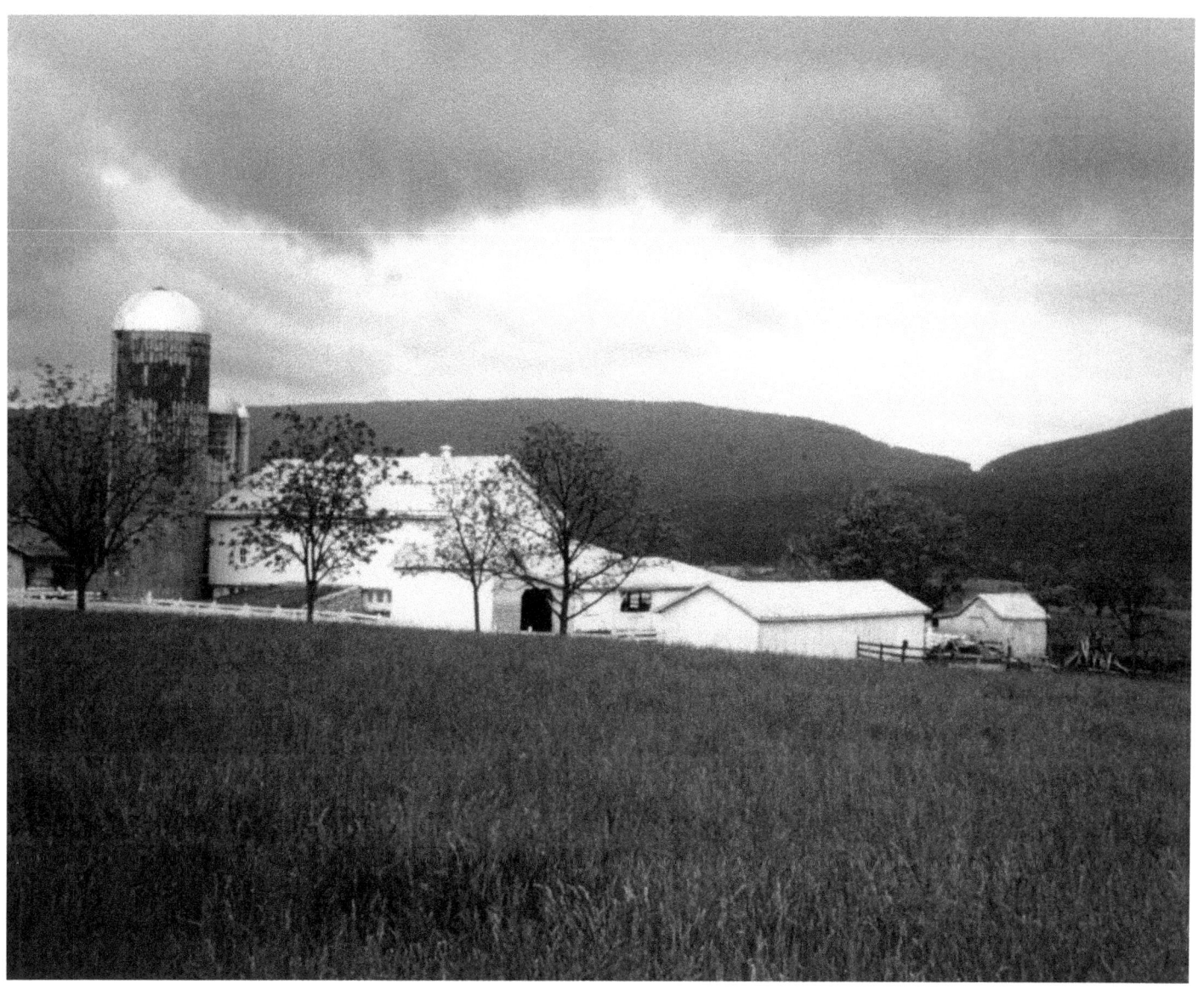

New Market, Virginia, lies in the upper Piedmont region of the state, not far from Manassas. Like Manassas, it was the site of an important Civil War battle. This scene shows a prosperous farm near New Market in the 1970s.

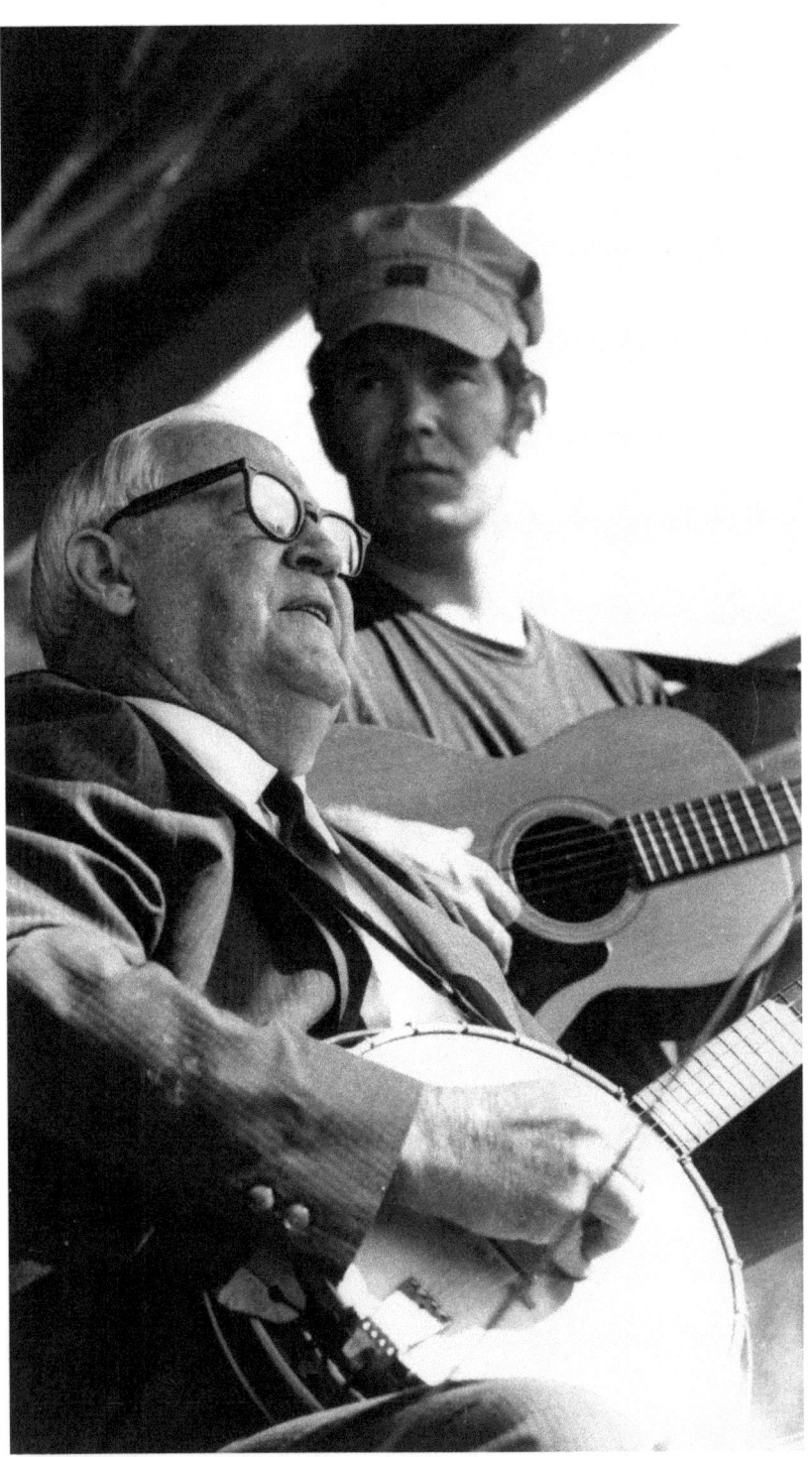

This fellow plays the banjo in the three-finger, up-picking style, at an Appalachian music festival sometime around the 1970s. Across the region, an Appalachian identity movement emerged at that time, which combined music with cultural revivalism and social justice activism.

Kings Mountain National Military Park, in Blacksburg, South Carolina, commemorates the battle of King's Mountain, a turning point in the American Revolution. In September 1780, mountaineers mustered as a volunteer militia at Sycamore Shoals, on the Watauga River, in upper east Tennessee, having heard that British major Patrick Ferguson was threatening to invade the mountains. Traversing the Blue Ridge, they used guerrilla tactics to defeat Ferguson's army of Loyalists on October 7.

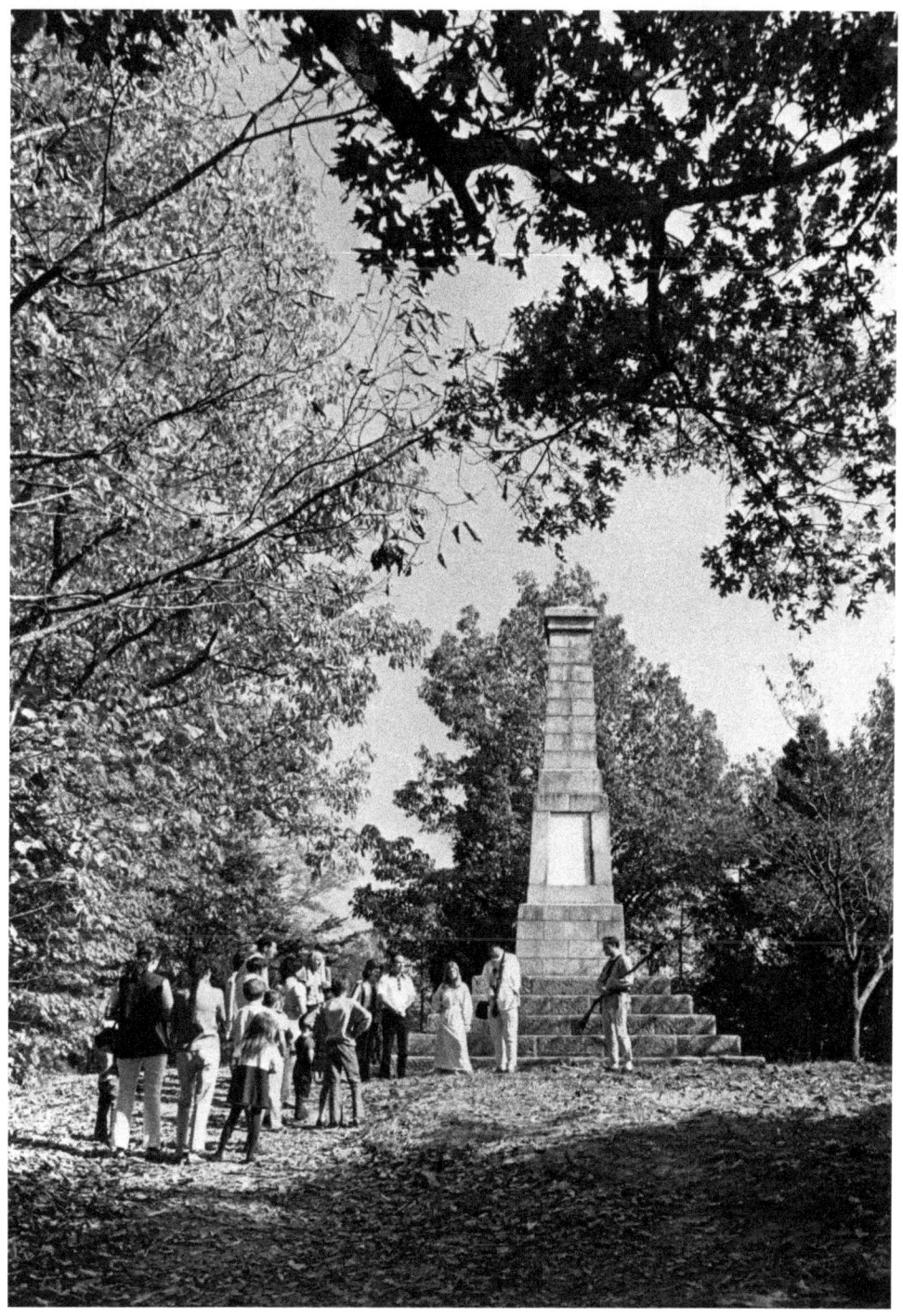

NOTES ON THE PHOTOGRAPHS

These notes, listed by page number, attempt to include all aspects known of the photographs. Each of the photographs is identified by the page number, photograph's title or description, photographer and collection, archive, and call or box number when applicable. Although every attempt was made to collect all data, in some cases complete data may have been unavailable due to the age and condition of some of the photographs and records.

HISTORIC PHOTOS OF
APPALACHIA

Appalachia: The place and its people have long inspired a special fascination among travelers and commentators. The rugged, ecologically rich mountains, at once forbidding and inviting, have provided a place of retreat and exploration for lovers of natural beauty and outdoor adventure, while the region's resources have long lured both capitalists intent on creating wealth and regular folks just looking for a steady wage. The inhabitants native to the region have often been held up as pure, strong, and self-sufficient on the one hand, and derided as primitive, backward, and exotic, on the other.

Not quite south or north, east or west, the region continues to defy easy classification. Yet it emerges in *Historic Photos of Appalachia* as both distinct and as familiarly American. The nearly 200 photographs included here portray the region's land and people in all their distinctive and sometimes surprising specificity—including views of towns, houses, and farms; families at home and on the job; railroads, mining, and logging; and beautiful streams and mountain landscapes.

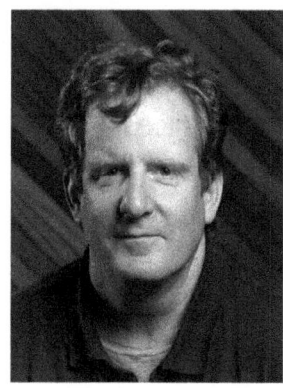

Kevin E. O'Donnell is a professor of English and the Director of the Environmental Studies minor at East Tennessee State University. A native of Cleveland, Ohio, he has lived and worked in Johnson City, Tennessee, for fifteen years. He has written articles on environmental history and nature writing, and is co-author of a book on nineteenth-century travel writing from Southern Appalachia.

WWW.TURNERPUBLISHING.COM

www.ingramcontent.com/pod-product-compliance
Lightning Source LLC
Chambersburg PA
CBHW052135170526
45162CB00003B/16

* 9 7 8 1 6 8 4 4 2 0 9 0 2 *